REDISCOVERING
AMERICA

P 340   His most significant American
discovery had been a way to love
the land and to extend that love to
the society at large.

Also by Frederick Turner

BEYOND GEOGRAPHY:
The Western Spirit
Against the Wilderness

REMEMBERING SONG:
Encounters with the
New Orleans Jazz Tradition

Edited by Frederick Turner

GERONIMO:
His Own Story

THE PORTABLE
NORTH AMERICAN INDIAN READER

REDISCOVERING AMERICA

John Muir
in His Time
and Ours

Frederick Turner

Sierra Club Books
San Francisco

The Sierra Club, founded in 1892 by John Muir, has
devoted itself to the study and protection of the earth's
scenic and ecological resources—mountains, wetlands,
woodlands, wild shores and rivers, deserts and plains. The
publishing program of the Sierra Club offers books to the
public as a nonprofit educational service in the hope that
they may enlarge the public's understanding of the Club's
basic concerns. The point of view expressed in each book,
however, does not necessarily represent that of the Club.
The Sierra Club has some sixty chapters coast to coast, in
Canada, Hawaii, and Alaska. For information about how you
may participate in its programs to preserve wilderness and
the quality of life, please address inquiries to Sierra Club,
730 Polk Street, San Francisco, CA 94109.

LIBRARY OF CONGRESS CATALOGING-IN-PUBLICATION DATA
Turner, Frederick W., 1937–
Rediscovering America.
Reprint. Originally published: New York;
Viking, 1985.
Bibliography: p. 351
Includes index.
1. Muir, John, 1838–1914.   2. Naturalists—
United States—Biography.   I. Title.
[QH31.M9T87   1987]   333.7′2′0924 [B]   86-24885
ISBN 0-87156-704-0(pbk)

Cover design by Bonnie Smetts

Printed in the United States of America

10 9 8 7 6 5 4 3 2 1

In Memory of
Peter Farb

Contents

Illustrations follow page 162.

Acknowledgments

My first debt, chronologically and other-
wise, is to my late friend Peter Farb, who enthusiastically encouraged me to attempt this book. Ronald H. Limbaugh, archivist of the
Muir Papers at the Holt-Atherton Pacific Center for Western Studies, University of the Pacific, has been unfailingly generous, both
with his time and with his great knowledge of the Muir Papers.
Thanks are due also to the members of his staff, especially Berenice
Lamson.

I was cordially assisted by the staffs of other institutions holding
Muir materials or items of related interest. These include the Yosemite National Park Research Library, with special thanks to Jack
Geyer; the State Historical Society of Wisconsin, with special
thanks to James Hanson and Harold Miller; the University of Wisconsin and its archivists Bernard Schermetzler and F. Frank Cook;
the Huntington Library; the Beinecke Rare Book and Manuscript
Library, Yale University; the Bancroft Library, University of California, Berkeley, with special thanks to Mary-Ellen Jones; the
Widener and Houghton libraries, Harvard University; the Cape
Cod Community College library, with thanks to Gregory Master-
son; the Martinez (California) Public Library; the John Muir National Historic Site, Martinez, with special thanks to P. J. Ryan,
Armando Quintero, Margaret Plummer, and Linda Moon Stumpff;
the California Hospital Medical Center, Los Angeles, with thanks
to Vicky A. Ryan and Joan Flynn of its Medical Records division;
the Military Service Branch, National Archives, with thanks to
Brenda Beasley Kepley; the Tennessee State Department of Conservation, with thanks to Terry Bonham.

Many individuals helped me along my way, and for what they
freely gave, the mere mention of their names seems poor recom-
pense. However, my sincere thanks to Millie Stanley, T. H. Watkins, Honora Moore, John Hay, Robert Card, Sr., Stephen B.
Oates, Clara Gee Rymer, Grant Barnes, Nelson Lichtenstein, Eric

Simmons, William Cadman, Robert E. Fletcher, Dr. John Talley, Eugene Newmann, Holway Jones, Dr. Gulden Mackmull, Harry Kearns, Roy Harvey Pearce, William A. Williams, and Charles A. Reich; to Lucille Adler for special examples; and to Elise R. Turner, who has cheerfully borne all the changes attendant to so long a labor.

The John Simon Guggenheim Memorial Foundation assisted me with a handsome grant while I was in the early stages of this work.

Chronology

1804 Daniel Muir born, Manchester, England.

1813 Anne Gilrye born, Dunbar, Scotland.

1833 Daniel Muir marries Anne Gilrye, Dunbar.

1838 John Muir born, Dunbar, April 21.

1845 Potato crop failures trigger famine in Europe. *The Condition of the Working Class* by Friedrich Engels.

1849 Emigration of Muir family to America. California gold rush.

1857 Muir family moves to Hickory Hill farm, Wisconsin.

1860 John Muir leaves home for Madison; meets Jeanne Carr; Lincoln nominated by Republican party, elected in November. Extinction of California jaguar.

1862 Muir in second year at University of Wisconsin; hires out as teacher for part of year. Homestead Act. Morrill Act. Death of Thoreau.

1866 Civil War over. Muir returns to America from Canadian exile, goes to Indianapolis.

1867 Muir's thousand-mile walk to the Gulf. Coal Land Act regulates sale of U.S. coal-bearing lands.

1868 Muir sees Yosemite for first time; he is thirty.

1871 Muir deep in glacial studies; publishes "Yosemite Glaciers." Visit of Emerson to Yosemite. Great slaughter of passenger pigeons in Wisconsin.

1872 Muir begins to write for *Overland Monthly;* meets William Keith; visits Oakland. Yellowstone Park established.

1876 Muir lives with Swetts in San Francisco; "God's First Temples" heralds his emerging voice in conservation debates. Centennial Exposition. Little Big Horn.

1879 Muir engaged to Louie Strentzel; leaves on first Alaskan expedition. Edison's incandescent bulb glows forty consecutive hours.

1880 Muir marries Louie Strentzel, April 14.

1881 Muir's daughter Annie Wanda born; Muir's health poor due to domestic worries; accepts invitation to go to Alaska aboard *Corwin.*

1882 Death of Emerson.

1885 Death of Daniel Muir.

1886 Muir's daughter Helen born. Haymarket Riot.

1888 In July, Louie writes Muir on trip to Northwest, urging his return to literary and conservation work.

1890 Muir completes two articles for Robert U. Johnson of *Century,* signaling his return to public life. Death of Dr. John Strentzel. Wounded Knee. Official Census notes disappearance of American frontier.

1892 Sierra Club founded. Forest reserves created in three states.

1894 *Mountains of California,* Muir's first book, published.

1896 Muir with Forestry Commission. Death of Anne G. Muir. McKinley v. Bryan.

1901 McKinley assassinated; Roosevelt becomes president and Muir writes him about American natural resources. *Our National Parks* published.

1903 Roosevelt camps with Muir in Yosemite. Death of F. L. Olmsted. Flight at Kitty Hawk. First federal wildlife reserve established.

1905 Death of Louie Muir. California recedes Yosemite to U. S.

1906 San Francisco Earthquake - april 18

1908 Secretary of Interior Garfield grants Hetch Hetchy to San Francisco. Creation of Muir Woods National Monument. Muir is seventy.

1911 *My First Summer in the Sierra* published. Death of William Keith. Muir departs on long-deferred South American expedition.

1913 *Story of My Boyhood and Youth* published. Death of John Swett. Hetch Hetchy formally granted to San Francisco, thereby ending lengthy dispute.

1914 World War I begins. Muir dies in Los Angeles, December 24.

1938 Don Beattie, born - April 18 (100 yrs after John Muir)

*REDISCOVERING
AMERICA*

Prologue:
Peru Again

Through the American summer of 1848 Con-
gress thrashed about in the moral wilderness created by the terri-
torial acquisitions from President Polk's Mexican War. The issue
the new lands raised into stark view was slavery—its limits and its
future—and over the factional forensics in Washington there now
loomed the thunderhead of sectional conflict.

During these months another state came into the steadily expanding union: Wisconsin, a free state, was added to balance the
newly acquired slave states of Florida and Texas. The acquisition
required the swindling of the tribes native to the new state, but this
was so minor a matter, judged in the scale of national controversy,
that it was generally ignored.

Eighteen forty-eight was also an election year, and in summer's
heat conventions were held at Baltimore, Rochester, Philadelphia,
and Buffalo. Hysterical and self-congratulatory as these gatherings
were, the platforms adopted by the Barnburners, Free-Soilers, Lib-
erty Leaguers, and others prophesied the collapse of a national
house increasingly divided against itself.

On August 19, the New York *Herald* ran a lengthy item on that most intriguing of the Union's new acquisitions, California. Buried some 2,000 words and thirteen paragraphs into this early specimen of California boosterism was mention of the gold discovered the previous winter at Sutter's Mill on the American River. This rich vein, the writer said, was only three feet below a surface of soft rock and sand and was so extensive it was safe to predict a "Peruvian harvest of the precious metals as soon as a sufficiency of miners &c can be obtained."

The article with its almost perversely obscure reference to the California strike did not engender a gold rush, nor did it by itself even confirm the first whispered rumors to reach the East. It did, however, add by its language a significant bit to the gathering force of those rumors. The adjectival characterization of the strike as "Peruvian" was a mother lode itself, calling up peculiarly American desires and dreams of riches that waited somewhere beyond the hand-to-mouth realities of the known world: Argonauts, gold of Ophir, Cortés in Mexico, Dalfinger and Aguirre hunting the Gilded Man through South American jungles, the Pizarros looting Peru, where it was said they had captured a golden cable so heavy that 600 natives could barely lift it. . . .

For more than a century now, emigrating whites filling up the imponderable spaces of this New World had been forced by the persistent nonappearance of further caches of the fabled riches to reformulate their hopes on a more modest scale. By the middle of the nineteenth century the luck of the conquistadores seemed truly a matter of the past. But the old dream lived on in America and in the Western mind, and at the end of the summer of 1848 it was brought to quick life again. America, accidentally discovered on the way to Eastern riches, once more blazed out in the popular imagination as the land of the quick, lustrous strike.

As summer turned into fall, rumor continued to feed hope. On September 20, the Baltimore *Sun* ran a sensational story about the strike, and a few days thereafter the New York *Journal of Commerce* wrote that Californians were running over the country and picking gold out of it "just as 1000 hogs, let loose in the forest, would root up ground nuts." Now there were stirrings all along the eastern seaboard, in the South, and up and down the Mississippi Valley. By November, samples of California gold had found circuitous ways east, people held the palpable stuff in their palms, and the first ships put out for California.

At the end of the month, President Polk had in hand an official firsthand account of the strike, and when he delivered the last of his annual messages to Congress on December 5 he incorporated the glad news in an otherwise sobering discussion of the perils of the large, unretired national debt. Few if any of his listeners cared about the debt. In newspaper accounts of the message, the lead paragraphs dealt with the confirmation of the gold strike. The gold rush was on.

Had Sam Brannan, who announced the gold strike at Sutter's Mill, bellowed his news in the heart of London or in Edinburgh's Prince Street, the effect on the Old World could not have been more electrifying than the news contained in Polk's message. The word "gold" immediately leapt free of its context and flashed along the port cities of Europe, up the watercourses, and into the columns of newspapers and journals already crammed with alluring information on emigration. In the tiny North Sea fishing village of Dunbar, Scotland, even the dour master of the grammar school showed some excitement and allowed his pupils to exhibit some of their own. To ten-year-old Johnnie Muir this latest American news seemed almost too exciting to bear. In their reading book he and his classmates had already been awed by accounts of the vast American forests that contained such marvels as the sugar maple and by descriptions of the wonderful wildlife these forests harbored. Johnnie Muir had been especially taken with the descriptions of the fish hawk and the bald eagle by the Scots naturalist Alexander Wilson, who like so many of his countrymen had gone to the New World after the American Revolutionary War. The boy read Wilson's words over and over again until he knew them by heart. And now to be told there was also gold in this fabulous country! Visions of hawks, eagles, red Indians, huge trees oozing sweets, and gold glittering in the mighty gloom of the wilderness filled Johnnie Muir's head.

Such dreams may be the special and perishable blessings of childhood, yet there is good evidence that in varying degrees of vividness they were shared in these years by the adults of Dunbar and a thousand other towns and villages of the Old World and for reasons that had as much to do with European realities as American promises. At midcentury, the Old World seemed faded and chaotic, the New World bright with limitless prospect. The latest news merely made the contrast the more obvious and the impulse for emigration the more compelling.

The three decades since the Congress of Vienna had redrawn the map of Europe had seen an accelerating pace of social and economic disruption amounting to a cultural revolution. Every aspect of life from family relations to international trade was profoundly affected. What is now called the First Industrial Revolution was then a bewildering phenomenon of so many facets that not even the most farsighted social philosopher or statesman could begin to comprehend it all or predict the direction and consequences of the changes taking place. Only the great poets of the Old World could then correctly intuit some of the consequences of all this on the hearts and minds of humankind, and few were listening to them.

Well into the nineteenth century the old certainties of the medieval world, apparently long vanished in the smoke and blood of war and the political rearrangements of the intervening centuries, had survived as emotional preferences and habits of living for millions in the rural areas. Now even these were being utterly obliterated in ways more final than could have been accomplished by the blasts of cannons and the changes of flags. The very landscape that had nurtured the old ways of thought and life was fast vanishing into the pits of industry, swallowed up by the expanding industrial centers. And the old assumptions of a fixed abode, of place, of hierarchical obligations, and of home-centered labor were being roughly uprooted without effective alternatives in prospect. Village life was being deliberately sabotaged by those who owned the lands surrounding the villages and who now saw new ways to make those lands yield greater profit.

Agriculture, once the basic mode of life, was becoming increasingly consolidated and at the same time was becoming distinctly subordinate to the cities with their factories, ports, commerce. Even in the years when harvests were good, agriculturalists suffered because of lowered selling prices. And when crops were poor—as they often were in what were known in Scotland as the "Hungry Forties"—there was hunger and indeed famine, and not just in the newly spawned cities. Such had been the case in 1845, so it was again in Ireland in 1847 and 1848, and in the latter year the condition spread from Ireland to infect much of the Old World and to leave a scar on the European consciousness: such sights, such scenes of unparalleled, irremediable suffering could not easily be forgotten or understood as the bottom curve of some huge cycle. They must instead portend the end of something.

The year 1848 confirmed the general fear of crisis, for not only was there the agricultural failure and famine; there was also the attendant economic crisis. Eighteen forty-five and 1846 had seen wild speculation in wheat and railroads; then the huge wheat purchases had been followed by a bad harvest. In England business houses failed in droves, thirty-three of them in London alone in 1848.

Above all this hovered the specter of revolution on the Continent. In Paris the king had been forced to abdicate, leaving the Tuileries to the vengeance of a mob. There had been upheavals in the German and Italian states and in Hungary. In Vienna, even the grand political puppeteer Metternich had been forced to flee to England before the threat of mob violence.

Assessing the situation, the Edinburgh *Review* in its July-October 1848 number took a very Burkean view, admitting the real possibility of political collapse everywhere, a contagion emanating from France's "huge chronic ulcer," the "foul and purulent" contents of which were now disgorged upon all nations. Plainly, in order to deal with the mobs of unemployed and dispossessed, extraordinary remedies might be temporarily required, "among the rest, greater facilities to Emigration—a subject which has lately, and justly, claimed so large a share of public attention."

With the exception of the Irish, the Scots were perhaps the most susceptible to encouragements to emigration, and a man like Daniel Muir, Johnnie's father, had grown up hearing talk of American opportunities while all about him he was discovering evidence of his homeland's historic poverty and overpopulation. Daniel Muir was born in 1804, precisely the period in which a more general recognition had come to the Scots people of just how far their country lagged behind the community of modernizing nations and of how far it was likely to stay behind. Scotland's problems, exaggerated by the convulsions of the Industrial Revolution, were in fact endemic.

As early as the eighteenth century the Scots financial adventurer John Law (he of the Mississippi Company Bubble) succinctly identified the country's major problem: numbers of people, he observed, "the greatest riches of other nations, are a burden to us." The country was simply too poor to support a large population. Law's personal solution was to try his fortunes abroad as did ever-increasing numbers of his countrymen as the century wore on and conditions darkened. The years 1763–75 saw almost 25,000 Scots leave for Nova Scotia, Canada, and America, a figure that would later look paltry but in that time was of sufficient magnitude to become a major public issue.

From the Highlands, where barren gray rocks dropped precipitously into the waters of lochs and range behind range of mountains and hills bore only the tough furze and heather, the people came down to try their luck in the Lowlands, and then, finding the prospects there equally grim, went to America, about which the news was so unfailingly good. There were stories of the American soil's great, almost magical fecundity, of the inexhaustible resources, of space for a free life. And those who had seen the Glasgow tobacco dealers grow fabulously wealthy on a product of the American earth, sporting their scarlet cloaks and gold-knobbed canes, could not doubt the factual basis of these rumors. Journals like the *Scots Magazine,* which featured a special section on "British North America," and the Chambers's *Information for the People* and *Edinburgh Journal* catered to the rising interest in emigration to America. Crèvecoeur's *Letters from an American Farmer* enjoyed a sustained popularity after its first publication in 1782. In it Crèvecoeur had written extensively of the Scots immigrants descending from the "high, sterile, bleak lands of Scotland, where everything is barren and cold," lands that "appear to be calculated only for great sheep pastures." He retailed the representative history of one Andrew, an honest Hebridean, who arrived in America pale, emaciated, and virtually without resources yet who in the course of four years became "independent and easy."

They were still coming down from the high country and out from the Lowlands forty years after Crèvecoeur wrote, for the conditions that sent the emigrants to the New World were only intensifying. The Highland clearances that had begun in the 1780s had by the 1820s increased in scope and ruthlessness as thousands of Highlanders were thrown off the land to make room for sheep. So too with the agriculturalists of the Lowlands, where consolidation and modernization were squeezing out the small farmer. Even the once-prosperous weavers of Glasgow, Paisley, Renfrew, and Lanarkshire now felt the pinch as thousands willing to work for almost any wage crowded into the industry. After 1815 the weavers became the most prominent occupational group in the emigration movement, and in Lanarkshire alone they had organized thirty-two emigration societies.

Growing up in that Lanarkshire district, Daniel Muir would surely have noticed all this, would have heard the talk of the New World and of the plans of the emigration societies. Daniel Muir's flight from the backcountry to Glasgow around 1825 was part of the larger pattern and was the first step in his own eventual emigration.

Muir had been born in Manchester, England, where his soldier father was then stationed in the British army. Shortly after birth Daniel had been orphaned by the deaths of both parents, and the baby with his eleven-year-old sister Mary was taken back to the father's home region of Lanarkshire and raised there by relatives.

In nearby Glasgow, despite some feeble child-labor statutes, small children regularly worked thirteen-hour days, and in the cotton mills of Lanarkshire similar brutalizing routines were in force. So it is not difficult to imagine that life for the orphan Muir children on the farm near Crawfordjohn was anything but idyllic. There on the high moors, surrounded by steep mountains that suffered but a few bleak villages and some lead mines, Daniel Muir "lived the life of a farm servant," as his son John was later to write in an obituary notice. He continued in this when he moved to the neighboring sheep farm of Hamilton Blakley after his sister Mary had become Blakley's wife.

Given the numbing routine of such a life and the absence of parental affection, it is a little surprising that Daniel Muir should ever have displayed much joy in life or any interest in its non-utilitarian dimensions. Yet at some point in his calcified maturity he confessed to his son John that on the Crawfordjohn sheep farm he had taken pleasure in carving little images out of whatever materials were at hand. He had also made himself a fiddle and had learned to scrape across its catgut strings the tunes of hymns and ballads. The native Lowlander is said to be an outwardly dour type who conceals the warm romanticism that bubbled out in Burns and Sir Walter Scott, and if circumstances deny him any effective outlet for the romanticism and demonstrativeness within, the result can be a grim, crabbed character. So it proved with Daniel Muir, and whatever his talents for life, for art and music, they were crushed out of him in the monotonous grind of agricultural servitude. He gave up the carving, though the fiddling and singing lingered on for a few years as a pathetic, vestigial remnant of the suppressed side to his character.

The most significant event in Daniel Muir's Lanarkshire apprenticeship to life was his conversion to a brand of evangelical Presbyterianism. Indeed, this was to prove the most significant event of his entire life and, it might be argued, of the lives of those who were to be his family and who would be forced to bear the burdens of his spiritual convictions. At some point in adolescence the Word in the dress of flaming, hellfired rhetoric was brought to the lonely farmhand, and he found in the love of Jesus something of what his earthly circumstances had denied him.

The specifics of the conversion experience are unknown, whether it came as the culmination of broodings while carrying buckets in muddy boots; or while in moments in his metic's cot before exhausted sleep; or whether some bellows-lunged marathon evangelizer reached the boy on a single, indelible Sunday. Nor is it known which brand of evangelical preaching among the many was decisive. The Scots have always been a divided people with a historical predilection for disputation and "hiving off" into a welter of small and smaller camps of opinion. This is particularly obvious in religious matters, where there exists a long, reddened record of religious warfare. The years of armed strife in Jesus' name were over by Daniel Muir's time, but the schisms and splinterings continued, and in the period 1806–20 there existed seven different

Presbyterian churches plus other smaller evangelical sects like the Glassites or Sandemanians.

What probably attracted Daniel Muir most in the message he heard was the addition of emotionalism to the ascetic piety of Calvinism and the displacement therein of the elitist doctrines of election and predestination. The most obvious source for this development was the influence of John Wesley, who in the course of his career made twenty-two proselytizing trips to Scotland; he gained few actual converts to Methodism through these, but his influence on the tenor of Scots religious practice was enormous. In a larger sense, this evangelical element was another of the myriad consequences of the Industrial Revolution, which had created new conditions for which the old modes and doctrines of worship now seemed inadequate. The poor, the dispossessed, the laboring masses, those like young Daniel Muir, needed some sort of fire in their lives, and evangelical religion with its odor of brimstone and its passionate promises of true equality in the hereafter gave it to them. As John Nelson, the English stonemason, told Wesley of Christ's poor, "No other preaching will do . . . but the fine old sort that comes like a thunderclap upon the conscience." Daniel Muir's conscience was struck in that way, and it remained so throughout his life. In his subsequent position as tyrant-head of his household and in his later career as a backwoods Wisconsin preacher and wandering evangelist, he would strive with a grim earnestness to direct God's thunderclap upon the consciences of his listeners.

In the meantime, he discovered that as one of Christ's poor this was a hard world to live in, and that some places might be harder than others. So in his early twenties he became part of that shifting, often confused mass of his countrymen seeking more hopeful prospects. But leaving the farm was one thing, a gamble Daniel Muir and thousands of rural people willingly took; accommodating oneself to city life was another. What Daniel Muir encountered in the Glasgow of the 1820s was enough to disabuse him forever of the idea that the city offered anything more than another version of the miseries of the backcountry. At the same time, having experienced the limitations of Scots life in both places, he may have recognized in the Glasgow episode the potential virtues of that even bigger gamble, emigration.

For Glasgow as Muir encountered it was fearfully over-crowded, having grown without plan more than 100 percent since the turn of the century. Sanitary conditions were hopelessly inadequate, and the old dread diseases like smallpox, typhus, and cholera had reappeared. Gangs of unemployed laborers, displaced rural folk—like Muir fleeing the farms or else thrown off them—aimlessly roamed the streets. Beggars clogged every corner. Hundreds of public houses ministered in their way to the despairing, and to get drunk was said to be "the short way out of Glasgow."

Another way out and one more congenial to Daniel Muir was to accept military service, as had his father before him. He took it, though it can have done little to ameliorate his view of life's harsh, regimented necessities. In the course of this tour he found himself on a mission as a recruiting officer to the fishing village of Dunbar.

How long Sergeant Muir stayed on this particular mission is now unknown, but it was long enough to meet, court, and marry a Dunbar woman and to persuade her to buy his release from service with some of her inheritance money. Muir took over the grain and feed store that was another portion of her legacy, and he was apparently in the process of turning it into a going concern when his wife died, leaving him in sole possession.

Given the conditions of the time and Daniel Muir's own situation, it would seem that this would have been the right, natural time for him to emigrate: he was alone and childless, a comparative stranger in Dunbar, and for the first time he possessed enough capital to make a good start in the New World. He must have seriously considered it, but Daniel Muir stayed on, and it may be that he did so because he had become involved with another woman. Early in 1833 he married Anne Gilrye.

Anne was a tall, serious-faced young woman who lived with her parents diagonally across the high street from where Muir had reestablished his business in a narrow three-story building faced with the Upper Old Red Sandstone so pervasive in the East Lothian region. The parents, David and Margaret Gilrye, both came from old and proud Highlander families and had done well in Dunbar, where David had sold meat until his retirement. They considered their daughter somewhat above the obscure young widower across the way who each Sunday could be seen turning to the right out of his store and marching with military resolution down the sloping street to the kirk on the hill. In that same kirkyard lay six of the Gilrye children, victims of various respiratory diseases, and it would have been natural for the parents to have been protective of Anne, eager to guard her against a bad marriage.

In order to marry her, Daniel Muir had to overcome the strong objections of the father, but the root of these was not social; it was religious. David Gilrye was a Church of Scotland man, satisfied with the state and practice of Presbyterianism within the established body and probably defensive toward enthusiasts like Daniel Muir who thought establishment worshipers not so much satisfied as complacent with dry formalisms. If David Gilrye intuited that such a man, all but consumed in his zeal and arrogantly sure that others of differing shades of opinion were no Christians, would make a hard husband and father, he was right. Anne Gilrye's life with Muir was hard indeed, and her comforts mainly those achieved through her connections with her children and in her private life, which she took care to shield from her husband. The marriage was to end many years later in separation.

Muir family tradition has it that Anne Gilrye was of a "poetical" nature in her maiden years, a euphemism generally indicating that thin indulgence sometimes granted young women to moon over ineffables and to write harmless verse in the period before life and its realities—husband, home, children—should begin. If she did once write poetry, none of it survives, but in her later letters to her son John there are suggestions of these conjectured youthful inclinations, and in the lines the work-worn farm woman wrote there is some evidence of that romanticism her son was able fully to express and that she could vicariously express through him.

But the woman was no silent cipher in the Muir household. When in 1834 the children began to come, Anne Muir did her best to protect them from the uncompromising rigidity of the father's beliefs and behavior. Had she been any less successful, Daniel Muir's tyranny and bigotry, unchecked and unleavened, must have produced corresponding deformities in the children. As it was, all were apparently sufficiently well adjusted—though all bore the marks of such a father—and for this the mother must be given considerable credit. In the pictureless, spartan house that Daniel

Muir insisted upon, Anne Muir taught her children how to endure, and how to express and enjoy themselves when the father was elsewhere. They all had to wear the harness of Daniel Muir's beliefs and character; she showed them how to wear it in some comfort.

PART
I

Apprenticed
to the Land

The
Lessons of
a Long-Distance
Runner

In the space of twelve years Anne Muir bore her husband seven children. Margaret came first and then Sarah in 1836; two years later John was born on April 21, and he would be followed by brothers David (1840) and Daniel Jr. (1843), and by twin sisters, Mary and Annie (1846). An eighth child, Joanna, would be born in America. Amazingly, considering the region's infant-mortality rates, all the children lived and were healthy in their young years.

At the time of John Muir's birth the family still lived in the house to which Daniel Muir had moved following the death of his first wife. In January 1842, however, Daniel Muir, described in the deed as a "corn dealer," bought the house next door. To the seller, Dr. Charles Wightman, he paid cash, suggesting either that he had been doing well in business or that he had been left a substantial sum by his first wife, or both. Immediately after obtaining the house and property, Daniel Muir made over the deed to Anne Muir "for the love, favor and affection he has and bears [her]. . . ."

John Muir's childhood home in Dunbar was separated from the house in which he had been born by a narrow alley. Tall and broad,

the new house had three stories topped by a slate roof out of which
protruded three dormer windows, the fronts of which looked out
on the high street, the rears looking beyond chimneys and gables
to the country westward. Daniel Muir conducted business on the
street-level floor while the family rooms were on the second. The
older boys, John and David, lived in one of the third-floor rooms.
In back was a long narrow garden, every inch of it in use. Flowers
were banked the length of its high gray walls, and three elm trees
were homes for robins. At the rear were several outbuildings and
a combination laundry and stable in which a neighborhood widow
had life-rent rights. Behind the Muirs' property ran a street used
by deliverymen and bordered by the sheds and warehouses of the
shops on the high street; at the far end was an abattoir, and from
their garden playyard the Muir children could hear the mortal
screams of the doomed pigs.

Among the thousands of scraps of paper John Muir left, the
littered accumulation of years of random writings and scribbled
notations, was this: "My first conscious memory is the singing of
ballads, and I doubt not they will be ringing in my ears when I
am dying." It is a rich and suggestive fragment and may indicate,
among other things, that in John Muir's early childhood years his
father had not yet become so soured as to put utterly away his
fiddle and his memories of those songs of his high moorland
youth.

Whoever the singer(s) John Muir heard, he could have had no
more direct introduction to his native culture and history than these
stark, deceptively simple tunes, so wild you can almost smell moor
and mountain and sea in them or glimpse the lonely vistas that went
into their making. The narratives the tunes carry are wilder yet, and
in them the somber Scots genius can be overheard brooding on the
long dark tale that is the national history and that formed the tough
national character so often remarked on—and too often misunderstood in caricature. Bright as Burns can be or Scott or James Hogg,
still that brightness gains from its contrast with the hue and tone of
Scots history, as these authors knew so well: Scott's introduction to
his *Minstrelsy of the Scottish Border,* for instance, is a skillful redaction
of those gore-spattered chronicles that lie behind the minstrelsy he
took such joy in collecting.

The themes of the ballads Muir heard and forever after carried in his head are variations on violence: murder, incest, fratricide, revenge, suicide. In "The Douglas Tragedy" the bride's father, seven brothers, and groom are all slain in combat. In "The Bonny Hind" accidental incest leads to suicide. "Mary Hamilton" tells of infanticide, "Lady Maisry" of fratricide. In "Young Hunting" a woman kills the king's son after she has gotten him drunk and seduced him; she herself is then burned at the stake: "An it took on her fair body/ She burnt like hoky-gren" (green wood). In "Gill Morice" a husband murders his wife's presumed lover and presents her with the head for a football only to learn that this was no lover but the lady's son.

There are also the border ballads celebrating the centuries of raiding and ambushing along the English-Scots border so close to Muir's boyhood home. The heroes of these—Johnie Cock, Johnie Armstrong, Hobie Noble—are all men who live and die by the sword.

And of course the sea: surrounded on three sides by it, the Scots had sea in their history, their blood, their imagination. The Atlantic, the Irish Sea, the North Sea—none are smiling waters, and the North Sea merges itself at last into the dark waters of the Arctic Ocean. So in much of the balladry Muir would have heard the sea is a vengeful tyrant, taking, holding, disposing. In "James Harris," for example, the shade of the dead lover returns from its watery grave to carry off the young girl to her destruction: only when they are well launched on the waves does she realize that the shade is really the Devil himself and those far shores to which they are hurrying the shores of Hell. The sea washes all through such wonderful ballads as "Kemp Owyne" and "The Lass of Roch Royal" and through what is arguably the greatest of all Scots ballads, "Sir Patrick Spens," which ends on the swell of tragedy:

> Have owre, have owre* to Aberdour,
>   It's fiftie fadom deip,
> And thair lies guid Sir Patrick Spence,
>   Wi' the Scots lords at his feit.

*Half over.

Such airs and the old but ever-current news they brought were part of the natural setting of Dunbar, exposed outpost on the North Sea with the Firth of Forth stretching to the northwest. The town seemed to drop directly off into the sea, and even in the most westward-lying sections you could smell it, salty in the nose, heavy with life and death. Running any of Dunbar's west-to-east streets would have brought Johnnie Muir and his friends quickly to land's end, where the waters gnawed at the town, its wharves and harbor walls. Here was the heart of Dunbar: the harbor with its old red stone walls whitened by the dung of the skimming gulls and cormorants and gannets whose cries punctuated the sea round of the day and rose to a shattering din at day's end when the catch was brought in.

For centuries men had lowered boats here and women had waited for them to come in with holds full of herring, though in Muir's time the herring had mysteriously disappeared and now the men went after whitefish, lobster, and crab. Here were the trim smacks riding at anchor or snubbed up to the dock, their decks salt-bleached, their bows, long oars, and masts battered. Dunbar children would quickly and easily have become familiar with the apparent jumble of the ropes, nets, and crates, able to identify their proper uses and the owners of the smacks and skiffs that were canted or laid hull-up on the shelly strand.

Amid all this were the weathered men, their eyes and faces screwed into an occupational squint against the North Sea winds and sprays, working at the ropes and sails with their rough, blunt hands, glancing up occasionally at the loitering boys, many of whom in their time might be expected to follow the sea. Every boy, Muir recalled of those harborside days, "owned some sort of craft whittled from a block of wood and trimmed with infinite pains—sloops, schooners, brigs, and full-rigged ships with their sails and string ropes properly adjusted and named for us by some old sailor."

Evening called the children home, away from the excitement of the harbor and shore, as it called the boats home, too, the catch to be unloaded, shiny, smooth-bodied, lying in waiting heaps; and the harbor now a bobbing forest of masts above which the headlands rose clear and naked.

In Dunbar Johnnie Muir would have been certain to pick up his full complement of sea lore from the talk of the harbor, from those of his friends whose fathers followed the sea, as well as from the ballads. Hearing "Sir Patrick Spens," for instance, a Scots boy on the North Sea would know that it was an ill omen for one of Sir Patrick's sailors to have seen the new moon with the old moon in its arms. Not surprisingly, given the climate, much of that lore dealt with such ill omens. Sailors said that a fleecy, mackerel-backed cloud with a capful of wind in it presaged a coming storm. So did gulls flying inland or a halo around the sun. Creaking furniture or a scratching cat were signs of bad weather on the way. It was bad luck to be wished well on your way down to your boat. The boys were especially mindful of the shellycoats, supernatural creatures said to haunt coastal pools and believed by Muir and his friends to devour unwary beachcombing boys. They never waded into such pools without first thrusting a stick into the murky depths to see whether it might be snatched from their grasp.

In fair weather the boys would wander the rocky shore past Long Craigs toward Belhaven Bay, the town's original harbor, where at the tide line there was a rich collection of shells—pelican's-foot, venus, Iceland cyprina, and banded wedges—and beautiful stones with strange, apparently ahistoric etchings in them—fossils—that made you ponder the mysterious. About their heads swung a variety of shorebirds such as shags, herons, oystercatchers, waders, terns, and eiders. The boys constructed homemade guns of gas pipe, then bought gunpowder and fired clumsy lead slugs at gulls and geese.

In foul weather the noise of an angry sea was brought to Muir and his family up on the high street. Then the whole town might be enveloped in a swirling, smothering mist, half rain and half spray, whipped up off the waves lunging below the hill. The clouds would wholly merge with the gray, flotsam-flecked sea, and rain, raking the old town, would polish the slate or stone roofs that now reflected their chimneys and stain the stone walls a darker gray or red. In the harbor the crafts would bounce high and sway wide at their anchors. In the kirkyard the slim and slanting stones darkened, and the many markers there to men and ships that had gone down in the "fashes of the flood" might seem to warn with a renewed urgency.

At such times Muir was learning more than the lore of the sea. He was learning of the fathomless power of the natural world against which men might build houses and harbor walls that were puny indeed and ultimately powerless. It was an indelible lesson, one that could be borne in on him again at any time, and often in later years it would be at the odd moment when he happened to sniff salt air once more.

But whereas in so many of his countrymen this lesson tended to produce a gloomy pessimism, a silent sense of life's rocklike necessities and swift, avenging accidents, in John Muir it produced quite the opposite: an imperturbable serenity and a natural unchurched reverence founded on an awareness that—storm or smiling sun—nature includes us; that like the fish or the gulls we too must be part of this world. Pessimism or, worse, fear was ignorance of this.

The more formal lessons began when he was not quite three. Scots parents did not coddle their children, a tendency partly the result of climate and culture and founded on a somewhat grim view of life's prospects. It was best to prepare children early for the hardness of the way that lay ahead.

The school to which Muir was so early sent was a representative one: disciplined, thoroughly structured, innocently harsh. It lay at the foot of a sloping street called the Davel Brae that ran down to the sea off the high street past stone and white stuccoed houses with little gardens like the Muirs' that spilled over walls topped with imbedded bits of broken glass to keep out intruders and passing schoolboys. Around the schoolyard ran a high wall appropriately made of the same materials as those protecting the harbor. For here, too, the sea was right below, and on stormy days its spit came flying into the yard or fell in admonitory taps on the roof of the schoolhouse. The master was one Mungo Siddons, who goaded his small charges to their tasks with a combination of threats, whippings, and encouragements, with rather more of the first two than the the last.

The Davel Brae schoolyard was an unsupervised, unofficial, but faithful extension of the school proper. Here too lessons for life were administered in the same harsh way: small boys were obliged to choose sides and fight each other like armies, using whatever ammunition was available—sand, sod, or snow. And there were individual battles: fistfights were daily occurrences, according to Muir, and there was no thought of avoiding them. For the great ambition of a small boy here was to become known as a good (that is, feared) fighter. Without understanding it consciously, the Davel Brae schoolboys were acting out a received vision of life as hard and relentless, as something from which one must not flinch but bear its greatest blows with a stolid countenance, and in their own way they were preparing themselves for this.

In every respect but Daniel Muir's excessive religiosity the daily routine in the Muir household was probably as representative of that time and place as was the Davel Brae school. Breakfast in the still dark of that northern latitude consisted of oatmeal with milk or treacle, spooned out of wooden dishes.* Then the children were off to school, the stiff sea wind in their faces, their book bags slung over their shoulders.

At noon they ran home up the slope of the Davel Brae, and the father would come upstairs from his shop to preside over the main meal of the day: vegetable broth, a piece of boiled mutton, a barley scone—all this consumed in the sacramental silence that Daniel Muir insisted upon as proper for the reception of gifts from the Lord. Then back to school for the afternoon lessons, the postclassroom education of the schoolyard, and, if weather and the season's daylight permitted, perhaps a cruise along the waterfront to the harbor.

A late afternoon snack at the Muir house consisted of a half slice of unbuttered white bread, a barley scone, and warm water with milk and sugar, a drink that was known, with characteristic Scots humor, as "content." After this John and David would cross the high street to the Gilryes', where in front of the ingle grandfather Gilrye would put them through their recitations. In the dark they would then come home to a mealy boiled potato, the inevitable

---

*In a reference to Scotland's historic poverty, Dr. Johnson in his famous dictionary defined "oats" as "A grain, which in England is generally given to horses, but in Scotland supports the people."

scone, and family worship, in which Daniel Muir took the leading role, praying long and fervently that he and his should not fall into the many temptations. And then to bed. If this seems a cheerless routine, it is well to remember that the lot of many children in factories and on farms at this time was immeasurably worse, and soon enough the Muir children themselves would have cause in the Wisconsin backwoods to think fondly of these days of comparative luxury and idleness.

And they found their outlets, particularly John and David, not only on Saturday and holiday excursions along the shore and into the country to the west but also at night after they had been put to bed. In the high-ceilinged third-floor room the brothers played at voyaging under the bed covers, imagining themselves on tall-masted ships scudding before winds that took them to America or other outlandish places as they worked their ways farther down into the smothering warmth of the blankets.

They also played more adventurous and forbidden games of daring they called "scootchers." John would formulate some tremendous scootcher such as dashing across the hall into the unused room where the first Dr. Wightman's ghost was said to be eternally busy at his dusty, greening retorts. One night John climbed out of a streetside dormer window and scrambled up to the roof ridge, where he sat in triumph with his nightgown bellying like a sail in a sea breeze. David's attempt to match this scootcher nearly ended in disaster, and he had to be rescued by his older brother.

At the age of seven or eight John Muir went on to the grammar school, a high-gabled stone structure bearing a telling resemblance to a church. In fact, the Dunbar grammar school was a secular arm of a Calvinistic culture. Its values were those of the old, unreconstructed Covenanters: the sanctification of work as the only activity morally and spiritually justifiable; an institutional understanding of the inevitable individual failings; and the consequent necessity of punishment, in this case administered with the tawse, a multithonged whip that was Master Lyon's only apparent indulgence.

The small scholars, Muir remembered, had to learn daily lessons in Latin, French, and English with additional obligations in spelling, arithmetic, and geography. All of this education was instilled with regular whippings. "We were simply driven," Muir said, "pointblank against our books like soldiers against the enemy. . . . If we failed in any part, however slight, we were whipped; for the grand, simple, all-sufficing Scotch discovery had been made that there was a close connection between the skin and the memory, and that irritating the skin excited the memory to any required degree."

In addition to these punitively administered school lessons there were equally severe ones at home, where Daniel Muir forced John to memorize a certain number of Bible verses each day; there was a whipping at the end of the recitation if he faltered. By the time John was eleven he said he had "about three fourths of the Old Testament and all of the New by heart and by sore flesh." It is another indication of the impress of Calvinism on the Scots mind that there seems to have been no thought there might be some strange incongruity between the motives of masters and parents and the methods they employed. It was simply assumed that a godly mind and an educated one would have to be thrashed into the children. This method was, as Muir said, the traditional Scots one "of making every duty dismal."

Naturally, the yard of the grammar school reflected the values of the school proper and the national culture. And as the demands and punishments of the school were more severe than those of the primary school, so were the schoolyard games. The individual fights were now often serious fistfights that resulted in bloody noses and black eyes. The evidence of the former, said Muir, could always be washed off in a fountain before going home. But the latter mark was more lasting, and it was no good to tell his wrathful father that the other boy had struck first. Whatever the case, Daniel Muir struck last, and so the boy was likely to suffer two beatings on any given day—three if Master Lyon had occasion to punish him.

Kindred diversions of the schoolyard included a game in which two boys would stand toe to toe and thrash each other's bare legs with limber switches, the object being simple, sober-faced endurance. The boy who winced or showed the least bit of discomfort was the loser and the object of savage ridicule. "Wee Willie Wastle," a game in which a boy would defend his sandhill against one challenger after another until knocked off it, was also popular. The game had its genesis in Cromwell's siege of the Castle Hume in 1651, during which he indeed knocked Willie Wastle off his castle.

Still, after all these thrashings at home and school, John Muir was later able to find some redeeming quality in it all, for, he said, the thrashings had been "admirably influential in developing not only memory but fortitude as well." Here, whatever the origins, were two qualities Muir was to need and display abundantly in those solitary adventures of his mature years for which he was now unconsciously preparing.

Cromwell and his defeat of Willie Wastle were facts of history, and as such Johnnie Muir and his fellows were compelled to learn them. But it is doubtful that such book facts were as exciting to them as that wider, more immediate history text that was their surroundings. Dunbar, geographical outpost though it was, had been a historic crossroads, and the crumbling hulk of Dunbar castle was both fact and metaphor of just how much history had been enacted here. A thousand years old, the castle lineaments were almost shapeless now, and little lawns of flowers and sod had grown in places where the masonry had at last grown tired of the centuries of effort and had sunk down to sleep. Through its remaining sagging arches the boys could see Bass Rock lumping up out of the Firth of Forth while the sea surged and ebbed through what once had been lower rooms but were now dangerous, sucking grottoes the boys dared each other to enter.

They knew in a general way the highlights of the castle's history, and in later life Muir could recite these: his college roommate recalled Muir scaring the Wisconsin youths with ghostly tales of the castle and its inhabitants. They might have known, for instance, that Edward I had besieged the castle in 1296 while its defenders hurled insults at the invading "Sassenachs," calling them long-tailed curs after the Scots belief that the English actually did have tails. And as good Scots boys aspiring to become soldiers themselves and perhaps recapture some of Scotland's lost glory, they would have known that it was this campaign that had ended in Edward's theft of the Scots stone of possession, the Stone of Scone, an action that launched the career of the great William Wallace. On the castle heaps the boys played Wallace, whose legend, Muir was later to note, was a sort of Scots Bible. They relived his great victory at Stirling Bridge, his single-handed slaughter of the Sassenachs as recounted in legend and ballad, and lamented his betrayal to the English, after which, said Holinshed in his famous *Chronicles,* the patriot chief was drawn and quartered and parts of him dispatched to various public places as a warning to potential Scots troublemakers.

Dunbar castle had also been the place of Edward II's retreat after the Scots had defeated him at Bannockburn, and this event, too, was transformed into a schoolyard and castle game. Indeed, so many battles had been waged here that the boys believed that every bone they found about the ruins was the last relic of some ancient warrior, martyred in Scotland's cause.

Daniel Muir did not approve of these informal lessons of the castle, the harbor, or the seashore. To him they could not prove anything but destructive, for in such random, unsupervised freedom John and David might easily learn bad words (which they did) and worse ways. He attempted to make a sort of prison-playground of the high-walled back garden and keep the boys in it whenever they had time on their hands. He was, of course, unsuccessful, and at some point he must have given up in all but a pro forma way. For when spring came to the Lothians and the birds—larks, mavises, and robins—began to call from the westward-lying meadows, the boys could not be kept home.

With their friends, Willie Chisholm, Bob Richardson, and others, they would go out into the countryside to hear the singers, run the country roads, snatch turnips from farmers' fields, whittle wood into whistles, perhaps catch a young lark and bring it home to a cage in defiance of the children's rhyme that warned against such behavior:

> The laverock and the lintie,
>   The robin and the wren;
> If ye harry their nests,
>   Ye'll never thrive again.

Perhaps they would go south out of town past the mysterious standing stone set alone in its field, an indecipherable reminder of ancient races who had inhabited this place before the old castle had ever been built; past Doon Hill, where Cromwell had littered the

sward with the bodies of Leslie's Covenanters, and on to Brunt Hill.
Then down its far side and on to High Wood and the meadowlands
along Elmscleugh Water. Or they might go out Bob Richardson's way by Belhaven and then westward to Beesknowe and
Grangemuir.

Whatever the route, whatever the consequences for a late return home, for John Muir the disobedience was creative and absolutely essential. Considering the ways in which his father's severity
compounded the confining regimen of the Dunbar schools, these
long runs and rambles into the heart of that landscape were mental
and spiritual escapes as much as they were physical ones. Here the
boy developed the intuitive ability to take instruction, comfort, and
deep pleasure from the natural world, an ability that did so much
to convert his childhood in Dunbar and in Wisconsin from blight
to lasting spiritual treasure. The runs began, as he would later
recognize, a lifelong pattern of personal salvation. Whenever the
deadening or seductive routines of settled life threatened his inmost
nature; whenever he felt the shadows of traditional obligations and
ways of thought spreading into his mind, then John Muir would
contrive some escape as now he did on the days of spring and
summer when with brother and friends he raced on out of the old
town.

Thus the real locus of his Dunbar memories is not the sea, wild
and wonderful as it was in its moods, but the hill country he could
see from his back window: the long, broad folds of the Lammermuirs, the deep greens, the copses like shadows, the brown, regular
lines traced by the stone walls. And as if in prefiguration of his
whole life—emigration, peregrination, and solitary explorings—it
was westward he was drawn, like his later hero, Thoreau, who
claimed that unconsciously his steps always tended westward.

Outward he and the others would go, first down the sloping
street under the kirkyard hill, outward into the Lammermuirs sung
by Scott and shepherds and birds. The land rose steadily away from
the coast, the roads bending inward, inward to the slopes, following
their imperative contours, hedges, stone walls, or just the trees
bordering them. On the ridges there were rows of beeches, their
massive, smooth and green-iced trunks standing separate while
their spreading branches interlaced into a dense braid with their
neighbors. Waiting out a shower in the shelter of these beeches,

they would listen to a burn gurgling into fullness at the foot of the hill, the grasses deep or cropped close where a flock of sheep browsed, looking like stars amid the greenness. There were the bird calls, too, the larks in the fields and the woodier notes of the copse singers. Then, the rain ended, they would run on again, passing the farm folk with their reddened hands and faces and shapeless dark clothing, hearing their threatening calls fading behind, smelling the hay in the ricks, the dung in the barnyards.

And among his fellows John Muir was perhaps a bit more given to moods. Sitting under the trees or running the roads or walking the meadows, he might have heard something more than they did, something *inside* the the raindrops, inside the leaves upon which they fell: a larger music, even a call . . . something that urged and compelled. A vision commenced here of life in its fullness, of a way of living that held infinitely more promise of excitement and mystery and enjoyment than that he was learning in town: books, school, prayers, and "content." There was something out there in the Lammermuirs, and like the name of the hills it was part of him, too.

Discovering
the New World

Sometime between the late fall of 1848 and early winter of 1849, Daniel Muir made the decision to emigrate to America. From what is known of his character, it is doubtful that he consulted with any of his family but simply announced the plan after he had made it. The factors, though, that led him to the decision are fairly clear, however obscure they may have been to the rest of the family.

The largest factor was the prevailing climate of opinion that so strongly favored removal to the New World, to which was added the news from California that had so excited schoolboys and adults alike in the waning days of '48. But in the immediate foreground was Daniel Muir's perpetually restless spirit that searched through the churches and splinter movements of his time for that perfect combination of zealotry and contentment. Now in his middle age he thought he had found it and was willing to risk all to go where a new sect flourished amid the edenic gardens of America.

He had become a convert to the Disciples of Christ through the exhortations of two brothers named Gray, one of whom had established the sect in Dunbar. The Disciples were still a small movement in Scotland, but they were ardent, and they drew a kind of cultural sustenance from the Scots predilection for "hiving off" into ever smaller splinter groups in religion and politics.

This movement, however, had come to Scotland from abroad, from the New World in fact, where it had its roots in the Great Revival that stirred frontier souls at the turn of the nineteenth century. The Great Revival was in itself the successor to the Great Awakening of the eastern seaboard, and like that earlier outburst it was characterized by an emphatic individualism, by emotional demonstrations of Christian belief, and by a radical anti-institutional bias—convictions close to Daniel Muir's heart. Mormons, Shakers, Rappites, Adventists, and Spiritualists all came out of it or were greatly strengthened by it, while the established denominations, the Baptists and Methodists, gained large numbers of converts at the expense of their more staid and hierarchical competitors.

What attracted Daniel Muir—and thousands like him—was the promise here of a reversion to the warm and simple ways of the primitive Christian church as it was believed to have been in the days of Christ's earthly ministry and just after. America, unfeatured, wild, innocently verdant, was clearly the chosen place for this reversion effort, the place where at last Christ's kingdom on earth could be established. So at least believed the Scots immigrant founders of the Disciples, Thomas and Alexander Campbell, and their American coadjutor, Barton W. Stone.

The Campbells and Stone joined forces in 1832, and thereafter the Disciples became a potent religious force all along the border of an advancing civilization. In Tennessee, Kentucky, Ohio, and Missouri, Alexander Campbell was a figure of almost legendary importance until the Civil War, and Mark Twain has recorded in his autobiography the excitement Campbell's arrival could generate in a sleepy hamlet of middle America. Where such a man as Campbell preached literal adherence to the text of the New Testament without frills or clerical interference and where there seemed such limitless opportunities for the advancement of both the cause and self, there Daniel Muir would go, throwing over as in a moment his prospering grain dealership, ripping up his wife's family roots and all his associations with his native land.

How much of the background of this decision the Muir children ever knew or understood is questionable. Probably the older four, Margaret, Sarah, John, and David, knew at least that their father was in the strong grip of a new religious enthusiasm; as the years went on and they saw him through an endless succession of these, they apparently learned a sort of ironic tolerance. Now, perhaps they merely accepted his latest involvement as one of the conditions of their lives without understanding how profoundly it was about to change their own destinies.

As for Anne Muir, she was probably simply told, and then Daniel Muir announced his plan to his in-laws. David Gilrye was vastly displeased and even alarmed for the welfare of his daughter and grandchildren. He now redrew his will so as to bar Daniel Muir from any inheritance and forced Muir to leave Anne behind with Margaret and the three younger children until a satisfactory home had been established. The old man knew enough of American realities to sense some of the perils of Daniel Muir's decision, and this in addition to his view of his son-in-law's capriciousness and restless spirit produced in him deep forebodings.

On February 1, 1849, Daniel and Anne G. Muir sold their property to Dr. John Lorn, a local physician, the deed of sale being officially recorded on the twelfth. On the evening of the eighteenth John and David were at the grandparents' hearthside where Grandfather Gilrye put them through their educational paces. Then the father came in from across the high street to announce that they need not learn their lesson this night for in the morning they would be off for America.

Fifty-eight years later John Muir recalled vividly his reaction to this lightning bolt of news: "No more grammar, but boundless woods full of mysterious good things; trees full of sugar, growing in ground full of gold . . . ." He instantly thought of the naturalist Wilson's hawks and eagles and of Audubon's awe-inspiring descriptions of flocks of passenger pigeons that filled the western skies like mighty thunderclouds. Here, suddenly, magnificently, was the prospect of millions of birds' nests and no gamekeepers in all the "wonderful schoolless, bookless American wilderness." John and David were delirious with delight, so much so (as Muir recalled in the unpublished version of this episode) that they could not work up a "decent regret" over leaving their grandparents. They promised to send grandfather a box of the fabulous tree sugar packed around with gold. But Gilrye had heard another side to the American story in the tales of terrific hardship and child agricultural servitude as recounted in the letters of immigrants. He knew, looking at these two small boys, wide-eyed in the firelight, that soon enough they too would be enlisted in the breaking of the new lands and that they might themselves be broken in the process. Poor laddies, he called them, and gave each a keepsake gold coin.

Grandfather's dour forecast was lost on the boys. In the dark street John shouted to some passing schoolmates that he was going to America in the morning. They jeered back their disbelief: the thing was incredible.

And yet in the next morning's gray light the Muir family with the Gilryes in attendance could be seen bundling down the high street, past the kirkyard (where soon David and Margaret Gilrye would join six of their children beneath a wide heavy marker) and on to the train station. The Glasgow train steamed in, Daniel Muir shepherded Sarah, John, and David aboard it, and they were gone.

In Glasgow there was a new stir to the city to which Daniel Muir had fled in his youth. The stir was the immigration trade, and docksides bristled with the thousands bound outward on errands of necessity and hope. Posters advertised swift passage to limitless opportunity, and the papers were filled with reports of the newest incentive, gold. A newspaper dispatch by electric telegraph told of discussions of a proposed railway across the Panamanian isthmus; another recounted the huge migration to California currently in progress from the eastern United States. There were dozens of items crammed under the heading "Ho! For California" and announcing the availability of passage to Chagres, of California mining boots, of daguerreotypes for those who wished to leave behind likenesses for family and friends, even of specially durable pens for those bound for the gold fields, these last items guaranteed to outlast a "cargo of quills."

There were other marks of the times that February day as the Muirs stowed their gear aboard with the other emigrants. One item in the day's news told of a fire in a cheap Glasgow theater that had so far taken the lives of more than fifty people. Another tallied ninety-two recent cases of cholera. In comparison with the brilliant prospects in the offing, the Old World must have indeed seemed old, dreary, and diseased to those—many of them newly married, so Muir remembered—aboard that bluff-prowed ship nudging down the Clyde in the gloom of a winter evening. But perhaps to none was the contrast more dramatic and exciting than to the boy, not quite eleven, who hung onto the rails as the lights of the Old World dropped steadily astern. The sea, woods, and meadows of the Lothians had created a hunger in Johnnie Muir for the wild. He was now bound for a place that promised to satisfy it fully.

As he recalled the passage years later, Muir found it a grand and glorious six-week holiday. There was, of course, no school with its dulling rote routines and cheerless martial tone. And there were probably no thrashings, either, for Daniel Muir (and Sarah as well) was seasick much of the time. John and David were thus much on their own and scampered about the tilting decks, dodging sea chests and sailors, and marveling at the great, rough expanse of water. They made friends with the sailors, learned at first hand the uses of those knots, ropes, and sails they had encountered as seaside boys in Dunbar. Now at last they were aboard a ship instead of merely watching them sail past on their much-conjectured destinies. But Muir also suggests that his delight in the passage was not shared by many of the emigrants, and even had he been silent on this, we know enough about such midnineteenth-century voyages to have drawn the inference.

They were often grim affairs. Ships plying the immigration trade were routinely overcrowded in defiance of the laws, and few health-care provisions were enforced during voyages that averaged about forty days (the Muirs' was forty-seven). Many captains kept their passengers virtual prisoners below deck, where fetid air, bad water, and tainted food produced "ship's fever" (typhus), dysentery, and other intestinal ailments. In the 1830s and '40s the ships brought cholera with them and the mortality was often frightful: passengers told of scores of bodies being dumped overboard. In 1847 seventeen thousand cholera cases were logged at Quebec alone; on the ship bringing Thorstein Veblen's father from Norway to Wisconsin in that same year, every child died en route.

There was sickness aboard the Muirs' ship, too, and John Muir

remembered the emigrants bravely attempting to keep up their
spirits by singing songs and swapping happy dreams of futurity
amid the smoky air of the hold. The Scots aboard talked of the
settlements made by their countrymen in Nova Scotia, along the St.
Lawrence, and in Ontario. They knew also of the sizable Scots and
Scots-Irish population of South Carolina and the junction area of
Tennessee, Kentucky, North Carolina, and Virginia. Apparently
Daniel Muir, though he too knew of these settlements, and though
he had hoped to settle amid a group of coreligionists, had shipped
with only the most general knowledge of American geography and
with no fixed notion of where he might settle his family. Most of
the stories he had heard were of Canada, but now he heard anecdotes of the relentless hardships of the Canadian wilderness, how
a man might sweat himself into an early grave grubbing out a
meager farm in the shadow of the endless forests. He heard too of
the open prairies suitable for farming that lay somewhere below
Canada's southern border. For years, Scots who had originally migrated to Canada had been moving south into the States for this
very reason.

In addition, Daniel Muir discovered some Disciples of Christ
among the emigrants, and from these he learned of settlements the
sect had made in the newly opened region of Wisconsin. In 1849,
the Disciples had established centers at Manitowoc, Center, Platte-
ville, and Waupun. Doubtless, it was said, more would be established (they were), for in this year Wisconsin's population was
growing at a faster rate than that of any state in the region. It had
succeeded Ohio as *the* place to settle. Daniel Muir's view now
shifted southward from Canada as the voyage continued, and by the
time they raised the port of New York he had determined to try
Wisconsin.

On the mild breezes of April 5, the Muirs' ship came to port. In
those days incoming foreign vessels were required to clear a Staten
Island quarantine station where the obviously sick were detained,
but then the ships proceeded directly to dock to disgorge their
passengers without any official reception process whatever. The
newcomers simply gathered their belongings and got off.

Waiting for them were the unofficial greeters: crimps and

sharks who would tote baggage at extortionate rates and disappear with it if not closely followed; others who sought to waylay the foolish in dockside taverns and spend their money for them; confidence men who for a fee would disclose to these land-hungry Europeans the finest piece of western land available anywhere; others who could arrange inland passage at what were described as rock-bottom terms. In the spring of 1849, business for these types was brisk. There was the uproar of the gold rush, and there were hundreds of thousands of innocent immigrants tumbling in—more than 200,000 this year of '49 into the port of New York alone. Viewing this unprecedented phenomenon from the vantage point of local journalists, Horace Greeley and Walt Whitman hoped these newcomers would not become trapped in the sprawling port cities and adjacent towns of the eastern seaboard but would get the right advice and head west.

Daniel Muir, with his eye now set on Wisconsin, did so, lingering but a day or two in New York before arranging passage up the Hudson to Albany. There the family saw evidence of the destruction caused by a great fire the previous summer, and there too they saw evidence of that almost ferocious energy of these Americans, who had already rebuilt much of the gutted area. Then along the Erie Canal to Buffalo. The opening of the canal in 1825—the engineering wonder of its time—had proved to be the major factor in attracting settlers like the Muirs into the Midwest, for it had put the ports of Lake Michigan's western shore on an all-water route to New York City. The canal also had the effect of inflating western New York State land values and so encouraging migrants to hunt farther west in search of cheaper real estate.

Buffalo was the gateway to the new region and in this year it would see more than a quarter of a million migrants pass through on their ways to the prairies. Here Daniel Muir made contact with William Gray, brother of that Philip Gray who led the Edinburgh chapter of the Disciples. Doubtless Gray gave Muir further information of the locations of Disciples centers and good lands in Wisconsin, and John remembered that his father also had a conversation then with a fellow grain dealer who told him that most of the grain received in Buffalo came from Wisconsin.

The Muirs took passage on one of the daily lake steamers out of Buffalo, jammed to its railings with a rough and travel-stained crowd of gold rushers and immigrants, each in his or her national dress, and five days later arrived at Milwaukee, where they joined yet another throng on the wharves and dockside streets and vacant lots. There amid the wheat, pork, and flour from the inland farms they haggled for oxen and wagons to take them still farther.

The Swedish novelist Fredrika Bremer was in Milwaukee about the same time and found it a beautiful town whose buildings were mostly of pale yellow brick with a populace dominated by thrifty German immigrants. But in 1849 hogs still roamed Milwaukee's streets, the municipal sewerage system was primitive, and there was (again) cholera. Even had Daniel Muir been disposed to stop here and set up again as a grain dealer, city property was dear, and all the best land on the outskirts had been snapped up by speculators. Those like himself who wanted cheap land were obliged to travel toward Madison and then strike northward through the middle of the state. Muir made a bargain at the port city with a farmer just in from Fort Winnebago with a load of wheat who, for thirty dollars, agreed to transport the Muir family and what John Muir called "our formidable load of stuff" to the town of Kingston some one hundred miles to the northwest.

And so they were off again on the last leg of their long trip, going now over the heavy, mired spring prairies, the oxen and wagon groaning and creaking under the grievous burden of immigrant belongings, many of them purchased in the misguided notion that nowhere in the wilderness beyond Buffalo could the necessities of civilized life be had. Atop the massed stuff—scales, weights, scythes, kettles, stove—sat the severe seeker, Abraham of his little flock, who had set his face toward what he hoped would at last prove his promised land.

The way was rough. Where there were roads these were usually not much better than the unimproved countryside, especially in springtime. Assuming a generally northwestward route to Kingston, they would have passed out of Milwaukee into a region of sugar maples (those treasure trees of which John Muir had heard), basswood, and oaks. Here and there were narrow little valleys with swamps and stands of black spruce and tamarack and hemlock. The junction of present Jefferson County and Dodge County was actually the best farming land the Muirs would have seen on their way to Kingston, but the immigrant father could not have known this, and there were no farms there to give him a clue.

So they kept their way through the oak openings, skirting the streams with their heavy thickets. Until a few years earlier, this portion of the country had been all but unknown to whites, but now a few settlements gave some cheer to anxious travelers—though probably the Muir boys were delighted by the areas they passed through that seemed most untouched. A man named Hyland had recently broken a wagon road from Watertown north to the center of Dodge County and had settled on the prairie there. Others had followed so that houses and barns now dotted the prairie, and all the quarter sections along Hyland's road had been taken. At Beaver Dam there was another small settlement and a sawmill in operation.

They went on through the sedgy meadows of southeastern Columbia County, then prairie and oak openings with the country beginning to roll now into knolls and hills, until at last they arrived at Kingston, hardly more than a huddle of houses with an inn at the crossroads. Alexander Gray, a bluff, hearty Scots settler near Kingston, readily agreed to help Daniel Muir locate on a suitable piece of land. Gray's farm was on a section road and he knew the lines of the immediate locale and the qualities of the soil. While their father was off on this business, John and David plunged into their own business of establishing childhood's intimacy with their new surroundings. Still in the fiction of America as a wild and wonderful playground, they explored the Grays' whitewashed farmhouse, the barn and outbuildings, the creek that ran behind—smooth and brown-watered with black snags on which snapping turtles sunned and drowsed. They played in the sandy road shaded by bur oaks, white oaks, and shagbark hickories. At the edges of the road ran remnant lines of the big blue stem flower that had once ruled the open lands of the whole Midwest. Meanwhile, Sarah was introduced to reality as Mrs. Gray gave her beginning lessons in the life drudgeries of a farm woman.

Gray and Daniel Muir picked out eighty acres of open woodland about six miles to the northwest on a knoll that sloped westward down through a glacial meadow laced with brooks to a small lake. On the brow of the knoll, Gray, Muir, and some neighbors joined in the quick construction of a bur-oak shanty that would serve as shelter for Daniel and the three children while a more substantial house was framed for the rest of the family.

In the meantime, life was a glorious and innocent exploration for the two immigrant boys from a Scots fishing village. They raced through the meadow, prying into tufts of grass and bushes in search of nests and burrows; climbed trees to inspect the birds' nests they had spied; poked along the brooks, marveling at the profusion of snakes, frogs, and turtles. Muir recalled, "This sudden plash into pure wildness—baptism in Nature's warm heart—"

> how utterly happy it made us! Nature streaming into us, wooingly teaching her wonderful glowing lessons, so unlike the dismal grammar ashes and cinders so long thrashed into us. Here without knowing it we were still at school; every wild lesson a love lesson, not whipped but charmed into us. Oh, that glorious Wisconsin wilderness!

In that spring of 1849, no white settler lived within a four-mile radius of the Muirs, nor was there a single man-made road in the vicinity other than the old Indian trail that ran through the marshy lands along the Fox River to the town of Portage. To children accustomed to the countryside of the Lammermuirs with its old farms and stone-walled fields, this new landscape must have appeared shaggy indeed, a true wilderness. Strange and wild-seeming birds like nighthawks and partridges bellowed and drummed in the woods. Fireflies spangled the unbroken fields at dusk. And on the far side of the long, narrow lake an occasional drift of wood smoke marked the encampment of some wandering Indian hunter: there were yet some Winnebagoes to be seen passing on their disconsolate ways through what had lately been their homeland. But the Muirs had not settled in the midst of a wilderness but instead on the edge of a rapidly advancing civilization, one that in Wisconsin was tearing into the landscape and transforming it into a recognizable, functioning part of an increasingly industrialized republic. In this year the line of white settlement had moved considerably west of where the Muirs now were, though to be sure north and northwest of their homestead was still Indian territory.

In the two hundred years since Jean Nicolet had met the

Winnebagoes in 1634—wearing his Chinese damask to be prepared for oriental potentates—Wisconsin had remained terra incognita to white America. Throughout much of this time the Winnebago, Menominee, Ojibwa, and Sac and Fox tribes had hunted, fished, gathered grain, planted corn, and buried their dead in ancestral lands, largely undisturbed by all but the advance men of civilization: stray white hunters, fur traders, and voyageurs, singing as they flashed their canoe paddles through the waters at forty strokes to the minute.

Nearly two centuries after Nicolet arrived, a census of the territory found little more than 3,000 whites among about 24,000 Indians. All this changed and rapidly so after the Black Hawk War in 1832. The old chief's people, the Sac and Fox, the Winnebago, and other tribes who were marginally implicated in the doomed resistance effort, were all severely punished. The decisive and bloody conclusion to the war and the subsequent tours on which Black Hawk was taken as a prisoner of war advertised the openness of new lands and the availability of titles to them.

By the following year, the forced land cessions of the tribes had opened all the territory south of a slanting line from Green Bay to Prairie du Chien to survey and settlement, and the Wisconsin land rush was on. Just as "Ohio Fever" had once threatened the depopulation of Connecticut, so now this newest contagion threatened to draw off not only the best of Ohio but even more migrants from the old northeast and western New York State. Organized as a territory in 1836 with a white population of 11,000, Wisconsin had 31,000 by 1840. By 1850 it had 305,000, and by the end of that decade it would have more than doubled this figure—a growth rate unchallenged anywhere except in California.

The transmogrification of the state from the year of John Muir's birth to his arrival there is an even more striking illustration of the multiform process that was changing the face and character of a continent. Black Hawk had died in the year Muir was born (and had been buried in the alien regalia of his conquerors), and in that same year one William Smith, a Philadelphia gentleman, published an account of his recent travels through the new territory. He mentioned the wild fecundity of the place, the herds of deer, the flocks of prairie hens that would start up under the hooves of the horses, the huge, luscious strawberries of the prairies, and the abundance of agricultural and mineral wealth just waiting to be tapped by enterprising settlers who were unafraid to plant themselves beyond the fringe of settlement.

Sketching the bright prospects of these new lands, Smith said the settler's land was

> purchased at the government price of one dollar and twenty-five cents per acre: land of the richest soil in the world. His prairie ground awaits immediate cultivation. His crops yield him from thirty-five to fifty bushels of fall wheat per acre, and from twenty to thirty bushels of spring wheat is calculated on as a sure crop; barley will yield from forty to sixty bushels, and oats from fifty to seventy-five bushels . . . .

This utopia lay in the future, however, for when Smith made his tour Wisconsin was indeed beyond the fringe, and only the lead-mining region of its southwestern corner had anything that could be said to be a dense population. Milwaukee was only a small village, the huge pineries of the north woods were all but unknown, and lumber for downstate construction was actually imported. Fort Winnebago (built under the supervision of U.S. Army Lieutenant Jefferson Davis) was the northernmost outpost of white civilization.

By the time Fredrika Bremer arrived in 1849 the changes were astonishing. Milwaukee was now a populous port of 20,000, and Bremer found immigrant groups scattered throughout the lower half of the state. They were thinly scattered, to be sure, and the state's roads were rough to the point of threatening bodily injury to stagecoach travelers, but Bremer also observed that it was "remarkable that in all directions throughout this young country, along these rough roads, which are no roads at all, run these electric [telegraph] wires from tree to tree, from post to post, along the prairie land, and bring towns and villages into communication." Milwaukeee was thus connected to Chicago and to the eastern seaboard.

To some the telegraph seemed an expensive toy, but its presence in the new land was a sure indication that American civilization had reached out to include Wisconsin in its fulsome, energetic embrace. Here once again was the national drama of the subjugation and obliteration of the wilderness. As a man, John Muir would see this drama as a tragedy. Now, a youth in the very midst of it, it was only life and necessity to him. Unwittingly, helplessly, he took up his part in it.

That first spring Daniel Muir hired a "Yankee" to help clear enough ground for crops to see them through winter. As the men worked, John and David pestered the Yankee with questions about the flora and fauna. They wanted to know all about the sandhill cranes whose choked cries sounded as if something had been cranked in their throats and to whom they could never get close before the big birds took air with astonishing suddenness, their wings white against the dense growth of woods. They wondered at the sound of partridge drumming, the meaning of the love song of the jack snipe and the song of the whippoorwill. The Yankee supplied only brusque answers to these and other questions, and there was so much to absorb in this new world, so many things for which questions could not even be formulated.

John Muir reveled in it all: the huge, portentous thunderheads, the clamoring chorus of peepers along the lakeshore, the spring flowers that burst forth in the watery meadow, and most especially the songs of the birds. But soon enough his schoolboy's vision of America as a vast playground where a boy might wander forever free, feasting his eyes and soul on endless beauty—a dream at least as old as settlement here—broke hard against reality: Muir's father put him to work in the fields clearing away brush for the advent of the plow and heaping it in great piles for burning. Nor did Father lose this opportunity to sermonize as the bonfires threw out blasts of white heat and showers of sparks. Think, he would say to John, just think what an awful thing it would be to be thrown into the midst of such a great, hot fire. Then think of hellfire that's so much hotter and that's reserved for all bad boys and for sinners of every sort who disobey God. Think, too, he added (as if this were not enough) of the infinitude of their sufferings, for neither will that hellfire ever die out—ever—nor will the sufferings of the sinners ever cease.

Then too Father once again took up his habit of childbeating. "The old Scotch fashion," Muir recalled, "of whipping for every act of disobedience or of simple playful forgetfulness was still kept up in the wilderness, and of course many of those whippings fell upon me." He described them as "outrageously severe," and they left their marks. Many years afterward in a letter to a boyhood friend, Muir offered some uncharacteristically personal reflections on this practice which, if it was indeed a national one, was in this case surely compounded by the father's cankered religiosity:

> When the rod is falling on the flesh of a child, and, what may oftentimes be worse, heart-breaking scolding falling on its tender little heart, it makes the whole family seem far from the Kingdom of Heaven. In all the world I know of nothing more pathetic and deplorable than a broken-hearted child, sobbing itself to sleep after being unjustly punished by a truly pious and conscientiously misguided parent.

"Compare," he then concluded, "this Solomonic treatment with Christ's."

The "Solomonic treatment" continued through spring and into summer, the cleared space in the oak opening gradually widening and the crops planted. When Daniel Muir wasn't plowing and planting he was hauling lumber from the Kingston lumberyard and supervising the construction of the permanent dwelling. At the end of the day the family would gather in the bur-oak shanty for the evening meal, and as the last bit of daylight lingered within the rough confines, they would kneel on the bare plankings in family worship. Muir evidently took some pleasure in remembering of these moments that he "too often studied the small wild creatures" that played about the devout scene, the field mice and beetles that used the interior of the shanty as if it had been made for them.

By fall when Anne Muir and the rest of the children arrived the house was ready. Of good pine, it stood stout, foursquare, and high with eight rooms; like its owner it was utterly without frills. Behind it was the bur-oak shanty, now converted to a stable for the boys' Indian pony, Jack. A barn and corral were at the foot of the hill leading down to the lake. John Muir said their wheat field was the first in the vicinity, and on that first evening together the reunited family strolled the borders of the field while Daniel Muir extolled the virtues of his frontier industry.

In his autobiography Muir did not spare readers when it came to descriptions of farm life, but he mentions none of that winter of 1849–50. They must have laid in enough corn, potatoes, and fuel wood to get by, they fed the stock wild hay, and for additional supplies they would have gone along the river road to Portage, a larger town than Kingston and about twelve miles distant. Here Muir had his first good look at American civilization along its cutting edge.

A rough settlement, Portage was strategically positioned between the Wisconsin and Fox rivers. At first it had been a fur-trading center in Astor's sprawling network, and then in the natural course of such things a military fort. Now, with the furbearing animals hunted out, it was a town supplying the needs of the local farmers and the red-coated lumberjacks bound north to the pineries or south out of them. The fort, as Muir remembered it, still stood within its stockade and was "painted a glistening white, still formidable although the last company of soldiers had departed three or four years ago to take part in War with Mexico."

There were perhaps 400 permanent residents when the Muirs arrived—Scots, Germans, Yankees from Vermont and Maine, a few blacks—and a shifting population of land speculators, canal boomers, lawyers, whores, theatrical troupers, lumberjacks, and Indians. As a boy from a Scots fishing village, Muir would already have seen his share of pubs and drinking, yet he remembered the freedom with which whiskey flowed in Portage and noted that the "many stores that rejoiced under the name of groceries and genral [*sic*] merchandise emporiums made their main profits out of whiskey." The streets were enlivened by Indian ponies at the hitching posts, Indian dogs everywhere, and frequent fistfights. There were cows on the common when the weather permitted. Twice weekly the stage arrived from Madison and pulled up with a grand flourish at the tavern of Uncle Dick Veeder. Here the stage driver, a kind of local hero in red-flannel shirt, high boots, and wide hat, would swing down to mingle with the crowd of lumberjacks and raftsmen who made Veeder's tavern their clubhouse.

With the coming of spring, 1850, life at what the Muirs called Fountain Lake farm began in earnest. Like so many other settlers, Daniel Muir was going to plant wheat as his cash crop: for a man struggling to get a claim into production, what with clearing, chopping, and fencing, wheat farming was the answer since it could be done in relatively careless fashion and on an extensive basis. So, much more of the Muir land had to be broken open and, as the eldest son, John Muir was drafted for the work.

As soon as the frost was out of the ground, the boy, though not quite twelve, was put to the plow behind the shambling oxen. The big handles of the shafts were about as high as his head so that all day he was obliged to trudge through the shearing furrows with his arms upraised, perhaps as many as eight or nine miles of walking before noon dinner. At the end of each row there was the task of hauling the heavy share loose from the gooey clods and setting it straight again for the return up field. At last the noon dinner and its hour of rest while his young muscles cooled and shrank so that, when called again to the work, he would go bent and hobbling at first like an old man. After another wearying round through the long afternoon, there was supper, the cows to be brought in, horses to be fed, worship, bed.

So it had begun: the patient, inevitable wheeling of the seasons and the years—a decade—and the boy driven relentlessly through them until at last he had emerged on the other side, work-hardened, accustomed to more than ordinary hardship, a man. But a man who had struggled and had managed to retain a youth's enthusiasm for the natural world that was the scene of his daily toil.

All his life he would remember with that primitive vividness the sights, sounds, and smells of the Wisconsin seasons. Spring announced itself with the shotlike reports of the lake ice cracking and breaking up. As the boy trudged the fields putting in the wheat, the corn, and the potatoes, his mind found refuge and instruction it would lay up for the harvest of maturity as he attended the mysterious emergence of the myriad life forms after the hard sleep of the Wisconsin winter. With the breaking of the ice, the loon, the great northern diver, sounded its utterly wild, wavering cry above the freed waters. Muir marveled at its apparently crazy, wing-dipping routes above the lake, how it would suddenly swoop, splash, and disappear beneath the surface and then emerge hundreds of yards farther on, beating the water from its feathers in flashing beads. Once he shot and wounded one of these magnificent creatures and brought it into the house, where he was able to study its anatomy at close range.

After the loons' appearance came the bluebirds, bright and

tuneful harbingers that told the sure advance of the new season on
the thawing land, then the song sparrows, thrushes—those grand
singers—the bobolinks, and the handsome red-winged blackbirds.
It was a memorable day to Muir when he beheld for the first time
the fabulous passenger pigeons of which he had read in Dunbar
days. They arrived on a spring day just after the snow had melted,
thousands and thousands of them, sweeping the woods clean of
acorns in a few minutes. Despite the fact that, as Muir said, every
"shotgun was aimed at them and everybody feasted on pigeon
pies," for years they kept coming, spring and summer, and no one
could have foretold that this apparently inexhaustible species would
be hunted to extinction by the turn of the century.

Far less spectacular but equally awesome in their grace and
clearly intelligent behavior were the flocks of Canada geese that
broke their northward journeys to alight warily in the Muir wheat
fields. After feeding on the young leaves they would mount again
into the softening skies and assemble into harrow-shaped formations, leaving the plowboy behind in the fields gazing after them
and musing on the mysteries of animal ways, perhaps already beginning to feel that "blind instinct" was not an adequate explanation
of the behavior of such wonderful creatures as these.

Through the gradually lengthening days he worked on, kept
company by birds busy with nest building and babies, the peepers
beginning again to sing in the rushy margins of the lake, and the
smaller creatures of the field who had come out into the warming
sun—like the gophers who ate so much of the seed corn before it
could sprout and whom Muir and his brothers were commanded to
kill.

Spring ripened into summer and with it came the hardest labor
as the heat intensified. The Muirs had settled far enough south in
the state to experience corn-belt summers: hot, hazy days of high
humidity punctuated by explosive thundershowers that cooled the
air only momentarily before the sun rolled out again from behind
the clouds to shine down fiercely on the wet lands. Such days began
for them at dawn when gauzy mists hung low over the waiting
fields, lake, and woodlands. Muir sharpened tools, fed the stock,
chopped stove wood, and struggled up the slope from the spring
under the slopping water buckets. Then there was breakfast, and
then the fields. In the early years before Daniel Muir bought cul-

tivators, all the cleared land had to be hoed, and the business of corn hoeing was a deadly, heavy one. Daniel Muir insisted that the hoes be kept busy at a machinelike, unvarying pace, that there be no talking or loitering when the children were in the field. Sickness was not allowed. Only once could Muir recall that he had been excused for illness, when he had a case of pneumonia from which he almost died. On another occasion, he had a severe case of the mumps but had to bear a hand anyway, though he often staggered and fell among the wheat sheaves.

In the deeps of the fields the sun streamed down on the boy and his brothers and sisters, the only shade being a solitary shagbark hickory or oak—underneath which they were forbidden to pause —and the occasional big and bossy Wisconsin clouds that drifted lazily across. Grasshoppers droned a steady, reedy accompaniment to the chink-chinking of the hoes. The friable soil was so hot the children scratched for cooler holds with their bare toes. When the breeze rustled the broad leaves of the corn, a heavy, milky smell engulfed the young toilers and seemed to intensify the heat.

If there was still enough light left after the evening chores, Muir and his brothers might have the luxury of fishing in the plank boat their father had made for them. Bullfrogs bellowed from the reeds, mosquitoes sang in their ears, and the placid lake was delicately laced with the zigzagged lines of the water bugs. The boys trailed their blistered, swollen feet in the darkening waters and trolled for pickerel and sunfish, black bass and perch.

Harvest was the hardest part of this hardest season. Wheat shatters quickly on the stalk, and it was watched anxiously as it ripened toward fullness, first the roots turning gold, then the necks, and at last the matured heads. Now there was a furious haste to cut and bind and store it, so Muir and the others were called from their beds at four in the morning and were in the fields at first light. All the long forenoon they relentlessly cut and bound, the oldest boy bent in cruel posture above the crooked snath, pulling the blade toward him through the bright stalks while the August sun crawled to the heaven of the noon dinner, perhaps announced to anxious eyes by the flutter of an apron from an upper window. Coming in to dinner, they would greedily seize upon the watermelons and muskmelons left cooling in the spring since morning. The sweet and juicy meats of these, Muir said, "were a glorious luxury that only weary barefooted farm boys can ever know."

At such times they worked the fields until dusk and sometimes even after and went to bed utterly drained. "In the harvest dog-days and dog-nights and dog-mornings," Muir recalled, "when we arose from our clammy beds, our cotton shirts clung to our backs as wet with sweat as the bathing-suits of swimmers, and remained so all the long, sweltering days" that were loaded with as much as seventeen hours of heavy labor.

Sunday afternoons were the only times they could call their own. After the Bible lessons, the Sunday school lessons, and the church services through which they struggled to stay awake, they could fish or swim in the lake or wander the nearby countryside in company with neighboring farm kids. In the early summer they might go strawberry picking or go after the dewberries or huckle-berries whose hearts, as Muir remembered them, were colored like little sunsets. They might roam as far as the wild-rice marshes on the Fox to get a shot at the fat mallards that feasted there in flocks of thousands. They might climb Observatory Hill, the highest point around, and gaze off at the blue Baraboo Hills to the west; or climb the loose, glacial slopes of Wolf Hill, up through the oaks and red cedars to the high fields cleared long ago by the Indians, inhabited now only by crows and red-tailed hawks whose sailing cries seemed to add distance and dimension to the increasingly cultivated land-scape that unrolled beneath them.

But best of all was the lake on the homestead. Ringed around with marsh grass and jeweled with white water lilies, its brown waters were so clear you could see bottom even at considerable depths, the sun rays filtering down through it in long, angled shafts. They drifted over it in their plank boat, watching the skittering of the water bugs, feeling the sun hot on their backs and luxuriating in the sense that they could cool off at any moment by simply dropping over the side. They fished lazily and learned to swim in a southern cove bordered with purple swamp thistle, cattail rushes, and tamaracks. Wading in here, their feet sank quickly and softly into the lime ooze. Then they pushed off, feeling the reeds trail the lengths of their bodies, tickling at last their toes until they were free of them and into deeper water.

When the wheat had been harvested and the hay as well, the pace of work slackened a bit and the weather too began to mellow toward fall as if in sympathy. John Muir now had to plow for winter wheat, chop wood, and shuck Indian corn. There was also the drudgery of stump grubbing, a task that fell to him as the eldest boy. Some days he spent more on his knees than on his feet, bent in the furrows over the tough old oak and hickory stumps, digging and chopping at the huge, gnarled roots. Splitting rails for fencing was another of his special chores, his father having tried it briefly and failed. Muir said he used to cut and split as many as a hundred logs a day of knotty oak, "swinging the axe and heavy mallet, often with sore hands, from early morning to night." Meanwhile, the colors came out in the woods, pumpkins turned bright against the slow fading of the grasses, and asters, goldenrod, sunflowers, and daisies put forth their special glows. In the shady portions of the meadows, ferns—to which Muir was especially sensitive all his life—unfurled their lacy banners.

Sometimes, too, more than these autumnal flowers glowed on the land, for in the early years of the Muirs' settlement great grass fires were a common feature of this season, as predictable as the turning of the leaves and the flowering of the late plants: huge expanses of prairie were swept up and the night skies reddened like an angry sunset. An English immigrant to Wisconsin in 1847 wrote excitedly back to the Old World about the sight of these prairie fires, which he described as burning "day and night for months together." As more and more of the country came under cultivation, the fires were confined, and the narrowing spaces between the plowed fields grew dense with woody growths that the fires had once checked.

On Sunday afternoons in the fall, John Muir and the others might go nutting in the leaf-showering woods where they especially delighted in hickory nuts. In the trees the birds began to gather on the stripped branches. The bobolink, whose song had been so fine a feature of spring's glad greening, now departed for southern rice fields. Muir noted that some species might hold convocations in the neighborhood for weeks at a time, and then one morning he would awaken to find them gone.

Few species stayed through the winter, but Muir knew those that did and cheered himself with their examples of fortitude. On winter mornings, many of which might be well below zero, his father's voice would sound in summons at six, and Muir would awaken to find frost on the coverlets. Hobbling down the cold stairs of the fireless house he would face his first task of the day: getting his aching, chilblained feet into shrunken, half-frozen cowhide boots. No fire was allowed at this hour where it might have lessened this agony. Stumping out on his morning chores, his feet in iron-like prisons, he would have to endure the pain until the temperature of his feet and that of the boots became adjusted and the leather grudgingly thawed and stretched.

In the fields or woods it was often bitter, but Muir warmed to his work of chopping or fencing, though the ax might rebound from the frozen wood as if he had swung it against iron. He remembered of these days not only the hard and "shivery" work but also the stark beauties of the season: "the wonderful radiance of the snow when it was starry with crystals, and the dawns and sunsets and white noons, and the cheery, enlivening company of the brave chickadees and nuthatches." Sometimes they would see Indian hunters running on the tracks of a deer or spearing muskrats at the edges of the lake. He might also occasionally accompany his father to Portage or Kingston or elsewhere in the immediate vicinity, for winter as a "slack" season was the preferred time for revival meetings, and Daniel Muir was much abroad in the snowy land, preaching his wintry doctrines and being preached at. On stormy days there was always work in the barn—shelling corn, making ax handles or ox yokes, mending harnesses—or they would sort potatoes in the cellar.

At last the ice that had boomed all winter above the surges of the waters beneath would begin to boom in a new and insistent way, then begin to crack, and at last to break up. Skies softened once again, and the voice of the loon was heard. Spring came to the oak openings and the cleared fields, and the old cycle rose again into its ascendant arc. Muir went on with it, captive to his seasonal chores but captivated, too, by the natural life of those seasons.

"After eight years of this dreary work of clearing the Fountain Lake Farm," John Muir recalled with a bitter asperity,

> fencing it and getting it in perfect order, building a frame house and the necessary outbuildings for the cattle and horses,—after all

this had been victoriously accomplished, and we had made out to escape with life,—father bought a half-section of wild land about four or five miles to the eastward and began all over again to clear and fence and break up other fields for a new farm, doubling all the stunting, heartbreaking chopping, grubbing, stump-digging, rail-splitting, fence-building, barn-building, house-building, and so forth.

Daniel Muir had spied out a tract of land that he thought would prove more fertile than the original homestead, and he had put John to the task of getting it ready for the move, which came in 1857. Meanwhile, the elder Muir had found a buyer for Fountain Lake farm in David Galloway, a twenty-eight-year-old Scot from Fifeshire who had settled in the area, then gone back to Scotland to bring over his parents and relatives. Galloway had fallen in love with Sarah Muir, and they were married in 1856. Galloway released his bride from the servitude of the fields, but the other children remained bound to their tasks.

A major factor that tempted Daniel Muir to the breaking of this new and much larger tract was the endemic immigrant disease called "land hunger." Most immigrants, even if they had some previous experience with farming as Daniel Muir had, possessed no background as landholders, and in the presence of such an abundance of cheap land as they now found in the New World they grew understandably greedy. Not content with living on small and manageable plots, many bought as much land as they could. A popular Wisconsin saying of the time was that "all the land a man rightly wanted was his own claim and any land that adjoined it."

In America, the Scots had gained and largely deserved a reputation as even more improvident in this regard, perhaps in part because their native agricultural practices had long been among the most benighted in the Old World. Here they were known not only for buying up more land than they could well manage but also for their wasteful methods of farming. Often they were ignorantly unconcerned with crop rotation and manuring and would exhaust one patch of ground, then another until finally they had worked out their entire claim and had to move on. Rather than cut trees for fuel and lumber and utilize the wood ashes for soap, Scots farmers often seemed content merely to girdle their trees and plant around them

while the trees slowly died. In Wisconsin, the contrasts between the
thrifty methods of the German immigrants and their Scots neighbors were embarrassing to the latter.

And this was the other factor in Daniel Muir's decision to move:
he had worked out his soil. The light and sandy grounds of Fountain Lake had begun to give out, the wheat yields dwindling steadily
from twenty-five to twenty, then to five or six bushels per acre.
Daniel Muir had tried corn, but here too the yield gradually proved
disappointing. So the answer seemed to be to buy another piece of
land and try there. In this fashion much of the state had become
exhausted as a wheat-producing region by the time of the Civil
War. After the war the locus of production would move into Iowa,
Minnesota, and then North Dakota. Hamlin Garland's story is
typical of this general pattern: born on a Wisconsin wheat farm on
the eve of the Civil War, Garland had moved with his family to
Iowa after the war, and they had ended up raising wheat again on
the prairies of North Dakota in the 1880s.

But this ignorant prodigality and disregard for the future was
not confined to wheat or to any one national group: all the resources of the region were at the mercy of these mental habits and
all groups were to one degree or another implicated. Wood, so
plentiful that early settlers positively delighted to see stands of
timber consumed by the annual fall grass fires, was everywhere
used up in the most wasteful of ways. The land, so it was said, was
made for farming, and cutting timber simply and self-evidently
opened more land for agriculture while it also produced jobs, capital, and useful products. Hardly anyone out there knew enough to
worry about the long-range effects of deforestation, and the few
who did, like Professor Increase Lapham of the state college at
Madison, were dismissed as cranks. Any settler could tell the professor that there was more wood in Wisconsin than could well be used.
But the pineries of the great north woods, hardly known in the year
of Muir's birth, were by now being rapidly sawed to bits. Portable
steam-powered saw mills and larger permanent installations sent
out an estimated two hundred million board feet in 1853, and a
decade after the Civil War the end of the timbering up there was
in sight, a thing that would have seemed incredible but a few years
previous when the rivers out of the pineries were choked with
fabulous log jams.

Daniel Muir was no exception to these wasteful habits of mind and the wasteful practices they engendered. He too ordered the spendthrift cutting of timber on his lands and then refused to use what he had cut to warm his house and so provide for the health and comfort of his family. "The very best oak and hickory fuel," John Muir recalled of his Wisconsin homesteads, "was embarrassingly abundant and cost nothing but cutting and common sense. . . ." However, instead of constructing ample fireplaces to accommodate large logs of these slow-burning woods as a household defense against the Wisconsin winters, Daniel Muir ordered the felled timber "hauled with weary heart-breaking industry into fences and waste places to get it out of the way of the plough, and out of the way of doing good." Meanwhile, the Muir family shivered about what John Muir remembered was a miserable little kitchen stove with a firebox "about eighteen inches long and eight inches wide and deep—scant space for three or four small sticks . . . ." Yet if Daniel Muir was both niggardly and wasteful with his own timber, there was a persistent rumor in the Muirs' neighborhood that he ordered his eldest son to poach timber from government land that lay in a swale west of his new claim. If he did so, Daniel Muir at least had the sanction of popular custom, the practice being widespread, the poachers accounting the timber as actually free and the sale money from it a kind of windfall.

Of all this and its consequences for the region—lowered water tables, droughts, proliferation of pests, exhaustion of the soil—Muir at the time knew little, though he could surely lament the wasting of those "heart-cheering" loads of wood. Like the others he was caught up in the seemingly inevitable process of breaking the land for civilization and profit.

Looking around him, he could see other families likewise bound to the soil, other children like himself and his brothers and sisters laboring at kindred tasks through the seasons: planting, plowing, chopping, even poaching wood. Perhaps his father was more severe in his demands and in the way he enforced them, but in truth all the immigrants drove themselves and their families much too hard. Nor did they seem to know any better in this regard than in agricultural matters, where the rule of hard usage also prevailed. As many of them had no previous experience with landholding or with the principle of usufruct, so many like the elder

Muir had had too near and numbing an experience with child labor to recognize how it could surely blunt and blight the new generations. In the Lanark mills of Daniel Muir's time children regularly worked a thirteen-hour day, six days a week, and spent their Sundays cleaning the machinery. Well into the nineteenth century it was common practice in the British Isles to employ women and small children in the pit collieries where like beasts they hauled carts by iron chains about their middles. To those with such knowledge the labor of the farm seemed neither cruel nor unusual.

To outsiders it might, as it did to Fredrika Bremer. Watching the midwestern farm families, bent and sweating in their chosen servitude, she wondered whether these new Americans, so determined on freedom and prosperity, would ever awaken to the far grander opportunity their new lands and situation offered: the chance to turn toward the sun, to open themselves to the possibility of regeneration as the vanished aboriginal races evidently had.

In the middle 1850s as his father prepared yet another agonizing grid of work for him, John Muir was not quite ready for such thoughts. And yet he could hardly have been oblivious to the human consequences of this furious industry. He could see some of those consequences in the deepening lines of toil and resignation in his own mother's face, in her hands. He knew that his sisters Sarah and Margaret were now in chronically poor health and that the first and greatest gift David Galloway had bestowed on the former was to take her out of the fields forever. He himself bore the humiliating title of the "runt of the family" since among these tall, angular folk he was somewhat undersized for a teenaged boy; later, he would claim that overwork had stunted his growth.

Like the people, the countryside seemed to be taking on the look of age, seemed to be becoming a facsimile of that Old World the immigrants had so willingly left behind for this new one. The land was filling up, and whereas the Muirs once had been virtually solitary, now all the neighboring quarter sections were taken up. There was a graveyard now, too, and Muir watched it entered upon and filled with its own settlers for whom the New World had not opened onto new vistas of life but had led instead to premature death: Graham, McReath, Thompson, Maitland, Whitehead. . . . "The generations," wrote another midwestern child of this time who survived into old age, "cannot utter themselves to each other until the strongest need of utterance is past." William Dean Howells had seen the wasting of the human resources of the region, and he had lived long enough to see in the next generation writers like Edgar Lee Masters and Hamlin Garland give voices to those silent ones beneath the blurring markers of hundreds of rural burying grounds, writers touched nearly enough by the whole breaking process to conceive their mission as the writing of the somber annals of these victims of ignorant industry and innocent rapacity. Now the maturing Muir could only feel the injustice and the pain and vaguely ponder the meaning of it all.

Terms of
Challenge

———————

The new homestead lay about five miles south-
east of Fountain Lake, and the Muirs christened it Hickory Hill
since the house site was atop a hill thickly studded with hickories.
Here they raised a stout two-story frame house with a wing running
off it in back. Behind the house they built a high, broad barn that
backed up on the woods. The views on the other three sides were
fine: the land's gentle rolls lent variety to the eye, and here and
there were heavy copses of virgin timber.

John Muir had already cleared the near fields in those months
before the family moved, and when they did so the farm was
already in production. Western land hunger had plunged the nation
into a financial panic in this year of 1857, and the consequences of
soil misuse were becoming evident throughout the Midwest. Still
the Muirs were hoping to prosper on the new farm as they had not
on the old, one family's version of the national notion that somehow a new situation would inevitably be better than the one left
behind.

But the new start began badly for John Muir, began, in fact, almost fatally. Unlike the old homestead, the new one was far from any surface water, and Muir was ordered to dig a well behind the house and a few yards from the barn. He soon tapped into a stratum of close-grained sandstone; the Muirs tried blasting through this, but they were unskilled at it, and so finally Daniel Muir gave his son mason's tools and told him he must chip his way down to water.

The work went on at a painful, inching pace. Each morning Muir was lowered by bucket and windlass into the slowly deepening shaft and left to work in this cramped, airless place until he was hauled out again for the noon dinner. Then, back down again until supper and chores. One morning as he was lowered into the shaft —at this point about eighty feet deep—he was all but overcome by carbon dioxide that had collected overnight at the bottom. As the fatal fumes invaded his lungs and numbed his brain, he could faintly and confusedly hear his father shouting down to him to get into the bucket, but he was already so weak that it seemed easier to settle against a wall of the shaft and sleep. As his father continued to shout, frantically now, Muir somehow summoned awareness and strength enough to clamber into the bucket and was hauled out, unconscious and gasping for breath.

There was no more work that day or the next, and while he lay in the costly luxury of his sick bed, Muir was visited by William Duncan, who had been a miner and stonemason in Scotland. "Weel, Johnnie," Muir recalled him saying, "it's God's mercy that you're alive. Many a companion of mine have I seen dead with choke-damp, but none that I ever saw or heard of was so near death in it as you were and escaped without help." Duncan taught Daniel Muir to air the shaft each morning with a splash of water and frequent stirrings with a bundle of brush and hay. Then the work went on.

Ninety feet down, Muir struck a "fine, hearty gush of water." They had their well now but at a price Muir would feel all his life; later he claimed that a peculiar rasping feeling in his throat was a lifelong reminder of the incident.

Nor could Muir ever forgive the fact that his father "never spent an hour in that well." The episode served to deepen his resentments against Daniel Muir's tyranny. But whereas the boy had few effective defenses against that tyranny, the young man had been developing some in the last years at Fountain Lake, and he continued to do so now at Hickory Hill. Things had slowly been changing in the Muir family, and especially between the father and his eldest son. For one thing, Daniel Muir had now completely retired from active participation in the running of the farm and left things to John. He still gave the orders, of course, and supervised the work, but henceforth he would devote himself to his religious pursuits, attending every revival meeting in the vicinity, and traveling about two counties as a preaching elder of the Disciples of Christ. When at home, he would sit by a strategically located study window where, his Bible in his lap, he could watch his children at their labors in the fields below.

Sarah's departure for her own household on the old acreage had also made a difference, for she had been a second, mediating mother in the household, and the loss of her counsel and helping hand was felt. Now John began to draw closer to Maggie, four years his senior and a sympathetic listener to whom he commenced to confide both his misgivings and vague ambitions.

The major difference, however, lay in the altered relations between Daniel Muir and John. This was not the boy who had been set to the plow in the spring of 1850. He had been seasoned and toughened by seven hard years in the fields, woods, and barnyard, and he had crossed the invisible divide into young manhood: lean, self-reliant, and increasingly thoughtful. He still deferred to his father and obeyed the orders so peremptorily given, but for some time now he had been freed of a particularly galling part of the paternal tyranny, for even Daniel Muir, so convinced of the spiritual necessity of corporal punishment, had come to feel it was unwise to continue beating John. The master-serf relationship between the two now became an undeclared battle between them. On the surface of it, there was the continuous crackle of verbal skirmishing in which the younger man often enjoyed an advantage, but beneath this lay John Muir's mortal effort to preserve an essential part of his character as he had come to understand it.

His experiences with the natural world of his Scots childhood had given him a kind of psychic and spiritual base, and in his early years at Fountain Lake he had drawn sustenance from this during the apparently endless days of his servitude until the kinship he felt for nature had deepened into a genuine need. This was the boy—now the young man—who had successfully cheered himself in the frosty fields of midwinter Wisconsin by watching the brave peckings and chirpings of the nuthatches and chickadees. This was the young man who had become intensely interested in some of the very things that had made his life so hard: the thick, gnarled oak and hickory grubs, for instance, that would toss the plowshare out of its furrow when it ran up against them. But rather than cursing their existence (though he may have done this, too, on occasion), Muir made an informal study of the roots and marveled at what he discovered of their life history.

But the farm, and specifically the life he was forced by his father to lead on it, threatened this essential affinity and presented Muir with the first and perhaps the greatest psychic challenge of his life: how in this circumstance to preserve his love of nature. Placed in an adversary, exploitative relationship, an unremitting hand-to-hand combat with the land, he began in his adolescent years to imagine some way of being and thinking that would allow him to continue to love that with which he struggled.

As any farm child knows, it is easy enough to talk of the bucolic splendors of the country when one has never known the round of agricultural labor, and it is quite another to love nature when one has to work with it each day of the year. Hamlin Garland had to learn this lesson and later wrote about it in his story "Up the Coulee." Here a man who had fled the Wisconsin farm of his youth returned to visit his mother and brother. Riding the train through the countryside toward his old home, he found the land beautiful, a serene and timeless garden of happiness. But then the train came to a halt at the little warped farm town, the man swung down, and the landscape stood still. In the barnyard of the homestead the city man was confronted by the mud puddles, the dung, and the spectacle of men and boys trying to milk the cows stamping and lashing under the pitiless attack of flies. And then he knew why he had left; only from the city or the rolling train could he love this land and its life.

Muir could not leave; he had nowhere to go. So if he was to

keep intact his love of the natural world, he would have to find a way to do so in the very jaws of circumstance.

Perhaps inevitably, Muir's earliest response to the challenge of the farm took the form of a desire to excel at his imposed tasks: to do the work better and faster than anyone else, especially his father. Doubtless such a response was in part a bequest to him from his Scots childhood, where a sort of heroic stoicism had been thrashed into him at the Davel Brae school. So at Fountain Lake Muir had sought to rise above the deadening affects of his labor by competing with himself and all others. "I was," he remembered, "foolishly ambitious to be first in mowing and cradling, and by the time I was sixteen led all the hired men." So too with plowing, where he strove to keep his share exactly trimmed and to draw a straighter furrow than anyone, and with rail splitting and stump grubbing. Even the digging of the well that almost became the digging of his grave was subsequently transformed into a source of stubborn pride, for he had sunk it straight and plumb and had built a "fine covered top over it, and swung two iron-bound buckets in it from which we all drank many a day."

This earliest response deepened into the character trait of a lifetime: Muir would actively, relentlessly seek out adversity and hardship, would relish almost any physical challenge, and would punish himself severely for real or imagined failures to be equal to any circumstance. He would also take boastful pride in his victories over himself, as he did in these years when, for instance, he spent hours one day diving over and over again from the stern of a boat in the deepest part of Fountain Lake to conquer his fear of drowning. Each time he plunged into the water, he addressed himself with "Take that!" Never, he reflected of this incident, "was a victory over self more complete. I have been a good swimmer ever since. At a slow gait I think I could swim all day in smooth water moderate in temperature." Later he would see the connection between such behavior and the Scots Calvinism in his background, but this was the view from old age, and by that time he had spent half a century seeking challenges and meeting them successfully.

Soon enough, however, Muir felt the rub in this sort of response, for its main product was compounded misery. Without giving up his competitive attitude, he began to overlay it with another response, as if aware even so early that such behavior could not ultimately save him, and that as a way of being, of going through the world for the rest of his life, it had clear and stark limitations. Something more was needed.

About the age of sixteen, while still striving to lead all the hired men, Muir asked his father for a mathematics book, and Daniel Muir, normally suspicious of all learning other than the study of Scripture, warily consented. Perhaps it was understood between them that Muir's study of it would be of use in the management of the farm. Whatever the spoken arrangement, Muir's underlying motive was to bring to his living a dimension it had heretofore lacked: formal intellectual exercise. Thoughtful from an early age, he had been so cut off on the farm that he had no other tools than his native wits with which to think about life. The rote learning of the Dunbar days was dead, and his acquaintance with the Bible was not yet the sort that would allow him the grand vistas it opened onto history and myth, to say nothing of the thunderous music of its language.

Even among his peers Muir was singularly isolated by the regimen his father imposed, not only without books and schooling but without regular converse with others outside his household. He had his Sundays—or parts of them—to visit with neighboring boys and girls, and Independence Day and New Year's, but otherwise he saw little of the rest of the world.

Comparing Muir's life at this stage with those of two of his contemporaries—Samuel Clemens (born 1835) and William Dean Howells (born 1837)—is one way to understand how pitifully limited Muir's outlets were, how much he was thrust onto himself and his inner resources, and what a far and lonely way he had to travel to come into his own. Clemens and Howells had also been middle-class midwestern boys and were almost his exact contemporaries. But they had been village boys from families of more liberal views, and their awareness of the world of their time and their access to it had been immeasurably greater than this backwoods youth whose pleasures were mostly those of his own devising, whose awareness of other American horizons was limited to occasional trips to Portage and to the casual talk of his immigrant neighbors in the minutes before the commencement of revival meetings.

But now he had the math book, and he took to it with a hunger that is the unmistakable sign of intellectual starvation. "Beginning at the beginning," he was to recall, "in one summer I easily finished it without assistance, in the short intervals between the end of dinner and the afternoon start for the harvest- and the hay-fields. . . ." Then in quick succession he took up algebra, geometry, and trigonometry, satisfying himself that he had made some real progress in each.

It was not, of course, simply mathematics that gripped him, though he found that he was good at it. At bottom this was an effort to intellectualize his existence and so lift himself above its routines. Surely nothing can so deaden aspiration and imagination as the cheerless prospect of yet another lengthy chore ahead after having spent so much on the one at hand—another field to be worked that you can see from the one you are currently working. But now as he labored, Muir mulled over mathematical problems; soon he had other matters to ponder as well.

About the time he was racing through his math books he discovered the wonders of literature. His immediate guides were two neighboring Scots boys, farm kids like himself but from families who prized learning and books. David Gray and David Taylor, Muir learned to his astonishment, not only had access to good books but had actually committed favorite lines to memory. More than this, they wrote poetry of their own, and Davie Taylor even sang some of his own verses. To Johnnie Muir the fact that two boys so like himself and living so near could possess such privileges, develop such talents, was almost incredible.

The first time Muir heard his peers discussing literature, the "twa Davies," as Muir called them, were talking of Dickens. They were in a swamp, discharging their families' neighborhood civic duties by building a corduroy road across it, and there amid the mire and the sweat was a sudden music that transformed the whole scene into something utterly different. Davie Gray and Davie Taylor were now not just day hands mucking about in swampy waters, cutting logs and fitting them: they were artists, men of literature.

Muir had, of course, known both music and poetry: he had

those old ballads running in his head and blood, and he had most likely also heard his father play the fiddle and sing the ancient airs in the days before that stern patriarch had put music away as an unseemly frivolity. After he had escaped the farm, he would write back to his sister Mary that there must be something at least mildly poetic in the family since "Mother made poetry when first acquainted with father and I think that father must have made some verses too. . . ." Still, belles lettres were hardly a part of the strait life of that household, where even casual talk at mealtimes was discouraged as sacrilegious. And as for frankly imaginative prose—novels—this was little less than lies.

Now with the help and examples of Gray and Taylor, Muir discovered lodes of inspiration and reflection. With an even greater avidity than he had displayed in taking to his mathematical studies, he plunged his mind and heart into literature, borrowing books, saving small sums to buy his own, forming part of a neighborhood lending library. He read Shakespeare, and the Romantic poets—Cowper, Thomas Campbell, Mark Akenside, and others. He saw the Bible with a new eye and heard its verses as treasures of sound. Perhaps closest to him was the great apologist Milton, whose lines in *Paradise Lost* he would remember forever. He memorized and savored images and whole passages, spoke them aloud to himself in the fields and woods or during some chore at the house, and applied them to the landscape through which he moved, learning, as Campbell had written, to "muse on Nature with a poet's eye!"

What Campbell and the others gave him was not an appreciation of the natural world; he already had that and better and deeper than almost any of them. It was rather their gift of reflection that was significant: reflection on the meanings of life as these were manifested in nature and, perhaps equally significant at this stage, the reflection of himself in their words. For in the pages of the poets he found expressions of that mystical affinity he had himself experienced since childhood when the "magic of Nature first breathed on my mind," as his countryman Campbell had written. Here in print and bound between covers—and codified thus—were confirmations of his own deepest predilections and intuitions. There had been others like himself! And not only that, but some of them had been famous. The effect of this discovery on Muir can hardly be overemphasized, for it gave him a view of himself that had been utterly unobtainable before and that would prove a source of continuous encouragement. Campbell's once-famous *The Pleasures of Hope* is only the most obvious example of the effect of the poets on this young farmer. In truth, all of them were hope bringers, as tangible as those sweet-songed bluebirds that announced spring.

Like Gray and Taylor, Muir now also began to write verses, though about what must remain a mystery since all but two specimens have been lost, and one of these survives merely as a reference to its subject matter. But the reference to his elegy on the death of an old tree in the neighborhood does indicate the influence of the Romantics for whom this subject was a favorite.

He read novels, too, but these had to be consumed in secret. Still, he managed to get through several of Scott's, which he borrowed from William Duncan, smuggling them into the house under his clothing and turning their pages in moments almost as precious as the books themselves.

He also began to get his first sense of the vast reaches of history through his reading of Plutarch and Josephus as well as John George Wood's then-standard *Natural History.* Ultimately this scale of vision would rival the Romantic humanism he was now imbibing and encourage a cosmic vision in which man himself was almost lost, a tiny, puny creature distinguished mainly by his outsized claims to dominion over the earth. But now literature and history harmonized to broaden Muir's scope of thought and provide him with creative ways to think about the world and himself in it.

Once it became known in the neighborhood that Daniel Muir's son, Johnnie, liked to read books, help and encouragement came to him from unsuspected sources. A number of Scots immigrants nearby were intellectually active and a few had brought with them modest but good libraries. Now they began to come forward with offers of help and, equally as vital, with words of encouragement, words that fell with the sweetness of benediction on ears long tuned to the rasp of criticism. In particular Mrs. Jean Galloway (David Galloway's mother and a woman Muir was to remember as a second mother to him), William Duncan, and Dr. William Meacher took active interest in Muir's development. Duncan had perhaps the largest library in that neighborhood, and he often suggested to Muir that he come by and browse in its treasures.

The neighborhood situation, so fortuitous to Muir, was not as extraordinary as might appear. The Scots had a proud and ancient intellectual tradition, and figures of the Scottish Enlightenment had been potent influences in the thought of the entire European community. In the New World, Scots immigrants had been conscious of the need to carry on that tradition, and so in the eighteenth century, while some Caledonians were blazing trails and creating homesteads in woodlands, others were maintaining intellectual ties with the Old World and vitalizing the life of the mind in the New. Cadwallader Colden, for example, became an active and systematic botanizer in upper New York State and kept close ties for years with the great Linnaeus. Moreover, his treatise on the Iroquois confederacy, *The History of the Five Indian Nations* (first published in 1727), is a mine of ethnographical information. Another who sent a steady stream of information about the New World to Linnaeus was the Charleston doctor Alexander Garden (for whom the gardenia is named). In addition to making important early studies of epidemics of yellow fever and smallpox, Garden was also interested in the medicinal properties of local plants and wrote Linnaeus of the vermifuge qualities of pinkroot. And John Lining of that same city made early observations on the relationship between forest clearances and regional climatic conditions, a relationship of which Wisconsin settlers in Muir's century were still ignorant.

Nor was the keeping of the Scots intellectual tradition confined to formally educated immigrants. Travelers along the edges of the advancing American civilization constantly remarked on the presence of books, newspapers, and almanacs in the often rude homes of the settlers, and many of those on the very fringes were the hardy Scots. In Muir's own reminiscences of his neighborhood there is further evidence, for the substance of the debate he described there on the whites' treatment of the Indians shows the settlers were familiar with the arguments of such Scots philosophers as William Robertson and Adam Ferguson, who had addressed this same tangled problem.

For Muir the importance of the existence of the Scots intellectual tradition on the frontier is obvious, for without the help of its carriers, such as Duncan, Meacher, and the Gray and Taylor families, it is hard to see how Muir, wholly unaided, might have found his way into the life of the mind. What is less obvious is that through the help and example of these people Muir was making another crucial discovery: that the Scots had a parallel tradition of the intelligent, intellectually curious workingman. William Duncan, miner and stonemason, was perhaps the nearest example, but as Muir went on with his reading and his conversations with his neighbors, he discovered other examples, and all his life he was to continue to do so and to take a special, telling pride in them. Hugh Miller, the great Scots geologist of whom Jean Galloway spoke to Muir, had begun his career as an untutored laborer in a stone quarry, and one of his most important collaborators had been Robert Dick, a workingman from Thurso who gave Miller his own collections of fossil fish. David Douglas, whose explorations of the Pacific Northwest added so much to the fund of knowledge of the New World, had been the son of a stone mason and had begun his botanical studies as the apprentice to the head gardener at Scone Castle. So even now Muir began to see that a life of manual labor—if indeed this was to be his lot—need not mean a brutalized, mindless existence, that it might be possible to go on with one's studies even as one wore the harness of repetitive chores.

But perhaps it was not absolutely given that a workingman remain fixed in that physical place where life had put him. For Muir was learning too in these days that his countrymen, those wandering Scots, had adventured in virtually every land on the globe. He had known in his Dunbar school days of the great Alexander Wilson, who traveled in the New World when it was yet a vast, unmarked wilderness, and doubtless he had heard tales of those hundreds of Scots who had fanned out through the breadth of the continent as trappers, scouts, and fur traders: Alexander Mackenzie, to take but one example, who explored an unimaginably vast area of the Pacific Northwest.

He read too of the exploits of Mungo Park, the Edinburgh surgeon who explored the Niger for eighteen months, during which he endured fabulous privation merely for the chance of "rendering the geography of Africa more familiar to my countrymen." Park's heroism made a deep impression on Muir; it seemed wonderful to be willing to suffer and dare so much in so disinterested a cause. And there was buried in the midst of *Travels in the*

Interior Districts of Africa an episode that may well have given Muir much to muse on, not only on the Wisconsin farms but in after years. Park had just been stripped and robbed by a band of Foulahs who took his horse and compass, leaving him utterly destitute and alone. "I saw myself," he wrote,

> in the midst of a vast wilderness, in the depth of the rainy season —naked and alone, surrounded by savage animals, and men still more savage. I was five hundred miles from the nearest European settlement. All these circumstances crowded at once on my recollection, and I confess that my spirits began to fail me. I considered my fate as certain, and that I had no other alternative but to lie down and perish.

At this moment of almost terminal despair Park experienced an epiphany when his distracted eye happened to fall upon a small moss, the extraordinary beauty of which so compelled his admiration that his spirits suddenly soared. Could the Being, asked the marooned adventurer, who placed this magnificent little thing here in this obscure part of the world, "look with unconcern upon the situation and sufferings of creatures formed after His own image? Surely not!" The natural manifestation of divinity conquered despair and brought resolution, the will to survive, and Park struggled onward to a small village where two shepherd guides took him to safety. It is an odd occurrence in a narrative so crammed with adventures and suffering that almost all the incidents save this one cancel each other. The young man who read it had already been rescued often enough from his own homely despair by various manifestations of nature and the force that lived through it, and he would not have missed the parallel.

Muir read another book of travels that made a deep impression on him during these years and for a long time thereafter. Alexander von Humboldt's *Personal Narrative of Travels in the Equinoctial Regions* described the young adventurer's fearless probes into the heart of South America, searching along mosquito-blackened watercourses, mute amid a welter of unknown tongues, for the principle he felt must unify all flora, fauna, and geological formations.

One day excitedly—and unguardedly—talking to his mother of

Humboldt and Park and describing to her some of their experiences in the jungles of places scarcely on any map, Muir heard her words of quiet encouragement. "Weel, John," he recalled her saying, "maybe you will travel like Park and Humboldt some day." In her necessarily careful way she would often so encourage her son in his nascent enthusiasms, usually when Daniel Muir was absent. But on this occasion her guard, like her son's, must have been down, for Daniel Muir heard the exchange from his study and cried out what his son remembered as a "solemn depreciation, 'Oh, Anne, dinna put sic notions in the laddie's heed.'" In Daniel Muir's mind, there was no thought of travel for his eldest son and still less of that son's spiritual change. And yet, under his unforgiving gaze, this was what was happening.

Of course Daniel Muir sought to bully John about his reading. He himself read only Christian literature, little more than the Bible and rigorously screened commentaries on it, and he felt that other kinds of texts were less than useful. Occasionally John was able to talk his father into accepting the household presence of texts in no way related to Christian doctrine. Plutarch, for example, was allowed since Daniel Muir was persuaded the ancient historian might be able to shed further light on the question of proper diet, just then vexing the senior Muir because of the graham bread fad that had visited the Wisconsin backwoods. But Daniel Muir dug in his heels at Thomas Dick's *The Christian Philosopher.* The offense was given in the title's word, "Philosopher." Philosophy in the father's lexicon meant sophistry, but in truth Dick's work was an earnest attempt to defend Christianity and reconcile it with nineteenth-century scientific advances. The effort was common at midcentury, and indeed Hugh Miller in his *The Footprints of the Creator* (1847) had recently framed a brilliant geologically buttressed refutation of fellow Scot Robert Chambers, whose *Vestiges of the Natural History of Creation* (1844) contained striking anticipations of Charles Darwin.

Despite Daniel Muir's objections, his son read Dick in secret, and the argument of this book must have been of more than casual interest, for John himself had entered a struggle with orthodoxy that was to continue well into maturity. His earliest efforts were directed toward defining for himself the tenor and tone of his own practice of the faith. He had been early immersed in Scripture, of course, and in childhood had been coerced into memorizing huge quantities of it. Nor did the gradual emancipation from paternal tyranny that was now in process include anything approaching a thorough rejection of so firm-set a heritage. But there are a few indications that Muir was now beginning to consider in an informal but nonetheless serious way just what sort of Christian he could continue to be. Such spiritual probings would find an uneasy coexistence with his acquired religious enthusiasm and Scriptural literalism, and it might be argued that he never really wrestled with his faith to the point where he felt finally blessed as Jacob had been by the departing angel. Perhaps he did not need such a contest.

In any case, available evidence suggests that in his young manhood Muir argued with himself about the quality and practice of his faith and that the argument was strenuous enough so that he projected it upon others. He could be in these years a jackleg preacher to his peers, zealous to bring the message of Christ's love to those he sensed were slipping from rigor. He wrote several hortatory epistles on the subject to a friend named Bradley, one of which has survived.

It was written in the form of a parable of a young man, lost and freezing in a blizzard at night, who was taken in and befriended by a benevolent stranger. Now, Bradley, Muir wrote, wouldn't you love and honor that kind man forever? Wouldn't you hold his memory in the warmest corner of your heart? Then how much more do we owe Jesus for His eternal, unfailing love of us?

The letter, which dates from 1856, is of interest not only as it indicates how deeply Muir's orthodoxy was set, but also because it indicates that he had been reading and responding to much more than religious literature. The prose is polished if stilted, and the imaginative evocation of the young man's predicament is so convincing it seems as if the writer were unconsciously more interested in the composing of it than in the message it was to convey. Here is evidence of a mind beginning to range and to range away from that orthodoxy it yet professes.

The major problem Muir faced in his religion probings was that of reconciling Christianity as he had observed its practice with the way it appeared to him in Scripture. Perhaps it would also be necessary to find a way of reconciling the Old Testament with the New.

His father, of course, was a New Testament man who had taught all his children to love Jesus and to admire and emulate the greatest Apostle, Paul. And yet Daniel Muir's behavior seemed decidedly un-Christian at times and was surely at variance with the mild and loving example of Christ. The elder Muir appeared to be more nearly the patriarch of the Old Testament: severe, implacable, capable of shocking acts. Angered at the way the boys' Indian pony, Jack, would chase the cows in at sundown on the Fountain Lake farm, Daniel Muir had once ordered John to shoot Jack. He had relented then, but he had himself killed one of the boys' favorite horses by relentlessly driving it twenty-four miles over hot, sandy roads to get to a revival meeting. Muir never forgot the way that doomed animal had lingered on in its suffering, how it would pathetically trail after the children, bleeding from the nostrils, gasping for breath, mutely pleading for some form of relief before it fell over and died. More than half a century later, when he detailed the episode in his autobiography, he used it to indict the Christian attitude toward the rest of creation. Looking back, he suggested that even then his attitude toward birds, beasts, and plants was radically different from the teachings of "churches and schools, where too often the mean, blinding, loveless doctrine is taught that animals have neither mind nor soul, have no rights that we are bound to respect, and are made only for man. . . ." This is almost surely the superimposition of the developed view of maturity onto the earnest questionings of youth. But it would be a mistake to assume it is only that. By his teenage years Muir had evidently come to a deep feeling of kinship with the rest of creation, a feeling that took him beyond the confines of orthodox Christianity. Possibly he was led in this direction by his own sufferings and so came to see that the farm's draft animals suffered too, that the brave chickadees and nuthatches also felt the sting of winter, and that even the plants had their seasonal joys and sorrows.

He got none of this from his father, whose view of the earth and of all earthly life was unrelievedly grim. Daniel Muir incessantly enjoined his children to regard themselves as soul-sick sinners in the eyes of an angry God and to view the world as a vale of sorrows and a place of snares through which the undeserving pilgrims were fated to pass on their way to judgment. Old-time Scots Calvinism had held that one sure way to recognize a sinner was that he delighted in looking at natural objects, for such objects were fated for eventual destruction, and so to delight in them was an offense against the Lord. The eyes, it was said, were prone to fifty-two divinely appointed ailments, one for each week of the year.

To a young man who had come to embrace the natural world, such a view would have been wholly inappropriate, even repugnant. Much more congenial was the outlook of those new-found Romantics whose exaltation of the self and of the divine sublimity of the natural world made such sweet sense to him after a childhood in the bleak barrens of crypto-Calvinism. The poets' views as expressed, for example, in the lines of Mark Akenside (one of Muir's youthful favorites) were much nearer his own than those he heard in his father's voice and in the marathon prayers offered up in Sunday services. He, like Akenside, knew solitude and the calm healing of nature

> When, all alone, for many a summer's day,
> I wander'd through your calm recesses, led
> In silence by some powerful hand unseen.

Sitting through those Sunday meetings at which his own father often presided in awful solemnity, clad in ministerial blacks and praying with tight-shut eyes for almost an hour at a stretch, Muir chewed windflower seeds to stay awake and perhaps to fill his mind with a paradise of flowers instead of the smoke of brimstone. And in these hours he must have been thinking about how he might continue to believe and to practice Christianity in a way different from that he was in these Sabbath moments experiencing.

Was it possible that some central essence of Christianity could be segregated or extracted from Christianity as commonly practiced and preached? Was there a way of belief that ran in another direction than this strait one so hedged about with negations and clouded with doom and destruction? Lines from a poem that Muir wrote at this time suggest that the young man now viewed the local religious practices with a somewhat detached and critical eye. In an apostrophe to the old log schoolhouse whose patient walls have borne the "blasts of strong revival," Muir wrote that human souls, too, have suffered these blasts, and that while souls were being saved, they were also being "pulled, and twisted/ All out of shape, till they no longer fitted/ The frightened bodies that to each belonged."

And yet, what were the alternatives? Clearly unbelief was out of the question. Not only was the force of all Muir's training against this but, even more significantly, so were his own observations and inclinations. Already he had been touched by the profound mystery of existence, witnessing it in the springtime rebirth of plant life, in the intelligence and feelings of animals, in the wonderful regulation of the whole natural world. His readings of Shakespeare, Milton, and the Romantics had reinforced his conviction that divinity was the source of this mystery, though there was some difficulty in reconciling Milton's views of that divinity with those of the Romantics, who were certain it was visible in the petals of a flower. No, unbelief was impossible for him, and it is unlikely he ever seriously considered it.

But such substitutes as spiritualism or phrenology were also impossible. Somewhere along the years to young manhood there had entered Muir a tough, knotty skepticism. He knew mystery and felt drawn to it. He also felt he knew the difference between mystery and humbug. And of the latter there was plenty along the advancing frontier of the Middle West in the years before the Civil War. Fredrika Bremer in her tour there in 1849 remarked that the hottest topics of conversation were spirit rappings and Jenny Lind. Muir's reminiscences of his Wisconsin years make it clear that his neighborhood was visited in its turn by the crazes that swept the rest of the nation: phrenology, the graham-bread regimen for the repression of animal appetite, and so on. None left more than a negative trace on Muir and in a typical exchange between father and eldest son he was able to disabuse Daniel Muir of his new adherence to Sylvester Graham's bread-and-vegetable diet by quoting Scripture. When the Lord hid Elijah from his enemies, Muir reminded his father, and sent the ravens to feed him, He did not send the prophet graham bread and vegetables but meat. And surely the Lord knew what was best for His own prophet in distress. Daniel Muir had to admit that He did.

So Muir was first and forever a Christian, and even if the fit of the faith was uncomfortable in places and had to be considerably altered to fit his own spiritual needs, it served well enough over time. Christianity might have its blindnesses, and he would define these sharply in coming years, but it was surely better than unbelief, better by far than any of the cults or splinter sects of his day. To say, as some of these did, that they dealt in the occult or the spiritual was not enough to interest him, and indeed he was to prove intolerant of San Francisco spiritualists when he was invited to their seances in the 1870s.

He believed in mystery and generally was content not to attempt to trace spiritual matters to their putative sources, recognizing that certain things could never be understood or explained. On the other hand, he was eager to solve certain kinds of mystery, to see how things worked. So in these farm years he made patient observations of animal habits and learned the secrets of the shrike, how it went about its fatal work of gopher hunting. He devised, too, an ingenious experiment to discover how the honeybees fixed the direction and distance of a food source from their hive. And still thousands of mysteries remained, for he could not feel that in seeing partway into any of them he had thereby exhausted and drained a phenomenon. His experiment with the bees provoked more wonder, not less. So in this way he was led from mystery to mystery with a deepening, widening religious awe, one that went far beyond the confines of conventional Christian practice. There would always be a certain amount of orthodox baggage that he carried within him, and in these years of coming into his own it was often burdensome enough—to himself and to others. But it would become lighter and lighter over the years so that in his late years some would call him a mystic or a pantheist.

The graham-bread episode gives another glimpse of that verbal skirmishing that was the exterior of the battle between father and eldest son. Behind its issue of proper diet there lurked the larger issue of who should define the terms of Muir's life, and Daniel Muir saw to it, as much as he was able, that the terms were of his own devising. At Fountain Lake and then at Hickory Hill he ran his farm with a military regimentation that left no room for irregularities of behavior and that sought to proscribe those of thought. Muir had to squeeze his reading and nature investigations into whatever odd and stolen moments he could find after the chores had been completed.

The moments were few and precious. In winter when the short days and cold weather precluded any out-of-house activity, Muir had to read under the very eyes of his father, and there was almost no time for it. Daniel Muir's strict rule in this season was that all should retire immediately after the end of family worship—presumably so that all would be fresh for the next day's toil. Occasionally on retiring the elder Muir would fail to notice the rapt reader's candle for perhaps five or ten minutes, "magnificent golden blocks of time," as Muir remembered them, "long to be remembered like holidays or geological periods."

One such evening as Muir hurriedly read at some text, his father called out to him from the darkness of his bedroom that John *must* go to bed along with the others, that he was tired of having to issue a separate order to John every night. If you must read, he added, get up early in the morning to do so. Here again the challenge, and Muir went upstairs into the cold dark, wondering how he could possibly meet it, how he might shake himself awake well before he and the other sleepers heard that stentorian voice from beneath the stairs summoning them to another day.

In the blackness of the bedroom Muir awakened hours later, how many he did not know, and, as he recalled it, "rushed downstairs, scarce feeling my chilblains, enormously eager to see how much time I had won. . . ." Holding his candle to the little kitchen clock, Muir read the incredible news its face gave back in the flickering light: it was only one o'clock. He had gained five hours on farm life. "I can hardly think," he was to say, "of any other event in my life, any discovery I ever made that gave birth to joy so transportingly glorious as the possession of those five frosty hours."

It was too cold in the night-and-winter-bound house for Muir to resume his reading, and he knew well enough that his father would begrudge him a fire, reasoning as the elder man would, that Muir would have had to take the time to chop the wood for it that he should have put in otherwise. No, it would all have to be done on his own time, every bit of it. So Muir went down into the mealy gloom of the cellar where, amid the potatoes and the cast-off, rusting tools, he set to work on an invention he had begun sometime previously: a self-setting sawmill. By the thin and wavering light of the candle he worked joyously through the remaining hours of night, hardly conscious of the cold or the damp or of the cramped and jumbled conditions of his shop. Here in this time and place and under the very floorboards of the paternal bedroom, he was again, if fleetingly, the arbiter of his own existence. Not merely a farm laborer, he was an *inventor,* at work on a device that in the very working at it would enhance his life. So he kept at it through the bleak winter mornings, rising with the incredible regularity that is the sure sign of a desperate determination to descend into the cellar and with his improvised tools fashion his inventions into realities.

At Fountain Lake, where the nocturnal work was first begun, and then at Hickory Hill, the sound of that subterranean hammering and the patient rasp of the homemade saw told Daniel Muir that his challenge had been accepted.

The self-setting sawmill was, to be sure, only a small-scale model, hardly of practical use. And in any case, it was not a device that would benefit Muir in the exercise of his daily tasks. But that was not the real goal, anyhow. The sawmill served the same purpose as his mathematical studies and his reading in elevating him above the circumstances of his life. Damming a small brook, he positioned his device and saw it work.

To Muir the act of arising so early and for such a purpose was almost equal in significance to the work he would then undertake, for it was a triumph of the will over the flesh, of himself—John Muir —over his circumstances. With that pride that often comes from such lonely efforts and that in him could occasionally come close to braggadocio, Muir looked back years later on this act of sustained heroism: "Many try to make up time by wringing slumber out of their pores. Not so when I was a boy, springing out of bed at one o'clock in the morning, wide-awake, without the shadow of a yawn, no sleep left in a single fiber of me, burning and bright as a tiger springing on its prey." Eventually he developed an ingenious sort of clock which would (had he needed it) assist him in his risings. At its appointed hour the contraption would cant the bedstead forward and noisily dump the sleeper onto the floor. Doubtless here, as with many other of his inventions, Muir was simply amused by the idea of the thing, its practical value being a secondary consideration.

Once fairly started on this course of inventing various wooden devises, Muir felt himself powerless to stop, and at an ever-increasing rate he fashioned waterwheels, door locks, latches, hygrometers, pyrometers, a barometer, an automatic horse feeder, and a huge thermometer with a scale of such amplitude it could easily be read from the barn where it rested to where Muir plowed in the fields below the house. He also devised a kind of guillotine for decapitating the farm's ravenous gophers, though, as he wrote his brother David in 1870, he was satisfied to remember this invention as his least successful.

Now his mind ran on clocks. He had taught himself the time laws of the pendulum by reading about them, and during his daily tasks he imagined how they might be applied to the construction of a clock. He began to whittle the works from pieces of hickory he carried with him as he did the mending and fencing and carpentry about the place, stealing minutes to do so whenever he was out of sight of the man who sat all day in the corner room poring over Scripture.

When the machine was almost completely assembled and hidden amid the tools and lumber of a spare bedroom, Maggie Muir came upon her father on his hands and knees regarding the strange thing he had accidentally discovered while looking for a tool. That evening at supper when Daniel Muir broached the subject, John had reason to fear he would be ordered to destroy his invention before he could complete it and discover whether it worked. But Daniel Muir contented himself with nothing more than another severe lecture in which he said that he wished John to follow the example of Paul, who said "that he desired to know nothing among men but Christ and Him crucified." On this occasion, anyway, Muir prudently refrained from engaging his father in debate and soon thereafter finished his clock. Like his other inventions, it worked.

Now that his clockmaking was out in the open he went on with it in a kind of joyous fury. He made one with a pendulum bearing an inscription pleasing to Daniel Muir, "All flesh is grass"; and another so huge its two-second pendulum was fourteen feet long. Here as with his other inventions he was unwittingly manifesting larger impulses at work in the nation. The pace of American life had measurably quickened in recent decades, and the country had taken as an article of faith Ben Franklin's maxim that time is money. On the Muir farms, it was not, but Daniel Muir was determined every minute of it should count. John Muir was determined it should be improved.

There were other reasons why Muir was preoccupied with time as the decade of the 1850s closed. His own life, he had come to feel, was passing. His recent arrival at young manhood had made him aware of his own mortality, and this was further encouraged by his reading of the Romantics, who dwelt so lovingly on this theme. Then too the juxtaposition of his time of life with the apparently endless round of farm labor made him feel that his span of years was not only short but that it was even now growing shorter—as it so tragically had for some other newcomers who like himself had entered the New World full of bright hopes but who now lay beneath the kirkyard sod, all hopes stilled. Soon it might be too late for him. Too late for exactly what he did not know; only that he knew now and perhaps had suspected for years that he was not meant for this.

Such feelings of personal crisis are a predictable psychological feature of this passage of life—which is one reason why they could be so prominent a theme in Romantic literature. And yet in Muir's case the feelings were more than the predictable ones of a young man troubled about his destiny or the apparent lack of one. They were rooted instead in a realistic assessment of his predicament, and they were the more acutely felt since he could hardly express them to anyone, not Maggie, nor his mother, nor David. Here he was, of age, and still stuck on his father's farm and under a regimen that threatened the very center of his being. He had, so far as he knew, no prospects for anything different, no formal education, no training, no credentials of any sort, and no contact with the outside world other than his Scots immigrant neighbors.

But he was no ordinary farmer, and he knew it. His impulses and inclinations had been different almost, so it seemed, from that very moment he had plunged himself so joyously into the new earth of Wisconsin, and he had strengthened and nurtured these impulses and inclinations through the solitary and partially defensive exertions of his late teenage years.

He passed through those years almost wholly unafflicted with what he would a few years hence call the "colt & calf" exchanges between girls and boys. While his peers and even his younger brother David were engaging in the prim and terribly earnest rituals of rustic courtship, Muir appears to have maintained an almost scornful indifference to the entire business and regarded such behavior as frivolous. Perhaps, half in daydream, he had thought of himself as a Park or Humboldt, solitary, unwived, free, moving toward great adventures unencumbered by emotional commitments. Perhaps too he understood that to enter here into a relationship that might become serious would further bind him to a locale that could hold nothing for him but more of what he already knew. Whatever it was he obscurely wanted, it was not here.

And doubtless what he had observed of marriage in his own home made him wary, he who identified so closely with his quiet, patient mother, he who had been compelled to watch her suffer under the same harsh tyranny as if she had been but one of the children. Was this what marriage meant: to be a commandant to one's household? The young Muir could not but feel such a destiny intolerable for himself.

But as with the other choices he was now struggling to define, the cost was dear. It was a loneliness deep and perhaps at last irremediable. In avoiding the possibility of close companionship, Muir was constructing another sort of prison for himself, and at forty he would see its precise confines. For the moment, he could do nothing but shy from relationships that threatened to ensnare him in the bonds of emotional responsibility and the sustained commitment of his personal presence.

His growing sense of loneliness and estrangement was accentuated by his habit, begun about the end of the 1850s, of taking long, restless night walks when the weather permitted. These can only have intensified his sense of difference, not only in relation to his own family but in relation to all of the world with which he had made acquaintance. It was one thing to read of the solitary musings of the Romantics and quite another to be abroad in the night when all others were sunk in sleep.

In this tight local culture he was odd and seemed likely to become even odder. He knew, even as he pretended indifference, that others in the neighborhood considered him so. Many young-sters passed through the vale of adolescent estrangement, but Muir was now even more essentially estranged from his world at twenty-one than he had been at fifteen. He had shown a lessening interest in those things that interested his peers the more; had sparked no girls; had shown no interest in his personal appearance or in the way others might regard him. Probably he had never even shaved, his long, silky beard straggling into being on his cheeks and chin. He was still curiously involved with bees, birds, plants, and other natu-ral phenomena that his contemporaries had long since banished to the unvisited world of childhood. Even his hilarious, outsized in-ventions in a way stigmatized him: they worked, all right, and they marked him as a sort of genius. But what sort of thing was this for a young man to be doing? Where could it possibly lead?

William Duncan continued to show interest in these inventions and to encourage him, stopping by the Muir house occasionally in the evenings to chat with John and to inspect his latest piece in the cellar workshop. And Mrs. Galloway too still believed in his star, still felt that he was destined for something out of the ordinary. But to others, even those who came around the farm to marvel at his whirring mills, ticking clocks, and gigantic sensitive thermometers, he must have seemed peculiar. In his debates with Daniel Muir he had developed a sharp and disputatious tongue, and he was capable now of using it on others, taking a certain pleasure in the very strife of verbal combat and in besting conversational opponents. Perhaps he would end by becoming a local crank: gifted in a wayward, impractical way, isolated, at last soured.

His mother wanted him to become a preacher, but he could hardly express to himself, let alone to her, all the misgivings he had developed about the practice of Christianity and its formal observ-ances. He knew, however, that he had become more unsuited for that vocation than anyone could have guessed. He had vague thoughts of becoming a doctor, but if anything these seemed more unrealistic than his mother's thoughts of the ministry. How indeed might he set out on this avenue without formal education, without connection to any academy?

About the only thing he could realistically see for himself was a position in a machine shop. The machine age had been a fact of life in Wisconsin even before the Muirs had migrated there, and now Case, Easterly, Rowell, Van Brundt, and other companies were in full production of various farm machines. In small villages throughout the state specialty manufacturers were turning out products to mechanize virtually all aspects of farm labor. No one had to tell Muir he was good with tools and machines; he had found this out for himself. But William Duncan did tell him that with his skills he would be assured a welcome at any shop in the country. Still Muir delayed. He knew times were tough in the wake of the national panic of 1857; perhaps what welcome he might have had would now be denied him as shop owners tightened their belts along with everyone else. Besides, he dreaded what he knew would be a painful scene with his father, who would refuse to bless the departure of his eldest son and best worker. And, once he had departed, how would the farm be managed by the others? Would he not be selfishly dumping an intolerable burden on his mother, Maggie, David, and the others left behind?

So he stayed on. Spring came once again to the rolling lands, and the young man observed his twenty-second birthday. There were increasing rumors from the southern states of secession. A man named Lincoln from a neighboring state was nominated for president by the new Republican party, and harvest time came with its heat. . . .

At the end of August 1860, William Duncan made one of his frequent calls at Hickory Hill, but this time he had something definite to discuss with John Muir. If Muir really wanted to get on in a machine shop, he ought to take his inventions to the State Agricultural Fair just about to open at Madison. Once people saw Muir's work, Duncan reasoned, John would receive all kinds of offers. To Muir, hesitant, poised, this was obviously *the* moment. He determined to go.

As Muir had foreseen, Daniel Muir refused his blessing, and when Muir asked him whether he might count on money from home if the need should arise, this was refused too. Once you leave here, Daniel Muir told his son, you're strictly on your own. Such, Muir reflected, was his reward for ten years of hard labor. He had about fifteen dollars he had saved and the gold piece Grandfather Gilrye had placed in his small hand so long ago. It was a slim chance he was taking, yet he would have to take it. Who could say when a better one would come?

He packed his hickory clocks, a thermometer, and the works for his early-rising device into a sack and said his good-byes. David was allowed to drive him the nine miles to Pardeeville, a place Muir had never seen, where he would catch the train to Madison. There at the tavern on the main street he and David parted, the younger brother turning the wagon sharply and then plodding slowly back down the street until at last he was gone from view.

John Muir stood on the porch of the tavern, a lean, shaggy-bearded man, with a sack beside him. He was setting out.

PART
II

Into
His Own

Books of Life,
Drums of Death

The shirt-sleeved farmer just off the train from the country and lugging an oddly shaped bundle was one of hundreds who arrived at the fair grounds in Madison that early fall day in 1860. Exhibitors, spectators, and officials mingled together on the spacious grounds downhill from the state university. A high fence ran around the perimeter, and the judges' stands and the railings of the race course boasted new coats of whitewash.

The *State Journal* for September 25 listed the schedule of featured events, including a plowing contest, band performances, and the expected appearances of notables such as Professor James Hall of the state geological survey. Philip Waldron, it reported, would be showing a prize buck and six lambs; C. H. Williams of Sauk City, a shorthorned bull named Paris; Louis Woodworth of Bristol, apples, pears, sweet potatoes, and beets. According to the *Journal* there was still room for exhibitors in the Hall of Fine Arts. Already a variegated lot had assembled there, including one man all the way from Chelsea, Massachusetts, with a "patent portable hand printing and letter copying press." Others were showing embroidery, fanning mills and other types of farm machinery, tobacco, mittens, and art work. Among the exhibitors in the hall was listed "John Miron, Millard, Marquette Co., 2 clocks, 1 thermometer."

The *Journal* had some of the facts right, anyway. Muir had been readily admitted to the grounds and the hall once his peculiar inventions had been seen. Within a few minutes he had set the clocks in working order and had rigged up his early-rising machine while a line of the curious formed to see how it might work. Everything did work, of course, and so well that a *Journal* reporter wrote up Muir as "An Ingenious Whittler":

> While at the Fair Grounds this morning we saw some very inge-
> nious specimens of mechanism, in the form of clocks, made by
> Mr. JOHN MUIR, of Buffalo, Marquette County. They were
> without cases, and were whittled out of pine wood. The wheels
> moved with beautiful evenness. One registered not only hours
> but minutes, seconds, and days of the month. The other was in
> the shape of a scythe, the wheels being arranged along the part
> representing the blade. It was hung in a dwarf burr oak very
> tastefully ornamented with moss about its roots. We will venture
> to predict that few articles will attract as much attention as these
> products of Mr. Muir's ingenuity.

So, he was something of a hit, if an odd one, and the secretary of the State Agricultural Society was impressed enough to send an emissary to look over the inventions and make a recommendation to the fair officials: they were so unusual they fit into none of the judging categories, yet evidently they were worthy of some sort of commendation. When Mrs. Jeanne C. Carr arrived at Muir's booth on her errand of inspection she found a line of small boys, including her two sons, waiting to take their parts in the experiment of the early-rising machine. Mrs. Carr was impressed not only with the inventions but also with the patience of their inventor and his very evident fondness for children. Boy after boy would climb into the bed, shut his eyes, and await the working of the clock that would cant the bed forward and drop him out onto the ground to the cheers of the others awaiting their turns. And all the while the bright-eyed, shaggy-bearded young inventor cheerfully answered the pestering questions of the kids. Mrs. Carr reported back with a recommendation of a special cash prize.

Muir was wholly unused to the entire spectacle—the crowds,

the level of activity, and most especially the flattering attention—and he seemed stunned for a few days. Then, as he steadied himself, he saw that the greatest wonder of the fair was not on the grounds but on the hill above them. The three large buildings of the university seemed wonderfully compelling. He had seen grand buildings before, of course, like Lord Lauderdale's castle at one end of the old high street in Dunbar, but nothing recently so imposing as the just-completed University Hall that dominated the campus hilltop. What sort of incredible, privileged life, he wondered, went on within those walls?

Meanwhile, the news of his success had gone back to Hickory Hill, and Muir hastened to assure the folks that his head hadn't been turned, that in fact he had not even read the favorable notice in the paper. Possibly he had not, for his father's lessons had been deeply implanted. Still, here was a young man hungering for some sort of recognition, and for the first time he had it. The temptation to enjoy it must have been great. In a letter to his sister Sarah at the beginning of October, he confessed this, adding rather pathetically that she knew how tempted he would be by this situation since he was so very fond of praise.

Among those lauding the backwoods inventor was a Norman Wiard, himself an inventor whose improbable contribution to American technology was a steam-powered iceboat that promised to solve the problem of winter travel on the upper Mississippi. The *Lady Franklin* had already been exhibited—but not tested—in the East and had drawn considerable attention. Now it was here, and Wiard recognized that Muir could be useful to him. The young farmer was obviously untutored in formal mechanical arts, but just as obviously he had talent. Wiard offered to instruct him in mechanical drawing and give him access to textbooks in exchange for Muir's serving as mechanic on the *Lady Franklin*. He was also to work in Wiard's machine shop and foundry at Prairie du Chien, whence the boat was to be launched that winter.

Muir accepted this offer, though apparently there were others. Probably he would have wished to enter the magical-seeming university rather than a machine shop had there been any way to do so. But he was a man without money and without the prospect of getting any, and besides, Wiard's offer was precisely what William Duncan had predicted: Muir's inventions had indeed opened the door to a machine shop. He *ought* to accept, and he did so, though not without some misgivings, some of which he kept to himself and some of which he wrote to Sarah. Was Wiard, for instance, possibly a Catholic and thus another potential source of improper influence?

The arrangement with Wiard was to be strictly a trade— Wiard's instruction for Muir's services—with no cash involved. This meant that in Prairie du Chien Muir would have to find the means to board himself. He found lodging at a small hotel in the midst of town where he did chores in exchange for a room and meals. Near the end of October his mother wrote him in care of the Mondell House, telling him that his father had at last been successfully prevailed upon and was sending him a trunk of store-bought clothes to replace his homemade country ones.

Life at the Mondell House was pleasant enough, though by now Muir was thoroughly homesick. Mrs. Pelton, wife of the owner, quickly became a surrogate mother to him—not the first nor the last older woman who would willingly accept this role—and there were a number of young people then boarding at the hotel, including the Peltons' niece Emily, with whom Muir established a friendship.

In this first, belated experience with the wider world Muir was discovering the discrepancies that existed between that world and the view from Hickory Hill. For one thing, he was learning that, despite his rustic appearance and manners, he had a certain charm. People liked his directness, his earnestness, his cheerful energy. Isolated as he had been, this new view of himself must have been about as surprising to him as his reception at the fair. His father had said that if John found him a hard taskmaster, he would find strangers in the big world a good deal harder yet. It was not so; in fact, those strangers seemed to think more highly of Muir than his own father had, and they treated him with greater consideration. The lesson implicit in this was not lost on Muir. The world was not so hard a place as he had been led to believe, nor was he so poor a specimen. He was ignorant of much, to be sure, and he found out daily just how ignorant of worldly ways he was. But he had strengths, too, and one was in simply being who he was; he need contrive no special effort to ingratiate himself with people. Being John Muir would be quite good enough.

Surely he was innocent and rough-hewn enough to have at-tracted derisive attention, but Muir was fortunate in his associations at the Mondell House, where the Peltons and their boarders liked him and overlooked his gaffes and his offenses against the customs of the house. They also bore with good grace his relentless pursuit of the self-improving studies which disturbed their early mornings with the heavy clatter of the early-rising machine. Harder for them to bear was Muir's lack of patience with what he thought the silly behavior of the young residents. As at Fountain Lake and Hickory Hill, so at Prairie du Chien he again found himself beyond coy courtship, chitchat, and parlor games. Driven by a sense of the brevity of life, of his own late beginnings and uncertain destination, he could not abide such apparently criminal wastes of time. Returning to the hotel one evening, he found the young folks at play in the parlor and when requested to join them solemnly and priggishly rebuked them with words out of Solomon: "My son, if sinners entice thee, consent not." More like Elijah than Solomon, he smothered that evening's festivities, as he said in a letter to Sarah and David Galloway, and concluded that such behavior had given him a great character for sobriety.

The Mondell House boarders forgave and went on with their entertainments though doubtless wary of offending the young man in their midst, a complex, puzzling combination of stiff sobriety and natural cheerfulness that was his legacy from family and nationality.

November came to the old French trade outpost, stripping the oaks, hardening the road ruts in the onset of winter. At the end of the first week there had been the national elections, splintered by sectionalism into a welter of parties and candidates, heavy with portent. Wisconsin went for Lincoln, and so, barely, did the country as a whole, though in the South neither Lincoln nor the Republican party appeared on any state ballots. In the North a tellingly heavy vote had been cast for secessionist presidential candidate John C. Breckinridge. None knew whether there would now be war, but all felt that the elections had decided *something*. In South Carolina, Alabama, and Mississippi people welcomed Lincoln's victory, for it had cast matters into such sharp contrast that this political defeat could appear as an emotional relief.

As for Muir, the war worries everyone now more openly voiced dovetailed with his own emerging sense of anxiety. Wiard and

Prairie du Chien had not after all proved a channel opening into wider opportunities but instead a backwater. Whatever it was he was meant to do and be, this was not it. Wiard was absent much of the time and had given his apprentice but a single lesson in mechanical drawing, and the routine of the machine shop had not been a great deal more inspiriting than the round of farm labor Muir had left behind. In a letter to his seventeen-year-old brother, Dan, dated November 19, Muir discussed these concerns of time, opportunity, and vocation, advising Dan to stay home and read up on mechanics and philosophy, and especially to read the Bible since his time on earth was to be terribly short. Nor should Dan be so anxious to get away from the farm, Muir wrote, for a machine shop in Prairie du Chien was not heaven, however it might appear from Hickory Hill. Indeed, Muir guessed, the routines of the shop did not teach much to help you get ahead. Original inventions would probably come out of freedom from such routines and maybe even out of a kind of ignorance of the mechanics of industrial production. For one so unacquainted with the ways of the world, to say nothing of the patterns of American industrial life, it was a shrewd guess, and it suggests Muir was being guided by some vision of himself and his destiny, however obscure. Already this vision had driven him from the farm; presently it would take him out of the machine shop and back to Madison and the university on the hill.

With winter, the river froze over, and so came the appointed time for the trial of the *Lady Franklin.* The boat broke down, nor was there anything its inventor and his apprentice could do to make it run, some fatal flaw in its design dooming it to immediate extinction. Probably by this point Muir had made up his mind anyway to go back to Madison; he was without prospects there, but really he had none here either, and he was haunted by the memory of the university.

On December 20, the event so many had seen as inevitable occurred: South Carolina declared itself out of the Union. A few days thereafter Muir received a fine friendly letter from David Galloway advising him that he was being much too stiff and sober with the young folks at the Mondell House and gently suggesting that he relax and enjoy himself a bit. Galloway also remarked that, however homesick and stranded Muir might be feeling, he could hardly be in a worse situation than Galloway himself, who felt doomed to grub an existence out of the soil, dawn to dusk, for the rest of his life. From this perspective, wrote Galloway, Muir looked pretty well set up.

Muir did not need to be reminded of this truth; whatever might lie ahead for him he would not retreat into farming. By the first weeks of the new year he was in Madison, a handyman now, hanging about the edges of the university and wondering how he might possibly enter that life. He made a few dollars selling his early-rising machines and a few more addressing circulars in an insurance office. He tended stock and ran errands, but still he had to live very close to the bone, and in a letter to his mother he confessed that his health was not good. Probably he was not eating regularly.

As Muir recalled it many years afterward, his university experience began with a casual conversation with a student who recognized him from the fair. When Muir learned it was possible to board oneself at the university for as little as a dollar a week and that many did so he summoned his courage and went to talk with Professor John Sterling.

Sterling was acting as chancellor due to the chronic illness of the incumbent. Even had the young man petitioning him for admission been less impressive, the chances are Sterling would have admitted him to some status anyway. The fact was that in 1861 the University of Wisconsin was in desperate financial circumstances, had pared its expenditures to the absolute minimum, and would have welcomed almost any addition to its slim roster of paying students. In addition to the ill health of its chief officer and its heavy debts, it had to contend with hostile legislators down the hill who missed few opportunities to remark on the quality of instruction, the behavior of the students, and that very financial instability they were themselves so much responsible for. Some legislators had been suggesting that the university be closed and its pitiful funds distributed to other institutions in the state.

The faculty consisted of the chancellor, five professors, and one tutor who were paid a total of $7,100; one of the professors is shown in the university books as augmenting his pittance by supplying the school with wood. The student population the year Muir entered was 180, down from 228 in 1859–60.

The halls of learning that had so impressed the knowledge-craving farmer the previous fall were University Hall and two other buildings that combined student residences, lecture rooms, laboratories, and mess halls. Muir was assigned to North Hall, a large sandstone structure with accommodations for sixty-five boarders. When Muir moved into his first-floor room that winter the heat was supplied by two big wood-burning furnaces in the basement. Residents hauled their own water from an adjacent well, and there was a set of noisome outdoor privies in back.

Among other allegations of the hostile legislators was that the university was a haven for children of the rich. No charge could have been more ludicrous. Tuition for a twenty-week term was but six dollars, and there were additional charges amounting to ten dollars for room and fuel. But even at such modest rates, many students had to board themselves while still others had periodically to suspend their studies for lack of funds.

In Muir, Professor Sterling saw a familiar problem, then. Muir was poor and, except for a few weeks at the old country school-house memorialized in adolescent verse, he had had no formal schooling since his Dunbar childhood. His letters to his family in these first months after leaving home reveal the vigor of his mind but also the weediness of his grammar and other consequences of his lack of formal instruction. Such spotty schooling was so general among students in the Midwest at this time that most institutions of higher learning had preparatory schools attached to them. These were usually—as at Wisconsin—staffed by the same men who taught the university-level courses, and after a successful probationary period students were admitted to regular status.

Such was the case with Muir. The university's second term in 1860–61 began February 6, and at some point between then and the close of the term at the end of June Muir was entered as a first-year student in the scientific program.

This assignment was only approximate: from the outset Muir was regarded as an original who defied classification. That he quickly made such an impression is suggested by Jeanne C. Carr. In notes she made years later, she remembered that her husband, Ezra S. Carr, professor of chemistry and natural history, had returned home one day after his lecture and had remarked that John Muir had been in attendance "& would probably remain for a scientific course of study, making a specialty of Geology." But, she added, he did not take any regular course of study "but daintily picked such crumbs of literature and science as suited his needs."

In fact, it is not known exactly what courses Muir did take during his two and a half years at the university, though it seems that in this spring of 1861 he took either chemistry or geology from Professor Carr and Latin from Professor James Davie Butler. But such fragmentary records as have survived from his time there indicate that he was never other than a first-year student. Hungry as he was for the learning he could get, he would define for himself the terms of that learning. He could not have said upon what basis he picked his courses nor what it was that he was thus preparing himself for, but he was determined that the way should be his own.

He was poor, certainly, and even among others in similar straits he was known as particularly impoverished, existing on little more than graham crackers, porridge, and water. And he was rough and wholly unsophisticated, even among the Wisconsin students of that day, with his beard so shaggy and unkempt he wrote his sisters that he had been advised by a fellow student to burn it off. Invited with others to a reception at Professor Sterling's, he had become so intrigued with the workings of a piano that he had actually climbed into the instrument for a closer inspection, then had climbed out again and rejoined the company. As a witness to this episode remarked in explanation, it was all right with everyone there since it was John Muir.

While Muir studied and starved through the last of winter and on into spring, the North and the South made conciliatory gestures toward one another. These came to nothing. Fort Sumter in Charleston Harbor seemed the probable point for actual hostilities, and when the supply of gestures had been exhausted the firing commenced with the explosion of a mortar shell that lit up the predawn darkness high above the fort on April 12. Within days the critically necessary state of Virginia had joined itself to the secessionists, and the lines for the great and awful contest were irrevocably drawn.

Like most of the country the state of Wisconsin was remarkably unprepared for this. It had about 2,000 men with some semblance of military training, but most of these had not drilled for several years. It owned fifty-six ratty tents, six outmoded cannons, and a rusty miscellany of flintlock muskets, pistols, sabers, and swords. Nevertheless, the First Wisconsin Infantry was ordered to assemble at Milwaukee by April 27, and in the flush of patriotic and sectional enthusiasm there was a stampede of young men to get into this regiment. Perhaps the show would be over so shortly only the first men to go would ever see action. Who knew? The whole thing— though all the signs had been there for many months—seemed so astonishing once it had actually begun. As recruiting agents hurried by horse and buggy through the Wisconsin countryside, they found in these spring days no lack of willing innocents. It is a telling comment on the life of the farm that many boys from the back- country would volunteer for battle merely to get away from home, would express satisfaction with army food and accom- modations, and would find the standard seven-hour drill day a restful surprise.

Whatever he might have wished, Muir could not have been unaffected in the midst of the terrific uproar. Wisconsin and the whole North were afire with rallies, speeches, and impromptu parades. On campus, students were beginning to drop out to enlist for three-month hitches. Portage, like dozens of other small com- munities, instantly mustered its own company of volunteers who clamored for action. If Muir felt at the outset that actual hostilities were a tragedy, he probably also felt that for him they were an unlooked-for impediment. What would it mean for his plans for study?

He tried hard to keep his mind on matters more germane. Writing his sisters, Mary, Anna, and Joanna, in May, he said noth- ing about the war craze but dwelt on things close to his heart. He described for them his habit of perching with a book in the bough of an old basswood tree that hung over the shore of Lake Mendota, dreaming down at the waters or up at the birds and leaves. He described for these country girls the sounds of the city waking up, where "instead of two or three roosters crowing you hear about a hundred all at once. And then the locomotives whistle so loud you would almost think the ends of their whistles were in your ears." And he mentioned the botanizing of other students, adding that while he himself loved flowers he had no time to study them.

But if he was as yet ignorant of the formal study of plants, he was an avid gatherer of them, and he told the girls how he kept his room brimming with them: "Ive got a fine posy at my nose here in an old ink bottle. And Ive got a peppermint plant and a young bramble in an old glass bottle and on the shelf, (the topmost one) stands my stew pan full of brambles 2 or 3 feet long and slips of gooseberry bushes and wild plum and I dont know all what—, and further along you may see my tin cup in the same business, they keep fresh a long time in water. . . ." Outside in a "fine grove" the thrushes whistled to him "just as they do on the black or burr oaks at Hickory[.] I always keep my window open and so I can hear them fine. . . ."

In May and again in June before the close of classes Daniel Muir relieved his son's poverty considerably by sending two drafts for forty dollars each, but after commencement exercises on June 26 Muir walked the forty-five miles to Hickory Hill to save the train fare, passing through small farming villages like North Leeds and Wyocena in summer's deep dust with big hard maples shadowing stretches of the road. When he neared Hickory Hill he paused to change from his dusty clothes into some fresher ones and combed his hair and beard. The disguise failed to fool the old family collie, who came bounding down the long slope of the farm lane to meet him—a welcome that moved him so that he wrote about it a half century later.

Immediately Muir settled into the worn routines of farm labor, but with this difference: his father agreed to pay him seventy-five cents a day for his work. And there was a greater difference still: now Muir could see his hard work—cradling four acres of wheat daily and shocking it—in perspective. Like the fields themselves that had once appeared endless to a small boy working in the midst of them, there were borders he could see to this experience. He was not doomed (like David Galloway) to sweat out his life here amid the rustle of the wheat and corn. However tentatively, belatedly he was out in the world, and he meant to stay out. The wages he received from his father were put aside to assure his return to that world in late summer.

At the end of July the news of Bull Run came to the farms and hamlets of the northern hinterlands like a cloud of acrid smoke drifting over the landscape and shadowing it with the portent of a long and costly war. What had begun as a picnic—and literally so at Bull Run, where holiday crowds including congressmen and senators had come down from Washington to view the fighting from a hilltop—had developed into a series of shocking setbacks. First Fort Sumter, then Big Bethel, and now Bull Run where the Confederates had turned an apparent defeat into a disgraceful rout of the Federals, who ran all the way back to Washington and there threw up panicky defenses. There in the capital's muddy streets under an all-day drizzle that panic had been visible to all in the haggard faces, the suddenly staring eyes, the empty drunkenness of the officers crowding the saloons and hotels. In the tall grass and under the shattered trees of Mathews Hill at Bull Run the corpses of Americans lay soaking, the first real harvest of this thing no one yet comprehended. Trying to put the best face on the disaster, Ralph Waldo Emerson wrote a friend that the war "with all its defeats & uncertainties is immensely better than what we lately called the integrity of the Republic, as amputation is better than cancer." Many were not so sure, including, no doubt, members of the Second Wisconsin who had been in the battle and the ensuing rout.

At the end of August, Muir packed his meager effects, took his hard-earned dollars, and returned to Madison. This time he had the solace of the company of his younger brother, David, who entered the preparatory branch just as Muir had months before.

The town was vastly changed now, and nowhere in it could you escape the fact of war. On the farm you could insulate yourself from it to some extent, and when news of it came, as in the aftermath of Bull Run, you could always go out into the fields or the barns and busy yourself with immediate tasks. Then the war would seem very remote. Not so here. The fairgrounds, which the previous autumn had been devoted to the arts of peace and productivity, had been transformed into Camp Randall, a tract of canvas tents, dust, smoking cook fires, and the clatter of arms. New bars and newly conspicuous brothels had cropped out on the streets surrounding the camp, sure signs of a bonanza of sorts. And up on the hill the serene remove of university life, which had so appealed to Muir, was now punctuated by the sounds of military drill. The students had organized a company and, encouraged by the university, they drilled daily. The war even invaded Muir's own room, for Professor Butler's little boy, Henry, would come there and make fiery patriotic speeches to Muir from atop a stool.

There were noticeably fewer students, too. Some had enlisted, but many others had not returned for the fall because they were needed at home to fill in for those who had gone. Still others who might have entered had been discouraged from doing so. In consequence of all this the university had revised its calendar, providing for more frequent recesses and making it possible for those who wished to teach school during the university year to do so while still completing a year's course of study. There was an anticipated shortage of primary school teachers in the state, and the Muirs among others would take advantage of this opportunity to augment their funds.

A student who knew Muir during this school year noted that he was "not a very regular attendant at church" but that he read his Bible regularly (along with his school texts and his Burns) and said his prayers morning and evening. Now in the new martial atmosphere of Madison Muir made another sort of profession of faith: he began making regular visits to Camp Randall, where he gave spiritual advice to the young men drilling for something that would require more of themselves than any militia sergeant could instill. His immediate concern seems to have been the bars and brothels that had sprung up around the camp like some rank growth. Celibate, abstemious, and perhaps overly proud master of his own body, Muir lectured the recruits on the necessity of living a clean life so as to be fit for the great struggle ahead, for civilian life afterward, and especially for the final judgment that awaited all men, whether cut off quickly in youth and battle or in the fullness of years.

In such lectures there had to be more than a whisper of that priggishness so obvious a few months before at the Mondell House, and yet there must have been something more, for Muir met with a generally favorable response. What interested and moved those with whom Muir talked may well have been less the specifically Christian aspects of the message than a view of existence that somehow comprehended Bible and battle both. Removed as he was from the rage of war, sectional sympathies, even national patriotism, Muir saw the war at a critical distance amounting almost to a cosmic objectivity. A letter to Mrs. Pelton at the Mondell House written after he had seen the Seventh Wisconsin off to the front indicates that Muir had imagined all the terrors the soldiers would soon be facing and that he felt profoundly the sacrifice of the young men, mowed down like stalks in the field but their flesh worth less than the stalks, belying in a way that motto he had carved on his scythe clock: All Flesh Is Grass.* In his mind he saw them charge the "enemy" positions, saw the shell bursts in their staggered ranks, shattered limbs, strewn brains. He saw the dead on the fields but disregarded the color of their uniforms. In this view the ostensible causes of war faded to a ridiculous insignificance; violent death of the young was all.

Meanwhile with characteristic determination he flung himself back into his self-designed curriculum, improvising where he found the university deficient in either instruction or facilities. Having become interested in chemistry through Professor Carr, he sought to remedy the university's lack of laboratory facilities by purchasing out of his own pocket acids, retorts, tubing, flasks, and bell glasses and rigging up a small, makeshift lab in his North Hall room. His diligence and imagination in this gained him in this year the reputation of the school's best chemistry student.

His regimen was as spartan, as relentless as ever, and in his sector of North Hall everyone hearing the thumps of the stone weights and the bedstead knew when Muir arose in the predawns. Through the days he drove himself at a pace that inspired both awe and amusement in his fellow students. Even his own diversions were colored by this personal sense of urgency. He devised what came to be known as the "loafer's chair," a split-bottomed contraption that concealed beneath it an old horse pistol loaded with a blank charge. The loafing victim was led to seat himself here only to leap up when a spring touched the pistol trigger. A good joke, but with a symbolic grimness to it. More elaborate but of a kindred character was a huge study desk he invented. Its legs were carved into representations of little books, and beneath its surface cog-wheels moved a cart filled with texts Muir was studying. At me-

*In fact the Seventh Wisconsin and the "Iron Brigade" of which it was a part suffered one of the highest casualty rates of any unit in the Northern forces.

chanically set intervals the book on the desk's surface would be clapped shut and dropped down into the cart while the next one would be shoved into place from beneath. Muir would load up the cart with texts, set the mechanism for a certain number of minutes per book, lock the thing into working order, and stow the key in some inconvenient place. Then he would seat himself and work doggedly through all the books in the allotted time span.* As with his earlier inventions on the farm there was considerable playfulness in the study desk. No doubt Muir had no practical need for such an elaborate device to enforce good study habits. And no doubt, too, it was amusing, as a contemporary witness recorded, to see Muir "sitting at that desk as if chained, working like a beaver against the clock and the desk." What was less amusing to the "beaver" was his persistent sense of mortality, the clicks of the study desk, the ticks of the scythe-armed clock, and the martial beat of the drums on the campus grounds combining to form the theme of his days.

How much of this sense of urgency amounting almost to desperation was apparent to those who knew Muir is a question. To some he must have appeared distinctly odd just as he had to some in the old neighborhood of the farm, sharing but few of their callow concerns, pursuing with a fierce dedication his own lines of thought and investigation. He could be amusing with his bizarre inventions, his pleasure in a practical joke, and his fund of stories from Scotland that he told in a rich burr. On the other hand, the inner drives and tensions must have occasionally erupted. The sharp tongue and tendency toward disputatiousness developed in combat with his father had not vanished in the father's absence, nor would they ever. Many years later in memorial exercises held in Muir's honor on this same campus, the famed naturalist John Burroughs would be quoted to the effect that these qualities made Muir often prickly company. Burroughs recalled Muir's "biting Scotch wit and love of contradiction," his characteristic relish in a verbal contest.

Indeed, any sort of contest brought out the deep competitive-

---

*The study desk, about nine feet high, is on permanent display at the State Historical Society, Madison. It is one of the very few of Muir's inventions that have survived, and so intricate is it that since some of its pieces have been lost no one has been able to determine how to replace them and set the desk in operation.

ness in Muir. Badly beaten by other students in a knife-throwing contest, Muir went into such assiduous practice that he was soon able to utterly vanquish his late tormentors. For the most part, however, he appeared friendly enough, and the man who became his room-mate in the spring of 1862, Charles E. Vroman of Stoner's Prairie, thought him the "most cheerful, happy-hearted man I ever knew."

By the time Vroman met him, Muir's singular ways had firmly established him as a campus character. Acting Chancellor Sterling directed visitors to Muir's curiosity of a room and Sterling was once disconcerted to find that Muir had used a distinguished guest to demonstrate the early-rising machine: Sterling arrived moments after the demonstration to find the guest sitting on the floor. Others, too, came to see the wonderful contraptions and chat with their inventor, Sterling's wife and Mrs. Carr among them. Vroman thought he was being given a glimpse of the university's museum when he was shown to the North Hall room on the spring day he entered the university. "The room," he remembered, "was lined with shelves, one above the other, higher than a man could reach. These shelves were filled with retorts, glass tubes, glass jars, botani-cal and geological specimens and small mechanical contrivances. On the floor, around the sides of the room, were a number of machines of larger size, whose purposes were not apparent at a glance, but which I came to know later." The floor was littered with sawdust and shavings and in the midst of all this was a young man sawing boards and busily adding to the clutter.

As Vroman became acquainted with his roommate, Muir told him something of his youthful hardships and his lack of opportuni-ties for study and improvement; perhaps he told others also, in which case his driven behavior would have seemed more explica-ble. In any case, Vroman at least did not find Muir intimidating. The picture he gives us is of a poor, hard-working, but essentially cheerful man whose energy and imagination made him both in-structive and delightful to be around.

That spring Muir had returned to Madison after a three-month hitch as a rural schoolteacher. He had done well, his affection and sympathy for younger people and his lively imagination making him a natural success. He had not, as he wrote Sarah and David

Galloway, relished that portion of his duties that called for him to be the disciplinarian, and when he had to use the hazel his voice shook for hours after.

Back in Madison, it was his turn to take instruction—and not from a professor but from a fellow student, a somewhat pompous fellow named Milton Griswold who occasionally declaimed with what Muir remembered as a "fine emphasis" that imparting knowledge was his greatest enjoyment. One day Griswold gave Muir a casual botany lesson by pointing out the similarities between the pea flower and a leaf from the locust tree beneath which they stood. The fact that it was this student who introduced Muir to the formal study of botany is of small significance (though when Muir had become a national figure Griswold achieved minor fame as an indispensable part of the legend). Muir had been powerfully attracted to the life of plants since boyhood and at the university had kept his room filled with clippings. No doubt he would eventually have taken Professor Carr's course in the subject. But he remembered Griswold's message all his life, as if here a door in a wood had magically opened to him, admitting him to undisclosed wonders.

He was immediately seized by the lesson's implications, both on personal and educational levels. On the personal level, it reconfirmed his interest in the natural world and its largely unsuspected life. Here, as in his readings of the Romantic poets, was a kind of justification of his own predilections. The mystery he had sensed in the natural world had been felt by others and had actually been the subject of systematic investigation. So personal inclination met educational practicality, for in the revelation of botanical study Muir intuited that his "play" might also become his "work." In the fields of home he had done his best to make the brutal drudgery recreational, had interested himself in chickadees, oak grubs, the look of winter mornings, had invented gadgets that symbolically lightened the load. But after all, it was just work—and very hard work. Nor had the routine of Wiard's shop and foundry been much better: there the work dulled you rather than releasing your better energies. But with botany the actual work of hunting, collecting, and analyzing plants was the same to him as play, releasing aesthetic impulses, inspiring imagination, revelation after revelation unfolding as in the opening of a flower's petals.

And how providential, too, was the fact that Muir should find this study in the very heart of the New World, surrounded by forests, meadows, and bogs brimful of discoveries waiting to be made. He could hardly have articulated any of this on that spring day beneath the locust, but it was all there in that moment—as he himself said late in life when he reflected back on the experience and described it as an epiphany. At the time all he had was an intuition that he had been given a glimpse of something large and wonderful, and he turned to it.

He carried his new treasure with him back to the farm, but that summer he worked the wheat fields of the old Fountain Lake place, now owned by Sarah and David Galloway. Daniel Muir had suddenly decided to lease Hickory Hill and move into Portage. With John and David both gone, Sarah and Maggie married, and young Dan threatening to leave, Daniel Muir had seen that his farm could no longer be worked by the family. For his oldest son the decision was a blessing, for at Fountain Lake he no longer had to contend with the constant pressure of his father's presence, and after the sweaty work of the day his time was wholly his own. He used it to study botany.

He had brought back a text on the subject and went quickly through it, but best was the field study. At noon, coming in from those fields where he had served his apprenticeship to manhood and farming, he now pursued an apprenticeship as a naturalist, gathering plant specimens and storing them in cool water. After the finish of the day's chores he said he "got to work on them and sat up till after midnight, analyzing and classifying, thus leaving only four hours for sleep. . . ." By the end of a year, he recalled proudly, he knew the principal flowering plants of the region.

That this study had no specific or practical end made no difference to him, though it may well have appeared another vagary to others, and in the summer of 1862 such peaceful and academic pursuits seemed especially out of tune with the times. The South, improbably, was beginning to assume the offensive against the muscle-bound forces of the North. In July, Lincoln issued a call for 300,000 volunteers—to serve not three months but three years. But the way the northern forces had been deployed thus far made many skeptical that the military situation would be remedied by purely numerical additions. And as if to accentuate the pervasive warlike atmosphere of the times, there was a terrible event in neighboring Minnesota. In the middle of August the Santee Sioux rose up in a bloody protest against slow starvation on their reservation, killed an estimated 700 whites, and cleared settlers out of a large portion of the state.

Muir kept on with his lamp-lit studies, and when harvest was made he packed up and once again headed back to Madison, where the fall term opened under the clouds of war. Lee had driven into Maryland, and then came Antietam, a sanguinary stalemate on a scale to shock the toughest veteran. Union General Joseph Hooker called it the most "bloody, dismal" battlefield he had ever seen, while a Confederate counterpart, gazing upon the sun-blackened faces of the putrefying corpses, exclaimed, "Oh it is revolting to humanity & why all this Can't be prevented. Oh, my God, Can't this cruel strife be brought to an end. . . ." On that battlefield men of the Sixth Wisconsin had been so quickly shot down by the dozens that they preserved formation as they lay upon the grass. Reports of these casualties were now coming back to Madison and mingling there with rumors that the university itself would shortly become a war casualty and be forced to close its doors.

Muir wrote Sarah and David, alluding to the crisis of the university and observing that the war seemed farther from an end now than ever. Leaves, he wrote, have their time to fall (still dwelling on the image of the scythe in the hands of the Reaper), "and though indeed there is a kind of melancholy present when they . . . are plucked from their places . . . , yet we hardly deplore their fate, because there is nothing unnatural in it. They have done all that their Creator wished them to do, and they should not remain longer in their green vigor. But may the same be said of the slaughtered upon a battle field?"

Still, in the midst of all this Muir said, he loved his studies more than ever and was beginning to see that this was no short-term adventure he had begun. Vistas continued to open before him so that he thought of going on to further study, if not at Wisconsin then at "some institution which has not yet been wounded to the death by our war-demon."

The idea owed much to Muir's contacts with Ezra and Jeanne Carr and with Professor James Davie Butler, all of whom by now considered him a friend as well as a highly gifted student.

The Carrs had followed him with interest ever since the state fair, and for the past year he had been coming to their home to do chores and to help Jeanne Carr look after her two boys and their little friend Henry Butler, who often played with them there. Gradually this arrangement altered, and Muir began to visit more as a friend and scholar than as hired help. He still performed chores and played with the boys, but there were other times when he came just to talk with the Carrs and still others when he came to read in their well-stocked library. He was, he made it clear, grateful for their interest in him, for their friendship, and for the gift of reading privileges, but he also seems to have indicated that he could accept all this only on the assumption that he and the Carrs were essentially equals. Thus on those occasions when he came to use their library he would have his privacy.

Nor would the social intercourse between him and his benefactors be entirely free otherwise. From a late, undated fragment Jeanne Carr wrote on Muir, it is possible to surmise that the Carrs offered to let Muir board with them but that he refused what must have been a splendid opportunity for so poor and ambitious a student. More than comfort and convenience, more even than access to the books he so loved, Muir cherished his independence and his privacy. These had cost him much to obtain, and he meant to keep them. So, after reading in the library with its busts of great figures in the history of thought, Muir would depart for his North Hall room and there in chosen isolation eat his meager meals. I would have welcomed him into my home, wrote Jeanne Carr, but no quail "ever hid her nest more effectually—or more truly enjoyed its privacy."

On any terms Muir was blessed in his friendship with the Carrs. Not only did they interest themselves in him and his future, but personally, socially, and intellectually they were wonderfully equipped to assist the young man on whatever way it was he was determined to go. Ezra Slocum Carr was then a handsome, clean-shaven man in his early forties, like his younger wife the descendant of a long line of New Englanders. Before turning to the study of chemistry and geology, Carr had been trained as a doctor and had taught medicine in New York and Pennsylvania. More significantly for Muir, Carr for years had been associated with those in the forefront of the earth sciences and had read and absorbed the theories of the best minds of the day: Lyell, Agassiz, and the brilliant, cantankerous James Hall, whom Carr had known in New York and then in Wisconsin, where he worked under Hall on the state geological survey from 1857 to 1862.

Carr was one of a new breed of earth scientists that had emerged in the past three decades. When he was born, geology was hardly a science in America, and its cardinal tenet was that the Noachian deluge explained everything about the way the earth looked. Many geologists were theologians or else possessed inviolable fundamentalist backgrounds and for this reason preferred theory to actual field investigation. Gradually, however, in the 1820s and 1830s the work of Hutton, of Guettard, and of Desmarest began to make an impression in the New World. In the 1840s the influence of Lyell and Agassiz became noticeable, especially after both men came to America and lectured widely. Hutton and those who came afterward shared the basic conviction that fieldwork should take precedence over armchair theorizing and especially over the faithful, uncritical acceptance of religious dogma passing for scientific truth. All believed that the history of the earth could be explained without reference to divine or even natural catastrophes. The forces that could now be observed at work were the same as those that had always operated.

Their influence began to be apparent in the state geological surveys of the 1840s and 1850s and in the work of such Americans as Hall, James Dwight Dana, William Mather, and David Dale Owen. These men and those they trained—like Ezra Carr—were beginning to give the American nation its first authentic views of its geophysical base. It was an exciting time to be at work in this field, and Professor Carr communicated this to his students at Wisconsin.

Carr's list of texts for his geology course included works by transitional figures like Edward Hitchcock and Thomas de la Beche, plus up-to-date studies by Lyell and the various state geological teams. But beyond the readings, Carr taught his students the

supreme virtue of *looking,* of painstakingly scrutinizing the landscape to see what it had to tell. Under him Muir sharpened his
already acute faculties of perception and began to read the landscape as if it were a book with a story it was waiting to divulge. Later
he was to pay tribute to Carr in this favorite metaphor, saying that
it had been Carr who had first opened to him the great book of
nature.

But though Ezra Carr was a crucial mentor for Muir, Jeanne
Carr was even more essential to his development, and ultimately it
was her influence that was to prove the more significant. She was
in her mid-thirties when she and Muir became friends, a strong-
jawed woman with thin, precise lips and something haunted and
haunting about her eyes. With her big, billowy dresses and high-
piled hair, her children, home, and well-known husband, Jeanne
Carr appeared the epitome of New England Victorian woman-
hood. Beneath this lay unsuspected capacities for wonder, passion,
and sorrow.

From her Vermont girlhood she had been intensely attracted to
nature: out of sight of her parents' house in Castleton, the small girl
loved to take off her shoes and stockings and race barefoot through
the high tickling grass of the cow pasture. She collected flowers and
plants in profusion and by the age of nine had assembled a large
herbarium. Her parents seemed to find her interest in nature
vaguely troubling.

The marriage to Ezra Carr had not proved the fount of happiness she had hoped, and perhaps, as she half suspected, she had
hoped for too much. Early, she found household duties irksome,
though telling herself such duties must be hers and were conse-
crated of God. But between caring for two small boys, tending the
garden and house, and waiting on Ezra, she was often so tired at
the ends of days that she could not even thank God for His gifts.
In a journal she kept from an early year of her marriage she exclaimed, "Oh wherefore this fearful Sacrifice of time to the petty
nothings of daily life!" At church one Sunday, when she ought to
have been attending the sermon, her mind lapsed, and she dreamed
of rhododendrons; she wished she could simply *be* like the lilies of
the field.

Perhaps this was only the natural reaction of a young and gifted
woman to the exigencies of marriage—she hoped so. But Ezra did

not make her adjustment any easier, and she confided to her journal that some days his behavior was so dour and imperious that she hoped merely for a smile, and often hoped in vain.

Yet if Jeanne Carr was smothered by her social roles, she was also a person of great energy and imagination. If she was to be a captive of sorts, she would learn how to exercise certain kinds of freedom. She served on commissions, juries exhibitions, read much in contemporary affairs, and took a leading role in the life of the arts in Madison. In the course of years she developed a network of intellectual connections just short of amazing which included some of the day's brightest minds.

In Muir, the lean, reclusive, handsome man twelve years her junior, she sensed a fitting confidant for her truest impulses and inclinations. Much as she gave to her family and her community, she had much more that could not thus be given. And here was John Muir. He was, as she quickly discovered, wary and, burned by the type of marriage and family life he had known too well, especially wary of enduring emotional commitments, but she was patient with him, compassionate, and clearly willing to give him what she had.

Among the many gifts she had for him was an easier way to love God, one which paid due tribute to His power and glory and His presence in the world but which at the same time released the worshiper from the negative dimensions of Christianity: the Calvinistic image of the tyrannical, inscrutable God; the fearful sinner with the sword of judgment suspended over him; the awful yawn of hell. These were dimensions Jeanne Carr, descendant of seven generations of Puritans and raised in a home atmosphere of pervasive religosity, had known herself, but she had also encountered the force of liberal Christianity in New England, the emancipating influence of William Ellery Channing and those who had followed his lead. It had been Channing who made the major public breakthrough against the doom-haunted version of Christianity, remarking in a famous sermon of 1826 that surely God would not have created this beautiful world only to overshadow it with a gallows of judgment. Surely, he taught, we have badly misconceived God's nature, for His visible creation plainly showed that the essence of that nature was love, not anger.

Jeanne Carr had also personally known Emerson, that most radical of Christians, and had taken to heart his message of an in-dwelling divinity. The world as Emerson came to understand it was a world of light, not darkness, and the phenomena of nature revealed to the contemplative soul the presence of a divinity of which that soul was an equal part. Emerson's message must have received a glad welcome from Jeanne Carr—as it did from many Americans from the late 1830s on—combining as it did an unshakable cosmic optimism with a profoundly religious view of the natural world. Here were release and identification and joy. Through Emerson, some portion of that which haunted Jeanne Carr and looked out of her eyes was dispelled.

In Muir, Jeanne Carr could see herself as she once had been, could see in fact earlier generations of pious Christians. No doubt part of his charm for her was his unemancipated Calvinistic Christianity and what she sensed could develop out of it—a tremendous intellectual and spiritual potential waiting to be released from a shackling orthodoxy. When she met Muir he had in fact already begun to think beyond that orthodoxy, yet it still held him, as he had testified at the Mondell House and Camp Randall. Jeanne Carr was to be his guide to an acknowledgment of those thoughts, to an understanding of their fullest implications, as well as to those yet to come.

From James Davie Butler, Muir received a further dosage of Emersonian influence. Butler taught classics, but he too had been touched by the intellectual currents of his native New England, especially by Emerson. Probably he had heard the great man lecture, for Emerson had toured extensively in the Midwest and Wisconsin since 1850. Butler's course descriptions as contained in the annual regents' reports are decidedly Emersonian in their emphasis on the vital connection of language to things and on the acquisition of knowledge as a matter that should have practical consequences.

Like Emerson, he urged on those who would be truly men of thought the importance of keeping commonplace books, and of committing to their pages aphorisms and epigrams snatched from the circumstances of daily life. These entries, he said, should resemble the honeybee: "short, sweet, and with a sting at the end"—so like Emerson's own style. Dante, he told his students, had kept a commonplace book, and so had Jonson, Bacon, Locke, and Macaulay—all the giants of thought. Muir did not immediately act on this part of Butler's instruction, but within months he would begin to keep a botanical journal.

The most immediate consequence of the influence of the Carrs and Butler was Muir's decision in the spring of 1863 to take up the formal study of medicine. The war, too, obviously figured in the choice. Muir had said much to the soldiers at Camp Randall about the need for strong Christian foundations as a response to war, yet now, when he sought an appropriate response of his own, it was not to study theology, which would have led to the pulpit, but medicine.

In his university years Muir's most candid letters went to Sarah and David (where Daniel Muir would not see them), and it was to the Galloways that he broke this news. In June he wrote them saying that he would not be returning to Madison in the fall but would go to Michigan to study medicine. Little more than a week later he wrote to say his plans had altered slightly: after further consultation with Professor Carr, he had decided to take some medically related courses at Madison before going to Michigan. As it happened, he did neither. Instead at the end of the month he and two friends went on a geological and botanical excursion down the Wisconsin River and into Iowa.

By the end of the school year Muir was thin and exhausted, the result of his customary impoverished circumstances and his increasing anxiety about a proper personal response to the war. Even though he had just announced his plans for medical study, the war seemed so terrible and life so uncertain that the plans almost seemed more fanciful than realistic. What he most needed now, he thought, was a long walk and a good look at the natural world that war or no lived out its own immutable cycles. Distraught and faced with dilemmas so large as apparently to defy individual resolution, Muir turned briefly and intensely to nature.

When he emerged near the end of July he had regained health and spirits in hiking the valley lands, clambering about the cliffs, poking through the green dells. Then the war had seemed very far away and his own choices mercifully postponed. A letter he wrote Sarah and David from Madison before coming to help them with the harvest rang with energy and enthusiasm and gave a prophecy of the wonder-charged prose that would flow from Muir in his Yosemite years. Writing of the Wisconsin Dells, Muir described them as the "most perfect, the most heavenly plant conservatories I ever saw. Thousands of happy flowers are there, but ferns and mosses are the favored ones." Expressing a conviction that would become almost a literary tic over the years, he said no human language could ever do justice to such scenes, but the joy of the "happy finding of dear plant beings" repaid all efforts—including this vain one of attempting to describe them in words.

This then had been an escape into the heart of nature, and brief though it was, it had proved successful beyond Muir's best hopes. It was both lesson and omen, and perhaps he thought over its implications as he toiled through the harvest at Fountain Lake. What if you could simply escape the war, mounting social pressure to settle down, family squabbles—all of it—and simply wander off into the American wilderness? Perhaps in these days of summer's end he thought back on Wilson and Audubon, whose adventures in the then-fabulous wilderness had so moved him in his Dunbar youth. Somewhere at the very core of the New World experience the dream of escape into wildness still existed, returning to haunt him when the press of civilization seemed especially heavy. In the mental distance the American dreamer, archetypal escape artist, could see the great forest standing in wait.

But in these days there was much talk of "duty," and Muir was sensitive to it. The faculty at Madison had warmly supported his decision to go on to study at Michigan and had written letters of recommendation for him. The Carrs and Butler in particular were expecting him to make good on a decision they had so much encouraged. Then there was the family talk about his duty to make a choice *now* and settle down: get married; go into business; become an inventor, machinist, preacher. Whatever, something must be done. He was now twenty-five, well past the age at which such decisions ought to have been made. Even young David had settled himself after his brief fling at schooling, was clerking in Portage, and planning a fall wedding. Muir and his father wrangled seriously during these summer months, and it was almost impossible for the son to visit his parents in Portage; doubtless a great issue in the fights was what the elder Muir would have to have seen as his son's strange and dilatory behavior.

And, as always, there was the war that now seemed to be entering a new and even grimmer phase. In March Congress had passed an Enrollment Act under which all male citizens twenty to forty-five years old and all aliens of these ages intent on becoming citizens became eligible for military duty. Henceforth the federal government would run a real draft. It was still possible to avoid service by payment of a commutation fee, through medical disability, or by providing a substitute, but with the Enrollment Act an iron mold had been set: the North would simply crush the rebels with the sheer force of superior numbers, and it meant to raise those numbers quickly.

In the wake of the Enrollment Act there had been savage draft riots in Troy (New York), Boston, and especially in New York City. There 105 people were killed in four days of mayhem; many had been blacks, and some of these tortured and mutilated. Nor was Wisconsin exempt from this reaction. The state was profoundly divided over the war and the draft, those first heady days of salutes and patriotic fervor seeming to have happened with another people in another time. In this summer of '63 there had been near riots over the draft in Dodge County adjacent to the Muirs and two enrolling officers had been wounded by gunfire. One of their assailants had been escorted home by a marching band after posting bail.

Resistance to the act spread. Of the 292,441 names drawn in the July draft, more than 52,000 paid the commutation fee; another 26,000 furnished substitutes; and almost 40,000 failed to report at all. In Wisconsin as elsewhere antidraft, antiwar sentiments were especially marked among immigrant groups—though the state did have all-German and all-Scandinavian groups serving with distinction. Many immigrants felt a sense of betrayal about the whole affair: surely this was not what they had torn up their roots for. Others felt the war was not really their business, that it belonged to the Yankees. Still others felt the national government had no claim on their services. What was the national government, anyway? Had not the seceding states exposed it as a fiction? And in this summer that fiction looked thin enough with the rebels all the way up into Pennsylvania. Underneath all this and embracing many groups in the North was the antiblack sentiment that surfaced in the New York City draft riots. To march off and perchance to die to free the "niggers" was not especially appealing to many in Wisconsin and elsewhere.

In Wisconsin draft dodging was becoming an increasingly popular solution to the imposition of the draft. Those who went north into Canada or west where the draft did not reach were said to have "skedaddled." Muir's youngest brother, Dan, had done so and was now somewhere in Canada. Irresolute, Muir stayed. After harvest, he went to build a house for his sister Maggie and her husband, John Reid. By then he had missed the opening of the fall terms at both Madison and Ann Arbor.

Then and also in later years, Muir supplied various reasons for his failure to go to either campus. To some friends he explained that he had been forced to wait at home to see whether his name had been drawn in the July draft; to others he said he had been detained by lack of funds. And in a letter written in December to Dan in Canada he gave both of these reasons and a third as well: he was saving his money and would leave America altogether in the spring. He would go back to Scotland where a peaceable man might have rest.

This suggests that Muir felt under so many pressures simultaneously that he could supply no single, wholly rational answer. Perhaps all the reasons were in some sense true, but among them the escape to Scotland was truest, precisely because it was an escape. For that is what he now felt most in need of: an escape mostly from the war, but also from his family and their pressing expectations, and from the necessity of choosing some line of work—a decision he felt deeply if obscurely disinclined to make. As he had thought about it through the summer and fall, he did not want to become a doctor any more than he had wanted to become a machinist or remain a farmer. At the turnings of each of these paths off the road of his life he had balked, and the pressure had been building incrementally. What made it all the more difficult for him was that he could not say (or was it "admit"?) what it was he wanted to do. As a teenaged farmer struck by the adventures of Humboldt and Park, he had fantasized kindred adventures. His little excursion along the Wisconsin River valley had given him a foretaste of such delights and of the feelings of inner peace and contentment he so much desired. But what kind of ambition was this? What sort of life goal? He could hardly voice it to himself; he could not at all to others.

In notes he made sometime in the next decade Muir said that at this point in his life he felt that he was *on* the world but not *in* it, a brilliant, personal shorthand for his feeling that he had yet to penetrate to the mysterious marrow of life itself. He felt himself a sort of shadow figure, enacting motions that touched nothing, affected no one, tormented, as he said, "with that soul-hunger of wh' we hear so much nowadays, that longing and vague unrest regarded as proof of immortality." This was the time of life, he continued ruefully, borrowing Milton's diction, "when all the world is said to lie before us for choice." A few friends kindly watched him as he rummaged through the "half dozen old ways in which all good boys are supposed to walk." But when at last even these friends found it time for him to make a commitment, Muir had said, " 'No, not just yet.' "

So, through that winter he worked for his younger brother David, splitting wood, meditating escape. He studied Scots history and manners, still keeping open the option of return to the homeland, and also French, Latin, and anatomy. At the end of February he wrote his friend of Mondell House days, Emily Pelton, saying he frequently stayed up past midnight working through his day's collection of botanical specimens. He told her of his presentiment that he was shortly to leave home, this time for good.

Meanwhile the shadow of the draft inched closer. In February Lincoln issued a call for 500,000 to serve three years—or the duration—to replace the men of the original federal regiments whose three years were now up.

That moved him. He too would "skedaddle," would go to Canada, plunge himself into its woody shadows, its meadows and bogs. He would not stay to be ground between the millstones of war and social pressure.* He would find this life, this earth upon

---

*Apparently Muir was never drafted nor was his brother Daniel. The consolidated enrollment lists and other pertinent draft records for the Second Congessional District of Wisconsin contains no reference to either of the Muirs.

which he now felt he moved so superficially. He would say definitively to the world of his time, "No, not just yet."

On March 1 he wrote a brief, touching note to Emily Pelton, telling her he was leaving home, and ending, "I feel lonely again." Then he was off.

+ Meaford, Ont. is in the pretty Beaver
Valley off Georgian Bay — the Bruce Trail
runs the B.V. & is on the Niagara
Escarpment its entire 430 miles from
Niagara Falls to Tobermory, the tip of the
Bruce Peninsula — in the peninsula the
escarpment drops 100-300 feet to the Bay
+ there are many ferns including one, the
Harts tongue Fern found in a small region
here + (Seattle?) + Scotland — the escarpment
has much unique plantlife — a reason for Johns

The Eye
Within

Thirty years after Appomattox when Stephen
Crane wrote *The Red Badge of Courage,* he imagined his protagonist
Henry Fleming fleeing the horrors of battle, "resolved to bury
himself" in thick woods. "He went far," Crane wrote, "seeking
dark and intricate places." So it was with Muir in March 1864, but
with this crucial difference: Crane's character fled to the forest in
blind terror and cared nothing for it except as it might serve as a
hiding place; Muir sought the forest as a place of both refuge and
nurture. Henry Fleming, wrote his creator, "could not conciliate
the forest." Muir, with his different attitude toward it, succeeded
in doing so, and what might have been a haunted, fugitive interlude
became instead a creative retreat.

The comparison between the fictional character and the man is
not, however, without its instructive similarity, for like Henry
Fleming, Muir was escaping the rage and din of war as much if not
more than he was fleeing from the gathering pressures of home.
Much later he was evasive about the two years he spent in Canada
and about the reasons why he had chosen that particular locale for
his first extended immersion in the natural world. About all he ever

being there?

said of the period is contained in an autobiographical fragment in which he wrote that after

> earning a few dollars working on my brother-in-law's farm near Portage, I set off on the first of my long lonely excursions, botanizing in glorious freedom around the Great Lakes and wandering through innumerable tamarac and arbor-vitae swamps, forests of maple, basswood, ash, elm, balsam, fir, pine, spruce, hemlock, rejoicing in their boundless wealth and strength and beauty, climbing trees, reveling in their flowers and fruit like bees in beds of goldenrods, glorying in the fresh cool beauty and charm of the bog and meadow heathworts, grasses, carices, ferns, mosses, liverworts displayed in boundless profusion.

For a man who had so astonishing a recall of detail and whose voluminous notebooks were carefully preserved through years of hard travel and perilous adventure to form at last the bases of every book he wrote, there is not much here. He did take botanical notes from the Canadian period, but he left them with a friend in Indianapolis in 1867 and never asked for their return. It is possible that he made some further travel notes that were subsequently destroyed by fire, but Muir never cared to go back and fill in the gaps.

From what has survived in fragmentary notes, stray references, and his Canadian herbarium with its identifying slips, it appears that Muir made for the Canadian border by the most direct route from Portage, going up through Michigan and crossing at Sault Sainte Marie. In the next two years he came close to U.S. territory on several occasions, as when he and Dan camped and botanized around Niagara Falls, but not until the war was well over did Muir reenter the States. In his laconic reprise of the Canadian years, "Great Lakes," should be understood as referring to the Canadian shores of lakes Huron and Ontario.

"Freedom" refers to the temporary but effective respite that Muir purchased by going north. If to be confined to Canada was still in some sense to be a captive of the world and its pressures, yet there was a boggy, green sort of freedom to this sojourn, and Muir was the man to make the very best of it. Shadowed as these years were by the war and by his own anxieties, and shadowy as he preferred to leave them, they formed a significant part of what retrospectively can be seen as an apprenticeship.

It is unknown what the solitary sojourner of that first spring told the few he encountered as he trooped the swamps and forests of the North Channel and then went south along Georgian Bay. Probably with his Scots accent he could easily have passed as a native Canadian, for these woods and small clearings were dotted with Scots immigrants, many of them second-generation refugees from the industrialization of the homeland and the Highland clearances— one day Muir even found folk from Dunbar and passed happy reminiscent hours with them.

But human contacts were few in these first months of his voluntary exile, and there were long, lonesome stretches where Muir was forced onto his own resources. Tramping through uncharted miles of green, moist woodland with his tiny bundle of effects, he collected and entered his specimens: moosewood, hornbeam, goldthread, Dutchman's-breeches. At day's end he often found himself utterly alone and without more than a crust of bread for supper, the last remnant of a loaf purchased from some woods wife miles and days behind.

There were also days he spent in swamps, splashing knee-deep through opaque waters, surrounded by the tangle of fallen and decaying branches, enveloped in a deathlike, brooding silence while on high the sun wheeled through a sky that seemed attached to another world. Here indeed he was dead to the world—or it to him—saturated in a wildness that took no cognizance of the frenzied doings of humans, where events were not those of the moment but were instead measured in the endless, imperceptible suspirations of a life that only casually included this spattered traveler. On such days the lessons this world had to impart seemed especially intense and significant, for in the swamps nature seemed uniquely, unassailably itself.

He was to remember one such day all his life. He had been wading for days through streams, bogs, and swamps of ever greater difficulty when one morning he entered a huge tamarack swamp that he could see would take him the better portion of that day to negotiate. Hours later, just when he seemed most weary and his feet numb with the icy waters of spring, he made a discovery. In a bed of yellow moss just above the surface of the swamp waters he came upon Calypso borealis, the Hider of the North. No other plant was near it. The dense stand of tamarack crowded close on all sides. One leaf and one small white bud reposed there on the moss bed like a welcome and a benediction. So unexpected was it and so surpassing its beauty here in the monochromatic swamp that Muir sat down beside it and wept. In the very center of his loneliness, here was this joyful beauty, fully at home. Perhaps, sitting beside it with the wall of tamaracks shutting off the rest of the world like a dense curtain, he thought back on one of his heroes, Mungo Park, who in similar circumstances had been transported by the beauty of a flower in an African forest.

By May he had penetrated beyond the southernmost tip of Georgian Bay and was in other swamps around the Holland River. Meanwhile, a thousand miles to the south in another wilderness, armies crashed into each other in a welter of underbrush and smoke; in the aftermath a doctor treating the Wilderness wounded at Fredericksburg noted that for four straight days he had done nothing but amputate arms and legs.

Muir spent June near Bradford, Ontario, with a Scots family named Campbell. He took advantage of the long days of early summer to botanize at dawn before his chores and then again at evening, poking through the swamps, collecting, pressing, and classifying treasures that mystified the high-spirited, bluff Campbell men. They called him "Botany" and played an unintentionally grim practical joke on him when they told searching British officers that "Botany" was a deserter from their army. Muir had to do some quick talking to convince them he really was but a wandering botanist.

In July he left the Campbells and worked southward toward Burlington Bay, then east again toward Niagara Falls. In early September he was joined there by Dan; apparently the parents in Portage relayed messages to their sons and so arranged this rendezvous. While they camped and botanized Dan mentioned a pleasant place he had worked before meeting John, a sawmill and factory on the shore of Georgian Bay, Ontario, near Owen Sound. Muir was by now short of cash and, even more significantly, the severe Canadian winter was near. The mill and factory sounded attractive as a place to hole up, and so the brothers went to the little town of Meaford, passing through the huge stands of hardwood at which the settlers hacked, year by year grubbing out tiny clearings in which to plant their potatoes and wheat.

The Muir brothers received a good welcome at the mill and factory owned by William H. Trout and his partner, Charles Jay. The Trouts were Scots and also Disciples of Christ, and in Dan's elder brother they saw a skilled, valuable addition to their operations. Muir knew woodworking and had an evident mechanical bent that Trout and Jay saw they could put to good use in the factory where they turned out rakes, brooms, and fork handles.

The Trouts must already have known why Dan Muir was in Canada, and in later years William Trout said it was his understanding that John was there to take care of Dan and was under a "positive order" from his parents to remain with Dan until the war ended. This, said Trout, did not at all coincide with John's feelings, "yet especially for his mother and Dan's sake he complied."

They settled in for the winter, a lively, talkative group that included another Trout brother and two sisters, plus Charles Jay and various visiting relatives of his. William Trout suggests that at first Muir struck them all as a bit odd with his queer stock of knowledge, his naturalist activities, and his daily habits, which included the inevitable early risings (assisted by one of his machines) and his voracious reading. He read before the rest were up, Trout recalled; he read at the noon meal, and again at supper and after. He was also given to lecturing the group on various subjects, but they, too, had opinions, and there was a good deal of spirited but congenial exchange.

The immediate work at hand was the construction of an addition to the factory, and the Muir brothers assisted in this until late spring or early summer of 1865, at which time Dan returned to the States. The war had come at last to what now could appear as its inevitable conclusion, and young Dan had had enough of Canadian exile. He was homesick for his family; John was not.

So, he stayed on through the summer, taking a leave from his work to retrace a portion of his solitary route of the previous year, botanizing as he went. In the fall he was back at the mill and now entered into a contract with the partners to turn out 30,000 broom handles for a Toronto firm. The contract also stipulated that Muir was to have the freedom to make such improvements in the factory machinery as he could devise, a provision that Muir had insisted upon. William Trout did not believe he could make any improvements, since Trout was himself something of an inventor and considered the self-feeding lathe he had installed a "nearly perfect instrument," as he put it. Muir knew better, for he had been in his habit of imagining inventions while he went about his workaday tasks, and he was already confident that he could indeed improve on Trout's device.

He worked on the design of his invention obsessively through the late fall. If, when he had come north to Canada, he had said to the world and its vocational pressures, "No, not just yet," here was evidence that he carried more than a little of that world's culture within him like some virus. Instead of filling the pages of his herbarium with drawings of plant specimens, he now filled them with sketches of the invention. He wrote Jeanne Carr that his mind was so preoccupied with plans for inventions that he was fit for little else. Night and day the problems of design gave him no rest, evidence enough of a powerful emotional and spiritual conflict within. How suddenly far away seemed those silent, solemn lessons of the swamps and woods and of that single blossom of the Hider of the North. Here in the mill and factory, for better or worse, was the reality of his time.

By February 1866, he had perfected his designs for the improved lathe and also for a machine that bored and drove rake teeth. He set them in operation, and they worked famously. So absolute was the improvement in production that Muir turned 23,000 of the 30,000 broom handles in a single day. William Trout, looking back to this astonishing mechanic's work, called him a "real live inventive, designing mechanic" whose machines it was a delight to see at work.

But in the very midst of this triumph there was the naggingly familiar question: was this to be how he would spend his little time on earth? The broom handles mocked him with their dull and common utility. He tried consolation by philosophizing in a letter to Jeanne Carr that cleanliness was a great virtue, and so in his small way he had contributed to the world's welfare by turning out cheaper broom handles. The world would perhaps be better swept now.

It was no good, and he knew it in the act of composing the letter and so rushed on to other equally hollow and self-deprecatory claims:

> I have also invented a machine for making rake teeth, and another for boring them, and driving them, and still another for making the bows, still another used in making the handles, still another for bending them—so that rakes may now be made nearly as fast again. Farmers will be able to produce grain at a lower rate, and the poor to get more bread to eat. Here is more philanthropy, is it not?

Then he added, disconsolately, "I sometimes feel as though I was losing time here. . . ."

Time in the guise of death continued to haunt him even with the great killing of the war over. Perhaps, brooding on the fact of those as yet untotaled deaths he felt some guilt at having survived. Writing to Jeanne Carr of the many things he wished to do with his life, he confessed to fears he would die before he could accomplish any of them. The John Muir whose machines hummed so productively in the little factory at Meaford amounted to nothing, really, weighed in the scales with his unrealized greater expectations. "How intensely," he wrote, "I desire to be a Humboldt!" Perhaps to no one else—even to himself—could he have made so frank an admission. "Happy indeed," he said to her in the same letter, "they who have a friend to whom they can unmask the working of their real life. . . ."

At the end of February, his contract completed and the new handles stacked for seasoning in the factory, a blizzard howled in and that night the factory took fire and burned to the ground, a total loss. Trout and Jay would begin again, but they would have to do so without their master mechanic, for the fire and its destruction of all his efforts had shown Muir just how dissatisfied he had become with his condition here. He had had enough of the Canadian woods and waters; and if, as it seemed, he was compelled by the times and his own talent to spend his life amid the whir of machines, he thought he could do better in an American commercial center than in retired little Meaford. Besides, he had quarreled with the Trouts over the proper way to worship God, and perhaps the disagreement was bound to grow worse as Muir pursued his own convictions. He now took a greater delight, as he told his sisters and Jeanne Carr, in reading the power and goodness of God in the phenomena of the natural world than in the words of the Bible. To the Trouts, who like his father stuck close to the letter of the Scriptures, such an attitude veered toward some kind of paganism.

He looked at a map of the States, searching for some city centrally located where his talents might be welcomed. Indianapolis was in roughly the same region he was familiar with, and as an important railroad center it was certain to have its machine shops. Also, as he noted, it was surrounded by forests of deciduous hardwoods; in his spare time there he could pursue his hobby of botanizing.

The partners figured they owed Muir $300 as per their agreement with him, but he would stand for no more than $200. In any case, at the moment the matter was academic since the fire had financially destroyed them and they could spare no more than his train fare to Indianapolis. He took the balance as a promissory note, and with that and his herbarium he left.

Reentering the United States at the age of twenty-eight, he seemed to have little enough to show for an apprenticeship. But in his head and heart he had about a thousand miles of wild landscape, and he had learned that he could survive very well beyond civilization.

Indianapolis was indeed a railroad town and so had its share of machine shops and factories. The city had early been a center of the expanding national rail system, had survived an extravagant binge of railroad speculation in the 1830s, and was now known (at least locally) as the "Railroad City," a title that would soon be successfully disputed by Chicago.

Like many another urban area in the North, Indianapolis had profited greatly by the war and had come out of those years a different community. Little less than half a century before the site had been a dense forest of oak, walnut, and ash—the trees that drew Muir. The city's lots had been cleared and streets laid out by the simple and characteristically wasteful expedient of felling the trees and burning them in grand bonfires. Municipal growth through the

1830s, '40s, and '50s had been steady if moderate. Then the war
came, and suddenly Indianapolis was a center through which passed
thousands of troops, government officials, and camp followers.
Businesses flourished, factories opened, rail lines expanded. Sections of downtown streets grew pavings and were lighted, though
most were still dirt that in summer had to be tamped down by
mule-drawn watering wagons. Horse-drawn streetcars ran through
the commercial section, and a home had to be established for
"friendless women" who had run afoul of official civic morality.
When Muir arrived, the city was in the midst of an unparalleled
growth that would double its population in the decade that had
begun with the war.

   In this bustling place he quickly found work. The firm of Osgood and Smith was the oldest manufactory in the city and the year
before Muir's arrival had bought the patent for the famous Sarven
carriage wheel. Located near the Union depot in the heart of the
commercial district, Osgood and Smith turned out the wheel and
a variety of carriage implements in addition to items like staves,
barrels, and plow handles. Muir knew about such items and how
they were made, and he got on as a sawyer at ten dollars a week.
After a few weeks' uncomfortable transiency, during which he told
his family he dared not unpack his bag so unsure was he of his living
conditions, he found quiet, clean lodgings with a fellow Scot and
sawyer named Sutherland. As summer came on he settled into the
life he believed he was fated to lead.

   But while professing an acceptance of that fate, at the same time
he was capable of railing against it, almost as if the force of culture
were a person or thing that bullied him into a way of life he would
not otherwise have chosen. Writing to Sarah in May, he admitted
his love of solitude but also the presence of this strange drive that
had brought him to where he now was, in the sawdust-filled factory
loud with the industrious, productive whir of circular saws and
lathes. "Much as I love the peace and quiet of retirement," he
observed,

> I *feel* something within, some restless fires that urge me on in a
> way very different from my *real* wishes, and I suppose that I am
> doomed to live in some of these noisy commercial centers.
>   Circumstances over which I have had no control almost com-

pell me to abandon the profession of my choice, and to take up
the business of an inventor, and now that I am among machines
I begin to *feel* that I have some talent that way, and so I almost
think, unless things change soon, I shall turn my whole mind into
that channel.

"I almost think," he had written—"almost." In the same letter he
described for Sarah the remnants of the great forest that had comparatively recently covered the noisy commercial center in which
he felt doomed to live. It is now in about full leaf, he wrote, and
he had been walking out in it in the dewy hours before breakfast.
There "among the beautiful flowers and trees of God's own garden, so pure and chaste and lovely," he could not help "shedding
tears of joy." They must also have been tears of sadness, for in truth
his nature studies, that "profession" he longed to follow, had become a hobby. He lived in the city now and his life was circumscribed by the round of factory work. The brief hours of morning
visits to the fields and woods were hours stolen out of a life that
seemed, almost mysteriously, to be running him.

He wrote Dan in the same vein, saying, and here without the
qualifying "almost," that since his talent apparently lay in machines
and mechanical inventions, "I just think that I will turn all my
attention that way at once." He expressed surprise at the lack of
inventiveness among the machinists he had encountered and mentioned by way of example the work of one of the more inventive
among them, a man whose hub lathe Muir felt he *"very naturally"*
could improve.

By early summer Muir's wages had more than doubled (though
he was working "double time," as he told Dan), and his Madison
friends, the Carrs and Butler, had arranged a contact for him with
the socially prominent Merrill family. Catharine Merrill and her
nephew and sister took Muir up immediately. Butler had written
this unmarried woman of middle age that if she would walk the
fields with Muir, she would find that "Solomon could not speak
more wisely about plants." Trying the advice, she found it so, and
by the end of summer Muir was head of an informal group of nature
worshipers that roamed the still unimproved spaces beyond the
burgeoning city. Sundays he took a class of working-class children
out into God's gardens, preferring here as he had in Canada this

kind of spiritual instruction to that offered in conventional Sunday schools.

These activities kept him in some contact with the world he loved, but at the same time he was being pulled ever more steadily into the business of the factory. Osgood, the original partner, and C. H. Smith early on recognized that here was no ordinary laborer, and like the good businessmen they were they were determined to keep him through progressive inducements. Muir had apparently originally told them his stay with the firm would be brief, only long enough to earn him sufficient cash to fund his Humboldtian dream of a South American excursion. But management was now offering him the position of foreman in the sawyers' shop; and, if that should go well, perhaps beyond lay the possibility of a partnership in this most prosperous firm, the only one of its kind between the Midwest and the Rockies. Muir was tempted.

Summer merged into fall; cholera and ague, which had plagued Indianapolis during the hot months, now faded. Dan had visited and apparently had worked briefly for Osgood and Smith but then had gone home again. Plans were afoot in the city for the first national convention of the Grand Army of the Republic, to be held in November. A sawyer in the shop caught his hand in a saw, mangling it horribly. And Osgood and Smith commissioned their prize sawyer to make a time-and-motion study of work in the shop to determine how productivity might be increased.

South America, always a dream, now came to seem an even more unreal possibility and the belts and lathes, saws and wooden hubs, more and more real and necessitous. One day Dan sent him a package of ferns from home, and crushed and cramped though packing had made them, their verdurous scent almost drove him wild with longing and with memories of the Wisconsin countryside. He wrote Dan back immediately, begging him to send more, adding that he felt impelled to quit his work and become a fern gatherer. But then, reality again: "I mean now Dan to give my whole attention to machines because I *must*[.] I can not get my mind upon anything else—. . . ."

In December he presented Osgood and Smith with the fruits of his time-and-motion study. It was a curious document, a combination of thistly Scots mother wit, mechanical talent, and a shrewd grasp of managerial detail. Studying the operations of the shop,

Muir discovered much wasted motion, unnecessary delays, fruitless consultations between workers, and a general lack of coordination. His remarks on the need for a central, organizing authority that would regularize and rationalize all aspects of production indicate clearly that he understood the essentials of what was then internationally known as the "American System." Here was a philosophy of factory production that in thirty years had revolutionized the economy of the Western world and had made an upstart nation preeminent among the world's manufacturers. Without formal training and without an abundance of actual manufacturing experience, Muir had grasped the vision of the total factory as a machine in itself, where laborers, machines, and products were interchangeable, smoothly functioning parts.

There was something cold and mechanically neutral in such a vision despite the presence in Muir's charts of his characteristically vivid and candid diction.* And this, too, was a part of the "American System," for the vision of the factory and its personnel as a machine had little room in it for human concerns; efficiency of production was the driving concern, and much else was sacrificed to this. In this kind of production, standardization and interchangeability were the revolutionizing concepts, and these had the tendency to rob workers of their humanity and the products of their individuality. There was in Muir's study of the workers a clinical detachment; the men were analyzed almost exclusively in terms of their failings, and while this was doubtless necessary in an exercise such as he had been set, still it is a bit surprising from one who had so much blood in his own veins and who knew from hard personal experience the mind-numbing consequences of repetitive labor. It was another indication that Muir was good (almost fatally good, considering his truest inclinations as he understood them) at this work, and could be an outstanding success at it.

In a section of his study labeled "Chart of one days Labor," he graphed the rise and decline of a day's production, showing its poor beginnings in the mornings when the men were sluggish and disin-

*Describing the inefficient arrangement of the felloe racks, he wrote that a worker stacking felloes was obliged to "poise them singly over his head like a Tartar balancing a lance." He also lectured his employers on their wastefulness, much of which he thought could be prevented "with half the forecast of a harvest mouse."

clined to "take hold" of the work, as he put it; the slackening on either side of the noon dinner hour; and the precipitous decline after lamps were lit in early evening. "Lamplight labor," he observed, "is not worth more than two thirds daylight labor." During the days there were occasional irregular spurts of productivity, "shameful angular projections," as he termed them, occasioned by the periodic appearances of the overseers in the shop. Here indeed is the managerial eye, and no doubt Osgood and Smith were pleased with the clarity and precision of their man's vision.

Spring began to break upon the midwestern landscape, and as its first harbingers showed themselves, Muir was poignantly reminded of how estranged he was in a daily way from the wild world of his dreams. He got out maps of the southern states, of the West Indies, South America, Europe, and studied them longingly, fantasizing a tremendous botanical excursion that would take years—and would take him far from this world in which he functioned so smoothly.

But the greater portion of his time and thought were taken up with the work of the factory. Writing home in February 1867, he told his family in exasperation, "If you knew how much I had to do you would not complain about the number of letters I send you [.] I send far more letters home than elsewhere [.] I *cannot* write oftener."

On the evening of March 6, he worked late. New belting had been installed on one of the machines and in the course of the day's operations had stretched. In order to tighten it, Muir had to undo its heavy lacings and was using the tang end of a file to do so. After a hard pull and the sudden release of the lacings, Muir's hand, armed with the file, sprang upward, the tang point glancing into his right eye at the edge of the cornea. For an instant he stood there stunned, his hand over the eye in belated, futile protection. Then he walked to the window where the wan light of an early spring evening filtered in. Slowly withdrawing his hand he saw in its cupped palm the drippings of the aqueous humor. Even as he gazed in horror the sight in the eye began to fail and soon was gone altogether. An assistant present at the scene heard him remark in a half whisper, "My right eye is gone, closed forever on all God's beauty."

He had sufficient self-possession to walk home "steadily enough," as he recalled it, but within a few hours the shock sent him trembling to bed and soon thereafter the left eye failed also in sympathetic reaction. He was a blind man.

The next day a doctor was summoned and, examining the wound, judged that Muir had lost the right eye, though the left would eventually resume its functions. Two days later Muir wrote his mother in scrawling, slanting lines:

Dear Mother
    While connecting a machine belt I accidentally thrust the point of a file into my right eye last wednesday and there is damage [.] I am completely prostrated and the eye is lost [.]
    I have been confined to bed since the accident and for the first two or three days could not eat or drink a mouthful but I am a little better today and hope to be at work again in a month or two [.] I am condemned by the doctor to a dark room for some weeks [.] I am surprised that from apparently so small a shock my whole system should be so completely stunned [.]

He was now free from pain, he continued, and kind friends were doing their best to lighten his gloomy hours by reading to him. In a few weeks, he ventured bravely, "I will be ready to look the world and the truth (?) in the face well as ever and I mean to make this long rest profitable as possible [.]"

There was soon better news. The Carrs and Professor Butler had learned of the accident and through the Merrills sent a specialist to examine Muir. After reassuring Muir about his left eye, the doctor said that the right eye, too, would recover much of its function. It had been badly damaged, true, and sight would never again be perfect, but Muir was young and vigorous, and the doctor gave him reason to hope that eventually he would be able to see about as well as ever.

There was other news, too, though whether to Muir it sounded as good as it might have to others was a question. Osgood and Smith had visited him in his dark room and had told him that they were building a new shop and that he would have charge of it. Writing his mother of this, Muir remarked that henceforth he would not have to work as hard as previously.

But the real message on the import of his accident and subsequent developments went to Jeanne Carr. To her he confided that he would gladly have died on the spot "because I did not feel that I could have the heart to look at any flower again." Now, to his inexpressible joy, he found that his sight was gradually returning, that his left eye had recovered and his right eye could distinguish shadows. Soon, he said, "I wish to try some cloudy day to walk to the woods where I am sure some of Spring's fresh born is waiting." There was no talk here of future factory responsibilities.

As ever, she understood him better than anyone, perhaps even better than he himself, writing him that God had given him the "eye within the eye, to see in all natural objects the realized ideas of His mind." Then she added, significantly, that God having given Muir this great gift of sight beyond sight, He would "surely place you where your work is." In these dark hours, forced by injury to think back on his life and the way he was leading it, he heard in her words that unfailing voice of compassion and, more, intuitive sympathy, telling him what he knew was so: that he had still not found his place, his work. In the moment of the accident perhaps he had seen that clearly for the first time, the eye within suddenly, paradoxically, opened on the glaring truth that he was still not *there,* busy commercial center and ascending career or no. Then in those first grim afterdays as the shock ebbed a deeper one intruded: that he would simply be another nameless casualty of this age of machines, like the sawyer of whom he had written, the man's hand mangled and forever useless; and he, never to have really experienced the fullness of the natural God-made world. Here lay the inmost, shuddering horror of the accident.

So, lying in his bed and slowly recovering amid flowers, the voices of readers, visits of his Sunday school children, he began meditating: not a return to the factory, ready manfully to look that busy world in the face and get on with his career, but a final escape. Little by little, the blinds had been raised, admitting more and more light, into his eyes, into his mind. He went back to his plans for a walking tour of the southern states and from there to South America. He read and was charmed by an illustrated brochure of California's Yosemite Valley—there, too, were mysteries he might experience.

The slow regeneration of his sight was wonderful, and it was also mysterious. Who knew whether it would continue or even whether the eye might fail again. He feared future blindness, feared also the prospect of the life he would then be forced to lead amid what he styled significantly the "shadows of civilization's defrauding 'duties.' "

His first tentative excursion into April's fields decided him: his work was not in the factory; with what remained of his sight he would escape into nature and there store up enough of flowers and sunlight and wild landscapes to last him the remainder of his life, whatever might happen.

To the surprise and dismay of his employers he resigned his place, closed up his spare affairs, and set off for Portage in the company of Catharine Merrill's eleven-year-old nephew, Merrill Moores. Muir would complete his recovery up there among family and friends, and then he would be gone, south into the wilderness and the tropics, and then still farther south into the hot, unknown life of South America.

The man and the boy went up through the center of Illinois, the man testing his eye on the flowering remnants of those grand prairies that once had covered the whole central region of North America. There was still a cloud over his eye, but he found he could take in the large picture of the landscape and that in general his powers of observation were undiminished: seven miles southwest of Pecatonia, Illinois, he noted 200 different plants in 200 yards: Rudbeckia hirta, four varieties of aster, Phlox pilosa, Amorpha canescens . . . ; he drenched himself in their spring life with the relish of one redeemed from darkness.

Either on the Illinois prairies or possibly later in the summer in Wisconsin, Muir took notes for an essay he never completed. In it he expressed his joy in his reviving powers of sight, writing of the inexhaustible glories to be discovered in the smallest area of the natural world. In any area, he wrote, no matter how limited in scope, "we are full gladly willing to be fenced in upon it for all eternity." The smallest plot of ground is in reality "ten thousand-fold too great for our comprehension, and we are at length lost, bewildered, overwhelmed in the immortal, shoreless, fathomless ocean of God's beauty."

Summer passed quietly with Muir botanizing at Hickory Hill and around Sarah and David Galloway's new farm at Mound Hill. On a tip from the pioneering Wisconsin conservationist, Increase

I. Lapham, he went to the Wisconsin Dells in search of the fern
Aspidium fragrans and found it there. He visited the Carrs and
Butler in Madison. He seemed mostly to be gathering himself,
quietly, surely, as for a great test.

Then in August it was time to go, and he had the distinct
presentiment that this would be a real leave-taking, that he would
never again call Wisconsin home nor even use it as a base, as he had
been doing these past weeks. His life, still obscure enough in its
direction, was clearly taking a critical turn toward somewhere. In
this context, good-byes to mother, brothers, and sisters had an
added poignancy, and so, in its way, did his parting from his father.
The two had fought on and off through the summer, the elder man
regarding the younger's nature studies as a species of sin; the son
retorting that in the fields and woods he was a good deal closer to
God than his father was, however much the latter might read his
Scriptures and Foxe's *Book of Martyrs.* Now at the moment of parting, the old man asked him if he had not forgotten to pay for his
lodgings. Muir handed over a gold piece, last tribute to be exacted,
remarking that it would be a long time before he would venture
home again. Then he was gone, taking the first of those long strides
that would carry him through woods, over mountains, and along
the savannas of the South.

From Indianapolis he wrote two valedictory letters, one to Dan,
the other to Jeanne Carr. "I mean to start for the South tomorrow,"
he wrote Dan on September 1. "I feel touches of the old depressing
melancholy which always comes when I leave friends for strangers.
I do not know where I shall go, nor when I shall return. . . ."
Appended to the letter was a kind of informal will in which he
parceled out his meager possessions and made an accounting of the
money he was owed by various parties. Mother, he stipulated, was
to have her choice of things; to his father he left nothing.

Then to Jeanne Carr he wrote again of his fate, except this time
he saw himself impelled into the wildernesses of the globe rather
than imprisoned in the sort of noisy commercial center he was in
the act of leaving: "I wish I knew where I was going. Doomed to
be 'carried of the spirit into the wilderness,' I suppose. I wish I
could be more moderate in my desires, but I cannot, and so there
is no rest."

The next day found him in Jeffersonville on the Indiana-

Kentucky line. He walked through Louisville "without speaking a word to anyone," as he wrote in a journal he was to keep of this adventure. "Beyond the city I found a road running southward, and after passing a scatterment of suburban cabins and cottages I reached the green woods and spread out my pocket map to rough-hew a plan for my journey." He traced a general route south and east with Florida as its terminus and then made his first entry in his journal: "John Muir, Earth-planet, Universe."

The
Thousand-Mile
Walk

―――――――――

It was a true departure, and it was also the
beginning of one man's singular rediscovery of America, the America that had been sheer potential in the European mind before its
existence had become known and that, having been discovered,
had then in a curious way been disregarded.

He did not, as he had written Jeanne Carr, know just what was
driving him, nor where that drive would take him. The map he now
spread in the shadows of the Kentucky oaks told him only locations
and place-names. But he knew at least that, wherever he was going,
he wanted to arrive there by the "wildest, leafiest, and least trodden
way" he could contrive. The ultimate destination was not on any
map—probably never would be. He would simply have to go on
in trust, whatever the cost in loneliness, dislocation, and the baffled
disapproval of the world.

After inscribing his journal so bravely, "John Muir, Earth-
planet, Universe," he essayed an analysis of his existential situation
as he presently understood it, this as a way of establishing bearings
at the outset. He seemed to be, he wrote, one of those who are

driven by tidal impulses that must be obeyed. In some persons, he ventured,

> the impulse, being slight, is easily obeyed or overcome. But in others it is constant and cumulative in action until its power is sufficient to overmaster all impediments, and to accomplish the full measure of its demands. For many a year I have been impelled toward the Lord's tropic gardens of the South. Many influences have tended to blunt or bury this constant longing, but it has outlived and overpowered them all.

Here memory could take him all the way back to Dunbar and to the stories he had read there of Wilson and Audubon, of their wonderful birding adventures in the wilderness. What a long and circuitous trail led from those schoolbook pages to where he presently sat, a kind of fledgling Humboldt bound on a voyage south! And yet, as his journal entry suggests, he was aware of the connections, and, even more significantly, he was now prepared to act on them and trust their direction.

There were more connections present than he could at the moment fathom, for just as the trails of the precursory explorers had helped lead him to where he now was, so where he would now go, making his own trail, would be through terrain traversed by another kind of explorer he would never admire, those who had opened this country to white settlement. Through Kentucky, Tennessee, the tip of North Carolina, Georgia, and Florida he would unwittingly follow the tracks of men whose motives for exploration would be forever foreign to him and whose vision of the wild New World was radically exploitative and predatory. Boone, De Soto, Ponce de León—legends in the lore of the nation that claimed title to the lands they had explored—had been after other things than the flowers, birds, and mysteries of nature that had inspired Muir's heroes.*

Here in Kentucky it was Boone. Beginning as hunter and trap-

---

*There was one exception, and in later years, after he had succeeded in defining for himself what sort of explorer he cared to be, Muir would discover William Bartram, an explorer after Muir's own heart and one, significantly, not included in American legend.

per in Shawnee lands, he had become a wilderness guide, a wilderness breaker, blazing a road well into the interior of the state; and he had lived to become a failed, embittered land speculator whose bones rested not many miles east of where this new explorer now was. Muir took no reck of Boone, either at this time or at any other. In a vague way they shared the hunger for "living room," space, the freedom to saunter unencumbered through the woods, the sense of thus having escaped civilization for a time—but that was all.

Muir surely had the sense of having just escaped, and in the journal entries he was to make on his walk the word occurs with a telling frequency. And like one who feels fortunate to have escaped some imprisoning thing or force, he did not spend long over his map but quickly lost himself amid the cavernous overhangs of the oaks. He traveled light, too, as if in carrying much worldly baggage he might be overtaken by that world again. He had been advised not to carry much cash, since the South was said to be filled with roving bands of guerrillas still in arms this long after Appomattox. Accordingly, he had no more than thirty dollars in his pocket.* He wore a tough gray suit that would not readily show stains and carried a plant press and small rubber bag containing a few toilet articles, a change of underwear, and three essential books: Burns's poetry, *Paradise Lost,* and the New Testament. By the end of the first day he had covered twenty miles along river bottom lands and put up in a "rickety tavern."

A few days later, heading due south, he entered the region of the Kentucky caves, first Horse Cave, which a local resident informed him had never been fully explored. Muir was astonished to learn that, though the famed Mammoth Cave was but a few miles distant, his informant had never bothered to visit this natural marvel and in fact considered it nothing more than a big hole in the ground. Here, as the traveler observed, was one of those "useful, practical" men such as he himself was supposed to be and was in

---

*He left $100 with his brother David in Portage for use when he should send word that he needed it. Evidently, the word was somehow delayed in transmission when Muir wired for the money from Savannah, for he had a hungry wait of almost a week before it arrived.

flight from becoming, one "too wise to waste precious time with weeds, caves, fossils, or anything else that he could not eat." Muir had met this attitude often enough among the backwoods people of Canada not to recognize and characterize it here. On this journey he would meet it again and again. At last it would begin to seem something almost native to the culture, a mental and spiritual habit that could not have been less than astonishing to him: for Americans to be in daily contact with their magnificent landscape and not be touched by it or even mildly interested in its most spectacular features. What had gone wrong, or where was the reason for this slothful insensitivity? In the journal entries of this walk Muir began to formulate this and kindred questions, but all his life he was to remain mystified by the phenomenon.

On September 9, he passed out of Kentucky, the "greenest, leafiest State I have yet seen," the "master existences" of which were the oaks. "Here," he wrote with an exuberance that is utterly absent from such spare inventories as Boone and his contemporaries cared to leave, "Here is the Eden, the paradise of oaks." In the hills about Bear Creek, seven miles southeast of Burkesville on the Tennessee line, he wrote Jeanne Carr, giving her a more precise itinerary as he had now worked it out. He would be bearing south-southeast and told her he meant to pass through Kingston and Madisonville, Tennessee, then down through Blairsville and Gainesville, Georgia. From Georgia he would go to Florida and "thence to Cuba, thence to some part of S America but it will be only a hasty walk." He asked her to write him at Gainesville, for he was already letter-hungry.

The next day he saw the Cumberlands, the first mountains ever for him, running on a line northeast to southwest, the chain that until Boone and the Long Hunters had seemed a natural and permanent barrier to further westward expansion. Up through "luxuriant tangles" of trailing vines he climbed—and steadily upward, too, for six or seven hours, "a strangely long period of upgrade work to one accustomed only to the hillocky levels of Wisconsin and adjacent states."

On the way up he had his first brush with the moral wilderness

that had grown up in the wake of the war: a lone horseman over-
took him, reined in, and engaged him in conversation, asking
where Muir was from, whither bound, and at length insisting he be
allowed to carry Muir's bag. When Muir finally consented, the
horseman increased his gait and disappeared around a bend in the
trail, where Muir came upon him investigating the contents of
the bag. Disappointed in its meager holdings, the stranger returned
it to Muir and soon went back the way he had come.

Holding a southeastward course, he passed through the "thrice-
dead" village of Jamestown and was told there what he subsequently found to be true: that the whole region from there into
North Carolina was wild and depopulated by the war. Lodgings
would be hard to come by. Luckily, he found shelter in what was
said to be the last inhabited house between Jamestown and North
Carolina. The man of the house, a shaggy blacksmith, inquired of
the traveler what his business was in these lonesome parts, and Muir
told him he was a plant gatherer, down here on a visit to get
acquainted with as many of the southern species as he could. The
man was aghast: what would so evidently strong-minded a man as
Muir be doing gathering plants? This surely was not a man's work
in any times, but in these hard times *real* work was required of
every man able.

Across the dinner table on which sat a hard-won meal of corn
bread and fatback, Muir cited Scripture to his host, reminding him
of Solomon, who had considered trees and flowering things worthy
of his capacious mind; and of Christ, who said the lilies of the field
held wisdom enough for anyone. As in similar arguments with his
father, Muir convinced the blacksmith, at least temporarily, that
flower gathering had some kind of legitimacy.

In the morning he was on his way once more, wading through
stretches of "showy flowers"—goldenrod, out with the onset of the
southern autumn, asters, and, along the banks of streams, laurel and
azaleas. That afternoon he had his first real encounter with southern
briers after a road he had been following petered out in desolated
fields now choked with these trailing, toothed vines that tore at him
like "man-catchers."

After fighting his way back out of the briers and onto another
road, he had his first encounter with those other man-catchers

against whom he had been warned: bushwhackers. Coming toward him were ten men mounted on scrawny horses. The riders with shaggy hair hanging to their shoulders, were as gaunt and unkempt as their mounts. Muir saw instantly that the gang had already spotted him, saw too that he could not hope to escape them, and so walked straight at them, the distance between the lone, unarmed stranger and his fate diminishing speedily until at last he was upon them. He fetched out a hearty "Howdy," found a space between riders, and briskly walked on through. "After I had gone about one hundred or one hundred and fifty yards," he wrote,

> I ventured a quick glance back, without stopping, and saw in this flash of an eye that all ten had turned their horses toward me and were evidently talking about me . . . and whether it would be worth while to rob me.

To his relief he was not followed, "probably because the plants projecting from my plant press made them believe that I was a poor herb doctor, a common occupation in these mountain regions."

At dusk he found a woods cabin inhabited by blacks willing to share their pole beans, corn bread, and buttermilk, after which, grateful for the feeling of food in his belly, he made his little camp in the "great bedroom of the open night."

September 12 found him descending the east slope of the Cumberlands. Here he had to ford several water courses, including the Emory River, "a wide cool stream" beside which he lingered for hours, marveling at the play of the water over the smoothed rocks, the moss-covered boulders on the banks, the shady coolness of this place where every "tree, every flower, every ripple and eddy of this lovely stream seemed solemnly to feel the presence of the great Creator." He gave thanks there to that Creator for having allowed him to enter so sacred a sanctuary and worship in it.

He was working almost due south now, passing through Kingston, where he paused long enough to send back his plant collections to his brother in Portage, and then on to Philadelphia. Here and there he began to get heart-lifting glimpses of the Unaka range of the Smokies. On the fourteenth he walked into a full view of them, a "magnificent sight," rising up from the valley with scarcely perceptible foothills clothed in their name-bestowing cloak of smoky haze, the united suspiration of more than a thousand native species of flowering plants. Here in truth were mountains, the loftiest (as he would later learn) this side of the great and legendary Rockies.*

Walking the road south from Philadelphia, he was compelled by this spectacle to stop often and breathe deeply, as if even at this distance he could smell the mountains or taste the magic there was in them. At nightfall he found a cabin inhabited by a hunter, prospector, and storyteller who loaded him up with tales of "b'ars," deer hunts, gold mines, and other wonders of the mountains. The man successfully prevailed on Muir to spend a day or two with him by promising he could lead Muir to a mountain summit where he would see "all the world on one side of the mountains and all creation on the other." The traveler, already entranced by the mountains, readily agreed. Perhaps, too, he was a bit footsore: he had been averaging twenty-five miles a day, and it would be good to have a rest and see something of these smoky wonders at the same time.

So he spent the next two days with his genial host, botanizing and rambling in the mountains. He encountered descendants of the Scots and Scots-Irish who had migrated into the mountains, hollows, and coves a century or more before, some of them coming from western Pennsylvania, some moving westward from Virginia and North Carolina until they found in the Smokies that abundance of game, natural solitude, and immunity from legal and governmental restraints that was congenial to them. Muir saw them, "wild, unshorn, uncombed men coming out of the woods, each with a bag of corn on his back," bound along the green, serpentine mountain trails for the gristmill.

They lived lives out of another century, he thought, and in the prodigal tradition of their ancestors cleared their little homesteads, girdled the trees and left them to rot, planted corn patches on the precipitous slopes, and when their land was worked out—which it soon was—"put out the fire and called the dog" and moved on. Much of what they raised as corn became whiskey, the making, consumption, and sale of which they regarded as their supreme

---

*The Unaka range has 125 summits exceeding 5,000 feet; ten that exceed 6,000.

inalienable right. The rest of the crop they fed their feral hogs and made into corn bread. As an old man, Muir told an admirer that he had had close experiences with these hogs. The mountain folk, he explained, had the custom of letting their hogs run wild, but to keep them from straying too far the owners would call them in the mornings, and the hogs would come rushing down to the clearings for their bit of corn. "I'd hear a shout," Muir recalled, "away down the valley somewhere, then the crackling of the brush all round, and those razorbacks would come charging down the hillside right through my little camp and right over me if I didn't look out—snorting and squealing, blind mad to get at that corn."

Witnessing their tradition-bound lives, Muir thought the mountain folk prisoners of the past, "as if laws had been passed making attempts at improvement a crime." It was, he concluded, "the most primitive country I have seen, primitive in everything. The remotest hidden parts of Wisconsin are far in advance of the mountain regions of Tennessee and North Carolina." The volume of Burns he carried in his bag spoke to Muir's sense of this place:

> A country where savage streams tumble over savage mountains, thinly overspread with savage flocks, which starvingly support as savage inhabitants.

Even his host, inhabitant and local historian of the region, seemed to admit to this primitiveness, recalling with an enlightened disdain the old-fashioned times that still seemed to linger here. But at the same time he shared the identical land ethic of those who were less progressive than he believed himself to be, seeing in the impoverishment of the land the hand of God. This is all according to divine plan, he told Muir, for the Lord foreknew this condition and had providentially prepared something else for His people here. "He meant us," Muir quotes the man, "to bust open these copper mines and gold mines, so that we may have the money to buy the corn that we cannot raise." To which his guest would add in his journal the laconic line: "A most profound observation."

But the highlight of the brief stay was nothing human or historical: it was the mountains. Climbing into them on September 18, he felt their magic for the first time. From a peak he did indeed get a sudden view of the world and creation; his geographical view extended from the Cumberlands into North Carolina and Georgia. But it was more than geography that moved him here: it was the cosmic overview he now had.

> Such an ocean of wooded, waving, swelling mountain beauty and grandeur is not to be described. Countless forest-clad hills, side by side in rows and groups, seemed to be enjoying the rich sunshine and remaining motionless only because they were so eagerly absorbing it. All were united by curves and slopes of inimitable softness and beauty.

The sight moved him to reflections on the divinity manifested here —not that providence-working divinity of whom his host spoke so familiarly, but a divinity whose earthly presence was visible in scenes of natural splendor such as he now beheld:

> Oh, these forest gardens of our Father! What perfection, what divinity, in their architecture! What simplicity and mysterious complexity of detail! Who shall read the teaching of these sylvan pages, the glad brotherhood of rills that sing in the valleys, and all the happy creatures that dwell in them under the tender keeping of a Father's care?

"Who shall read the teaching of these sylvan pages?" he asked in his journal, and the posing of the question, here in the Smokies, some way on a grand nature excursion of indeterminate length, may be in some sense rhetorical: Muir may already have begun to develop an answer. Perhaps it was he, John Muir, who was meant to be such a reader, using that eye within the eye that Jeanne Carr had said was his special gift. Perhaps *this* was to be his life's work. If he did indeed entertain such a thought, it would have been as immense in potential as the scene was in extent. Here certainly was a new vista unobtainable anywhere else.

The next day, loaded with warnings from his host about the mountain brigands who lived like beasts and would murder a man for five dollars, he headed south. At Madisonville the land swept upward in a broad fold, and south of that place he could see the tree-lined ridges of the foothills; beyond in the blue and misty distance loomed the huge dimensions of the Unakas. At this point

he turned eastward to meet the mountains that seemed to curve
obligingly toward him. Perhaps he crossed Gee Creek before following the green Hiwassee River on its southward course into
North Carolina.

Here he was on the traces of De Soto. Fresh from participating
in the sack of the Inca empire, the conquistador had fitted out a
large expeditionary force to plunder the supposed aboriginal kingdoms of the American southeast. By the time he and his men,
horses, slaves, and pigs had forded the Hiwassee near where Muir
now sauntered, the fear must have been upon them all that they had
been terribly misled, that here there were no jungle kingdoms, no
empires, nothing precious to them. And so they thrashed and battered their way through this landscape, trying with increasing desperation to get out of it. If Muir gave their fatal folly a thought or
heard the ghostly rustle of their old intrusion, he did not record it.

His mind dwelt on another kind of kingdom where riches lay
about on every hand and free for the observation. Along the Hiwassee, which he could see sparkling through vines and trees, birds
called and butterflies fluttered through sun and shadow. If he
paused to write in his journal or steep himself in the scenery,
sunlight coming through the rich tangle of vegetation dappled the
lined pages of his book. Mountains rose steeply all about him, and
on their wooded slopes—sheer masses of green—he could see
breezes at play, bending limber trunks back and forth as in a choral
dance. Though it was now late September, summer colors still
dominated the slopes with only here and there a droplet of gold
splashed into the deep green or else an intense, tiny point of red
from a berry bush. But there was an autumnal look to the haze on
the summits, making them appear even bigger and more solemn.
Big crows cawed and flapped through the distances, and there was
a hush on the land after the heat and growth of summer and before
the blazing decay of true fall.

Where the trees along the river banks thinned out into small,
sedgy meadows he had glimpses into the far distance where blue
humps of mountains ranged one behind another, on and on. Before
him the river spangled over its stones, providing thrilling contrast
to the deep shade of the rock overhangs and the thickets of laurel,
briers, rhododendron, oak, locust, and pine. In little openings
where the sun penetrated through the tangle, a small tree or berry

bush blazed like an untended fire, a new season already upon it.

He had longed to see this part of the country, and what a providential way he had chosen to see it!—in secret, along this most wild, leafy, untrodden way, the sound of the birds and the river in his ears, the forest mold of unnumbered ages underfoot, and the bouquet of bark and ferns in his nostrils.

On September 23, he passed out of the mountains and into the low, sandy, pine-dotted savanna that stretched across Georgia to the coast and the city there that took its name from the geography. On his way to Savannah he crossed the trail of that kindred soul, William Bartram, one of those singular explorers in early American history for whom the natural beauty of the land itself was riches enough and who sought no empires or thought to found any. Bartram had passed this way on his extraordinary four-years' journey (1773–77) that took him 2,400 miles through the Carolinas, Georgia, and that Florida for which Muir was bound.* Here was one like Muir excited by the language of birds, the hunting habits of spiders, and the secret life of plants, one with the deep interest and patience to examine small things and see their relationship to the larger scheme.

Like Bartram, Muir was remarkably sensitive to plant life and like Bartram too he confided to his journal that for all of human arrogant bluster not much really was known of the secret life of plants, "their hopes and fears, pains and enjoyments!" Now in Georgia he began to notice that he was entering a region where he was himself wholly ignorant of the plant life. "My flower companions were leaving me," he wrote, "not one by one as in Kentucky and Tennessee, but in whole tribes and genera, and companies of shining strangers came trooping upon me in countless ranks." On the Chattahoochee River he feasted on a new delicacy, muscadine grapes. He met too with strange and handsome grasses and the long-leafed pine, a cypress swamp, and, most impressive, Spanish moss (Tillandsia). He spoke in his journal of these new phenomena as if he were making the acquain-

---

*In 1897, Muir's friend, Charles Sargent, gave him a copy of Bartram's *Travels,* which he eagerly read and pronounced "v. interesting."

tances of wonderfully rare human beings, and this signals a different tone to these jottings than is present in his earlier recorded
nature raptures: an aboriginal tone, call it, in which the distinctions prevalent in Western civilization between men, plants, and
animals begin to be broken down and are replaced with a kind of
mystical reverence for all forms of life.

The farther from the known world of the Midwest he went, the
deeper he seemed to be penetrating another world. It began to
close in around him as he followed the Savannah River south
through solemn cypress swamps. At dusk on the first day of October
the deepening strangeness occasioned feelings of "indescribable
loneliness." He felt feverish as he bathed in a black, silent stream,
nervously aware of the possibility of alligators.

That night he found shelter at a planter's house set amid cotton
fields. Though the family seemed fairly well off, they kept their
house dark except for the guttering light from a pitch-pine fire—
perhaps a lingering precautionary habit from wartime.

The war intruded on his thoughts also on the following night
when he stayed with a Dr. Perkins and his family, for they filled
their guest with stories of its horrors. Muir found the family refined
of manner and hospitable "but immovably prejudiced on everything connected with slavery."

On October 8, he reached Savannah, expecting to find letters
from home and a package of money that he had requested his
brother to send by express. However, there was nothing awaiting
him, and feeling "dreadfully lonesome and poor" he took lodgings
in a mean hotel.

Two days passed and still no money. He had just enough money
left for some crackers, but he could no longer afford even the
shabbiest room. But where to camp? Like many northern whites
who professed some sympathy with the recently emancipated
slaves, Muir really knew little about them and was afraid of them.*
And in Savannah they seemed to be everywhere so that he was in

*As late as 1908 in the Pelican Bay manuscript of his autobiographical remin-
iscences, Muir referred to blacks as "niggers," though at some point before his
death, still hoping to write a sequel to *My Boyhood and Youth,* he went back through
the typescript and wrote "Negro" for most, but not all, of these references. In the

a quandary as to where he might be safe. Wandering past the last of their quarters and leaving behind the rice fields, he came to the salt marshes and islands of the river. Here he heard the screams of bald eagles, the caws of crows, the tumbling notes of warblers, and crossing a stream entered an old cemetery. Reflecting that folklore had it that blacks were afraid of ghosts, he decided that this would be the perfect retreat while awaiting the arrival of his money.

Bonaventure Cemetery had a peculiar magic to it as well as a kind of topical appropriateness, and this combination provoked a startling meditation from the stranded, lonesome traveler. The grounds had been laid out in the previous century by a Colonel John Mulryne, who graced his mansion with a long avenue of live oaks. The mansion was a ruin now (it had burned during one of the colonel's lavish dinner parties), and the grounds had become a cemetery, but the live oaks had survived everything and were impressively decked and dripping with Spanish moss. The "long silvery gray skeins, reaching a length of not less than eight or ten feet" and slowly waving in the wind, produced on Muir "a solemn funereal effect. . . ."

Accompanying the funereal moss in the cemetery was the cumulative effect of the war stories Muir had been hearing as he walked farther and farther into the South, no longer now merely the seat of rebellion and battle but a living place. And not only the stories, vividly as these must have given him the reality of the thing, but also the sights created by war: the desolate fields, aimless, overgrown roads, and the faces of blacks and whites who had been through it and could never forget it.

Beyond these sights and the faces there was the felt presence of those hundreds of thousands whose lives had been violently cut off. Sitting in Bonaventure Cemetery amidst the tombs, the trees, and the waving mosses, he could hardly have escaped confronting

---

journal of the thousand-mile walk he used "Negro," "negro," and "nig." Many otherwise liberal-minded Northerners also used the term "nigger" during the Civil War era and after. Whitman, for one, used it through the 1870s at least and hotly denied the war had anything fundamental to do with the "nigger question" (Justin Kaplan, *Walt Whitman: A Life,* New York, 1980). The widespread use of the term probably reflected more than linguistic usage: Wisconsin joined most of the rest of the Northern states in 1865 in rejecting the proposed enfranchisement of the ex-slaves.

this great, central fact and its corollary: that he was alive. Whatever else the war had been, whatever else it might have meant—a senseless game like his old Dunbar schoolyard battles, as Muir may have thought it; the amputation of a cancerous member of the body politic, as Emerson thought; or something altogether other, as it might prove—the central fact of it was death, death on an unprecedented scale.

Yet here on the very grounds of death there was life. And not just his own, but the magnificent natural profusion of flowers, trees, mosses, birds. The cemetery was in reality "a center of life." He gazed on it "awe-stricken as one new-arrived from another world." All of it, he wrote, the "rippling of living waters, the song of birds, the joyous confidence of flowers, the calm undisturbable grandeur of the oaks, mark this place of graves as one of the Lord's most favored abodes of life and light."

Here was a paradox: the apparently irreconcilable opposition between life and death was in truth resolved by simply *looking* at nature itself. If you looked with a steady, calm regard, you could not find the dread opposition. In the unmediated presence of the natural world, life and death were not opposites; they were the same thing. All was process, all was cyclical, and the tombstones and statuary surrounding him were monuments to a mistaken cosmology. Amid these shades he wrote that instead of the "sympathy, the friendly union, of life and death so apparent in Nature, we are taught that death is an accident, a deplorable punishment for the oldest sin, the arch-enemy of life, etc." The use of the clause "we are taught" suggests that Muir's thoughts ran back on his own history, to his crypto-Calvinist upbringing, the lugubrious lessons of kirk and school, to those bonfires in the cleared fields of Wisconsin in the lurid light of which his father had depicted the terrors of death and damnation. Haunted by death through childhood and into manhood—a haunting intensified during the war years—he had not been capable of trusting what lesson nature had patiently been teaching. But

let children walk with Nature, let them see the beautiful blendings and communions of death and life, their joyous inseparable unity, as taught in woods and meadows, plains and mountains and streams of our blessed star, and they will learn that death is stingless indeed, and as beautiful as life. . . . All is divine harmony.

The meditation, judged in large historical and cultural terms, might seem a modest enough achievement for a twenty-nine-year-old man. The inseparability of life and death and their reconciliation in nature had been a theme of the Romantics for over half a century, and Muir had first encountered it in reading them. By the time Muir wrote these words the theme in Europe had become a literary and philosophic cliché and along with other Romantic ideas had yielded to the hardness of the new Realism. But judged in the context of Muir's personal history, the meditation evidences a major break-through against the inhibiting intellectual and spiritual influences of his childhood and adolescence, and for him its implications were to prove incalculably great.

It had been a long time in preparation: the musings of the young man laboring in the fields of the home farm and discovering the forbidden pleasures of literature; college readings and the influ-ences of Professor Butler and the Carrs; the solitary testing in the Canadian outback. Then this long walk, this escape from success as his culture had defined it, into the heart of nature, to this cemetery in the burned-over American South where personal and national history converged. What adds to the significance of the occasion is that the meditation was also an obvious and direct refutation of the very viaticum with which the pilgrim had prepared himself for this journey: next to Muir as he wrote was his rubber bag containing his Burns, his New Testament, and his Milton. Burns was safe enough from the revolutionary direction of Muir's thinking, but the great apologist and the New Testament were not. For Milton's epic is based on a Puritan reading of Scripture and dramatizes how death came into the world as, in Muir's words, "a deplorable punishment for the oldest sin," disobedience. Sin equals death, and death is horrifying as the angel Michael reveals it to Adam in a vision of a "Lazar-house" filled with those dying of spasms, torture, madness, and grief, over which stands "triumphant Death."

Take away this conception of death and the central drama of Milton's poem disintegrates—and not only that portion based on

the events of Genesis. For Milton shows us that the new dispensa-
tion, Christ's entry into history, is to redeem all mankind from
death. Without Christ mankind

> Must have been lost, adjudg'd to Death and Hell
> By doom severe. . . .

So here by the logic of Muir's thought the New Testament was
called into question, or at any rate the interpretation of Christ's
mission as salvation from death. Muir neither called the New Testament into question here nor disavowed Milton, yet the thrust of his
entries is unmistakable. He could continue to appreciate the Gos-
pels and revere Christ and His teachings, but he would also dis-
criminate and learn silently to ignore those interpretations of the
New Testament that had become offensive to his own beliefs.
Paradise Lost would remain for him a great poem, sustained by
the sheer magnificence of Milton's language and the largeness of
his conception, but it would not be the same again: it would
be literature and not a beautiful redaction of divine and absolute
truth.*

As for the other half of the Bible, it was probably no mere
matter of a traveler's convenience that he did not bring along the
Old Testament. It is more likely that he had by this point already
lost most of his interest in it and in its terrific, wrathful Father, so
like his own; lost interest also in its obsessive emphasis on obedi-
ence through fear. The image of divinity purveyed in the New
Testament would have been much more congenial, both in terms
of his needs and in terms of his personal development during the
past decade. For in these years he had discovered many more
evidences of divine love than of divine wrath, and the former were
not merely more numerous; they were far more impressive. His
experiences in the natural world had already indicated to him that
such beauty could only be the expression of an indwelling, abiding

---

*Muir would love Milton all his life and, nearly blinded himself, would
cherish the blind poet's evocation of light as the incarnation of divinity: ". . . since
God is light, / And never but in unapproached Light / Dwelt from Eternity . . ."
(Book III, 3–6). Compare Muir in this undated journal fragment, possibly from
1871: "Light. I know not a single word fine enough for light . . . holy, beamless,
bodiless, inaudible floods of light" (Linnie Marsh Wolfe, *John of the Mountains: The
Unpublished Journals of John Muir,* Madison, 1938, 1979).

divine love. So, gradually, he had abandoned the creed of his father, had abandoned, too, the creeds of those whose lights led them to emphasize inevitable sin and inevitable punishment, who viewed this world as a place of trial and temptation possessing little intrinsic interest.

Now that he sensed powerfully, immediately the oneness of existence, the way was prepared for the last vestiges of his orthodox Christianity to fall away. Not immediately, however flashing this graveyard meditation, but surely and steadily, leaving at last no place for the old fear of death in a spirit filled to its capacity with wonder.

Other such declarations of independence soon followed, as if having come so far he could now go all the way, truly cut loose.

Leaving Savannah when the belated arrival of the money package allowed him to do so, he made for Florida, destination of his long-deferred dreams, dreamland, too, for the misguided conquistadores who had styled it the "Island of Flowers." He went down from Savannah by coasting schooner, avoiding the impenetrable swamps that stretched between that city and Fernandina at Florida's northernmost tip. Discovering there that the state was so "watery and vine-tied that pathless wanderings are not easily possible in any direction," he followed a railway embankment southwestward, heading for the Gulf. Then, amid the shocking profusion of tropical flowers and fruit that he had longed to see and come so far to find —magnolias, palms, and the wonderfully strange palmetto—it was the dangerous and loathsome alligator that provoked further observations on the order of the universe.

After remarking that many "good" people sincerely believed the alligator created by the Devil, Muir wrote that this was simply not so, and that merely because we could presently find no good use for these creatures was no reason to suppose they had none in the wider plan of things. Indeed, he insisted they did have some as yet undiscovered place in the large plan: if we only knew more of the plan, could see some of its outlines, we would see how all things fit into it and fit into each other as well. Instead, our ignorance begot a blasphemous arrogance that sealed us off from kinship with the rest of creation:

> How narrow we selfish, conceited creatures are in our sympa-
> thies! how blind to the rights of all the rest of creation! With what
> dismal irreverence we speak of our fellow mortals! Though alliga-
> tors, snakes, etc., naturally repel us, they are not mysterious evils.
> They dwell happily in these flowery wilds, are part of God's
> family, unfallen, undepraved, and cared for with the same species
> of tenderness and love as is bestowed on angels in heaven or saints
> on earth.

Nor was this all, though surely it would have been quite enough
for those "good" people he had in mind. For in the alligator Muir
was prepared to see and assert greater wonders than the orthodox
view could admit: "Honorable representatives of the great saurians
of an older creation," he called them in clear refutation of the static
Christian view of the earth's history.

In Muir's university years evolution was hardly a universally
accepted theory, especially in the American hinterlands. But he had
encountered it there, probably through Ezra Carr, and evidently
had been influenced enough to accept its essential view that the
earth was dynamic and still in process. Yet, as so much evidence
reveals, he had retained his strong belief in the divine origin of all
things. William Trout, the Disciple of Christ with whom Muir came
to have serious religious disagreements, said that though Muir was
then much involved in the new sciences, he saw God's hand in all
creation—as accurate and succinct a judgment of Muir's position on
evolution, both in these years and after, as we are likely to get.

But what is of greater interest in the entry than Muir's current
views on evolutionary theory is the radically non-anthropocentric
tone of it. If Muir was not at this point a thoroughly convinced
evolutionist, neither was he a crypto-Christian scientist, admitting
to the evidence of changes in the earth's history while holding onto
the orthodox Christian view that the world had been created ex-
pressly for man and that all natural history pointed plainly to man
as the Lord of Creation. Both the so-called "catastrophists" and the
later "progressionists" had in this way sought to reconcile the
emergent dynamic view of natural history with Scripture, insisting
that all changes indicated the Creator's intention of establishing the
human species as the apex of His works. At this point Muir seems
to have shared almost nothing with the catastrophists, and whatever

he may have shared with progressionists like Hugh Miller and Louis Agassiz, he emphatically rejected their central contention that man was the measure of creation, preferring instead a far wider, more generous view in which man was one among many forms of life, each of which had a special mission to perform.

For him this more generous, inclusive view was to prove crucial, for it allowed him to see the whole natural world in so warmly sympathetic a light that he was granted insights into its workings forbidden those who viewed the world from the summit of an assumed human superiority. Such people, Muir wrote a few days later, ought better be called "creation's braggart lords" than "Lords of Creation." He had, he asserted, "precious little sympathy for the selfish propriety of civilized man," and if there should ever chance to occur a war between man and the wild beasts, "I would be tempted to sympathize with the bears."

On October 23, pursuing his way Gulfward and still in the piney woods, he caught a whiff of a vagrant sea breeze, and suddenly all thoughts of magnolias, palms, and the thousand bright blooms of Florida fled his mind. In on that salt scent poured Dunbar, its rocky coast, the humpbacked shape of Bass Rock rising mysteriously out of the choppy Firth, "and the old castle, schools, churches, and long country rambles in search of birds' nests." The instantaneous flood of these associations astonished him. "We cannot forget anything," he wrote, and memories long dormant can, on a breeze, "flash into full stature and life with everything in place."

The old associations mingled strangely with new ones when several miles thereafter he actually beheld the "burnished, treeless plain" of the Gulf, stretching away into a distance seemingly bordered only by sky. Like Balboa viewing another ocean for the first time and seeing it as a highroad to the riches of Cathay or Cipangu, Muir now saw beyond the horizon to the West Indies, South America, and who knew where else. On this shore he had come to the end of something and the beginning of something else. He had walked to the end of America, and in doing that had walked to the end of a phase of his life, too; further destinations lay beyond, and he was in no mood to be contained now by mere geography. He felt himself on his way. . . .

But the harbor at Cedar Key was empty, and so for the moment further adventures would have to wait on practical considerations. Should he walk down the west coast to Tampa or to Key West, where he would be sure of a ship to Cuba? Or should he wait here at Cedar Keys and "like Crusoe" pray for a ship? Mulling this, he learned at dockside that a schooner was due in to carry lumber from a local cedar mill along the Gulf coast to Galveston. He searched out the mill owner and learned from him that it would be two weeks before the schooner would sail. But Mr. Hodgson told Muir that if he wished to wait, Hodgson would employ him in his mill and make that wait worth his while. Muir would wait, though how long it would turn out to be he then had no way of guessing.

The next day he botanized along the slender beach, feeling unaccountably sluggish and heavy of limb. He bathed in the surf, thinking it might revive his energies; perhaps he was merely tired from his long walk and those restless nights of little sleep in the damp lands of Florida. But two days thereafter a malarial fever broke upon him with the sudden and resistless violence of a tropical thunderstorm. Returning from the little town to the mill hands' bunkhouse, he fell unconscious on the trail and lay there undiscovered from midafternoon until night. When he came to, the stars were out; he could see them, could see also, dimly, the trail. But which way lay the bunkhouse? He was so feverish he could only guess and started off in a staggering gait, hoping that he was going the right way. At intervals he blacked out and fell again and again but had sufficient presence of mind to will himself to fall with his head pointing in the assumed right direction.

In the early morning hours he finally reached the bunkhouse, but the night watchman, hardened to the drunken behavior of the mill hands, ignored Muir's pleas for help and went on his rounds. So it was left to the sick man himself to struggle desperately to the haven of his bunk, lurching and falling and eventually tumbling into it.

"I awoke at a strange hour on a strange day," he recorded later, "to hear Mr. Hodgson ask a watcher beside me whether I had yet spoken, and when he replied that I had not, he said, 'Well, you must keep pouring in the quinine. That's all we can do.' " Muir had been unconscious for days and had been meanwhile transferred to the Hodgsons' home, where Mrs. Hodgson supervised his care. Muir said the chief medicines were quinine and chamomile, both administered "in sorry abundance," and that for three months he suffered from edema, night sweats, and such terrific weakness that he could scarcely walk but rather crawled about. And so it went, on into January 1868, a period he characterized with spare feeling as "a weary time."

Here was a near death that on another plane of reality was also a symbolic one: at land's end, journey's end, to have so utterly dropped out of the world of his time, as though this were the real, fitting conclusion to the odyssey that had taken him away from all he had known and to some sort of threshold. So, when he could get out a bit on his own, he returned immediately to the beach, both threshold and place of departure.

All day he would lie under a moss-dripping live oak at the edge of the wood and watch the "thousands of waders of all sizes, plumage, and language" pecking an existence out of the sands. Some days the Hodgsons' boy would take him sailing; they would skip amid the nearby keys as the Gulf breeze fanned his hot temples. When he got a bit stronger, he would sail out himself and on the blue expanse think about a ship that might soon come to his rescue and carry him onward toward the ghost of Humboldt and that great continent that still loomed in his thoughts—South American rivers running through wonderfully tangled jungles, strange bird languages he would learn, and in the distance, mountains rising out of tropic lands to dazzling white peaks.

In his decrepitude, lying in the shade at the meeting of beach and wood, he liked to gaze on the "lonely old herons of solemn look and wing" that rested in favorite oaks, "old white sages . . . drowsing away the dull hours between tides, curtained by long skeins of tillandsia." White-bearded hermits, he thought, "gazing dreamily from dark caves could not appear more solemn or more becomingly shrouded from the rest of their fellow beings." Perhaps he felt some kinship with these old birds, so shrouded and cut off was he now from the life he had left behind as well as from that he dreamed of living, that seemed to lie tantalizingly beyond him.

He sketched in the pages of his journal and made some entires and waited—for a ship, for health and strength—while tides came and went. Wan and weakened as he was, one day something moved him to literary vigor, perhaps the sudden, full force of the trans-

forming experiences of the last four months. He wrote like one
who had survived something terrific and who could thus speak of
life from a unique perspective. "The world," he commenced, "we
are told was made especially for man, a presumption not supported
by all the facts." Both those who tell us this and those who credu-
lously accept it also believe that they are somehow on intimate
terms with the Creator and know His inmost intentions. All this is
the thinnest fiction, Muir countered,

> and it is hardly possible to be guilty of irreverence in speaking of
> *their* God any more than of heathen idols. He is regarded as a
> civilized, law-abiding gentleman in favor either of a republican
> form of government or of a limited monarchy; believes in the
> literature and language of England; is a warm supporter of the
> English constitution and Sunday schools and missionary societies;
> and is as purely a manufactured article as any puppet of a half-
> penny theatre.

Not only is the passage amusing with its image of God as a somewhat pompous Anglophile politician, but it is also a serious rejection of the popular image of God that had succeeded the grim, Old
Testament deity of earlier times. And while Muir had himself
thrown off this older image as neither suitable to his spiritual needs
nor confirmed by his personal experience, he found the newer,
more benign image if anything less accurate.

It was not just a matter of arriving at an appropriate conception
of God, important as this surely was; there was something else
involved here. For Muir now saw that neither view of divinity—
the punitive God of Wrath or the benign politician—could lead to
an appropriate view of God's creation. For him, God's visible work
was the important thing: it was so glorious, so tangible, so various
that no one need wrangle in the sloughs of theology. Nature was
all you needed to know of God.

As he had noted before the onset of his fever, it was the an-
thropocentrism of orthodox images of divinity that caused the problem. As long as God was viewed as having created the universe with
man in mind, so long would all creation be viewed and valued
purely in terms of its usefulness to the self-styled lord of creation.
Sheep, in this plan, were created specifically to provide wool for the

clothing necessitated by the sin in the Garden, whales for oil, hemp "for ships' rigging, wrapping packages, and hanging the wicked. Cotton is another plain case of clothing. Iron was made for hammers and ploughs, and lead for bullets; all intended for us. And so of other small handfuls of insignificant things." On the other hand, everything not "useful" or apparently inimical to man's interests, such as wild beasts or poisonous minerals and plants, was considered the creation of the Devil.

Nor was it, he noted with asperity, the godless or the pagan who espoused such meanly utilitarian views. Instead it was the "fearfully good, the orthodox," the very same who cried out " 'Heresy' on every one whose sympathies reach a single hair's breadth beyond the boundary epidermis of our own species."

Benighted and arrogant though we are, we claim souls for ourselves only, he continued, while denying soul life to all the rest of God's creation. "Plants are credited with but a dim and uncertain sensation," he wrote, "and minerals with positively none at all. But why may not even a mineral arrangement of matter be endowed with sensation of a kind that we in our blind exclusive perfection can have no manner of communication with?"

The idea of plant and mineral sentience, common to "primitive" cultures the world over, had in fact been one of the hardest heresies missionizing Christians had to extirpate, and it is somewhat startling to meet it here in the thought of one whose background was so strongly Christian. And yet he had been led to it quite naturally and by his very acceptance of divinity. For how could you truly contemplate the phenomena of the natural world *without* believing that all things had their germane purposes and their own deep lives to lead? How could you clearly and cleanly experience the variety and beauty of that world without becoming impressed with the truth that it had its own moods, cycles, behaviors that took no heed of human observation and had been going on without human assistance through unnumbered aeons? In the face of mountains or the mountain ash, human arrogance was sickening. It was far more likely that the mountains and their red-berry bushes were equal with humans in the eye of the Creator and had as essential parts to play in the master plan.

True, the universe would be incomplete without man, but it was equally true that it would also be "incomplete without the smallest transmicroscopic creature that dwells beyond our conceitful eyes and knowledge." In writing that, Muir was stating the bedrock principle that would in time become the basis of the American environmental movement; here in his journal it was meant as a statement of conviction, something he intended to live by.

Glad now to be finished with these heartfelt literary exertions and able to turn from "ecclesiastical fires and blunders," he concluded with a sort of serene apocalypse:

> This star, our own good earth, made many a successful journey around the heavens ere man was made, and whole kingdoms of creatures enjoyed existence and returned to dust ere man appeared to claim them. After human beings have also played their part in Creation's plan, they too may disappear without any general burning or extraordinary commotion whatever.

On an early January day, Muir climbed to the rooftop of the Hodgson house to watch the sun setting in the glitter of the Gulf. This evening there was an added feature to the grand spectacle, for Muir saw the white sails of an incoming schooner. Lost in his fever, Muir had of course long since missed his ship to Texas; he would not miss this one if it should be bound for some place that would serve his larger plans. Weak as he was, he walked to the harbor soon after the ship's arrival and booked passage to Cuba.

The *Island Belle* hit a storm en route to Havana, but the frail landsman surprised the captain by apparently reveling in the smash of the waves and the roaring of the winds. He kept topside, holding to a rope to keep from being washed overboard. The cold wind and ocean spray were wonderfully soothing to Muir, and he was sorry when, on January 12, they sailed into harbor at Havana under the booming of the bells and the cannons of Morro Castle.

Muir immediately noted the mountains rising right behind the port and, consulting his map, saw that they ranged spinelike down the center of the island. He had long dreamed of mountains in tropic lands, but now that he could actually see them he found himself too weak even to attempt any climbing. A mile walk through Havana's sultry streets quite exhausted him, and he was grateful to return to the haven of the *Island Belle.*

For a month he became a beachcomber. In the mornings a sailor from the schooner would row Muir ashore, and he would take the broad cactus common past Morro Castle, on out of sight and sound of the city. Along the beach he gathered shells and plants in happy solitude, wandering slowly, pressing plant specimens, resting frequently in the shade of bushes and vine heaps until the sun began to lower. Then either a member of the *Island Belle* crew would come for him, or else he would hire a boat to take him out. After rest and supper, the traveler would reveal to the captain and bemused crewmen his treasures of the day: flowers, shells, and the recitation of quiet, intense adventures in the cactus thickets, sunflower swamps, and at the verge of the rolling breakers.

In the early part of evening he dreamed awake on deck as the schooner swung easily at anchor, looking up at the stars, out at the city lights and the bobbing lights of the vessels in the harbor. By ten o'clock he was in his bunk, the harbor waves tapping at his ear. He dreamed of heavy heat, entangling vines, and of breakers that chased him up the beach to Morro Castle.

After a month of this—pleasant, though limited as it seemed to him—he had rash thoughts: though his health was really no better than it had been when he had taken ship and seemed not likely to improve soon, he was close to South America, closer than he might ever be again.* So he looked for a ship to Colombia or Venezuela, from which place he could strike toward the headwaters of the Orinoco, thence south to a tributary of the Amazon, and from there "float down on a raft or skiff the whole length of the great river to its mouth."

More than the logistical flimsiness of the plan there was the flimsiness of his health. He was reasoning apparently that, poor as his health was, he ought to try this Humboldtlike excursion before it grew any worse. But he could find no ship bound for South America and so was forced to turn his thoughts north and west rather than south. He thought of New York, not the city but the

---

*While recuperating at Cedar Key, Muir drew a graph he called a "health line" showing his fall into fever, his approach near death, and his recovery. This latter is a long, gradually ascending line punctuated with two sharp relapses. The chart indicates that, when he went to Cuba, Muir was only slightly improved from that point at which he judged he was out of danger (original manuscript of *A Thousand-Mile Walk*, Muir Papers, Holt-Atherton).

port, and of a ship from there to California and the Yosemite Valley, of which he had read briefly in those other convalescent days in Indianapolis. There, as he had surmised months ago in a letter to Jeanne Carr, he might hope to learn humble but exciting secrets of nature's life.

Such thoughts mingled with images of February's frost and snow in the temperate zones, winds and weather cold enough to blow fever's dregs clean out of him. When the *Island Belle*'s obliging captain pointed out a trim schooner loading oranges for New York, that was what he felt he needed. The schooner sailed the next day, and at daylight, without proper papers, Muir, his plant press, and his rubber bag of books, journal, and personal effects were stowed beneath hatches. Nattily dressed port officials came alongside as the schooner paused at Morro Castle but did not board, and thus the stowaway left the tropics. Muir recorded that the ship was so laden with oranges that the captain and crew were obliged to negotiate the decks on planks laid above the massed fruit.

He spent his days looking at the sea, thinking of its deep and as yet undiscovered life, speculating like Darwin before that "we may at length discover that the sea is as full of life as the land." He had time, too, to think back on Cuba, on its hot, seagirt life, and of new lessons he had been given there on its beaches. On tropic shores he had had opportunity for comparisons, the unforgotten North Sea and the green tropical one merging in his mind "to form some idea of the one great song sounding forever all around the white-blooming shores of the world."

And there had been another, closer lesson, one existing within that great seashore song of the watery globe. On a stretch of beach he had come upon a small, pink flower somehow clinging to a brown wave-washed rock. He had marveled at its ability to survive the rhythmic surge and suck of the surf, living its hardy, beautiful life beyond human care or comprehension. Nor was it an anomaly in its place, as might have been supposed: it *belonged* precisely where it was. So it underscored for him again and anew the inexhaustible adaptability of nature, how each bit of it was right and at home in its setting, nothing askew or amiss. "There is not a fragment in all nature," he wrote, "for every relative fragment of one thing is a full harmonious unit in itself. All together form the one grand palimpsest of the world."

Nights when the sea was choppy he resumed his habit of the *Island Belle* and stayed on deck, watching the break of the phosphorescent waves and treated now and then to the heavy thump of a flying fish landing atop the oranges, where it was instantly attacked by the ship's Newfoundland dog. On the twelfth day out they saw New York, and Muir felt the frosty winds sift through his "loosened bones." The "leafless, snow-white woods of New York," he wrote, "struck us with all the novelty and impressiveness of a new world."

PART
III

Rediscovering America

First
Summer

This was his second experience of New York, and it was about as limited as the first almost exactly nineteen years before when he had been deposited there by the immigrant ship out of Glasgow. Then he and his family had landed amid the frantic hustle of gold seekers bound for California; now Muir was on his own, and he was on his way to California, too. The place still beckoned goldenly to thousands of Americans while to him it seemed the very newest part of this New World.

New York was still as alien to him as it had been before, and as he waited for passage to Panama and thence to San Francisco he kept close to the docks and used the orange boat as hotel and haven. He took his meals at a waterfront restaurant and hardly dared venture out of sight of his schooner lest he become lost in the wilderness of buildings, narrow streets, and hurrying throngs.*He

---

*Perhaps on one of these waterfront days his eye might have fallen on one who had been in wildernesses of water and jungle and was now trying to feel at home here: Herman Melville was then in the early years of his long exile from the literary world and spent his days along the New York waterfront as a customs official.

saw cars with signs for Central Park and wanted to go there but was afraid he would not get back. In another of the small ironies that cluster about this brief stopover, the park's cocreator (with Calvert Vaux), Frederick L. Olmsted, was at this time in California, where he was superintendent of the newly created Yosemite Park.

Before sailing, Muir had his introduction to California when an enterprising dockside dealer talked him into buying a dozen large roller-mounted maps. Muir wondered aloud what he would want with these, and the dealer told him. The man assumed that Muir was bound for California to make money. Why else would anyone go there? And since everything there fetched twice the sum it could elsewhere in the States, it made sense to buy these wonderful maps and sell them in California at a handsome profit. There you had California neatly summed! A place where people went to make money in a hurry. Muir bought the maps but never said what he did with them.

Nor did he have much to say about the passage to California other than that he found it a "savage contrast" to his voyage from Cuba aboard the orange boat. Apparently, conditions aboard were crowded and the passengers a rough lot; mealtimes he found especially trying. Part of the time he spent scrawling notes in a small marble-backed notebook. Here he made further observations on the narrowness of human sympathies and on human arrogance, using the sea as a metaphor powerfully suggestive of human limitations. And his immediate situation filtered into the notebook, too, in the form of observations on human filth. Man, wrote the fastidious Scot, is the only unclean animal, and as civilization advances, so do the forms and complexities of filthiness. He was glad to be relieved of contact with his fellow passangers when the *Nebraska* docked at Aspinwall.

The railroad across the isthmus that had been but a newspaper rumor when the Muirs had put out from Glasgow in '49 was now a solid reality, and along it Muir stood on the car platform, visually immersed in the brilliant show of jungle foliage along the Chagres River. Sights that had passed all but unremarked by the gold rushers —and before them the treasure-laden Spaniards coming up out of Peru—made this explorer almost weep with ecstasy and to fervently pray that someday he might return here and experience such splendors in depth.

Muir, 1890. *(Bancroft Library, University of California, Berkeley)*

Only known picture of Daniel Muir, Sr., a painting done after his death by his daughter, Mary Muir Hand. *(Holt-Atherton Pacific Center for Western Studies, University of the Pacific)*

Photo of Anne Gilrye Muir taken at Portage, Wisconsin, 1863. *(Holt-Atherton Pacific Center for Western Studies, University of the Pacific)*

John Muir's "old grammar school," Dunbar, Scotland. *(Photograph courtesy of Allan Inglis)*

Muir with his sister, Sarah Muir Galloway, and her two children, in front of Fountain Lake House, c. 1863. *(Holt-Atherton Pacific Center for Western Studies, University of the Pacific)*

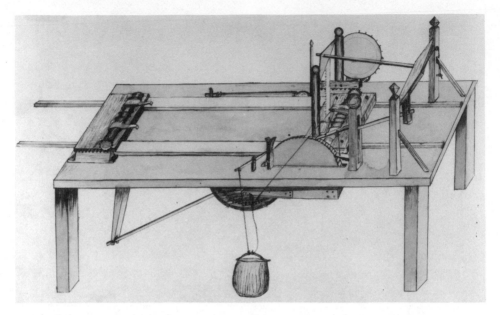

Drawing of a table saw by John Muir, 1860–63. Watercolor and ink. *(State Historical Society of Wisconsin)*

OPPOSITE, ABOVE: Ezra S. Carr, c. 1880. *(Holt-Atherton Pacific Center for Western Studies, University of the Pacific)*

OPPOSITE, BELOW: Photo of Jeanne C. Carr, during the time she was Muir's confidante/mentor, 1876. *(Holt-Atherton Pacific Center for Western Studies, University of the Pacific)*

First portrait of Muir, Madison, 1863. *(Holt-Atherton Pacific Center for Western Studies, University of the Pacific)*

Drawing from one of Muir's journals, showing lonely figure of the explorer toiling over snowfield toward Sierra minarets, c. 1878. Scale suggests Muir's view of humankind in large natural context. *(Holt-Atherton Pacific Center for Western Studies, University of the Pacific)*

Muir in San Francisco, winter, 1872, his first real trip down into civilization since 1869, and the beginning of his gradual return to it. *(Bancroft Library, University of California, Berkeley)*

ABOVE: John Swett, left, and Muir at Martinez, probably in the 1890s. *(Bancroft Library, University of California, Berkeley)*

OPPOSITE, ABOVE: Muir in his "scribble den" at Martinez house. Note set of damaged right eye. *(Bancroft Library, University of California, Berkeley)*

OPPOSITE, BELOW: Jeanne C. Carr and Ezra Slocum Carr in old age in Pasadena. *(Holt-Atherton Pacific Center for Western Studies, University of the Pacific)*

John Muir resting on the trail, 1895. *(Holt-Atherton Pacific Center for Western Studies, University of the Pacific)*

Muir, far right, with Sierra Club members on the trail, 1902. *(Holt-Atherton Pacific Center for Western Studies, University of the Pacific)*

Teddy Roosevelt and Muir in Yosemite, May, 1903. *(Bancroft Library, University of California, Berkeley)*

Muir with Louie and their two daughters, Annie Wanda, left, and Helen, on porch of Martinez home, 1901. Photo by Muir's good friend, C. Hart Merriam. *(Bancroft Library, University of California, Berkeley)*

Muir in his orchards at Martinez with family house in background, c. 1906. *(Bancroft Library, University of California, Berkeley)*

Muir in Petrified Forest, Arizona, 1905–06. Photo by Helen Muir. Note characteristic nailed boots. *(Bancroft Library, University of California, Berkeley)*

First view into Hetch Hetchy from Surprise Point. *(Bancroft Library, University of California, Berkeley)*

"Sweeping Back the Flood." Together with all the city's newspapers, *San Francisco Call* was a persistent advocate of Hetch Hetchy as city water supply and attacked any group that opposed this use. *(Bancroft Library, University of California, Berkeley)*

Wilderness sage, a late portrait by W. Dassonville, c. 1912. *(Bancroft Library, University of California, Berkeley)*

Then the long swing up the Pacific coast of Central America and Mexico, and again his thoughts were on the sea and the life it held. He wrote on light, too, the changing light on the sea, the sunlight on the coastal lands, phosphorescence at night; on March 17 he saw a heavenly light in the streak of a meteor. At last there was California and San Francisco, now a populous city that had been built on the gold trade.

Evidently, Muir found at least one fellow passenger congenial enough because the day after the ship docked he and an Englishman named Joseph Chilwell (who called Muir "Scottie") were on their way south out of the city bound for Yosemite.* "I followed the Diablo foothills along the San José to Gilroy," he wrote a few months later to Jeanne Carr in an extended account of the trip, "thence over the Diablo Mountains to the valley of the San Joaquin by the Pacheco Pass," and from there he took a leisurely, meandering way up into the Sierra Nevada and Yosemite.

It was the beginning of April and the valleys were in their splendor. The hikers saw broad wheat fields, orchards, vineyards, and alfalfa meadows, and the air was so clean and vital it seemed to have a positive taste to it. Both of them, Muir recalled,

> had lived on common air for nearly thirty years, and never before
> this discovered that our bodies contained such multitudes of pal-
> ates, or that this mortal flesh, so little valued by philosophers and
> teachers, was possessed of so vast a capacity for happiness.

Indeed, it really did seem a new world and they Adams in it, "new creatures," as he said, "born again; and truly not until this time were we fairly conscious that we were born at all."

As they turned eastward, hills piled upon hills before them, and

---

*In later years when his life was becoming legend, Muir liked to tell listeners that after arriving in San Francisco he had accosted a carpenter in the street and asked that astonished man which was the quickest way out of town. Where, the man was said to have asked, do you want to go? And Muir had returned, "Anywhere that's wild." More plausible—and less entertaining—is the version he gave to Melville Anderson late in life: that he had simply asked the man the nearest way out of the city and had been directed to the Oakland ferry. Muir knew well enough where he wanted to go and was carrying with him a pocket map of the state (Melville B. Anderson, "The Conversation of John Muir," *American Museum Journal,* March, 1915).

beyond these, mountains. Their way to the Pacheco Pass was accompanied by the shouts of quail and the song of a stream slipping over its pebbly bed, now brilliant in the sun and translucent air, now in shadow where its banks were bordered with dogwood and alder.

At the top of the pass Muir saw the Sierras for the first time. Though he was more than 100 miles from the snowy peaks on the axis of the range, they looked so smooth and bright to him it seemed "impossible for a man to walk across the open folds without being seen, even at this distance." More than 300 miles of the range were revealed to him at this first amazed glimpse.

Nor was this all, though it would prove best and most enduring in its hold on him. For at his feet lay the wide valley of the San Joaquin, "the floweriest piece of the world I ever walked, one vast, level, even flower-bed, a sheet of flowers"—the sight caused him to chase metaphors breathlessly—"a smooth sea, ruffled a little by the tree fringing of the river and of the smaller cross-streams here and there, from the mountains." Florida, he told Jeanne Carr, had been for him the land of flowers, but this was incomparable: "Here, here is Florida!" Here the flowers

> are not sprinkled apart with grass between as on our prairies, but grasses are sprinkled among the flowers; not as in Cuba, flowers piled upon flowers, heaped and gathered into deep, glowing masses, but side by side, flower to flower, petal to petal, touching but not entwined, branches weaving past and past each other, yet free and separate—one smooth garment, mosses next to the ground, grasses above, petaled flowers between.

He could hardly imagine that such a magnificent assemblage was permanent. Rather, "actuated by some plant purpose, they had convened from every plain and mountain and meadow of their kingdom, and that the different coloring of patches, acres, and miles marks the bounds of the various tribes and family encampments."

Then, as he waded out into this thigh-high lushness, the inquiring, curious aspect of his mind came into play, succeeding awe and bewilderment, and he began to examine the arrangement of the flowers and to discover the way they made their effect on the observer. At first glance, he noted, you are simply dazzled by the predominance of yellow flowers. "But to an observer who first looks downward, then takes a wider and wider view, the yellow gradually fades, and purple predominates, because nearly all of the purple flowers are taller. In depth, the purple stratum is about ten or twelve inches, the yellow seven or eight, and down in the shade, out of sight, is another stratum of purple, one inch in depth, for the ground forests of mosses are there, with purple stems, and purple cups."

Gradually they climbed beyond the sea of flowers and stopped at Coulterville, a tiny mining town in the Mariposa foothills that had managed to survive the rush and abandonment of the gold rush and now hung on as a way station to Yosemite. They bought tea and flour at Francisco Bruschi's general store, and Bruschi told them they would also need a rifle if they intended camping out in the mountains. So they bought an old army musket and a few pounds of shot. Thus provisioned, they made their way up to the great valley through Deer Flat and Crane Flat, subsisting on a diet of tea and unleavened cakes. This was fine for Muir but a miserable gastronomic trial for Chilwell, who complained about the prison-like fare of bread and water.

But Muir was after other things than mere comfort, and he mentioned no hardships whatever during this brief initiation into the majestic life of the mountains—other than having to endure Chilwell's complaints. The eight days he spent in Yosemite, sketching, exploring the falls, collecting plants; the camps made amid trees he could only call "noble" with a helpless repetitiousness; encountering the sequoias of the Mariposa Grove: all this engendered a hunger for more. At the same time, these experiences were profoundly humbling, and he hardly dared hope he might somehow have further ones in this astonishing landscape. Everything seemed so grand, so beautiful, that he felt he was not worthy of what he was seeing.

He carried this sense with him as he and Chilwell made their way back down to the San Joaquin. But more than this, he carried the majesty of the mountains within him. South America was still much on his mind, but now he had in the background of his thinking those looming peaks and the high secrets they held, and they were to stay in his thoughts, mysterious and compelling as some sacred story half recalled.

always

In the meantime there was the nagging necessity of bread. With a Thoreauvian sense of the spiritual dimensions of economy, he noted that this first Sierran baptism had cost him but three dollars. But some kind of grubstake must be acquired if he was to go up there again for a more extended exploration, and this meant the hot life of the valley: harvest in the grain fields at Hopeton; breaking horses; running a ferry between Stockton and Mariposa; and then sheepshearing with a gang of "Spanish, Indian, Irish, English, Scottish" shearsmen. He found this rough, dusty work but exciting in a way, and he made good money at it. His spirits were high and his health wholly mended as he wrote his brother David in mid-July. This was "splendid country," he said, where "one might truthfully make use of more than half of the Methodist hymn 'Land of pure delight' in describing it, and it flows with more of milk and more of honey than ever did old Canaan in its happiest prime." Characterizing these days, he was ready to call them the happiest of his life.

The tone was the same in a letter to his sister Annie a month later. The first California months had been "the floweriest of all the months of my existence . . . ," he told her. But there in the midst of a glowing description of the valley's flower-life was the familiar cloud again: what to do with this life. What did it mean that in his thirtieth summer he was still a wanderer, a shearsman among what he styled the "mixed, mongrel, unanalyzable elements of California society"? "I am always a little lonesome Annie," he blurted, "ought I not to be a man by this time & put away childish things [?] I have wandered far enough & seen strange faces enough to feel the whole world a home, & I am a batchelor [*sic*] too [.] I should not be a boy, but I cannot accustom myself to the coldness of strangers, nor to the shiftings & wanderings of this Arab life."*

just read it over!

*Robert Enberg and Donald Wesling (eds.), *John Muir: To Yosemite and Beyond,* prefer the date of August 1869 for this letter. In the archives of the Yosemite National Park Research Library the date given on the typescript of the letter is August 15, 1868, the assignment apparently that of William Frederic Badè, Muir's literary executor. This date seems the more likely in view of the letter's internal evidence. Muir seems to refer herein to events of the spring of 1868 when he and Chilwell wandered through the San Joaquin, and there is no

The matter remained on his mind during the next five months while he tended one of the flocks of a Snelling sheepman, John Connel, alias "Smoky Jack." His base during these months was a "dismal little hut" off the road between French Bar and Snelling, another ex-mining town. The job was decidedly a compromise for him since he had no interest in the sheep business, but it did provide him with a roof against the winter rains, some cash, and, most of all, an opportunity to take account of his situation and prospects. "What shall I do?" he wondered in the pages of a journal. "Where shall I go?" He considered the "palmy islands of the Pacific," and the Andes, but the attractions of California, for the moment anyway, were strongest, and he decided he would stay another year or two.

Thus his presence in Smoky Jack's filthy, sparsely furnished cabin with its blackened cooking utensils and leaky roof. On his first night he lay wakeful, thinking back on the ways that had brought him here, then drifted into a troubled sleep.

Light through the holes in the roof awakened him, and he went to the hearth to inspect what he hoped had magically become breakfast bread. But the mix he had prepared and set in the coals the night before was but a "sticky compost innocent of yeast or any inflating mixture," and it had remained as passive beneath the fire as "an Indian martyr" so that in the unforgiving morning light it was a solid black mass. It became extremely hard in cooling, he said,

> and looked like a cartwheel, and on attempting to cut out a section
> of it with a butcher knife it broke with a glassy fracture and I
> began to hope that like Goodyear I had discovered a new article
> of manufacture. My teeth were good, and I rasped on a block of
> it like a squirrel on a nut.

His resolution was at least as tough as his teeth, however, and within a few days he had learned the secret of sourdough baking. Henceforth, he said, "my bread was good."

The same resolution made him determined that this winter interlude should be a creative hiatus instead of a lonely, miserable

---

reference to his glorious summer in the Sierras in 1869. Surely he would have mentioned this if he were still up there.

exile. He would observe the changes of natural life here while attending to his ovine duties, and he would keep a journal of those observations, recording the coming of the rains to the browned foothills and the splendid, mysterious ways that local life responded as if to answered prayer.

Limited though his experience with the sheep business was, still it had been sufficient to show him that here was no Virgilian idyll of singing herdsmen and somnolent, browsing flocks, not even that sober, contented existence of the old Scots shepherds before the clearances. The shepherd whose duties he had assumed here had all but fled past him as Muir had approached the cabin, so wild was the man to get back to civilization. The forlorn disarray of the camp —ashes, discarded shoes, sheep skeletons and skulls—bore witness to the desperate, stupefying loneliness of the ordinary shepherd's life.

Not for him. If he was fated for the moment to be a shepherd, he would not become "sheepish," as he said he found most of his fellow shepherds. He would not suffer himself to become "so muddy and degraded." So he read Shakespeare in the foothills, wrote in his journal, and watched with minute attention the incredibly rapid renewal of life.

The first rains fell on December 18, and shortly after he wrote in his journal of the quicker life of insects and plants, the first, faintest tinge of green on the wavy hills. As the green infiltrated the burned land, he saw nature writing over the older lines of the past season, just as it had been doing since the first light, the earth seeming to him a huge palimpsest upon which were written and endlessly rewritten the lessons and laws by which all things lived. It would become a favorite metaphor, almost a literary reflex. He yearned to be able to read this palimpsest and drew the analogy between the natural world and the inner world of the individual by remarking that a man might consider himself fortunate if in his "calm days of reflection" he could regard with pleasure both the "upper and under lines" of his own palimpsest and so see his biographical integrity.

He read the local portion of the earth's grand manuscript with characteristic scrupulosity: on the tenth of January, while the flock grazed, he counted 550 mosses in a quarter of a square inch of a

creekside rock. Two weeks later he spied the harbingers of the host
of yellow flowers that would blanket these hills and then the first
white cress that, with the purple blossoms to come, would form that
triumvirate of color he and Chilwell had stepped into the previous
spring. At the end of January he heard the first frogs and was able
to call the month "without question . . . the most enjoyed of all the
Januarys of my life."

The rains continued into February, bringing new life even as
numbers of Muir's flock died in the cold and wet. As he watched
this—a hundred died during the night of February 10–11—Muir's
sympathies included these "poor unfriended creatures." "Man," he
asserted, "has injured every animal he has touched." On this same
day he noted the retreat of the snow line from the highest of the
foothills.

Then on the thirteenth, as he was singing "Highland Mary"
and often repeating the lines

> There simmer first unfaulds her robes,
> And there they longest tarry,

he suddenly saw "simmer" in the patches of gold on the plains. "I
left my sheep," he wrote,

> and went down into the Hollow to meet the lovely visitors in their
> robes of gold. They numbered about one million souls in five or
> six companies. I welcomed them to the world, congratulated
> them on the goodness of their home, and blessed them for their
> beauty, leaving them a happy flock in the keeping of the Great
> Shepherd, while I turned to the misshapen half-manufactured
> creatures of mine.

The encounter drew from him the surmise that if an evangelist were
to awaken in these fast-flowering hills, he might imagine he had
found Wesley's heaven.

In the following days he noted the appearance of the "go-
quicks" (small lizards), the earnest business of the squirrels, birds,
hares, and ants, the sure clearing of the skies. On the twenty-fourth
he watched the "wonderful effect of the setting sun in a sheep's

eyes," and on that same day he wrote Jeanne Carr, congratulating her on her family's recent move to California, this "magnificent land," as he called it.

Into March, he heard the first canaries on the thirteenth and saw the grass panicles open two days thereafter. Now he beheld the last rapid rush of vegetation, spring seeming almost to be engulfed by summer in a few days' time. Already he detected the beginnings of summer's burnt colors on the edges of the hills and the fading of spring's high, primal brightness. He had seen the cycle turn here, from the dead brown of December, through the coming of the rains, the greening and goldening, and now once more the coming of dryness and heat.

Maybe this was on his mind as a kind of grand background when he wrote Dan about his "plans," which were really no plans at all except to continue somehow what he had been doing, bearing witness to all of nature's doings. He might still go to South America, he said, and from there to Europe, but no matter where his travels might take him or how long, he feared he would never be ready to settle down into the accepted grooves of life. He was too captivated by nature to ever be "productive" as the world understood this. About the only thing he could think of that he might enjoy doing would be to "preach Nature like an apostle." But even that would perhaps be a problem, for Muir saw that if he should ever enter a pulpit with his message, "I fear I should be found preaching much that was unsanctified & unorthodox." Even in such vague imaginings he could not see a place for himself in the world.

June: the valley and foothills burned to dun and hot gold, the long, deep summer of the San Joaquin now on the land. In company with four other men, Muir followed a straggling flock of sheep eastward into the rising hills, heading for summer pastures in the Sierras. He protected himself as best he could from the fierce sun and the dust clouds that billowed from beneath the feet of thousands of sheep desperate for water, shade, green forage. But there was little he could do, and as the flock suffered so did he and his companions.

The owner of the flock was Pat Delaney, a lank priest manqué with a sharp, hacked profile like Don Quixote. Muir had worked briefly for him before, and "the Don," as Muir affectionately styled him in the pages of his journal, had taken a special interest in this odd vagabond. Now that Delaney was to move his flock into the mountains, he engaged Muir to assist him.

Muir accepted with alacrity, for as spring became summer he had heard with increasing clarity the call of the mountains. But his acceptance was not primarily based on his financial situation, as he later suggested. Had he been in need of cash, he could probably have earned more by staying and working in the valley. Indeed, before leaving the foothills he had sent money home to fund his sister Mary's break with their father, who in one of his religious rages had flung her precious sketches into a mud puddle to save her soul. And in any case, he would earn hardly anything for his assistance during this summer. More than money, he needed what Delaney's offer provided: a practical way of exploring the mountains, a loose, flexible work schedule, and a movable source of supplies. Muir was not to be the shepherd; "Billy" would take care of that dulling business. Delaney wanted Muir to see that Billy attended to business after the owner himself should depart for the valley. For the rest of the time, Muir was free to pursue his odd passions for sketching, plant and rock collecting, hiking, and simply sitting and gazing into distances.

Even in this mixed company of a Chinese, an Indian, and Billy, the swarthy shepherd in his drooping, oleaginous overalls, Muir must have seemed the most peculiar of the bunch. Whatever else the others may have known about him—and it probably was not much—they would have thought him distinctly different, this spare, handsome man who carried a plant press and a blue-paneled notebook that dangled by a thong from his belt and who stopped occasionally even in the oven heat of the hills to make pencil sketches. He was certainly no shepherd, so why was he with them? Why would anyone voluntarily follow sheep into the mountains and spend a whole summer up there away from the towns?

Only Delaney, college-educated and of an inquiring mind, understood a little about the extra hand, knew of his interests, and was impressed. An ex-miner who, as Muir described him, had been "overflowed and denuded and remodeled by the excitements of the gold fields," Delaney apparently sensed some deep drive in Muir and was respectful of it. He would do what he could to assist Muir in whatever it was he was after.

Muir could hardly have said himself what he was seeking as they set out in those first days of June. He knew, of course, something of what lay ahead and above, but he had not even begun to work out his relationship to that landscape. So for the moment, as they toiled up through tough chaparral, manzanita, and Ceanothus, with here and there the relieving green of a blue oak or digger pine, he was content to make fine-lined sketches and note their slow progress into higher ground.

On the third day out they were at Horseshoe Bend, where from the bench they could see a large section of the Merced Valley. Gazing at it in awe, Muir felt he "might have left everything for it." What wonderful, fulfilling, endless work it would be, he mused, to trace the forces that had gone into its making. As he looked and then made his hurried journal jottings, the dusty flock, the harrying dogs, and the trailing humans vanished from sight, and he was blessedly alone with his thoughts. And there, suddenly objectified in the distance between himself and the herd, was the gap he would somehow have to bridge: between the world's work and the "work" he would love to do. But for the time being, anyway, he would have to catch up to Delaney and his flock.

On the sixth day he entered the unmistakably alpine environment, leaving the foothills and their concerns below, leaving there too the lower flora as he came to the edge of a coniferous forest of yellow pine and even a few of the majestic sugar pines. The entrance immediately struck him as mystical—even if he would always shy from the use of that word—and provoked an ecstatic response in his journal: one so direct and vivid that among the many kindred passages he was to write over the years it stands out, almost blazes from the page with the authentic force of a conversion experience:

> We are now in the mountains and they are in us, kindling enthusiasm, making every nerve quiver, filling every pore and cell of us. Our flesh-and-bone tabernacle seems transparent as glass to the beauty about us, as if truly an inseparable part of it, . . . a part of all nature, neither old nor young, sick nor well, but immortal. Just

now I can hardly conceive of any bodily condition dependent on food or breath any more than the ground or the sky.

This moment and the view that inspired it seemed so utterly transforming that he wrote:

> How glorious a conversion, so complete and wholesome it is, scarce memory enough of old bondage days left as a standpoint to view it from! In this newness of life we seem to have been so always.

He stared astonished at the snowy peaks above Yosemite, seeming to see them for the first time in all their blue clarity. *Here,* he saw suddenly, here was the place he had been seeking and for which he was destined. Canada, the long Gulfward walk, Cuba, and then that first expedition into this place last spring—all had been an extended test, a novitiate. Now before him, magically, terrifically, lay a landscape that seemed to beckon him, that seemed to nod imperceptibly in his direction as if grandly assenting to his presence here. For him there could be no mistaking either the rightness of the place nor the call it made.

This much—and it was a great deal—he understood by early June, well before the company had reached the summer camp in a glacial meadow above Tuolumne Meadows. He was in his place, and here he would become a "mountaineer." But what did that mean, and what would it entail? What were the requisite skills of mountaineering? These were the questions his notes show him asking and beginning to answer, and the long, sun-filtered days of this first Sierran summer he spent defining for himself his new vocation and establishing an intimacy with the landscape wherein he would follow it.

In this process there were no trails for him to follow. No one in his known family history had ever been engaged in anything but sober, practical pursuits, nor had he ever met anyone who might have been called a naturalist, much less a mountaineer. Further, his Scots background with its heavy, insistent emphasis on productive work as a religious obligation was still a part of him, however much he had struggled to disentangle himself from the cerements of orthodox thinking. He well knew, of course, of those great explorers—Mungo Park and Humboldt and Charles Darwin—but they had been men of great learning and some means, had possessed credentials and various tangible and intangible supports, whereas he was wholly unknown, the product of an improvised, self-designed course of study and without any sort of support for the thing he now saw he wished to do.

Further, the famed explorers seemed peculiarly a European phenomenon. Here in America, which ironically had a much wilder landscape and grander field for such activity, it was hard to find examples of earlier rambling naturalists. There *had* been such men: Mark Catesby, Conrad Weiser, Bartram, Thomas Nuttall, and, in Muir's own time, John Wesley Powell (another graduate of a Wisconsin farm). But their traces were faint indeed; mostly they were men yet unsung, and at this crucial point Muir could not have taken much direction from any of them. There had been practical explorations with definite geopolitical ends in view as with Lewis and Clark, but few precedents for what he really had in mind. At bottom what he wanted for himself had no practical dimension to it, would result in no gift to the great world—empire, gold, or trade route. It would simply make him rich in spirit, and this was plenty for him.

The clearest expression of this singular ambition came in his entry of August 14. He had been gazing at Cathedral Peak and South Dome from the valley's rim and confiding to his journal that he would be content to dwell here forever doing nothing more or less than what he had done this day. Here, with nothing more than bread and water, he would delight in the spectacle of the "circling seasons," the songs of wind and water, the clouds and storms and calms. "I feel sure," he wrote, "I should not have one dull moment." Nor would such an existence be "extravagant." "It is only common sense, a sign of health, genuine, natural, all-awake health."

It may be that he had already been forced to defend such apparently aimless activity against the charge that it was "extravagant." Surely his fellows of the sheep camp would have found his patterns eccentric, to say nothing worse: walking abroad at night to listen to the wind play in the pines while the others lay gratefully rolled in their blankets; sleeping out on a rock in the middle of a stream; climbing trees like a very boy! And in truth, there was something boyish in his behavior: for this summer, anyway, he was allowing himself to obey the commands of whim and fancy, running here and there through this dazzling landscape, clambering up trees and mountain slopes, drinking mountain water, lying in lush meadows with closed eyes and listening to the land, sketching whole days on the rim of Yosemite. As soon as he had finished his minimal chores at the camp, he was gone, often not returning until dusk. Then he would perhaps show Delaney his visible treasures of the day—sketches, plants, rock samples—but the real treasures remained within, and he was content that they remain there, however he might appear to Billy and the others.

So there was a note of joyous defiance in the letter he sent Sarah in the midst of this summer, a note doubtless intensified by his awareness that he was writing from the Sierra wilderness back to a Wisconsin farm. After a brief but ecstatic description of his situation "far from the ways and pursuits of man," he confronted the issue of his behavior. He made a rhetorical feint in the direction of sober and civilized pursuits and then said he had discovered they were not for him. "I am a captive," he wrote, "I am bound. Love of pure unblemished Nature seems to overmaster and blur out of sight all other objects and considerations." Then this direct, defiant confrontation:

> I know that I could under ordinary circumstances accumulate wealth and obtain a fair position in society, and I am arrived at an age that requires that I should choose some definite course for life. But I am sure that the mind of no truant schoolboy is more free and disengaged from all the grave plans and purposes and pursuits of ordinary orthodox life than mine.

Then, as if he would seal off the matter forever, he concluded that on the day following he would be "among the sublimities of Yosemite and forget that ever a thought of civilization or time-honored proprieties came among my pathless, lawless thoughts and wanderings."

But while it was one thing to style himself a truant and an outlaw, it was quite another to actually enter on such a way of life and be comfortable enough in doing so that he might realize the potentialities he was certain lay hidden therein. Shepherding had provided his entrance here, but shepherding as a way of living in this landscape was clearly out, and not just because it was seasonal. Degrading as he had found it could be in the foothills, up here its inherent disadvantages were clearer yet, as if the alpine atmosphere had more sharply defined this, too. Being around Billy on a daily basis and observing the man's indolent and brutish behavior, he came to suspect that this sheepish existence had rendered the man almost insane. Worse even than this, however, was the evident fact that it had permanently dulled Billy to the splendors and lessons of the natural world. Passing with the flock through a luxuriant stand of ferns, Muir had felt sure no one could witness such an expanse of dense green beauty without being moved. Yet when he had asked Billy what he thought of these "grand ferns" the man had churlishly remarked that they were "only d---d big brakes." Later he tried to get Billy over to the rim of Yosemite to have that breathtaking experience, telling the shepherd he would be happy to watch the flock in the meantime. But Billy would not, remarking to Muir that Yosemite was "but a cañon—a lot of rocks—a hole in the ground—a place dangerous about falling into—a d---d good place to keep away from." Muir pressed him, earnest as a missionary, but partly also in the spirit of fun. Just think of the waterfalls you'd see, he urged, all those grand vistas. But Billy remained as stupid and sheepish as a flock on the edge of a creek: he would not be budged. "There is nothing worth seeing there anyway," Muir reported him as saying, "only rocks, and I see plenty of them here. Tourists that spend their money to see rocks and falls are fools, that's all. You can't humbug me. I've been in this country too long for that."

So Billy was proof against Muir's urging and against all those wonders Muir wished so much to experience, and Muir had to conclude that of all nature's voices the only one Billy heard was "baa." Even the voices of the coyotes that threatened the flock "might be blessings," he thought, "if well heard, but he hears them only through a blur of mutton and wool, and they do him no good." To think of himself becoming so beaten down and numbed through years of such work made him shudder. Maybe even seasonal shepherding was contaminating.

Nor would the life of a sort of modern-day mountain man do, a hunter, trapper, and guide. Muir made some entries in his journal of this summer that indicate that, as he went about defining what a mountaineer might be, he thought back on the old mountain men. How much he actually knew about them is conjectural, but if he knew anything—and his entries indicate he did—he knew enough to exclude them as useful models.*

True, they had been supremely competent in their wilderness world, and they had memorized its features with a depth and accuracy immeasurably greater than the primitive maps of their time. They had been heroic, too, in a way, and even as Muir was defining for himself his own kind of mountain life, the adventures of Tom Fitzpatrick, Jim Bridger, and Hugh Glass were becoming part of the national folklore. But the life of these adventures was blood. The very reason these men had gone into the mountains, forsaking civilization, braving great dangers, was to drown beavers in vast quantities for the European fashion trade. Nor had they stopped at this. Their work bred the habit of gross slaughter: not far from where the fledgling mountaineer now was a party of Hudson's Bay boys had killed 395 elk, 148 deer, seventeen bears, and eight antelope in a spree of sport shooting.

The mountain men had used up the country quickly and in the process put themselves out of business. The beaver trade, begun about 1820, was practically over by the year Muir was born, the streams trapped out and the beaver so few it no longer paid a man to take the necessary risks. Now the remnant survivors of the beaver trade were scattered over the huge landscape they had done so much to make known—and they were still in the business of killing: as buffalo hunters and as army scouts in the Plains campaigns.

Knowing some of this and sensing the implications of their ways, Muir found little to admire in them except their ability to exist in the wilderness. He lumped them with shepherds as men too

---

*Among Muir's papers is an undated article on Jim Bridger in which it was claimed, and with justice, that Bridger knew and memorized almost every portion of the Rocky Mountain country (Arthur Chapman, "Jim Bridger, Master Trapper and Trail Maker," place and date of publication missing, Muir Papers, Holt-Atherton). In *Steep Trails,* mostly written in 1888–89, Muir made further trenchant remarks on the mountain men.

coarse and brutal to appreciate what he called in a July 7 entry "Nature's fineness," and observed with some justice that both shepherds and mountain men would consider his appreciation of nature's wonders "bothersome and unmanly." Muir wanted nothing from the mountains but what they had so freely to give: lessons of life, not death. So for the most part he seemed in a cultural and historical vacuum; he would have to invent his vocation as he went.

As much as he was now given to understand of his vocation, he understood or maybe intuited that its chief requistite skill was vision. His background probably in part led him to this understanding, for ever since childhood he had been delighted by the look of things; after the accident in Indianapolis he had felt clear vision was more precious than ever. Now in the Sierras the views were so staggering, the scale so overwhelming, it seemed imperative to develop a kind of vision in some way equal to the landscape. Without an educated way of seeing you might be utterly defeated by the grandeur. When he and Chilwell had first seen the Sierras he had felt something like this: numbed and crushed by the immense spectacle.

Perhaps the way to a steady, comprehensive sort of vision might be to begin with careful inspections of near phenomena and then proceed to the integration of these pictures into ever larger compositions. In this way a living, interrelated view of the terrain might eventually be achieved, one that would permit you to live your best in it. So while he continued his sketching and his long rambles into the higher mountains, he was also looking with an almost microscopic intensity at the immediate landscape. Any portion of it, he found, however small, handsomely repaid his attentions.

He spent time in patient observation of the behavior of black ants, the way they established colonies, the terrific efficiency of their jaws. He measured the lengths and circumferences of sugar-pine cones. The tracks of a bear seemed great and suggestive as he followed them, and when he happened upon a bear browsing hip-high in a flowering meadow, he studied it in secret until he thought it would be good to see the bear's gait. He rushed out from hiding, supposing the bear would quickly retreat. When it defiantly stood its ground, Muir had the opportunity for a brief but stressful study of bearhood at close range. He made a study, too, of Nuttall's flowering dogwood, of water ouzels, wood rats and their curious, humanlike villages; wrote the biography of a raindrop; and sketched the aerobatics of a grasshopper above North Dome. Even the bear, he said, "did not express for me the mountain's wild health and strength and happiness so tellingly as did this comical little hopper." On a hike down Bloody Canyon to Mono Lake, he was careful to note the progression of the flora along the way: "at the head [of the canyon] alpine eriogonums, erigerons, saxifrages, gentians, cowania, bush primula; in the middle region larkspur, columbine, orthocarpus, castilleia, harebell, epilobium, violets, mints, yarrow; near the foot sunflowers, lilies, brier rose, iris, lonicera, clematis."

The more closely he inspected things, the more he began to enter the hidden world beneath the surfaces of natural phenomena. Thinking about bears and their diet, he entered imaginatively into their daily lives, seeing them in his mind's eye as they tore logs to shreds and roughly devoured ant eggs, larvae, parent ants, "and the rotten or sound wood of the cells, all in one spicy acid hash." In the aftermath of a mountain storm the trees fell silent, but only apparently so, for Muir had discovered what went on inside them. Their songs never cease, he wrote, for "every hidden cell is throbbing with music and life, every fibre thrilling like harp strings, while incense is ever flowing from the balsam bells and leaves." In an alpine meadow in August he was dazzled by the late-blooming asters, gentians, and goldenrods. Then, led deeper, he parted the grasses and glimpsed "the underworld of mosses and liverworts." And in unlikely locations such as apparently barren mountain summits he encountered hardy clinging plants of surpassing beauty. "Again and again," he wrote, "as I lingered over these charming plants, I said, How came you here? How do you live through the winter?" And the plants revealed their secret: "Our roots, they explained, reach far down the joints of the summer warmed rocks, and beneath our fine snow mantle killing frosts cannot reach us, while we sleep away the dark half of the year dreaming of spring."

Gradually those larger, more comprehensive views emerged out of his appreciation of how small things worked and fit into each other. Contemplating the morning dew in late July he was led from the spangled grasses to the stars:

> What pains are taken to keep this wilderness in health,—showers of snow, showers of rain, showers of dew, floods of light, floods of invisible vapor, clouds, winds, all sorts of weather, interaction of plant on plant, animal on animal, etc., beyond thought! How fine nature's methods! How deeply with beauty is beauty overlaid! the ground covered with crystals, the crystals with mosses and lichens and slow-spreading grasses and flowers, these with larger plants leaf over leaf with ever-changing color and form, the broad palms of the firs outspread over these, the azure dome over all like a bell-flower, and star above star.

He was led into the same kind of progression through his contemplation of the lacy patterns the mountain streams made over the massive terrain. These reminded him that

> everything is flowing—going somewhere, animals and so-called lifeless rocks as well as water. Thus the snow flows fast or slow in grand beauty-making glaciers and avalanches; the air in majestic floods carrying minerals, plant leaves, seeds, spores, with streams of music and fragrance; water streams carrying rocks both in solution and in the form of mud particles, sand, pebbles, and boulders. Rocks flow from volcanoes like water from springs, and animals flock together and flow in currents modified by stopping, leaping, gliding, flying, swimming, etc. While the stars go streaming through space pulsed on and on forever like blood globules in Nature's warm heart.

Now he felt nothing of that earlier defeated sense when looking into tremendous vistas. Scale did not numb or crush him because he had learned enough already to see that all things were related naturally and harmoniously to each other. Observing any one thing, you were quite easily led on to the next and the next, and so into infinity. When we try to pick out anything in nature, he wrote, "we find it hitched to everything else in the universe." There was a sense of community in this, a sense of shared life, that engendered joy and profound comfort. "One fancies," he said, "a heart like our own must be beating in every crystal and cell, and we feel like stopping to speak to the plants and animals as friendly fellow mountaineers." So, as the summer completed itself, he was able to write that the "best gains" he had made in these months were the "lessons of unity and the interrelation of all the features of the landscape revealed in general views."

By this time the great cycle had wheeled into Indian summer, making Delaney anxious about his sheep. It would not do to muse through these days and so be caught in the high country by the first snow. His odd extra remained unconcerned. For his part, as he wrote in his journal, he would be content to stay here "all winter or all my life or even all eternity."

On August 24, Muir noted a slight frost on the grasses of the long, narrow meadow, and the mountains appeared to him to be "growing softer in outline and dreamy looking. . . ." Late flowers now came out while others went to seed, and each day for him opened and closed like those late bloomers, noiselessly, effortlessly. In the golden days, hazy with the wind-borne seeds of another summer, he seemed to drift into an ever more serene repose—while Delaney watched the skies for ill omens—content to note the changing colors on the mountain slopes and those changes near at hand: the progressively heavier crops of hoar frost, the browning of the meadow grasses, the slow reddening of the clouds. With a firmer equipoise than he had yet experienced he watched the death of the mountain year and cheered it. Once we understand enough about nature's processes, he wrote,

> we soon cease to lament waste and death, and rather rejoice and exult in the imperishable, unspendable wealth of the universe, and faithfully watch and wait the reappearance of everything that melts and fades and dies about us, feeling sure that its next appearance will be better and more beautiful than the last.

In this lull, Delaney, with his eyes ever on the future, told Muir he would certainly be famous one day: such intensity, such purpose! It could not be for nothing. Muir sputtered a bit in his journal, but only a bit. He was playing for bigger stakes here than Delaney's opinion or any conjectured, future fame. At risk here was his life and how he would lead it. And he was determined he would lead it, and not it him—no life of "quiet desperation," as Thoreau had characterized the lives of too many. As to his "duty" and "influence," he now had come to feel that they would not fail somehow to be felt, even if, "like a lichen on a stone," he were to keep silent.

He would no longer lament his fate, for at the moment, anyway, everything seemed so clear and simple. The mountain year was ending and with it his mountain summer; he would have to fold his effects like the flowers of the meadows and go down with Delaney and the sheep. But his heart remained high, for he had determined that the lowland interlude would be but a brief one before the "good time coming, when money enough will be earned to enable me to go walking where I like in pure wildness, with what I can carry on my back, and when the bread-sack is empty, run down to the nearest bread-line for more." For now, he lacked the essentials he thought he needed to snug himself in up here and witness the coming on of winter, to see how the animals lived, "how the forests look snow-laden or buried, and how the avalanches look and sound on their way down the mountains."

They started down on September 9, Muir and Delaney following the flock and the loaded, clanging packhorses. If anything, Muir was even more disgusted by the "silly sheep" and the whole business of herding than he had been in early summer, for he had seen the harm the sheep did to the alpine meadows and it had gone to his heart. He thought to himself he would almost rather herd wolves than sheep.

Still, it had been shepherding that had opened his way into this place, and for that he would put up with much. "Anyhow," he wrote in summation of the entire experience, "we never know where we must go nor what guides we are to get—men, storms, guardian angels, or sheep."

The
Secret
Pass

When the seasons pushed Delaney and his
flock out of the Sierras in September, Muir vowed to his journal
that "I'll surely be back, however, surely I'll be back. No other
place has so overwhelmingly attracted me as this hospitable, Godful
wilderness." By mid-November he was climbing up through the
foothills in fulfillment of that vow, going to a place he had recognized was home.

When he entered Yosemite on a fall day, the valley brown,
crisped, waiting for first snow, he was an unknown itinerant laborer
looking for work. Five years later, when he left the valley for
civilization, he was a naturalist with standing in American scientific
circles, the acknowledged expert on the life of the Sierras, and a
writer of reputation. Dramatic as this change was in his fortunes,
yet the crucial events of these Yosemite years were inner ones, and
the period forms the most significant portion of Muir's intellectual
and spiritual life.

Its beginnings seemed prosaic enough when Muir and a friend
named Harry Randall hiked to Yosemite and found work with a
local hotelkeeper, James M. Hutchings. But appearances notwith-

standing, Muir himself recognized his entrance into the mountains as the fateful step it was to prove. Describing it to Jeanne Carr, he used the same kind of language he had employed when entering the Sierras the previous summer with the sheep. Then he had written, "How deep our sleep last night in the mountain's heart. . . ." And, more pointedly, "How deathlike is sleep in this mountain air, and quick the awakening into newness of life!" Now he wrote Carr, "I am dead and gone to heaven."

The similarities in wording here are not adventitious, for Muir realized he was indeed turning his back on the life and world of his time, was dying to that world and entering another (one more truly alive), a mode of existence which must prove the right one for him if his life were to make sense. He had served, as it must have seemed to him, a long apprenticeship; now was a time to enter directly into new life and without further preliminaries. So, in a real way, the stakes here justified the life-and-death metaphors, for Muir was betting that he had found life, had patiently, faithfully stalked it through shams and blind alleys and dispiriting backwaters to this place, and that in doing this he had escaped the deadening routines of the lowlands. So in his first Yosemite years the ancient motif of the one who dies to (ordinary) life in order to truly live found expression in his writings. On his first exploration of Hetch Hetchy Valley in the late fall of 1871, he wrote that "Wild wood sleep is always refreshing; and to those who receive the mountains into their souls, as well as into their sight . . . sleep is a beautiful death, from which we arise every dawn into a new-created world, to begin a new life in a new body." An undated journal fragment, probably from the year following, mused on death in high places, hazarding the guess that in them death would be found a species of pleasure. And the year after that he recorded a dream of death in the mountains, a death that was hardly fearful but seemed calm and "noble." Nor was it a matter of language only: there were numerous instances in these years when Muir actively sought out danger and even courted death, as if only by pushing toward the highest limits could he really *feel* that life he was so determined to experience.

From the first he seems to have been sensitive also to the archetypal mystery of mountains, the deep, compelling call they *for me too!*

have exerted through time, geography, and human cultures.* Something of this numinous sense of mountains first came to Muir when he strode the steadily rising hills of the Cumberlands in 1867, but it had become much more powerfully apparent with his Sierran entrance in the summer of '69. Then he had felt compelled to acknowledge that the "charms of these mountains are beyond all common reason, unexplainable and mysterious as life itself." Mountains are "fountains," he felt, "beginning places, however related to sources beyond mortal ken." In his Yosemite years he would write of the Sierras as being as holy as Sinai; of mountains so aglow with soul and life it seemed they had died and gone before the throne of God; of mountains wearing spiritual robes and halos like the aureolas the old painters put around the heads of saints.

At the beginning he had no more definite object in mind than the simple, joyful, thorough exploration of his chosen surroundings, that objectless object he had defined for himself the previous sum-mer: in a late autobiographical fragment, he said he approached his Sierran studies like a leaf in a stream. In January of his first winter in the valley he wrote that his ambitions seemed to him humble enough in that they were confined to the exploration of the earth and to the understanding of the story it had to tell. He would not wish, he said, to fly to the moon or visit the sun but would rather "hover about the beauty of our own good star." He would like, he continued,

> to study Nature's laws in all their crossings and unions; I should
> follow magnetic streams to their source, and follow the shores of

*Always mountains have figured in our imagination in grand opposition to the abodes and strategies of normal, lowland existence, as places of spiritual refuge, of withdrawal, and as the seats of the gods where humans might encounter divinity and be transfigured. Thus an incised clay fragment almost 4,000 years old tells how the huntsman of the gods came upon the door of the Sun in the moun-tains, entered it, and journeyed on into the mountains' heart where dwell the souls of the dead. The Hittites, who told this story, said that there in that unimaginably remote fastness the huntsman had been transfigured into a constellation, the one we know as Orion.

my favorite constellation!

our magnetic oceans. I should go among the rays of the aurora,
and follow them to their beginnings, and study their dealings and
communions with other powers and expressions of matter. And
I should go to the very center of our globe and read the whole
splendid page from the beginning.

To his brother Dan he confessed that he was living without what
the world would regard as a fixed and definite aim. He was simply
enjoying the exploration of nature in all its manifestations, and that
was aim enough.

His position at Hutchings's hotel and mill provided a good
base, though as the months went on he was to find that his duties
there were not without annoyance. The hotel had been almost
comical in its primitive facilities and its lack of privacy for individual
guests, and with tourism in the valley picking up Hutchings had
decided more civilized accommodations were necessary. He
wanted wooden partitions constructed to replace the bedsheets that
divided the hotel rooms, additions made to the main building, and
cottages built around it. Apparently a storm the year previous had
provided much fallen pine, and Muir and Randall were occupied
at first in building a sawmill and then in the construction of the
improvements; they also fed and tended the livestock and served
as guides to the valley. But in whatever spare time he could squeeze
out of his work days Muir continued his explorations of the Sierras
and of the valley that was their heart. And oftentimes he would
create two "days" out of one by going without sleep so that he
might explore as fully as he could. Hutchings, perhaps with some
calculation, worried to his valuable employee that he would ruin his
health with such exertions.

He saw his first snow in the valley in mid-December, a longed-
for spectacle that did not fail to match and even exceed his imaginings of it: the enraptured man rode out from Hutchings's to the
very end of the valley, glancing from side to side, and "thrilled
almost to pain with the glorious feast of snowy diamond loveliness." Through the winter days he noted the comings and goings
of those sky messengers, the clouds, the varied moods of the valley's grand god, Tissiack (Half Dome), the play of light on the
living stone of the valley walls. His characteristically close attention
to small details caught the first faint signs of spring in the croaking

of February frogs as they sat up to their throats in the blue sludge
of shallow ponds. March announced itself to him with huge cumu-
lus clouds that appeared to be additions to the mountains and in
butterflies that drifted like flowers in the wind. Then summer came
and farther rambles ensued, into Merced Canyon, for example,
where he wrote in his journal that he was giddy with the intoxicat-
ing beauty of his surroundings:

> A mild wind [he wrote then] comes up the canyon playing upon
> all kinds of leaves, upon each with a music for itself, and for the
> falls that are white in the rocks and for every creature that makes
> its home here. A willow shows endless shades of black, green, and
> silver white as the wind exposes the under side of the leaf. . . .
> Here and there are small patches of sand upon which are written
> the footprints of ducks and blue cranes and water-ouzels, ever-
> present in loving romantic dells where water blooms in white-
> ness. . . . I saw a little bluish wagtail, and abundant signs of
> grizzlies. . . .

He saw dawn come to the mountain peaks:

> Morning light rayless, beamless, unbodied of all its purple and
> gold. No outgushing of solar glory pouring in torrents among
> mountain peaks, baptizing them; but each pervaded with the soul
> of light, boundless, tideless, newborn from the sun ere it has
> received a hint of good or bad from our star. . . . The trees, the
> mountains are not near or far; they are made one, unseparate,
> unclothed, open to the Divine Soul, dissolved in the mysterious
> incomparable Spirit of holy Light! . . .

Drifting through mountains and valleys and along the courses of
rivers, he found magic in everything he encountered, from the
carcass of a dead bear to a microcosmic landscape he discovered in
a dew drop:

> In the calm morning I happened to look thru my pocket lens at
> one of the drops while admiring a dew-laden alder bush and was
> delighted to find the landscape in it in miniature—hills, trees,
> bushes, everything within sight, in infinitely fine colors and all.

At first there was no more system to his explorings than there was to any other dimension of his life here: he would merely decide on a destination and then, when opportunity offered, go there, learning the landscape on his way, discovering its reality, whether far-off mountain peak or a nearby notch in the canyon walls. In the course of these years he developed and refined mountaineering techniques that permitted him to go virtually anywhere, to penetrate the most formidable passes and scale untried heights.

On extended explorations in timbered regions Muir made use of a trusty brown mustang named Brownie. When he had to, Brownie could hop among boulders like a goat and was rock-steady in all terrains. He would load this remarkable beast with two thick blankets, eight or ten pounds of bread and crackers, a few pounds of oatmeal, a package of tea, and, occasionally, some cheese or a bit of dried beef. The provisions would be tightly packed in thick canvas bags that could withstand the pounding as well as the tearing of the underbrush. If Brownie stumbled and rolled, the bread and crackers would be dashed to meal, but they would still be edible. As for cooking utensils, Muir fashioned a kind of pot made of a tin can fitted with a wire handle so that it could be held over a fire, and he packed two of these, one for cooking porridge, the other for his tea.

The explorer himself wore baggy duck or denim trousers that allowed for ample play at the knee; the length of a stride, he found, was often of critical importance, and the trousers must never interfere with it. He found a belt better than suspenders, shoes better than boots. The latter would stretch and shrink when wet and dried and so would become too loose or too tight, whereas shoes could always be adjusted by their laces. They must come up well about the ankles and be heavily shod with round-headed nails. Nailless shoes, he found, would not last through a single excursion. A vest was essential as a carrier of small items; a woolen shirt and a brimmed hat completed his outfit. He might pack along a coat, according to the season and the heights to be encountered, but Muir found it flapped in the wind or snagged while climbing, and so it was always left at his base camp.

He carried a light ax, useful chiefly if he was crossing ice fields where steps might have to be cut; a watch, pocket lens, clinometer, level, aneroid barometer, thermometer, compass, pocket knife, and spectacles, which he used for protection when crossing glaciers or snowfields in strong sunlight. He took no gun, partly because it was so cumbersome and partly because the time taken in hunting game would be time taken away from life-enhancing pursuits. Besides, he enjoyed the company of wild creatures about his camps, and the thought of killing, dressing, and eating them was repugnant. For his needs, he found the regimen of bread and tea perfectly sufficient, and this light, portable diet allowed him to travel far and fast, giving him a freedom from the "bread-line" that was essential to the kind of life he wanted to lead.

Still, for all the freedom his techniques and self-discipline gave him, he came in these years to learn his limits. You could go without much sleep for days on end, he discovered, but you could not go two days without bread. The first day passed well enough except for a telltale weakness in climbing; but that night he found he was sure to dream of bread, a sign of real and dangerous weakness, and then the trip back down to the "bread-line" would utterly exhaust him. Once, returning from a long scramble in the region of Lyell and Ritter mountains, he had a dream of bread that mingled and mixed strangely with images of the glaciers he had been studying. In the dream he saw a wide, glaciated canyon filled with a foaming gray torrent and on its far side a magnificent lateral moraine composed of fine brown loaves, thousands of bread boulders that stretched into the distance. Before the occurrence of such dreams, and the dangers they warned of, it was better to break off exploring and travel down to stock up again.

Establishing camp became a routine, too. Finding some grassy area beneath the slopes, he would unload Brownie, gather his firewood, and select the choice spot for his bed, as level as might be had and preferably with a generous view of the sky and a bit of fir branch overhanging it. Fir boughs formed a spicy and elastic mattress. If a tuft of bryanthus could be found for a pillow, and if, moreover, he could hear the song of a stream, the spot was heaven. Sometimes he would arrange bouquets of scent for himself, mixing mint or goldenrod with the spicy fir. Then came dinner, his pot of porridge cooking over the flames and water for tea boiling in the other blackened and battered container. As the stars began to wink and the snows of the peaks gained in contrast to the growing darkness, he would put on more wood and in the rosy blaze go over his scribbled notes of the day, rewriting them into more coherent and usable form. Then the only sounds might be the cropping of the mustang and the snapping of the burning branches.

With morning light the first care was to find out if Brownie had been frightened away by bears. If not, he would stoke the embers, have breakfast, and then be off again while the sun was still lancing through the upper branches of the trees. So he would continue for weeks at a time until at last he could feel the bottom of the bread sack through the remaining crumbs.

Above the timberline he found he had to employ different techniques. Not even Brownie could traverse the terrain, and so Muir was obliged to become his own packhorse. Equipment and provisions were stripped to the barest essentials. After trying the upper slopes with a blanket tied to his waist, he found this too cumbersome and so went blanketless as well as coatless. He would forage for as many pine knots as he could gather and keep as big a blaze going through the icy night as he could. Oftentimes his bed was but a level arrangement of rocks, and on these he would huddle until the intense cold forced him up to tend the fire. Adding more pine knots, he would hover about the upstarting blaze, rubbing his limbs until some warmth had returned to them, then return to "bed." Through the night, as the temperature continued downward to dawn, his sleep became more and more broken until at last he could see with relief the whiteness of dawn and light on the peaks above. Singing a bit of a Scots ballad perhaps, or rolling out lines of favorite poems, he sought to cheer himself into full wakefulness, noticing a huskiness in his voice. His bones were sore, and he felt a general "torpidity" as he washed in the available water. A cup of hot tea and some steaming porridge completed what he called the "revival," and then the man straightened up as if he had been a bough bent by winter and was now responding to spring. His eyes lifted to the challenge of the peaks, and as if he were driven by some mysterious power, he would go swinging upward through snowbanks and over shattered ridges.

Through his development of such techniques and the will that went into them, Muir was granted views in the Sierras that few others had seen—and surely no other whites before him. There were penalties and prices to be paid for the visions he obtained—hardships, deprivation, the loneliness of evenings camped in the rapidly cooling grasses of high meadows or on the bare and rocky margin of some glacial lake—yet he did so willingly, gladly: the rewards were far greater. He was rich, he wrote Jeanne Carr in July 1870, "rich beyond measure, not in rectangular blocks of sifted knowledge, or in thin sheets of beauty hung picture-like about 'the walls of memory,' but in unselected atmospheres of terrestrial glory diffused evenly throughout my whole substance."

The grand reward was the establishment of an intimacy with a huge block of the natural world. The whole Sierran landscape and skyscape came brilliantly alive for him, spoke to him in syllables and sentences so that at last the old distinctions between subject and object, the knower and the known, the animate and the inanimate, man and the exterior world—all these were dissolved into a mutuality, which is to say a real relationship. Moving through the Sierras, Muir felt he was among friends, in company. He did not move among dead things—rocks, waters, trees—but among a shining, vibrant group of beings. There were inevitably feelings of longing for the company of other humans, for the sound of another voice than his own, for earthly love, but the sense he developed of a vibrant, breathing wilderness did much to assuage such feelings.

He had been greatly disappointed in the Indian tribes of the Sierras, the degraded and dispossessed remnants of which he occasionally encountered in his explorations, but to a significant extent his sense of the landscape was theirs. He believed in the secret life of plants and trees and also of rocks. Writing Jeanne Carr after the Inyo earthquake of March 1872, he said that he had "long been aware of the life and gentle tenderness of the rocks, and instead of walking upon them as unfeeling surfaces, [I] began to regard them as a transparent sky. Now they have spoken with audible voice *and* pulsed with common motion." Rocks, he observed in an undated jotting, "have a kind of life perhaps not so different from ours as we imagine. Anyhow their material beauty is only a veil covering spiritual beauty—a divine incarnation—instonation." He believed there was a natural rhythm in the landscape, that the arrangement of the rocks pointed it out. The mountaineer, hopping and striding over the rocks, was compelled to step to that rhythm if he wished to travel with ease.

The pantheistic tendencies evident in his thought since his long walk in '67 became accentuated in these years. Musing on the spirit in natural phenomena in 1873, he wrote that all of these "varied forms, high and low, are simply portions of God radiated from Him as a sun, and made terrestrial by the clothes they wear, and by the modifications of a corresponding kind in the God essence itself." He might as well have used the term "Great Spirit" or "Great Mystery" as some of the Plains tribes did, but in any case the names were of small consequence. Religion, about which he had bothered so much in the early years, now seemed a simple and natural matter for him. In a letter to Emily Pelton in 1872, he looked back ruefully but candidly on his jackleg preaching at the Mondell House in Prairie du Chien—inessential nonsense, as he now saw it, and he could on occasion be strikingly severe in his criticism of Christian behavior, as if the scars of that old fundamentalism were still too tender. Writing to young Catharine Merrill in 1871 on the subject of her Christian schooling, he said he had glanced through the school catalogue she had sent and felt exactly as if he had "looked into a dungeon of the olden times full of rings and thumbscrews and iron chains." Thank God, he exclaimed, for "this glorious mountain Yosemite barbarism." But for the most part he had done forever with church, theology, and theological disputes.

It was the same with other long-vexed matters like vocation and time. One's vocation now seemed a simple enough matter: what was it you *really* wanted to do? Find that out, he thought, and then do it. In the clarity of these mountain days he saw that it did not make any great difference in the world or to the world how he spent his life—and it never had. So long as he might be close to what he called the beating bosom of nature and so be true to himself—*that* was vocation enough.

And time had ceased to be a matter of great concern. He who had been obsessed with death and the brevity of the mortal span and who had once done a time study for his employers was now released into a geological time scale that mocked all other chronologies and revealed them for the petty things they were. Here was duration amounting to immortality; to live one day truly amid the rocks, to see all things clearly, was as much as you could ask of any lifetime.

So in the early portion of the Yosemite years the dominant feeling in Muir's letters and journal entries is that of release and freedom. The chronic tensions of the past were relaxed, he felt his body to be as sound and transparent as a crystal, and he was capable of almost incredible feats of physical skill and endurance. Late in life, he set down in casual form recommendations for those who would hike the trails and routes of the Yosemite region as he had done three or four decades before; a fine, easy two-day saunter is fifty miles, a three-day hike, sixty. A constant level of spiritual excitement amounting almost to ecstasy can produce an athleticism otherwise unobtainable. This was the Muir of the Yosemite years. For Muir the gateway into this freedom, this excitement, had been the mountain rock, the murmuring stream, the untouched stands of woods. Later he would write that between every two pine trees there is a door leading to a new way of life, and for him this was no literary conceit, no metaphor out of the Romantic credo; it was a living, literal fact.

Others dreamed of becoming the archetypal New World Man, escaped into the wilderness beyond the confines and the comforts of civilization: lone, womanless, released into a wildness, owing no formal allegiances. In America the dream persisted even as the possibilities of it were steadily abridged as the wild places where it might be achieved shrank before axes, plows, the steam-powered sawmill, the locomotive. Our great writers—Thoreau, Melville, Twain—lived enough of that dream to write of it imperishably, but very few actually lived the dream fully, deeply. Muir was one.

Though he had come into the Sierras without any more definite object than becoming a mountaineer, soon a sort of goal emerged out of his rapt observations. The overpowering majesty of the valley, with which he was confronted each morning as he stepped from his cabin door, made him hungry to discover how such scenery had been produced. By what agencies had it come into being? Divine in origin, still, what was the natural history of such splendor?

Oddly, though Yosemite had become a famous spot of natural beauty and was annually visited by hundreds, when Muir took up his studies no one had actually looked carefully at all the geological evidence of the valley in its geophysical context. The Spaniards had cared so little about the area that as far as is known they had never even bothered to come into it in all the years they nominally held its title. Nor had the mountain men cared about it or thought on the forces that might have gone into its creation. Under Joseph Reddeford Walker a group of them had trooped around its rim in 1833, perhaps the first whites to see Yosemite, but they were seeking with a weary impatience a way to the rumored big valley that lay somewhere still westward, and the chronicler of the expedition dismissed the valley with mere allusions. When Walker died in 1876, Yosemite was famous, and he had it carved into his tombstone at Martinez that he had "Camped at Yosemite" (an achievement of which he had grown increasingly vain), but there is no evidence that he or any of his roughened fellows cared any more for Yosemite than did Delaney's shepherd Billy, who had told Muir it was but a big hole in the ground and therefore a good place to stay away from.

In the wake of the Mariposa Battalion's 1851 incursion into Yosemite, following the Indians they were eventually to dispossess of a magic homeland, it might have been supposed that here as elsewhere exploring naturalists would take scientific advantage of what rifles had wrought. Not so: the valley was a spectacle about which idle and empty guesses could be freely ventured, but it still awaited authentic analysis. Then in the early 1860s, James Hutchings realized the tourist potential of the place and somewhat refurbished the old Upper Hotel. Tourists began to flock in, but *still* the valley's natural history remained largely unexamined.

Even the California State Geological Survey under Josiah D. Whitney failed to securely confront all the facts. At the time of his appointment in 1860 as director of the survey, Whitney was among the leading geologists in America. He was also a man of unquestioned probity, one reason why sponsors of the bill authorizing the survey had specified his appointment: there were numbers of venal legislators who believed the real purpose of the survey should be to locate precious metals and so make all of the insiders (like themselves) rich forever. Whitney would have none of this. He gathered an outstanding group of young, ambitious men, including William H. Brewer, Charles F. Hoffman, and Clarence King, and in the decade of the 1860s conducted extensive fieldwork in the state. The survey members did especially fine work in the Sierras and left their individual names all over its landscape, but because of Whitney's intellectual obstinacy they did not arrive at an accurate understanding of the making of Yosemite.

In their fieldwork for the summer of 1863, survey members encountered unmistakable evidences of glaciation in the mountains above Yosemite, and later Clarence King saw signs of what he thought might have been a 1,000-foot-thick glacier in the valley itself. But though Whitney admitted the presence of glaciers in the Sierras, he denied they had been a major factor in carving the landscape.

As for Yosemite itself, Whitney had publicly committed himself to the theory that the valley was the exceptional creation of violent forces. Specifically, he argued that at the time the whole Sierran block was uplifted and tilted westward, or possibly just after this, Yosemite had been created by a huge and sudden subsidence in which the valley floor sank due to the collapse of its support. Half Dome was the most spectacular and obvious evidence of this catastrophic event, the missing half having gone down with the rest of the valley. Whitney brushed aside his assistants' reports of glaciation above Yosemite, and he pointedly refuted King's report of glacial markings in the valley, saying that they proved nothing important about the formation of the valley. King and the others deferentially shut up, and Whitney refused to confront the facts themselves.

Muir, mill hand and tourist guide, had nothing at stake but his sense of the truth. He was a nobody; or, as Whitney would later style him when the great man found himself involved in an embarrassing controversy, he was a "mere sheepherder." So he had been, but he was far from the "ignoramus" Whitney claimed. He was singular in his freedom, having no reputation to defend, no theoretical position to uphold. He had wanted to learn this landscape so as to feel fully at home in it, and in doing so he had discovered how essential glaciers had been in its formation. The views he would eventually express on the formative role of glaciers here and in other, lesser "Yosemites," would bring him to the attention of the

scientific and literary communities, but these studies and their results were actually incidental to his larger ambitions. For him, and
despite a tremendous fascination with glaciers that lasted the rest
of his life, the discovery of the truth of the making of the valley was
a grand and fortuitous by-product of his spiritual ambitions. In the
end his discoveries turned out to be an appropriate metaphor for
his achievement of those ambitions.

When he had first entered the Sierras, Muir had seen what he
then believed the marks of glacial action in the "strange, raw,
wiped" appearance of the rocks and also in the deposition of boulders that had been carried along and stranded far from their original homes. A glacier, he thought, must have been responsible for
all this, and he recorded this "fine discovery" in his notebook.

He had been prepared to understand the evidence by his college experience at Madison, for the 1860s had been a period of
great interest in glaciers among North American geologists. Eugene Hilgard, John S. Newberry, Edward T. Cox, Sir William
Logan, and J. W. Dawson were all studying glacial action, and
surely Muir would have been exposed to some of this work from
one so current as Ezra Carr. Carr like his contemporaries had been
stimulated in this field by the arrival in America of the great Louis
Agassiz in 1848. Ten years of Agassiz's glacial studies in the Alps
had made European geologists "glacier-mad," as one of them put
it, and his American arrival had the same effect on geologists in this
country. Agassiz had successfully demonstrated that glaciers
moved, and he had gone on to discover how they did and what the
effects were on the landscape when they did so. Here was the latest
and perhaps the most spectacular application of the dynamic theories of the Scots empiricists, Hutton and Lyell, that had so revolutionized every aspect of earth science.

Muir was disposed by everything in his personal history to
accept the fullest implications of Agassiz's work and the dynamic
underpinnings of it. At the same time, everything in his past
caused him to reject Whitney's subsidence theory, for in the latter's hypothesis there lurked something of that dogmatic fundamentalism that had cost Muir so much. Whitney was a man of
modern science and hardly a study-bound theologian arguing
from Scripture to explain rock-hard facts he would not look at,
but in this instance at least Whitney had allowed himself to take

and hold a position dangerously close to that of the eighteenth-century catastrophists who had assumed the literal reality of the Flood and who argued that the way the earth now looked was the result of a series of divinely appointed catastrophes of which the Flood was the last and greatest. Through the work and influence of Hutton and Lyell the catastrophists had become passé, as Muir had learned at Madison, but what was especially significant for him in the dynamic view was the assumption that the forces that had produced the earth in its present form were still in operation, still acting in the selfsame ways they had from the beginning of geological time.

While this "uniformitarianism," as it came to be called, made scientific sense to Muir, it also had a powerful personal appeal for him in that it confirmed the presence of a loving, indwelling divinity like the one he had so delightedly found in the work of the European Romantics and in Emerson. God had not fashioned this beautiful world in a series of wrathy catastrophes and then gone away and left it. Instead, He had set in operation forces that had slowly shaped the globe, and in their continued operations one could feel and indeed see the presence of divinity.

Thus as early as his first spring in Yosemite Muir told Jeanne Carr in a letter that he "devoutly" disbelieved Whitney's subsidence theory. Soon enough he was telling anyone who would listen that glaciers, not some remote catastrophe, had carved the magnificent amphitheater on which they gazed. Tourists in the valley who were consigned to his care were likely to be subjected to stone sermons of an astonishingly enthusiastic sort. The man seemed to have a very personal stake in their education in nature, and especially so on this point.

In August 1870, Joseph Le Conte, a leading geologist, brought a group of his students from the University of California into the valley for some fieldwork. Jeanne Carr had told Le Conte of Muir's work, and when Le Conte met Muir there was an instant shock of recognition. Muir, dressed in his dusty mill clothes, formed a sharp contrast to the correct professor and his college boys, but one look into Muir's remarkable blue eyes and a minute of his talk were sufficient for Le Conte to understand that here (as he wrote later) was a man "of rare intelligence, of much knowledge of science, particularly of botany, of which he has made a specialty." As Muir led the party's expedition over the following five days, Le Conte learned that he was also deeply acquainted with the mountains, and Le Conte had ample occasion to marvel at the abilities of this unknown. "A man of so much intelligence tending a sawmill!" he exclaimed in his journal.

Muir guided the professor to locations where the glacial evidence was clear and unmistakable, and while Le Conte then confided to his journal that he would be inclined to attribute far more influence in the valley's formation to preglacial action, he did agree with Muir that glaciers had been at work here.* He came away profoundly impressed by this man of the mountains who, as he said, gazed and gazed on the natural world as if he might never "get his fill." But as astonished as Le Conte was by the depth and originality of Muir's mind, he was even more so by the passion of the man's attachment to nature and by the clear determination Muir showed to maintain his mountain freedom, even if it meant accepting such humble employment as that in which Le Conte found him. "I think," wrote the professor, "that he would pine away in a city or in conventional life of any kind."

The next year Muir met another emissary of the the academy, John D. Runkle, president of the Massachusetts Institute of Technology. For five days in early September 1871, Muir guided Runkle about the valley and into the mountains above it, preaching his glacial theory, as he put it in a letter to Jeanne Carr. "He was fully convinced of the truth of my readings, "Muir wrote, "and urged me to write out the glacial system of Yosemite and its tributaries for the Boston Academy of Science.

"I told him that I meant to write my thoughts for my own use

---

*Subsequent theory accepts Le Conte's reservation. Muir took the current view that there had been a single great glacial invasion and attributed all the work in the valley to it. It is now believed that water erosion and exfoliating granite played important roles in making Yosemite and that there were at least three distinct glacial invasions. Still, though subsequent theory has refined Muir's observations (and this largely through technological innovations that have made possible a much more comprehensive and accurate reading of the landscape), he was more nearly right about Yosemite than anyone else of his time (Francois E. Matthes, *The Incomparable Valley: A Geological Interpretation of the Yosemite,* ed. Fritiof Fryxell, Berkeley, Los Angeles, London, 1950).

and that I would send him the manuscript and if he and his wise scientific brothers thought it of sufficient interest they might publish it." So the terms were to be strictly Muir's own. And yet it was not so simple: others, especially Jeanne Carr, had been urging him to write up his studies, but he saw writing for publication as a compromise with what he regarded as his real work. Still, it *would* be a sort of validation of that work, of his life even, and however far he had succeeded in retreating from the world, he had not been so absolutely successful that he did not understand this really was an opportunity. And if everyone was fated to have to do the world's work in some form or other (as he was in running the sawmill and in guiding blasé tourists), then surely this was better work than most could hope for.

He wrote of his ambivalence in the same letter to Jeanne Carr in which he told of Runkle's visit. Some others, he said, had been urging publication on him, and "I am almost tempted to try it, only I am afraid that this would distract my mind from my main work more than the distasteful and depressing labor of the mill or of guiding. What do you think about it?" She had thought plenty about it, and shortly she would begin to show a forceful hand in the shaping of a literary career for him.

In the meantime, Muir had more important matters on his mind. The future would take care of itself; he was on the track of the past. On an October day of this year he discovered a living glacier at Red Mountain in the Merced group. Standing before its dirt-stained prow as before an altar, he shouted his joy to the sky. The grand event, the fulfillment of an intensely personal quest, also had a consequence of a distinctly practical, worldly nature, for here was incontrovertible evidence, and with it he felt willing to send an article to the New York *Tribune.*

He pieced the article together from letters he had sent to friends, the relevant portions of which he had made copies of. The article, "Yosemite Glaciers," appeared on December 5, 1871, and brought the surprised author $200, a goodly sum and especially so for a first published work. It was pure, authentic Muir, the oft-enraptured prose of the journals and letters suddenly brought to light as if the man had reluctantly opened his carefully compiled pages and let who would have a look. "I have," he told his unknown readers, been drifting about among the rocks of this region for several years, anxious to spell out some of the mountain truths which are written here; and since the number, and magnitude, and significance of these ice-rivers began to appear, I have become anxious for more exact knowledge regarding them; with this object, supplying myself with blankets and bread, I climbed out of the Yosemite by Indian Cañon, and am now searching the upper rocks and moraines for readable glacier manuscript.

There was a kind of Whitmanlike directness in this announcement, the writer, whatever his private feelings, daring to assume that what was of compelling interest in his own life would be of similar interest to anonymous readers. And, in the same way as Whitman, there was a long, shadowed foreground to this announcement and to this passage on glaciers, one of the finest Muir ever wrote:

There is a sublimity in the life of a glacier. Water rivers work openly, and so the rains and the gentle dews, and the great sea also grasping all the world: and even the universal ocean of breath, though invisible, yet speaks aloud in a thousand voices, and proclaims its modes of working and its power: but glaciers work apart from men, exerting their tremendous energies in silence and darkness, outspread, spirit-like, brooding above predestined rocks unknown to light, unborn, working on unwearied through unmeasured times, unhalting as the stars, until at length, their creations complete, their mountains brought forth, homes made for the meadows and the lakes, and fields for waiting forests, earnest, calm as when they came as crystals from the sky, they depart.

Now he was in the public arena, and once in, at least as a writer, he would let Jeanne Carr (and a few others) do with his words what they would. The *Tribune* printed his "Yosemite in Winter" on New Year's Day, 1872; his epistolary remarks on glaciers were read before the February, March, and May meetings of the Boston Society of Natural History; and in April he commenced a fruitful association with the *Overland Monthly* that would see him become perhaps that magazine's most popular contributor over the next two years.

Concurrent with this literary acceptance, and probably much more significant to Muir himself, was the accolade he received from the great Agassiz himself, to whom Muir had written of his studies. Agassiz instructed his wife to respond, telling Muir that he was the first man Agassiz had heard of who had an adequate conception of glaciers. Oddly, unexpectedly, and even against his expressed will, Muir was a "somebody" now, a success of sorts in the eyes of the world.

Had it not been for Jeanne Carr, Muir might never have taken the necessary steps to see the results of his observations into print. Literature had been a great discovery for him in adolescence, but when it came to creating literature himself, he saw suddenly the terrible limitations of language's ability to catch what was there in nature. In a fragment that apparently was to form a portion of his autobiography, Muir wrote that, while it was easy to enjoy nature, "it is not easy to tell about this. . . . One's feelings are always in advance of words, so much is deeply felt that is in its very nature indefinable, especially when we travel alone." Spirit was everywhere, shining out of rock, audible in the murmuring stream—and here was the impoverished recorder with his few, primitive tools, trying to get something of it down.

"Oftentimes," he wrote Jeanne Carr, just as his literary career was taking wing,

> when I am free in the wilds I discover some rare beauty in lake or cataract or mountain form, and instantly seek to sketch it with my pencil, but the drawing is always enormously unlike reality. So also in word sketches of the same beauties that are so living, so loving, so filled with warm God, there is the same infinite shortcoming. The few hard words make but a skeleton, fleshless, heartless, and when you read, the dead bony words rattle in one's teeth.

He called the articles she was urging him to write "dead bone-heaps," but said, a bit sadly, that he would do his best, both to please her and in the hope that the "bone-heaps" might at least serve as markers toward the reality beyond them. From the first writing was an unhappy compromise, both because it distracted him from his real work and because, like generations of Romantic writers before him, he knew too well how much more there was in nature than even the greatest artist could convey. Writing for publication was the world's work, not his, and if Jeanne Carr was his literary agent, she was also the agent of that world's intrusion into his mountain life.

She had followed him with an unwavering faithfulness from their first meeting on the fairgrounds at Madison; she had sought him out in his isolation in Prairie du Chien, encouraged and even mothered him at Madison, written him in his Canadian exile. During his first summer in the Sierras and after she had moved to California with her family, she had come looking for him again, but he had been truly inaccessible then and she had had to be content with letters. During the early portion of his Yosemite years Muir felt he owed her almost everything: she was his confidante, his teacher, his literary adviser, and just about his only authentic contact with the rest of the world. He called her his "dear, dear spiritual mother," and, perhaps closer, "my Carr" and "my ain Jean." By the end of his Yosemite years, after she had engineered a literary career for him and had been successful in persuading him to come down out of the mountains to accept it, he may well have felt that he owed her too much, had allowed her too much say in his life.

The legend of the love affair between Muir and Jeanne Carr is ubiquitous and undying. Even those who know little more than Muir's name—and do not know Jeanne Carr's at all—are convinced there was a love affair. The full truth of the relationship may never be known. The epistolary record of it is extensive, but it is far from complete, and some of the crucial letters that have survived have been mutilated by persons unknown. Near the end of her life and after she had apparently suffered some impairment of her mental capacities, Jeanne Carr gave some of her Muir letters to the writer George Wharton James, apparently with the implicit understanding that he might publish them. Muir made strenuous efforts to retrieve these and at last succeeded. Among his papers at the Holt-Atherton Library at the University of the Pacific is a large envelope on the back of which, in the uncertain hand of old age, are Muir's directions as to which of his letters to Jeanne Carr he wished destroyed as of April 1909. Seventeen letters are listed here by number and, to the right of these, such notations as "all," "a few sentences at last," "half off." In addition to these specified deletions there are at least thirty letters missing from the correspondence, dating from Muir's years in Canada, as well as numerous other deletions of extant letters, deletions Muir himself apparently never directed. The record, while full, is hardly complete.

What then is a good surmise? That whatever else may be, John Muir was the great love of Jeanne Carr's life, and that she was absolutely crucial in giving Muir and his great gifts to the world. But in doing this great service to the world—and perhaps to Muir as well—she lost him. Not just because once he was out into the world he had other claims upon him; nor even that he had outgrown the need for her and her guidance: at bottom, it may simply be that he could never quite forgive her for having brought him down from his freedom.

From 1860 when they first met, through all his travels, his wandering, obscure existence, he had relied on her for friendship, guidance, and love. And in the end, as he might have seen it, she had failed him, failed to understand his deepest desires as fully as he believed his ventured confidences should have guaranteed. As for her, she had feared (with reason) he might end as a hermit genius, crabbed, eventually warped by the lack of human intercourse. In later years Muir would find his boyhood friend and mentor, David Taylor, thus: his eyes still burning in his head, poems locked in his mind, drinking in the solitude of the Wisconsin woods for lack of a single kindred soul to whom he might express himself.

And doubtless, too, she had her own needs that he in some way could fulfill. Her papers indicate that she was a potentially talented author, was remarkably responsive to nature. Yet where was the outlet for this? Who was *her* confidante and champion? She began her autobiography half a dozen times and only once got as far as her early childhood. In one of the last, fragmentary efforts telling who she was and what she had meant, she wrote with a weary asperity that

> Mrs. Carr insists that she "has yet no individual history to speak
> of;" having been until her eighteenth year simply the eldest

daughter of Dr. Albert Smith of Castleton, Vermont, and of Caroline Carver his wife; and since then the wife of Dr. Carr, well known as a college professor and educator for some forty years; that she is noted for nothing except for the fact that her eyes have always been open. . . .

If he needed her, she had need of him as well to actually accomplish those things he was so capable of, those things she would not achieve.

He had relied on her also for protection against the rest of the world and particularly against other women, almost at times seeming to use her as convenient and conveniently safe female companion. In his first full Yosemite year complications had arisen between Muir and James Hutchings's young wife and then later in that same year with a visiting countess, Thérèse Yelverton. Then Muir had turned to Jeanne Carr for help, and in doing so had brought the full force of his long-denied emotional and sexual needs to bear. He had written *her* the love letters he might have written Elvira Hutchings or Thérèse Yelverton, love letters of a special sort in which a passion for the natural world displaces and mingles with another kind of passion; even so, there are occasions when words and phrases slip through that carry these letters close to the brink of Victorian indiscretion.

Whatever the truth of Muir's relationship with Elvira Hutchings in the winter and spring of 1870 and his relationship with Thérèse Yelverton during the summer and fall of that year, it is clear from his letters to Jeanne Carr that he was turning to her— safely married, safely removed in Oakland—for help and protection, and as a safe repository for powerful feelings. And it seems clear also that she understood and accepted her role. If she responded with some of her own emotional needs, who can be surprised?

Shortly after James Hutchings engaged Muir and Harry Randall to work for him, he left the valley for Washington, D.C., on business; he would not return until May 1870. On leaving, he gave Muir and Randall responsibility for the upkeep of the hotel and the additional charge of looking after his wife and three children. Elvira Hutchings was twenty-two years younger than her husband, a dreamy, ethereal young woman, as she was often described by contemporaries, and one who apparently shared Muir's interest in nature's smallest details. She came from an artistic family and was much interested in painting and in botany. Inevitably, perhaps, she and Muir became good friends, and it is likely that she confided some marital misgivings to Muir: an undated letter she sent him some time after the winter of 1869–70 adverts to troubled confidences she shared with him. When Hutchings returned to the valley that spring his relations with Muir took a decided turn for the worse, though they had never been especially good. Muir continued to work for him until the fall of 1871, at which time he moved to Black's Hotel westward along the valley. Then, in 1874, Hutchings closed his business affairs in the valley and with Elvira and the children moved to San Francisco.* There Elvira left him for another man.

That Muir was the precipitating cause of the breakup is entirely unproved and, in view of the chronology, unlikely, though around Yosemite the rumor persists. What is more likely is that Elvira Hutchings turned toward Muir in her unhappiness and isolation and that subsequently both felt an attraction that both resisted. For Muir an active romantic involvement with a married woman would have been morally impossible; and the ensuing obligations would also have prevented him from enjoying that essential freedom he had gained. Instead he turned to "Mrs. Carr" and wrote her letters in which human love and love of nature mingle so strangely and strongly.

He wrote one in the summer of 1870 using sequoia sap for ink, telling her that he and the "King tree . . . have sworn eternal love —sworn it without swearing, and I've taken the sacrament with a Douglass squirrel, drunk Sequoia wine, Sequoia blood, and with its rosy purple drops I am writing this woody gospel letter." After several more paragraphs of such impassioned writing, he descended suddenly into the personal, indeed the intimate, ending, "Therefore, my Carr, good-night."

*Hutchings's business in Washington was a legal battle for compensation for his land and the improvements made on it. Yosemite had been made a state park in 1864 and although Hutchings's claim was somewhat muddied, he was not alone in feeling that he was owed some compensation under the preemption laws. Eventually he was awarded $24,000, and it was after this that he left for San Francisco.

Things became even more complicated in the summer and fall, for not only was Muir still seeing Elvira Hutchings, but this was also the time that Thérèse Yelverton arrived in the valley. She began paying Muir a good deal of attention, and this appears to have intensified his emotional reliance on Jeanne Carr.

Thérèse Yelverton was an acquaintance of Jeanne Carr's and was also one of the most famous (some would have said notorious) women of that time, subject of a sensational British divorce case as the wronged wife of the bigamist Viscount Avonmore. She was vivacious, attractive, romantic, and she became so enamored of the blue-eyed miller/guide that she made him a character in a novel she was then writing. Her idealized portrait of Muir in *Zanita* strongly suggests she had developed more than a literary interest in him.

Muir was warily attentive to Mrs. Yelverton, willing to guide her to the valley's beauty spots and to share something of his enthusiasms with her. He apparently also responded to her request for help in the writing of her novel, though in what way is not clear. Perhaps he supplied her with information on the Yosemite locale in which *Zanita* is set. But if in these months of her residence in Yosemite he withheld himself from Thérèse Yelverton, he did not withhold himself in his letters to Jeanne Carr. "Would that you could share my mountain enjoyments!" he exclaimed in that summer.

> In all my wanderings through Nature's beauty, whether it be among the ferns at my cabin door, or in the high meadows and peaks, or amid the spray and music of waterfalls, you are the first to meet me, and I often speak to you as verily present in the flesh.

The previous Sunday, he continued, he had baptized himself in the "irised foam" of Vernal Falls, "and you were there also and stood in real presence by the sheet of joyous rapids below the bridge." He casually referred to Mrs. Yélvèrton and Le Conte, two friends she had sent him and for which he was, of course, grateful, but, he said, "I am *waiting* for you."

Maybe the most extraordinarily charged letter he wrote her was that he sent after spending part of the night of April 3, 1871, on a tiny ledge next to the thunderous shower of Yosemite Falls. He had wanted to spend the whole moonlit night up there, looking at the spectral-seeming valley through the mist of the falls, but he had been tempted to crawl even closer along a narrow sliver of stone to see things as the falls might themselves see them. The attempt nearly cost him his life when he was suddenly severely battered by an irregular deluge that fell straight down upon his head and shoulders. But wet, chilled, and dazed as he was he still could write: "Oh, Mrs. Carr, that you could be here to mingle in this night-noon glory! I am in the upper Yosemite Falls and can hardly calm to write, but from my first baptism hours ago, you have been so present that I must try to fix you a written thought." The thought was to "wish again that you might expose your soul to the rays of this heaven." Then the heady and maybe purposefully vague mixture of sentiments so characteristic of this stage of their correpondence:

> How little do we know of ourselves, of our profoundest attractions and repulsions, of our spiritual affinities! How interesting does man become considered in his relations to the spirit of this rock and water! How significant does every atom of our world become amid the influences of those beings unseen, spiritual, angelic mountaineers that so throng these pure mansions of crystal foam and purple granite.

Whatever this passage means and whatever else the full letter once contained (a portion of its penciled text has been erased), we have record here of a special, rare kind of intimacy and one that Muir perhaps cared to achieve with no one else. A comparison of the letters he would later write his wife Louie suggests at least the possibility that in some ways Muir never loved another woman as he loved Jeanne Carr when she was in Oakland and he in Yosemite.

And still, from quite early in the Yosemite years, Jeanne Carr was applying her special leverage to bring Muir down from the mountains. At the end of the ecstatic letter he wrote with sequoia sap he evaded a question she had put to him, writing instead: "You say, 'When are you coming down?' Ask the Lord—Lord Sequoia." About a year later, responding again to her pressure, he chided her thus:

> I feel sure that if you were here to see how happy I am, and how ardently I am seeking a knowledge of the rocks you would not call me away, but would gladly let me go with only God and his written rocks to guide me. You would not think of calling me to

make machines or a home, or of rubbing me against other minds,
or of setting me up for measurement. No, dear friend, you would
say, "Keep your mind untrammeled and pure. Go unfrictioned,
unmeasured, and God give you the true meaning and interpretation of his mountains."

But she ignored his stated misgivings, feeling she knew better, and
by the summer of 1872 was mapping his career in the most forceful
of terms. In late July she wrote him: "This is what you are going
to do. After the harvest time is over . . . you will pack up all your
duds, ready to leave [Yosemite] two or more years. . . . You will
live with us. . . ."

He felt this pressure, like gravity, and he was baffled that its
main source should be her. Others could be expected not to understand what he was doing up here, and a world in bondage could
be relied upon to begrudge one man his freedom. But from the one
mortal who had urged him to follow his instincts now to become
the advocate of another kind of "duty" . . .

He would not surrender so easily, even to her and her plans;
he would stubbornly resist success. A few days after receiving her
letter he wrote in his journal that what he really wanted was more
time up here, all the time there was, actually, to read this "terrestrial language." He did not wish to be hurried into anything, especially not a return to the world and to the solemn task of beginning
a career.* So, instead of coming to Oakland as she had directed, he
went the other way, higher up into the inaccessibilities of the Tuo-

---

*Here, as in so many other ways, one is reminded of Thoreau, whose life
seemed so aimless and fugitive and who felt and resisted the pressure to take up
his social responsibilities. In his thirty-fourth year, having by the world's standards
accomplished almost nothing, Thoreau wrote in his journal: "Me thinks my seasons revolve more slowly than those of nature; I am differently timed. I am
contented. This rapid revolution of nature, even that nature of me, why should
it hurry me. Let a man step to the music which he hears, however measured. Is
it important that I should mature as soon as an apple tree . . . ? May not my life
in nature, in proportion as it is supernatural, be only the spring and infantile
portion of my spirit's life? Shall I turn my spring to summer? May I not sacrifice
a hasty and petty completeness here to entireness there? If my curve is large, why
bend it to a smaller circle?" (Bradford Torrey and Francis H. Allen [eds.], *The
Journals of Henry Thoreau,* New York, 1962.)

lumne River Canyon and Hetch Hetchy and finally the very summit
of Mount Ritter. In a mood of exultant triumph, he wrote her on
the eve of this escape:

> My horse and bread, etc., are ready for upward. . . . This time I
> go to the Merced group, one of whose mountains shelters a
> glacier. . . . Ink cannot tell the glow that lights me at this moment
> in turning to the mountains. I feel strong to leap Yosemite walls
> at a bound. Hotels and human impurity will be far below. I will
> fuse in spirit skies.

On this expedition he was accompanied by three artists, one of
them William Keith, like Muir a native of Scotland and with whom
Muir would enjoy a close, rewarding friendship until Keith's death
in 1911. Muir had told them he would guide them to spots where
they would have all the landscape any artist could wish. As for
himself, he was bound for Mt. Ritter.

"Mount Ritter," he would later write, "is king of the mountains
of the middle portion of the High Sierra, as Shasta of the north and
Whitney of the south sections." Its 13,000-foot summit was
guarded below by steep glaciers and tremendous canyons, and as
far as anyone knew it had never been climbed. Moreover, at this
season (the last days of August), though the weather was still clear,
there was the ever-present danger of snow. For Muir, all the conditions were right for challenge: he would climb Ritter. In leaving the
artists behind, he told them he might possibly be gone as long as
a week or ten days if a storm should catch him.

The first day was pure pleasure as he climbed through ancient
glaciers, "painted meadows, late-blooming gardens, [and] peaks
of rare architecture. . . ." When he was high enough he obtained
a view over the top of the range and down into the Mono Desert
on the east, "lying dreamily silent in thick purple light—a desert
of heavy sun-glare beheld from a desert of ice-burnished granite."
Evening's long, admonitory shadows came to him on the rim of a
glacier basin at about 11,000 feet but still miles from his destination. Hacked, shattered peaks towered about him as he made
camp in a thicket of dwarfish pines. He found water for tea, gath-

ered firewood, and then readied himself for night. He was up many times during it, for he he had brought neither coat nor blankets.

Stiffened with cold, he welcomed the morning star, had his tea and bread, and, fastening a "durable crust" to his belt in case he should not get back to base camp that night, he set off for Ritter. The mounting sun set the peaks before him ablaze, and he was the only human in all that vast, eternal landscape of rock and ice, his iron-shod shoes making the only sound as he clanked upward.

At the foot of Ritter, Muir encountered one of the guardian glaciers. No, he said to himself, looking at the glacier and the slope rising above, no, the season is too late and the climb too hazardous to try this now—next summer. Yet, in a matter of minutes he found himself started on the ascent, climbing into a "wilderness of crumbling spires and battlements" that with each step seemed more and more to seal off retreat. To go back looked more dangerous than to press onward.

Eventually he was brought to a position where he really could not retreat without tremendous peril, yet facing him was an almost sheer cliff. Up it he went, feeling for each handhold with what he described as "intense caution." Then, about half way to the cliff's top, he was "brought to a dead stop, with arms outspread, clinging close to the face of the rock, unable to move hand or foot either up or down. My doom appeared fixed. I *must* fall."

"In any sudden exigency," Muir wrote years after in an undated autobiographical fragment, "a sound man brought face to face with danger will always do better than he anticipates. While in perfect accordance with nature [,] alone [,] free from perturbing influences [,] one is dominated by one's inner self whose existance [*sic*] under civilization is hardly dreamed of." With a characteristic wariness where mysterious matters were concerned—matters which might so easily be misconstrued by the credulous or by "adepts"—he guessed that these "hidden powers" were "only the accumulated experience of innumerable ancestors." So it was, however accounted for, in this instance, for after the rushing sense of imminent death on the glacier far below, then

life blazed forth again with preternatural clearness. I seemed suddenly to become possessed of a new sense. The other self,

bygone experiences, Instinct, or Guardian Angel,—call it what
you will,—came forward and assumed control. Then my trembling muscles became firm again, every rift and flaw in the rock
was seen as through a microscope, and my limbs moved with a
positiveness and precision with which I seemed to have nothing
at all to do. Had I been borne aloft on wings, my deliverance
could not have been more complete.

The mountain's difficulties hardly ended atop this memorable cliff,
for above it Muir found the face "still more savagely hacked and
torn." But that mystical moment seemed to leave a residue of
power that sent him on through an effortless climb to the summit.
     Looking south from that height, over the tumbled, formidable
expanse, he could see Mount Whitney. Westward his view comprehended the broad valley of the San Joaquin and those blue
coastal mountains that had kept him company when he first entered
California on his way toward a destination only gradually revealed.
Turning about and looking north, he saw Cathedral Peak in the
near foreground, then Mammoth Mountain and Ord, Gibbs, Dana,
Conness, Tower Peak, Castle Peak, Silver Mountain, and a towering host of others yet unnamed. To the east there was the Mono
Desert with its single long lake, Owens Valley dotted with craters,
and the mighty Inyo Range that rose to heights rivaling the Sierras.
Here truly was the New World, magnificent, intact, utterly itself.
And to one who would make the effort, climbing into and past
death's shadow, it would reveal itself unstintingly.
     Sometime previous Muir had read with delight and deep recog-
nition Thoreau's *The Maine Woods,* in which there is an account of
another man's search for the ultimate America. Atop Mount Ktaadn
Thoreau encountered what he had so patiently been seeking
through the years, that America lying beyond geographical discovery, beyond Columbus and Raleigh, beyond the red men, even: the
New World itself. And in its presence, Thoreau had been moved
to write:

Nature was here something savage and awful, though beautiful.
I looked with awe at the ground I trod on, to see what the Powers
had made there. . . . This was that Earth of which we have heard,
made out of Chaos and Old Night. Here was no man's garden,
but the unhandselled globe. It was not lawn, nor pasture, nor

mead, nor woodland, nor lea, nor arable, nor waste-land. It was
the fresh and natural surface of the planet Earth, as it was made
for ever and ever. . . .

Talk of mysteries! Thoreau had exclaimed. The real and fundamental mystery was just *this:* nature itself.

Muir did not need Thoreau to tell him this—though doubtless
it was good to feel that kinship across years—for he had made his
own discoveries, in woods, in swamps, in the carved and echoing
valleys, and here again, on the awful summit of an unscaled mountain with no least trace of mankind's existence. Here was that
America that had been in the making through eons, that existed
thus when the first humans had walked into it following game or
instincts, that awaited the accidental coming of white Europeans,
that a Scots schoolboy had read and dreamed of by a seaside
decades ago. "What canyons must be crossed," he wrote late in
life,

> what precipices ascended in reaching the summits at which we
> aim. What moats and walls, snow avalanches [,] rock avalanches
> & blustery storms defend the Alpine mansions we would enter;
> where are the most accessible slopes and passes? There are doors
> and ways opening and leading to every alpine mansion if we but
> know where to find them.

And he did.

Two months after his escape to Mount Ritter Muir found himself
in Oakland, lured there by Jeanne Carr with immediate assistance
by William Keith. It was, to be sure, a very brief trip, a kind of
scouting expedition in which the wild man of the woods (as he
imagined others regarded him) took a quick survey of civilization
and then fled in horror and confusion back to the mountains. In
retrospect, however, the venture appears as the beginning of the
end of his heroic mountain solitude, the beginning of that long and
perhaps always incomplete process of reconciliation with the world.
He would hold out in the mountains until the very end of 1874,
but the process had begun. In the intervening two years another

force for reconciliation was at work, joining Jeanne Carr—that of Emerson.

He had been an influence ever since Muir's Madison days when the Carrs and Professor Butler had talked much of him, and Muir had evidently read some of his essays, enough anyway so that when Emerson came to Yosemite in May 1871 Muir was as excited as he had ever been by the prospect of meeting another human being. (He said on one occasion that his greatest meetings had been with phenomena of the natural world like the Hider of the North but that even in that context Emerson was special.)

By the time of their meeting Emerson had finished his great work. Five years previously he had written in a poem that

It is time to be old,
To take in sail:—

Maybe it was the sense of having done just that that prompted him to take this trip into the West and to see with his own eyes what he had read so much about, what in fact so many of his best hopes for America were founded on: that great and inexhaustible land that ought to encourage the growth of a great, moral nation.

A select party of worshipers was convened in Boston to escort Emerson on his inspection of this geophysical fund of the republic, and as they trained across the American prairies that Emerson had seen on his lecture tours, the sage dipped again and again into his purple book satchel for volumes of poetry, manuscripts-in-progress, and German texts that he faithfully studied. At Salt Lake City they met Brigham Young, who seemed not to know who Emerson was and so unwittingly provided a measure of just how great, in extent anyway, this land really was.

Then California, which Emerson responded to as had so many others, jotting in his journal of "Asia at your doors and South America," but also of that "Inflamed Expectation" that haunted men here. In Oakland he met his old friends the Carrs, and since he was going to Yosemite, no doubt Jeanne Carr told him of Muir's presence there. Emerson was delighted with Yosemite, a place, as he said, that fully lived up to the brag made of it. But he was even more delighted with the rough-clad man who ran the sawmill.

Great as was the commotion made over Emerson and shy as

Muir was of social contacts, Muir's desire to talk with Emerson was such that he sent the great man a strangely worded note saying that El Capitan and Tissiack demanded that Emerson prolong his stay in the valley. The note prompted Emerson to seek out its author at Hutchings's sawmill, where Muir had built a small cabin high up at one end of the building.

"It was amusing," recalled Muir, "to see the old philosopher climb the hen-ladder into the 6 × 8 room . . . hanging over the stream." Muir showed Emerson his herbarium and sketches, and Emerson, like Le Conte before him, was immediately and profoundly impressed. Here in the flesh was that scholar-as-man-of-action of whom he had written, for whom he had called. Here before him was one who labored with his hands yet had his head in the stars. He could hardly have helped recalling Thoreau in the years when the younger man had been content enough to consider Emerson his mentor. The disciple had cut his path away from Emerson, had died early, and, as Emerson would have had to see it, unfulfilled. Now here was Muir, and Emerson's excitement at this unexpected western discovery had him "pumping unconsciously," as Muir said, and they had an afternoon of "fine, clear talk."

Emerson came back every day he stayed in the valley, and when his party had tired of the local splendors, Emerson invited Muir to accompany them on their ride out. Muir accepted on the condition that Emerson camp out one night with him in the Mariposa Grove where Muir promised to light a camp fire in the "great brown body of the Sequoias. . . ." At this suggestion, Muir remembered, Emerson became "enthusiastic like a boy [,] his sweet perennial smile became still deeper & sweeter & he said Yes [,] Yes [,] we will camp out. . . ."

They did not; the party of devoted friends would not hear of any plan that seemed so clearly to threaten the health of their hero. There had been snow in the valley during Emerson's visit, and no doubt this gave further alarm; Muir's plan was out.* They did

*Years later, Theodore Roosevelt, who took everything personally, wrote Muir from the White House that he had "always grudged Emerson's not having gone into camp with you. You would have made him perfectly comfortable and he ought to have had the experience" (Letter to Muir, Washington, D.C., January 27, 1908, Muir Papers, Holt-Atherton).

however stop for lunch in the Mariposa Grove, Emerson calling on various members of the party to recite poetry. Muir said he preferred the poems of Alice Cary to those of Byron because Cary's were far more moral; Emerson spoke of his student days at Harvard.

Then they left, Emerson riding in the rear. Where the trail dipped downward and westward, the old hero turned in the saddle and waved an affectionate farewell to the man standing alone among the giant, soaring trees. Then he was gone, and Muir felt a sudden, overpowering loneliness. *That* had been authentic contact, surely, and it may have made him realize then and in subsequent months just how much it meant to him, how much he was missing in his solitude. But for the moment, he roused himself into cheerfulness again, as he had in so many other cheerless circumstances through the years. He had made himself into a mountaineer, at home in a world where humans did not really count for much, where you had to depend on other resources. He made himself a cheering fire and shortly the voices of small woods birds spoke to him; he felt in the company of friends once more.

The meeting continued to have reverberations.* Muir wrote Emerson several letters and sent along plant specimens. Eventually, in February 1872, Emerson responded. He apologized for not having done so earlier and begged Muir not to imagine the delay a sign of anything other than the "singular disease of deferring, which kills all my designs. . . ." Then he launched directly into the subject he had opened with Muir when they had met: the debt a man of truth and intuition owes to society. On that occasion Emerson had told Muir that "society also has its claims on a man," as Muir remembered his words. Now Emerson wrote:

> I have been far from unthankful—I have everywhere testified to my friends, who should also be yours, my happiness in finding you —the right man in the right place—in your mountain tabernacle, and have expected [you] when your guardian angel should pro-

---

*It was as impressive to Emerson, apparently, as to Muir. To a list labeled "My Men" and containing the names of such as Carlyle, Agassiz, Thoreau, and Oliver Wendell Holmes, Emerson added "John Muir." It was the last name he was to add (undated fragment, Edward W. Emerson and Waldo Emerson Forbes [eds.], *Journals of Ralph Waldo Emerson,* 10 vols., Cambridge, 1909–14).

nounce that your probation and sequestration in the solitudes and
snows had reached their term, and you were to bring your ripe
fruits so rare and precious into waiting society.

He trusted, he continued, that already Muir had received his "signals from the upper powers" and would shortly roll up his drawings, poems, and herbarium and come to Emerson's Concord
home. Asa Gray would be nearby in Cambridge and Agassiz would
shortly return there from Tierra del Fuego; both would be available
to a protégé of Emerson. In a postscript Emerson said he was
sending a two-volume edition of his essays.

It was a handsome letter and a handsome offer from one of
America's most famous men, and it is a clear measure of Muir's
determination to stay where he was that he could refuse it. He did
so, but hardly blithely and not without continuing consequences,
for the summons from Emerson, carrying with it the burden of
moral duty, now joined with Jeanne Carr's more personal appeal
to make him once again take stock. In an undated fragment from
about this time, he noted that eight members of his family were
accounted "useful" members of society. Since that was so, he argued with himself, surely "one may be spared for so fine an experiment." "I will follow my instincts," he blurted, "be myself for good
or ill, and see what will be the upshot.

> As long as I live, I'll hear waterfalls and birds and winds sing. I'll
> interpret the rocks, learn the language of flood, storm, and the
> avalanche. I'll acquaint myself with the glaciers and wild gardens,
> and get as near the heart of the world as I can.

He had found, in Emerson's words, that "profoundly secret pass
that leads from fate to freedom," and he wished to stay on its far
side. And yet, here was Emerson himself urging that he return back
along that secret pass.

The Emersonian force continued its work through those
volumes he sent Muir. The second of these has been lost, but the
first bears sure evidence that Muir carried these books along with
him on his high, lonely explorations and that he read them with
scrupulous attention. The essays are heavily underscored and otherwise marked; there are a number of marginalia in Muir's hand

(almost all of them objections to Emerson's remarks about landscape); and the leaves at the end of the volume are filled with page references and passages that the reader found especially interesting.

In the words of a man who had himself deliberately turned away from the outer world to discover in the inner world his own secret pass to freedom, Muir found much to comfort him, particularly, of course, in "Self-Reliance," which is the most heavily marked essay in the book. There he read and marked the passage where Emerson had written:

> And truly it demands something godlike in him who has cast off the common motives of humanity and has ventured to trust himself for taskmaster.

And,

> Welcome evermore to gods and men is the self-helping man. For him all doors are flung wide; him all tongues greet, all honors crown, all eyes follow with desire. Our love goes out to him because he did not need it. We solicitously and apologetically caress and celebrate him because he held on his way and scorned our disapprobation. The gods love him because men hated him.

Muir also marked passages in which Emerson had said that one's genius might well lead one to the very edge of what the world would think madness, and that there was something almost insane about the works and acts of a man who is truly carried away with the force of an interior conviction. Men commonly regard such an inspired one as a "fool and a churl for a long season," Emerson wrote in "The Poet." Muir also marked the passage that included the observation that this general disapprobation "is the screen and sheath in which Pan has protected his well-beloved flower. . . ."

But Emerson also had much to say in these pages about the ultimate necessity of the hero's acting in this world. In his own life he had experienced the struggle between individual freedom and public service that inevitably involves the abridgment of freedom and maybe even its annulment. He had never quite resolved the conflict for himself, but he knew it to be fundamental, both to the individual's life and to the life of a democratic republic. For while

(saying recalled by Patricia Sun — to be a genius is nothing if you dont bring it into the world.

the development of the inner man was essential, it was also crucial
for the individual to bring the fruits of his sovereign individuality
to what Emerson called "the combatants and demagogues in the
dusty arena below." He had always been somewhat disappointed
in Thoreau on this account and had said as much in his graveside
eulogy of Thoreau in 1862.

Muir marked several passages in which Emerson addressed the
problem. In the so-called "Divinity School Address" Emerson had
said that it was a necessary consequence of true conversation with
one's soul to wish to impart the knowledge thus gained to others.
"If utterance is denied," he said, "the thought lies like a burden on
the man.

> Always the seer is the sayer. Somehow his dream is told; somehow
> he publishes it with solemn joy: sometimes with pencil on canvas,
> sometimes with chisel on stone, sometimes in towers and aisles of
> granite, his soul's worship is builded; sometimes in anthems of
> indefinite music; but clearest and most permanent, in words.

In "The Method of Nature" Muir marked the passage where Emerson had quoted Emanuel Swedenborg to the effect that "the spirits
who knew truth in this life, but did it not, at death shall lose their
knowledge."

Muir had a generous amount of social conscience; it was one
aspect of his Christian heritage. And there is no doubt that what he
heard from Jeanne Carr and then from Emerson had something of
that force and appeal to it, though in both it had an overlay of
Swedenborgianism that disguised and broadened the base. And in
marking the passage on the necessary relationship between knowing truth and doing it, Muir was perhaps acknowledging the unpleasant fact that for him escape could not be final, indeed should
not be. He believed he had found truth, had climbed high enough,
wandered far enough to meet it. Translating it to others was something else again, and he was not easily persuaded it was possible.

One thing was clear by 1873, however: that he had attained
something in his solitude that the world wanted. Early in the Yosemite years, when Jeanne Carr had urged him to give his gifts to
the world, he had said that what he had nobody wanted. Like the
mountain mystics of old, he believed that those below were too

caught up in the burdensome round of daily life to be able to attend lessons of eternity. But the ready acceptance of his essays and his growing reputation among distinguished writers and scientists made it impossible honestly to hold to this opinion. Odd as it was to him, and whatever it might mean, he *was* in some kind of demand. If that demand was easily enough avoided by the simple expedient of climbing so high that the demand itself ceased to be of consequence, losing its force in the rarer zones, yet there was a growing demand within him that could not so simply be avoided. Writing more and more clearly "open" letters to Jeanne Carr and carrying Emerson in his saddlebags, he pondered the possibilities of his return through the secret pass.

Civilization
and Its
Discontents

I suppose I must go into society this winter,"
he wrote Sarah in mid-November 1873 from Yosemite. "I would
rather go back in some undiscoverable corner beneath the rafters
of an old garret with my notes and books and listen to the winter
rapping and blowing on the roof. May start for Oakland in a day
or two." He had committed himself to writing up some of his Sierra
experiences for publication, and while this did not in itself make a
descent into the Bay area imperative, the commitment clearly symbolized something to him. The grand formative experiences in the
mountains were behind him now, and he would retail them as best
he might for an unknown audience. Perhaps he felt that to do so
in Yosemite itself would be wrong, a kind of violation of the spirit
of that place and of the intensely personal history he had enacted
there. If he had to come down into the world, forsaking the eterni-
ties amid which he had been living, then it might as well be the city
itself, locus and nexus of civilization.

Since summer he had been girding himself for this, and his
wilderness wanderings had about them an almost desperate quality,
as if he would compress into a final few months of freedom enough

memorable experiences to live on in an indefinite, cloudy future. Early in the summer he had guided a group including Jeanne Carr, his old Wisconsin friend Emily Pelton, and William Keith into Yosemite and above; then he had plunged directly into the high Sierras from early August to the beginning of September, an exploration, so he wrote Sarah, that was his "longest and hardest" yet. Returned from that, he immediately began an even longer and more arduous excursion to the Kings River region, Kern River, and ultimately Lake Tahoe lasting until the middle of November. In the course of it he covered more than a thousand miles, scaled unnamed peaks (including one that would become known as Mount Whitney), and tracked the glaciers to their homes. Emerson had once written, "Give me health and a day, and I will make the pomp of emperors ridiculous." Muir had marked the passage approvingly, but in actual experience of the wilderness, the wild heart of that nature both men celebrated, Muir had gone far beyond his intellectual mentor. Perhaps with this in mind, he wrote Jeanne Carr in the midst of the season's last exploration, "Give me a summer and a bunch of matches and a sack of meal and I will climb every mountain in the region."

But summer could not last forever, even for one whose hardihood extended the season of exploration well beyond its normal boundaries. By the middle of November, bowing to the season and the coming on of uncertain weather, he had retreated to Yosemite, whence he wrote Sarah of his reluctant descent into Oakland.

The plan had been for Muir to live with the Carrs (an old, fond hope of hers dating back to Madison days) while he composed his Sierra studies for the *Overland Monthly,* but when he arrived in Oakland he found the Carrs mourning the death of their eldest son, Ned, who had at last succumbed to a disease he had contracted on the Amazon. Here was the first of those events that were to shadow the rest of Jeanne Carr's life and that in fixed, inexorable succession would bring her the loss of a second son, her husband's loss of place at the university, and at last the failure of their hopes for a new life in Pasadena, where they had tried to establish an intellectual and artistic colony. But for now, Muir consoled the Carrs as best he could and took lodgings with other Oakland friends, the J. B. McChesneys.

McChesney was the principal of Oakland High School, a bookish man who like many on both sides of the Atlantic had been considerably taken with the cultural theories of Ruskin. "Mac," as Muir knew him, had earlier sent Muir some volumes of the British sage, which prompted a vigorous response from the recipient. "Ruskin is great," Muir wrote, "but not a great man, only a ready-to-burst bud of a man. He is fettered & bounded though his chain is long." Then deeper feelings bubbled forth, provoked by Muir's reading of *Modern Painters,* especially volumes one, four, and five, where Ruskin discusses the aesthetics of mountains. "I have never experiences his mtn. gloom wh doubtless is bogle humbug," the exasperated mountaineer wrote from Yosemite. "But the worst thing I find in his book is his lack of faith in the scriptures of nature." As earlier he had "devoutly disbelieved" Whitney's catastrophic theories of the valley's formation, so here Muir rejected Ruskin's contention that in the mountains man beheld the juxtaposition of God and Satan. "Here," Muir wrote, "I want to say so much that I cannot say anything. Onely [*sic*] he is an infidel to nature and knows nothing about her." Christianity, he continued, and "mountainanity are streams from the same fountain," and in reading Ruskin's heresies of "Mtn gloom & mtn evil & mtn devil & the unwholesome-ness of mtn beauty as everyday bread, I wish I were a preacher."

Now in Oakland he was to have his chance to be a kind of preacher, trying in his Sierra essays to convert readers to an authentic appreciation of mountains, ice, and the grand conformations of their landscape. It would not be an easy task for him, nor was he sanguine about success, but he settled to it with a grim determination that occasionally shows itself in a stiffness and formality of literary style that those who knew him well and had heard the remarkable torrent of his talk found slightly disappointing. Ever after, even when Muir had achieved literary fame, some of these friends would wistfully claim that the artistic genius of the man remained locked and lost in the talk of random evenings when Muir, glad of escape from the loneliness of his littered desk, would descend to the drawing room and tell of that beautiful wild world from which he came.

The days of literary labor in his upstairs room at the McChesneys' seemed both endless and confining to one who had accustomed himself to great blocks of sun- and air-filtered time where no clock kept hours and where none attended his schedule. Writing letters he had found easy enough, and when he had been in the grip of inspiration, as so often when writing Jeanne Carr, these had flowed out into long, rhythmic screeds. Writing for publication was another thing, and he quickly found it tough, agonizing work; his early struggles with formal composition now deepened into a genuine distaste for the work, a habit of mind that would last the rest of his life. Endless revisions were a telltale sign of this, and he formed the habit of writing on rough, cheap paper, leaving large spaces between his lines so that he could go back again and again, fussing with his periods until he abandoned them as the best of bad jobs. His friends brought this literary tic to his attention, but he could not break himself of it.

He took most of his meals at restaurants, dressed casually with always about him some sprig of greenery, a talismanic link with forsaken freedom, mulling matters of composition over with his meals. And when he simply could not keep himself at his work he would enter the McChesney family circle, especially if there were an opportunity to play with the McChesneys' little daughter, Alice. Then too there were visits from his friend and fellow Scot, William Keith, who would come over from San Francisco to cheer Muir, often bringing with him John Swett, a pioneer in California public education who would eventually offer Muir a place in his household while he completed the last of his *Studies in the Sierra.*

In May 1874 the first of the studies appeared in the *Overland,* and they kept appearing in the months following until with "Mountain Building" in January 1875 the series was complete. By that time, however, their author, his work done, had in September 1874 run away to the mountains and buried himself in them.

He had been trudging city streets on a September day, weary of his work and the city with its poisonous air, when he had chanced upon a bloom of goldenrod struggling up at the margin of a sidewalk. He gazed upon it with his old love now mingled with regret, and as he did so the weed brought home to him with sudden, irresistible force an awareness of how estranged he was becoming from the steady circumambience of the world beyond the city. The blooming of the goldenrod spelled the end of summer, and here

he was, still imprisoned in the city's lifeless routines! Muir went
back to his room, scooped up a bundle of clothes and notebooks,
and caught the train for Turlock.

"Shrunken and lean," as he described his appearance, he was
dazed by the motion of the train as it rattled down the Santa Clara
Valley, but the sight of a big glacial boulder stranded in a field at
the entrance to the Livermore Pass brought him to himself. At
Lathrop the passengers suppered and changed trains; there in the
last light Muir stood gazing on the harvested wheat fields, the new
moon hanging over them "like a sickle." To the north he could see
Ursa Major, and he picked out the Milky Way curving "sublimely
through the broadcast stars like some grand celestial moraine with
planets for boulders. . . ." He spent the night at Turlock and then
in the new, hot sun of a September morn set off on foot for the
Sierras.

Before he had walked ten miles he felt faint and footsore, and
still this labor was delightful to him after the rigors of writing and
the feel of dead pavements beneath his feet. "Any kind of simple
natural destruction is preferable to the numb, dumb apathetic
deaths of a town," he would write once he had reached the mountains. And quickly enough he lost the sense of this as hot, tiring
work, for he began to pick up the sights and sounds of his old home
at Twenty Hill Hollow where six years before he had done his
apprentice shepherding. The familiar flowers nodded patient greetings; a lark called; butterflies fluttered by his hot cheeks. He threw
down his bundle and surrendered to the land and the moment,
heedless now of the growing strength of the sun, the hour his
warning watch pointed, the miles yet to travel. He was, as he said,
"wild once more," and he cared for nothing but that. Everything
was brimful of excitement for him, and he spent uncounted hours
tracing the tracks of lizards and grasshoppers, recording in his
notebook their characteristic hieroglyphics on the sand. He caught
a field mouse, then freed it to watch it embroider the sandy soil with
its tiny tracks.

At noon he came upon a group of grangers at dinner in the
fields. Though his stomach was too tender from his diet of restaurant food to allow him to partake of their bacon and beans, still he
was glad to take buttermilk and water with them. He went
on refreshed to the "sacred" Merced and bathed in it, listening to

its song of mountain origins as it slid over the shining brown stones.

The next evening at Hopeton he caught his faithful Brownie, mounted him, and cantered through the fragrant fields to Pat Delaney's on the Tuolumne where his old benefactor welcomed him "in the old good uncivilized way, not to be misunderstood." In the morning he went on toward Coulterville, noting as he climbed the astonishing work of the hydraulic miners who had laid open huge sections of the Tuolumne banks in a mechanized, intensified continuation of the gold rush. At Coulterville he had a surprise. Where once he had entered that little place an unknown wanderer who knew only that he wanted to see Yosemite, now he found that he was a minor celebrity, for his Sierra essays had been read here, and he was told copies of the *Overland* had even penetrated Bloody Canyon and reached Mono.

That evening he and A. G. Black, the Yosemite pioneer, rode in moonlight up through a sugar-pine forest to Black's ranch above Coulterville, and Muir now felt truly at home. The keen wind that had mountain winter in it caressed his brow, and he could feel the rosiny forest taking the city's staleness out of him almost by the moment. As they rode on, the sounds of the forest were joined by unseen human voices rising in a chant, and Muir heard the falling boulder, the rushing stream, the tones of mountain wind in them. "That's the death song," Black said softly as they reined in. "Some Indian is dead." Shortly, they saw the barred glow of two large fires far into the woods and wisely forbore closer approach.

Higher and farther they rode, much of the time in such deep shadow that Muir simply had to trust Brownie to know the way. The far bank of the North Fork of the Merced glowed silver in moonlight, and the stream itself seemed to pronounce a "prolonged Aaaaaah," as if sharing Muir's release. Before sleep at Black's he wrote convalescent lines in his journal, speaking of himself as weary and seeking "with damaged instinct the high founts of nature." Compared to his present surroundings the vaunted advantages of civilization seemed more than ever a dangerous delusion. All those who lived below, he avowed, appeared to be "more or less sick; there is not a perfectly sane man in San Francisco." Then came this apostrophe, jagged, fragmented, as though its author were breathless with haste:

> Go now and then for fresh life—if most of humanity must go through this town stage of development—just as divers hold their breath and come ever and anon to the surface to breathe. . . . Go whether or not you have faith. . . . Form parties, if you must be social. . . . Anyway, go up and away for life; be fleet!

Here and in the few lines that followed Muir appeared to be addressing himself at the same time he addressed those still caught in the "pagan slavery" of the city. The new note here derived from the writer's sense that though he had escaped the city's slavery, still that escape could not be final. Tellingly, he compared his stay in Oakland to that near-fatal and compulsory descent into the well at Hickory Hill. And maybe the comparison was complete enough to include the recollection that after a brief convalescence from the "choke damp" he had been sent back into the fields and their waiting work.

There is much of the valedictory in the subsequent journal entries he made when he reached Yosemite the day following and also in the long, extraordinary letter he wrote to Jeanne Carr. In his flight from Oakland he had been quite conscious that he was fleeing her, too, her world and the literary and social connections she had so patiently forged for him. Sitting under his favorite pine at Black's Hotel, he wrote to tell her that as soon as he had recovered something of himself, her spirit had come up into the mountains and joined him there. On the moonlight-splashed slopes along the North Fork of the Merced he had felt her nearness. "I reached up," he told her,

> as Browny [sic] carried me underneath a big Douglas spruce and plucked one of its long plumy sprays, which brought you from the Oakland dead in a moment. You are more spruce than pine, though I never definitely knew it till now.

Yet, though he felt her presence, the farther he went into the mountains' heart, the more remote and insubstantial even the most intimate of human relationships came to seem. Describing his night trip up the river with Black, he wrote of his entrance into the magic woods where "a thousand arms were waved in solemn blessing," and also of the complete "absorption of one's life into the spirit of the mountain woods." Here no one could either hate or love, nor could one have "any distinctive love of friends. The dearest and best of you all seemed of no special account, mere trifles." He would not wish to appear ungrateful or cold, only changed, translated back into one different from him they had known. So he added that he had been rereading her letters, and these at least had not been diminished by his escape. "Altogether," he told her, "they form a precious volume whose sentences are more intimately connected with my mountain work than any will be able to appreciate." The valedictory note became more insistent at the letter's close. "None of the rocks seems to call me now," he wrote, "nor any of the distant mountains. Surely this Merced and Tuolumne chapter of my life is done." He signed this, "Ever lovingly yours."

It would not be so simple to sign off from this chapter of his life. Near the end of September, he wrote in his journal that the pines, rocks, and water ouzels seemed "true and immortal," yet somehow he felt satisfied to leave them "and labor in other fields." But he did not. Instead, he hung about the valley, visiting old haunts, delaying that return to civilization that he and all his friends appeared to regard as inevitable. Then on October 7, he wrote a short, definitive letter to Jeanne Carr, telling her where he had been and in more than one sense where he would be going. He had been in the Merced Canyon revisiting the scenes of the camping trip he had taken her on the previous summer with Keith and the others, and now he would go over the mountains "to Mono and Lake Tahoe. Will be in Tahoe in a week, thence anywhere Shastaward, etc. I think I may be at Brownsville, Yuba County, where I may get a letter from you." This proved an accurate enough physical itinerary, and there was included this other sort of itinerary which was to prove even more accurate:

> Civilization and fever and all the morbidness that has been hooted at me have not dimmed my glacial eye, and I care to live only to entice people to look at Nature's loveliness. My own special self is nothing.

So he went "Shastaward" and climbed the mountain on November 2, getting back to his base camp just as a big storm blew in. He was happily snugged in, surrounded by firewood, content with his notebooks and breadsack, when rescue came and he had reluctantly to accept it. As he wrote in a delightful letter to his "Dear Highland Lassie Alice" (McChesney), he had climbed Shasta in that season because he loved snow and mountains and storms, and his only regret was that he had been "rescued" and so prevented from experiencing the full and finest effects of the weather. Even on the wintery slopes of Shasta, so it appeared, he was not safe from civilization. The men of towns, houses, and comforts *would* seek him out and carry him back with them.

Pondering the matter in the following weeks as he explored in the Shasta region, he wrote Jeanne Carr on December 21 that he was feeling a "sort of nervous fear of another period of town dark, but I don't want to be silly about it. The sun glow will all fade out of me, and I will be deathly as Shasta in the dark." But, he added with the kind of grim optimism that would come to characterize him more frequently, "mornings will come, dawnings of some kind, and if not, I have lived more than a common eternity already."

At least in a heavy gale on the Yuba he was safe enough from the meddling hand of civilization, for no one but he would wish to be out in the forest in such weather. He had been exploring a valley that led into the Yuba when the gale blew up, but rather than retreat from the woods where he heard trees crashing "every two or three minutes," Muir sought out the very heart of the phenomenon: he climbed to the top of a 100-foot Douglas spruce, which waved and circled wildly in a flashing sea of pines. The great wind had come from the sea, and he thought he could detect in it the scent of salt, his mind ranging back to that day in the hot lands of Florida when he had smelled the Gulf and all his North Sea boyhood had come rushing back.

When the wind began to lower, he climbed down from his high perch and sauntered through the calming woods as the lowering sun changed the forest light to a deep amber. Later, in an essay he would write on this experience, "A Wind-Storm in the Forests," he noted that he had learned that trees like men were travelers:

We all travel the milky way together, trees and men; but it never occurred to me until this storm-day, while swinging in the wind, that trees are travelers, in the ordinary sense. They make many journeys, not extensive ones, it is true; but our own little journeys, away and back again, are only little more than tree-wavings; many of them not so much.

When Muir descended into Oakland again and took up lodgings with the Swetts, he was commencing a pattern that would endure for the remainder of his years. Henceforth he would be a man of civilization who would make periodic escapes into the wildernesses of the globe. But never again would he be a man of the wilderness whose time and travels were distinctly his own. He knew as much now and said so in a letter to Sarah in late February 1875. "I have not yet in all my wanderings," he wrote frankly, "found a single person so free as myself." But now that freedom seemed a thing of the past, for he felt "bound to my studies, and the laws of my own life." At times he felt "as if driven with whips and ridden upon. When in the woods I sit at times for hours watching birds or squirrels or looking down into the faces of flowers without suffering any feeling of haste. Yet I am swept onward in a general current that bears on irresistibly."

He spent much of the spring of 1875 writing up his recent experiences, his only escape a journey to Shasta in April with a party from the Coast and Geodetic Survey. The trip was a costly one for him. He and a companion, Jerome Fay, were trapped in a fierce storm on the mountain high above their base camp and were obliged to spend an interminable night in some shallow hot springs. They made it down to rescue in the morning, but Muir's feet were badly frostbitten, and he was to suffer the consequences for the rest of his life. As it was, he admitted to Jeanne Carr, he felt "battered and scarred like a log that has come down the Tuolumne in flood-time."

In April his essay "Wild Wool" appeared in the *Overland Monthly,* the result of his Shasta excursion of the previous year with some Scots sheep hunters. In many respects it was typical of what Muir had been writing for some years in his journals, in

letters to friends, and of late in periodicals. There was the same
delight in anything natural, the same fine descriptions of the wild
world, the characteristic microcosmic inspections that imply the
macrocosm. But there was something new too, a tone and intention suggestive of the altered circumstances of his life. In "Wild
Wool" the writer speaks as a man of civilization addressing his
fellows. Here he would try to do precisely what he had told Jeanne
Carr was his goal: to entice others to look at Nature's loveliness.
What he would like to gain, he said, is a "hearing on behalf of
Nature," Nature free, unimproved, unappropriated: wild Nature.
For pure wildness, the writer had discovered, is "the one great
want" of our civilization. The essay is strongly reminiscent of
Thoreau's posthumously published essay "Walking," where the
writer begins his discourse in the village, talking to his fellow vil-
lagers as one of them but one who would like to take them on a
"saunter" out of the village, so to speak "a word for Nature, for
absolute freedom and wildness. . . ." For Thoreau, too, "from
the forest and wilderness come the tonics and barks which brace
mankind."*

With the coming of summer he made for the Sierras once more,
but now in the company of others and with specific literary assign-
ments. Still, the venture was a tonic to him, however circumscribed,
and he groaned over the prospect of his return. From Yosemite at
the end of July he wrote Jeanne Carr that John Swett, "who is
brother now, papa then," and who had been with him on recent
rambles, was ordering Muir "home to booking." "Bless me," he
broke out, "what an awful thing town duty is! I was once free as
any pine-playing wind, and I feel that I have still a good length of

---

*Muir knew Thoreau's essay and greatly admired it, though not without
reservation. Sometime in the early 1870s he made journal remarks on "Walking"
and there perhaps intentionally misunderstood some of Thoreau's rhetorical strategy (Engberg and Wesling [eds.], *John Muir: To Yosemite and Beyond*, p. 160).
Much later, Muir purchased the 1906 edition of *The Writings of Henry David
Thoreau* and heavily marked the essay there (Muir's personal library in the Muir
Papers, Holt-Atherton). By the end of his life Muir knew Thoreau so well he could
quote whole passages from the works, especially *Walden*. Bailey Millard, who
knew Muir in his last years, reported that Emerson had said Muir would be the
perfect man to edit Thoreau's works (Bailey Millard, "A Skyland Philosopher,"
Bookman's, February, 1908).

line, but alack! there seems to be a hook or two of civilization in me that I would fain pull out, yet *would not pull out*—O, O, O!!!"

For the moment, anyway, he would use the full length of his line, refusing Oakland and booking and going instead on an extended, solitary exploration of the sequoia belt that took him from Yosemite in August to the White River in Tulare County by the end of October. But if at the outset he had thought of this as an escape from or deferment of city obligations, he was soon enough mistaken. The exploration was, of course, both of these, but he *was* at last on a length of line, and, moreover, he carried with him now the concerns of that civilization to which he belonged. So in the journal entries of these weeks there intruded a speculative concern for the appropriate relationship between civilization and the wilderness. And here there were few intellectual blazes to follow; for though many had explored the wildernesses of America, few had done so as carefully as Muir, and even fewer had cared to work out the terms of a potentially nurturing relationship between a civilization and its wild lands.

At the outset, Muir felt himself unprepared to develop what amounted to a land ethic, and indeed, long after he had become a legend and a symbol of the preservationist cause, there remained a kind of quizzicality to his public utterances, as if even after so many years in the highest reaches of public life he could not quite understand how such a task had fallen to him. But in the late summer of 1875, he felt compelled to make a beginning.

Once in the sequoia belt, he settled into established patterns, especially that calm waiting in the woods that he had learned was necessary to get at the magic of the place: not just to see the "wood-dwellers, winged or footed," who would only reveal themselves to the patient observer; but also to experience that deeper magic of the slow play of light and air in the trees, the fullness of a forest day from dawning to night. And once he had reentered the timeless circle of the forest he saw again how different was the pace and pulse of that world he had come to live in. "Talk of immortality!" he wrote, perhaps unconsciously again echoing Thoreau. "After a whole day in the woods, we are already immortal. When is the end of such a day . . . ?"

So, in these woods he was whole once more, but that wholeness was circumscribed as it had not been before, not only by thoughts of civilization but also by the incursions of that civilization into the woods: a cow walking through a meadow suddenly signified the coming commercialization of the wilderness and caused Muir to wonder whether it was America's destiny to use up every last one of its wild places. "I often wonder," he wrote in his journal,

what man will do with the mountains—that is with their utilizable, destructible garments. Will he cut down all the trees to make ships and houses? If so, what will be the final and far upshot? Will human destructions like those of Nature—fire and flood and earthquake—work out a higher good, a finer beauty? Will a better civilization come in accord with obvious nature, and all this wild beauty be set to human poetry and song? Another universal outpouring of lava, or the coming of a glacial period could scarce wipe out the flowers and shrubs more effectually than do the sheep. And what then is coming? What is the human part of the mountains' destiny?

The question continued with him through the sequoia belt, transforming the escape into a purposeful examination of what he believed was his civilization's greatest resource. And the examination was powerfully disturbing, since it suggested that here at least the human part of the mountains' destiny was to extract all of their wealth as quickly as possible, as wastefully as seemed expedient without a thought for the morrow—to say nothing of a thought for what other uses the mountains and their forests might possess. It looked as if the gold-rush mentality had simply shifted its object to timber. Near the southwestern extreme of the King's River sequoia belt he came upon Hyde's Mill, "booming and moaning like a bad ghost," churning out 2 million board feet a year—and wasting perhaps triple that, for the *Sequoia gigantea* shattered like glass when felled so that most of a tree would be rendered useless for commercial purposes. This was but one of five mills Muir found operating in or near the belt, and their cutting was not all, for the operators routinely burned the nonusable refuse so as to get farther in, and this destroyed the seedlings and saplings and prevented forest renewal.

Muir was not so removed from the realities of his time as to imagine that wood, and plenty of it, was not a great necessity. But what began gnawing at him among the giant trees—while the mill operators gnawed at the trees themselves—was the narrowness of his world's view of woods. The sequoias were popularly viewed simply as massive blocks of salable material and the forests as places of concentrated commercial potential. Such a view passed for sober realism. But there was another view that saw the sequoias as "antediluvian monuments, through which we gaze in contemplation as through windows into the deeps of primeval time" (this in *my view!* a journal entry of early September). And there was a view of forests as places where humans could, as in primeval days, feel divinity surrounding and encompassing them. It was for this reason that ancient peoples, including the Greeks and Romans, had preserved their sacred groves, and even recent peoples of the Old World had saved out sacred groves amid the cultivated countryside. The woods, towering above man, speaking of duration and the mystery of existence, were, so Muir wrote, a necessary "counterpart of man." Their beauty, he felt, "—all their forms and voices and scents —seem, as they really are, reminiscences of something already experienced. . . ."

Yet "how little note is taken of the deeds of Nature!" he wrote in solitary astonishment.

> What paper publishes her reports? If one pine were placed in a town square, what admiration it would excite! Yet who is conscious of the pine-tree multitudes in the free woods, though open to everybody? Who publishes the sheet-music of the winds, or the written music of water written in river-lines? Who reports the works and ways of the clouds, those wondrous creations coming into being every day like freshly upheaved mountains? And what record is kept of Nature's colors—the clothes she wears—of her birds, her beasts—her livestock?

He had yet to find, he wrote on September 10, the man "who had caught the rhythm of the big, slow pulse-beats of Nature." And still the busy world below beat on, ignorant of the real treasure it had in these mountain groves and thus willing that they be mined and milled speedily out of existence.

In early November, near the boundary of the sequoia belt,

Muir paused for a look back over the way of his thoughts. He imagined the moiling multitudes below in the cities and towns of America, dying slow deaths "for want of what these grand old woods can give." And though it might be futile, still he felt compelled to shout, "Ho, come to the Sierra forests. The King is waiting for you—King Sequoia!" Our crude civilization, he wrote, "engenders a multitude of wants,

> and lawgivers are ever at their wits' end devising. The hall and the theater and the church have been invented, and compulsory education. Why not compulsory recreation . . . ? Our forefathers forged chains of duty and habit, which bind us notwithstanding our boasted freedom, and we ourselves in desperation add link to link, groaning and making medicinal laws for relief. Yet few think of pure rest or of the healing power of Nature. How hard to pull or shake people out of town!

How hard, too, for him ultimately to avoid town: no snug cabin now in the snowy valley nor a hangnest on the end of a sawmill where after work a man might be content with his books and the blank, inviting pages of notebooks to be filled with thoughts meant for no one but himself. Instead, the Swett home on Taylor Street in busy, building San Francisco, where fully a quarter of the state's population lived chockablock in states of ease or unrest Muir could only wonder at. How hard once again to adjust himself to city routines, the unforgiving texture of pavements, the unnourishing fare of restaurants.

Swett was himself hard, a compactly built ex-schoolmaster with a schoolmaster's view of duty and intellectual discipline. He dared occasionally to bully his houseguest in an effort to get him to write down some fraction of that fund of nature stories Muir had in him. Once in civilization, Muir much preferred talking to writing and would gladly spend hours—and much imaginative energy as well —entertaining listeners with tales of water ouzels and windstorms. Swett knew the technique as avoidance and would actually order Muir up to his room to write what he had just so superbly told— and sometimes Muir would actually go.

When not wrestling with problems of composition Muir spent

hours walking the city's hills, catching from their summits vistas of the great bay. On its other side lay the flowered and tree-flocked hills of Marin County, and often Muir's truant steps would lead him to the ferry that would take him over there to wander in a green solitude seemingly far removed from the city. Sometimes, to, he would visit "Willie" Keith in the latter's amazingly cluttered studio, where amid a haze of smoke (some of it Muir's, for he had taken up a pipe) the two disputatious Scots would argue any subject that might arise. He spent time also with the Le Conte brothers, Joseph and John, the latter now president of the University of California, and also at the Oakland Public Library, where he had lengthy talks with Ina Coolbrith, librarian and literary lioness.

In January 1876, he gave his first public lecture, a talk on glaciers and forests to the Literary Institute of Sacramento. Despite his skills as an informal monologist, Muir was miserably uneasy at the prospect of a formal presentation. Keith, witnessing his friend's anxiety, suggested he take with him one of his mountain landscape canvases for company, telling Muir to look at the painting to cure his nervousness. It was, to be sure, an unconventional technique, but it got Muir over his initial jitters, and shortly he was launched on his subject. The speech was a great success, and Muir had now begun a career as a public speaker.

January was also the month he made another kind of entrance into that "dusty arena" of public discourse of which Emerson had written, for in this month Muir wrote his first essay on forest conservation. Like his first published essay, "Yosemite Glaciers," this was an astonishing debut. "God's First Temples: How Shall We Preserve Our Forests?" appeared February 9, 1876, in the Sacramento *Record-Union* and was inspired by Muir's autumn tour of the sequoia belt. He took his title from William Cullen Bryant's famous poem, "A Forest Hymn," as if he would openly and forcefully bring the insights of the Romantics to bear on the cultural problems of his time. The idea of the sacred grove loomed in the background of the essay, which moved from a deft and loving description of the high groves, down along the courses of the Sierra streams, and finally into the broad light of the lowlands—and legislation. The organization was at once so natural and easy that the reader was led to an assent that might not have been forthcoming from a more polemical approach. Yet for all its charm, this was a tough, uncom-

promising essay. Muir claimed that the destruction of the Sierra
forests was proceeding at such a rate that in the foreseeable future
the slopes would be stripped and the lowlands inundated with the
floodwaters formerly held and conserved by the forests' root systems. Nothing, he argued, in the whole bonanza history of California—not the wasteful practices of the gold rush, nor the
soil-stripping work of the wildcat farmers, nor even the destructive
operations of the hydraulic miners—equaled this calamity, for it
was essentially permanent and irreversible. The forests belts, he
said, were being "burned and cut down and wasted like a field of
unprotected grain, and once destroyed can never be wholly re-
stored even by centuries of persistent and painstaking cultivation."
The only thing that could possibly prevent the calamity was legislative intervention, hardly a popular remedy in these years when
most Americans seemed to believe that neither the federal nor local
governments should have any role in social planning.

Whether "our loose jointed Government" could organize itself
to stop the timber miners and the sheepmen who wantonly burned
the forests to create paths and pastures was a moot question, as Muir
knew, but his essay left the question hanging in the reader's mind.
There it might possibly join kindred questions relating to the future
of America, questions that hung in clusters like storm clouds as the
republic uneasily celebrated its first hundred years.

The thrust of Muir's *Record-Union* essay plainly revealed a sharpened awareness of the problems he had pondered on his exploration of the sequoia belt. What indeed would be the "final and
far upshot" for a nation that gobbled up all its wildernesses to
get at their resources? What would America be like without any
wilderness?
Some few, like Muir, were asking this and allied questions
about the future of what had once popularly been known as "Nature's nation." The questions had arisen ever since the force and
direction of the culture had become clear in the 1830s. Then, when
the "West" meant everything beyond the Mississippi, travelers into
it had predicted a time when it would cease to exist as a distinctive
region giving a special tone to the culture. The West was just
another name for wildness, as Thoreau had put it in "Walking," but

by the 1830s it was possible to see that wildness by any name would not be a part of future America, that the entire country would soon enough be made over in the image of the Old World. Audubon had seen this and said so. So too had George Catlin, who had gone even farther afield than Audubon, had seen the buffalo-dark plains and the amazing spectacle of American life beyond the farthest frontier, and had wanted some portion of the wilderness preserved from what he knew would be its eventual destruction. Even now as Muir began publicly to address the wilderness question an intrepid few were still searching out the vestiges of the wild New World as if in these alone might you encounter the soul of the continent: George Bird Grinnell, for instance, who was going among the Pawnee, the Cheyenne, and the Blackfeet and learning life from their perspective; or James Willard Schultz, who instead of taking the grand tour of the Old World went up the Missouri in a steamer to live and ride with the Blackfeet. Their elegaic books would not appear for some years, but the note of elegy for a vanishing or already lost New World was in the air, even if all but drowned out in the thunderous martial airs that accompanied the centennial celebration.

America no longer seemed "Nature's nation." The great, fecund wilderness had not apparently nurtured and brought forth a great people, as Jefferson, Crèvecoeur, and Emerson had hoped. Instead, the wild lands had been pillaged of their resources, and the nation had derived purely economic benefits therefrom. The moral and spiritual benefits that some had supposed would accrue to America from its wild lands had not, and Americans in 1876 appeared, if anything, more estranged from nature and from their lands than their counterparts in the Old World.

At Philadelphia, though, where the official centennial celebration was held, the dominant note was anything but elegaic. There all was energetically, even relentlessly optimistic, and the symbol of the republic at one hundred was not any aspect of the wilderness nor even the old icon of the plow—it was a machine. The Corliss steam engine stood thirty-nine feet high, weighed almost 680 tons, and could deliver an astonishing 2,500 horsepower. It supplied power for all the other mechanical marvels in Machinery Hall, and when President Grant, accompanied by the Emperor of Brazil, turned the crank that set the gigantic machine—and all the others, too—into smooth, regular motion a thrill of emotion swept through the crowd. Here surely was a symbolic tableau: Grant, the man of arms and iron will, now tragically miscast as a peacetime president and rather aimlessly presiding over that giveaway of the national resources subsequently to be known as the "Great Barbecue"; and the machine that towered above even so heroic a figure and that (as Henry Adams was later to note) the nation seemed fairly to worship as men had once gone down on their knees before mountains or colossal statues. William Dean Howells, who was there for Grant's ceremonial performance, somewhat ruefully admitted that the Corliss machine seemed more truly expressive of the national genius than anything else.

Maybe the machine *was* the truest expression of the national genius, and maybe the future lay with machines, but could the machine and a machine-oriented culture produce those moral and spiritual blessings that were the ultimate promise of American life —and that were supposed to have been naturally conferred by the American landscape? This was a question, a fundamental if publicly unacknowledged doubt, and beneath the fanfare, fireworks, and spread-eagle oratory of the centennial there was pessimism, frustration, and real anger about the present condition of the American experiment. Something significant seemed to have been lost over the hundred-year stretch, and since the war's end the loss, however identified, had become more generally apparent.

During the war's red years it had been possible to believe that all the slaughter and sacrifice were the necessary consequences of great moral contradictions that had long existed and that out of the war the nation would be reborn, rededicated to the deepest American dream: individual and collective regeneration in this still-beautiful land. In an unexpected way the reform movements of the previous three decades had coalesced in the abolitionist crusade that the war was bringing to a triumphant conclusion. Reform, genuine reform, had won the day and prepared the future.

It had not happened so. The war, instead of revitalizing American culture, seemed to have taken something vital out of it. A high idealism had been left behind on a hundred battlefields, and a new, hard-boiled and empty cynicism had survived. The same Howells who had pondered the significance of the Corliss machine noted the pervasive sense of loss that followed the Union victory. He recalled the talk of a long Ohio summer twilight at the beginning of the '70s when he had stopped at the home of James A. Garfield, then an Ohio congressman. In the course of the evening, conversation had turned to the great New England literary figures Howells had come personally to know, and Garfield became so excited by his guest's anecdotes that he had gone to the fences of the homes adjoining his to call the neighbors. The greatness of these men, the high idealism they had articulated for the nation, could still on occasion shed its glow down the corridor of years. But that had not been the end of the talking, for in the historical order of things talk of the war had succeeded talk of the New England giants. Garfield told his listeners of another summer's eve when with his command he had ridden into the valley of the Kanawha in West Virginia and had seen there what he took to be the forms of sleeping men in a green meadow. "Suddenly," wrote Howells,

> it broke upon him that they were dead, and that they had been killed in the skirmish which had left the Unionist forces victors. Then, he said, at the sight of these dead men whom other men had killed, something went out of him, the habit of a lifetime, that never came back again: the sense of the sacredness of life, and the impossibility of destroying it.

And Garfield had gone on to suggest that his was not an unsual reaction, but that a whole generation of Americans had suffered a similar loss and was now going through the motions of life inwardly crippled.

Loss, absence, enervation, the brooding feeling of spiritual vacuity—these were the feelings that actually succeeded the war. "We hoped," Emerson wrote, "that in peace, after such a war, a great expansion would follow in the mind of the country; grand views in every direction—true freedom in politics, in religion, in social science, in thought. But the energy of the nation seems to have expended itself in the war."

Not quite. There had, after all, been a great expansion after the war and great energy, too, but these were expressed in ways that mocked Emerson and the high-minded men and women of the prewar reform decades. The expansion and energy had gone into the making of the mightiest, wealthiest industrial nation on earth.

In the years between the beginning of the war and the centennial the great West had been thrown open to settlement and the incredibly rapid exploitation of its natural resources; a master plan had been devised and implemented for the construction of trunk rail lines spanning the continent; a wall of tariffs had been erected to protect fledgling industries; and huge numbers of immigrants had flocked in to work the mills and factories, to swell the cities, and to take up homesteads in the newly opened lands. Between 1863 and 1873 almost 3 million immigrants arrived, and more than 5 million more would join them by 1888. In virtually every area of the economy—copper, crude oil, cotton, coal, steel—production soared. New industries produced new products marketed in new ways and at such rates that Americans literally could not consume them fast enough.

In the year of the centennial the nation looked markedly different than it had before the war, and it sounded different with the thump of heavy industry and the welter of foreign tongues. It felt different, too. Henry Adams, that mordant and not always reliable observer of the national scene, thought that the whole cultural ground had shifted so that what had been a useful education up to 1870 was now rendered useless. Truly, this was a new world, one devoted, as he and some others believed, to the acquisition of wealth and power.

The great prewar voices of reform had been altered, muted, or altogether stilled by the terrific struggle: Whittier, Emerson, Thoreau, Brown, Lincoln, Theodore Parker, Melville, Charles Sumner. A kind of moral interregnum ensued within which began to appear a new class of leaders, not reformers but transformers, who would decide the shape and content of modern American culture. These were the financiers, entrepreneurs, and businessmen who had, like Muir, been born in the 1830s: Carnegie, Gould, Armour, Fisk, Morgan, Rockefeller, Hill, and Cooke (though he was born in 1821). Significantly, none had served in the war, and many had profited by it, especially Cooke, Gould, and Fisk. The millionaire, before the war a comparative rarity, had become by the centennial a conspicuous, spectacular feature of the cultural landscape and had conferred on an acceptant nation his supreme value—the acquisition of fabulous wealth.

The making of money had long been *an* American value, and in the twenty years leading up to the war men like Emerson and Parker had decried its steadily increasing importance. Now in the 1870s it had emerged as *the* American value, so thought Adams and others, including Mark Twain, who was to style the period the "Gilded Age," the first of several opprobrious sobriquets to be applied: Great Barbecue, Tragic Era, Brown Decades, Age of Excess. The making of money was deified by a subservient clergy, who explained the appearance of the new plutocrats as a sign of God's favor, and by economists (some of the more prominent of whom had begun as clergymen), who were moved to marvel at how perfectly the laws of the laissez-faire marketplace accorded with divine laws.

Was it for this kind of America the war had been fought, an America of blighted lands strewn with haphazardly cut rail lines, sprawling mines, careless slag heaps; an America showing the sure signs of unrest among the defrauded and exploited laboring classes; an America that existed for the new, would-be barons who were openly contemptuous of democracy? Whitman, who had seen the war closer and longer than almost anyone of his time, was aghast at the national scene of the '70s. He recalled with an indelible vividness the night scenes in the winter of '63 on the second floor of the Patent Office in Washington. There, amid the glass cases containing models of machines and inventions, lay row on row of the war's sick, wounded, and dying; their groans bounced and echoed off the glass and marble of the high-ceilinged room. Surely all that agony had meant more than the inhuman models within the display cases, yet when the great patriot came to survey the American scene a decade later, he was forced to wonder whether the war had been fought merely to ensure the ascendency of the captains of industry.

Victorious, Whitman wrote, over the only foe it need ever fear (an interior one), the Union's society appeared "canker'd, crude, superstitious, and rotten. Political, or law-made society is, and private, or voluntary society, is also." The "depravity," he continued,

of the business classes . . . is not less than has been supposed, but infinitely greater. The official services of America, national, state, and municipal, in all their branches and departments, except the judiciary, are saturated in corruption, bribery, falsehood, malad-ministration; and the judiciary is tainted.

The national spectacle of moral emptiness, "hollowness at heart," as he put it, was appalling, and he concluded that American idealism had vanished from the land: "The underlying principles of the States are not honestly believ'd in (for all this hectic glow, and these melodramatic screamings), nor is humanity itself believ'd in. What penetrating eye does not everywhere see through the mask?" With all the urgency his pen could convey, Whitman urged a searching examination of the national condition, "like a physician diagnosing some deep disease."

Muir, however estranged and even contemptuous of politics and their narrow, factional rhetoric, could hardly have remained aloof from the great questions and uncertainties of the '70s—as indeed his *Record-Union* essay shows he did not. And in his solitary city rambles he came into intimate contact with the jarring new contrasts of American life: the stupendous new wealth of Nob Hill, the imposing money temples of the financial district with their cast-iron facades, and the degrading poverty of the waterfront tene-ments at the foot of Russian Hill, where the "other half" lived. On his returns from his Marin County rambles, he would take his musing way through these mean waterfront streets where the little "Arabs" would hold out grimy hands, begging for one of the flowers he had brought back with him from the other side.

Too plainly the vaunted technological advances and "labor-saving" machines had failed to make life better and more meaning-ful for millions now crowded into cities and enslaved to the assembly line. An exhausting pace of work; brutalizing, often haz-ardous working conditions; low wages; and the ever-hovering threat of layoffs and wage cuts—these were the lot of working Americans in the new age. Muir had had his own taste of the emergent order in the Indianapolis carriage factory, and he could not have missed the large implications of developments since then.

As he walked the city's streets, he could see in San Francisco's uncharted sprawl the way a city created an all-encompassing envi-ronment for its residents, closing them off physically and psycholog-ically from larger and more natural realities. If you lived long enough in the city, it came to seem all there was to life, and yet everything told Muir that "all" would not be enough. What could make the difference in the lives of the toiling masses was the unimproved, natural world that lay outside the cities; yet, as he had written to himself, few knew anything of that world or went out into it. And at the same time, the wildernesses were vanishing into the hands of the exploiters, so that soon enough this precious recreational resource would no longer be available, and the city really would be all. That would be the "far and final upshot" of current trends, and from Muir's point of view it would be a disaster.

The peculiar thing to him was that no one in authority seemed to care much about the conditions of contemporary life. In his *Record-Union* essay Muir had styled the government "loose jointed," by which he apparently meant that it seemed not very well articulated and that it did not do much in the way of social planning. This was a kind epithet, for in fact the federal government was incredibly lethargic in this as in most other areas, its mission being to "let things regulate themselves"; the clergy and the academy were linked in unholy alliance with the power brokers and industrialists; the limit of employers' concerns for their workers was how to get more production out of them for less wages. As Muir and a few others like Whitman surveyed the scene, they might well have wondered who there was left in America to care about the quality of the common life.

Perhaps it was about this time that Muir wrote down his own concern, both for the natural world so quickly being used up and for those many who most needed the intangible resources of that world. Thinking of the lovely meadows of the Sierras, now ravaged by sheepmen and timber miners, he wrote on a scrap of paper:

> The flowers I used to watch and love are mostly dead, and all the open gardens are trodden into dust, but in craggy nooks and aloft in high fenced conservatories a thousand of the fairest and dearest still dwell safely. Pat, pat, shuffle, shuffle, crunch, crunch, I hear you all on the sidewalks and sandbeds, plodding away, hoping in righteousness and heaven, and saying your prayers as best you can, above the sand, beneath the fog, and fenced in by the lake and marshes.
>
> Heaven help you all and give you ice and granite.

Home

Summer 1877 found Muir afield again, principally in the Wasatch Range of Utah, California's San Gabriel Valley, and the Shasta region, where he botanized with two famous men, Sir Joseph Hooker and Asa Gray. And once again he traveled as a correspondent, sending back dispatches to the San Francisco *Bulletin.*

In Utah, he found, as ever, the mountains and rivers more compelling than the man-made scratches on the giant landscape. Still, in his public letters he forced himself from time to time to turn his attention to leafy Salt Lake City and the "Latter-Days," as he styled the Mormons. He heard Brigham Young preach in the Tabernacle; remarked on the loving cultivation of flowers among the residents of the city; and bathed in the great lake itself, a bracing, bouncing experience, as he described it.

The lean bachelor found Mormon polygamy to have a "degrading" influence on the men who practiced it. But the women, he said, seemed more married to one another than to their husbands and so made out to survive with some dignity. Probably the visit among people so determinedly devoted to marriage and the family made Muir reflect a bit ruefully on his own condition. Earlier in the year he had written Sarah on this subject, saying that it seemed odd and ironic to him that one so fond of home and domestic life "should be a bachelor and doomed to roam always far outside the family circle." Now again, at the end of this summer's rambles, he wrote her in a similar vein, saying that her domestic round was a blessed luxury he had to live without, and saying too that others, Mormons and close friends alike, seemed to pity his unanchored, drifting ways. On his way back to San Francisco from Shasta, he told her, he had stopped at Martinez, California, to visit his friends the Strentzels. "They pitied my weary looks," he wrote, fed him in the "most extravagant manner imaginable," and begged him to stay longer. On this visit anyway he would not.

On his return to the city he was almost assaulted with daily evidence that the long-simmering discontents of the working classes had come to full boil in the Bay area as well as all across the country. The national economy, operating like a runaway locomotive, had gone off the tracks in this year and was stalled in the hard times that would endure until the beginning of the next decade. The response of the corporations had been to lay off workers, cut wages, and rescind the pitifully few consessions they had granted their employees. As for the workers, their response was prompt and violent; appropriately for a generation that believed itself mortgaged to the railroads (as Henry Adams had written), it began with a work stoppage against the Baltimore & Ohio in July and quickly spread out of West Virginia to involve other lines and then other industries. In Pittsburgh there was a full-scale riot that included the killing of ten strikers by militiamen and the destruction of a vast amount of railroad equipment. From there strikes and riots swept westward to the coast.

In San Francisco ever larger crowds of the unemployed and disaffected had been gathering on street corners and vacant lots to listen to speakers inveigh against the concentration of wealth and the treatment of employees. Now as Muir resumed residence with the Swetts in the fall, the local grievances found a pyrotechnic voice in Denis Kearney, an Irish drayman who inflamed his listeners with descriptions of corporate irresponsibility and the economic incursions of the Chinese. America had entered into a period of cultural crisis; what would become clear in time was that the crisis would last on into the next century. These years would see more strikes and riots, two presidential assassinations, the formation of labor unions, the rise of splinter parties, and growing fears of a general revolution: precisely those phenomena that in the late 1840s had sent so many European immigrants hurrying to the New World.

Nor would Muir find the Swett home any haven from the intense questions of the period. The New Hampshire-born Swett had been branded in his formative years by personal exposure to Emerson and the impassioned reformer Parker and had carried that idealism on into his career in California public education. Now he and a group of others, including the Le Conte brothers and Ezra Carr, were meeting regularly with Henry George to discuss the trends of the time. Like George, Swett had become much impressed by the concentration of wealth and power. In the 1840s Parker had preached that a true democracy was possible only with a broad distribution of money and power, but since his day the process of concentration had greatly accelerated until the existence of an authentic democracy seemed threatened.

The national condition was nowhere more clearly and starkly illustrated than in California, where the rich bounty of the land had fallen with incredible rapidity into the hands of a comparative few and its resources selfishly plundered. Bayard Taylor, who had witnessed the gold rush, was astonished at the rapid transformation of the state within ten years of that phenomenon, writing that "Nature here reminds one of a princess fallen into the hands of robbers, who cut off her fingers for the sake of the jewels she wears." And Karl Marx wrote friends for information on California, for it seemed to him that "nowhere else has the upheaval most shamelessly caused by capitalist centralization taken place with such speed."

Swett was no revolutionary, nor were the others who gathered for evening discussions at George's modest home, though George warned in *Progress and Poverty* (1879), the book he began writing in the aftermath of the explosive summer of '77, of a greater explosion to come from the gathering "Huns" and "Vandals" if a more equitable distribution of wealth were not devised. Muir accompanied Swett to some of the Sunday evening sessions, but it is hard to imagine him taking an active part in discussions of political economy. There is evidence that initially at least he found Swett's commitment to social uplift a trifle jejune. Idealistic as he himself was, there was still a hard knot of Scots skepticism in him, nor had his self-willed exile from society encouraged a belief in the perfectibility of man. Emerson had caught that strain in Muir immediately, perhaps because the great man shared something of this tendency himself and had never resolved the contradiction it presented to his reformist views. And if Muir was now beginning to speculate on the republic and its future and to see it as in crisis, he was leery of political remedies or the panaceas of theorists like Henry George.

However, he surely would have agreed with George that American civilization had curiously, crucially failed to deliver real happiness to the great masses of people: in moments of deeper pessimism, as when he had fled Oakland in the late summer of '74, he had seen civilization as a kind of organized insanity. Something fundamental had gone awry, and in his extensive explorations of California he had seen much of the local evidence. The gaping economic contrasts of San Francisco were daily sights, of course, but in a way reality began beyond the city's perimeter. In the countryside the evidence of monopolistic concentration and exploitation was everywhere: in the valleys, where huge landholdings were held out for speculative harvests and where a new, aggressive, military approach to wheat farming was quickly wearing out the soil; in the foothills, where the hydraulic mining operations tore at hillsides, stripped them, and dumped the refuse into the streams, choking them and flooding the flatlands below; in the mountains, where the timber miners mowed down the forests like fields of grass.

When he wandered farther afield, as he did again in the summer of 1878 with the U.S. Coast and Geodetic Survey in Utah and Nevada, he came upon many other scenes suggesting in odd, recondite ways something historically, even endemically wrong with American culture. Nevada he found to be a sort of microcosm of New World history, "one of the very youngest and wildest of the States," as he wrote in the San Francisco *Evening Bulletin*. Even so, it was "already strewn with ruins that seem as gray and silent and time-worn as if the civilization to which they belonged had perished centuries ago." Go where you might, he continued,

> throughout the length and breadth of this mountain-barred wilderness, you everywhere come upon these dead mining towns, with their tall chimney-stacks, standing forlorn amid broken

walls and furnaces, and machinery half buried in sand, the very
names of many of them forgotten amid the excitements of later
discoveries, and now known only through tradition—tradition
ten years old.

Here were the marks of that mad haste and greed that had characterized the whole history of discovery and exploration in the
Americas, the whites running over a gigantic, magnificent landscape in a ceaseless effort to extract its wealth and leaving behind
their litter like a people in flight. Traveling southward from Austin,
Utah, down the Big Smoky Valley, Muir was confronted with a
spectral smokestack that looked grotesquely out of place in the
desert, "as if it had been transported entire from the heart of some
noisy manufacturing town and left here by mistake." He learned
from the ghost town's sole inhabitant—"a lone bachelor with one
suspender"—that the smokestack had belonged to a set of furnaces
that were to smelt ore that was never found. Around its base Muir
found the workmen's tools still lying "as if dropped in some sudden
Indian or earthquake panic and never afterwards handled."

Some of the ghost towns had been mere encampments, but
others had been real towns with substantial populations, and most
of them had not been abandoned because the local veins of ore had
been worked out but because of rumors that had come to them of
more elsewhere, rumors that sent the inhabitants flying off toward
another dream of riches. As in California, most had been disappointed; one in a hundred was successful, Muir guessed. The other
ninety-nine "died alone in the mountains or sank out of sight in the
corners of saloons, in a haze of whiskey and tobacco smoke." Taking a sly poke at current trends in popular Christianity where great
wealth was described as the inevitable divine blessing upon the
thrifty and industrious, Muir remarked that the "healthful ministry
of wealth is blessed," and that "surely it is a fine thing that so many
are eager to find the gold and silver that lie in the veins of the
mountains." But in this searching too many of the seekers went
mad, striking about them "blindly like raving madmen." Thus the
ruins left behind were not picturesque aspects of the Old West.
Instead, Muir would have his readers see them as "monuments of
fraud and ignorance" and "sins against science." The drifts and
tunnels so frantically, laboriously dug into the rocks were the "pray-

ers of the prospector, offered for the wealth he so earnestly craves; but like prayers of any kind not in harmony with nature, they are unanswered."

Modern mining methods, he noted, had greatly improved returns to investors, and the entire industry was now run on a scientific, efficient basis, as he was able to observe in a tour of the Richmond and Eureka mines at Eureka. But Muir was not entirely sanguine about even such modern operations, for deep in those mines he came upon the miners themselves, chipping away at the ore masses "like navvies wearing away the day in a railroad cutting. . . ."

In addition to the literary letters of this expedition, Muir was also in active correspondence with his friends the Strentzels of Martinez, and when the surveying party was at the Humboldt Sink, he wrote them of the litter left there by the dazed and panicked gold rushers of three decades ago. How hot it was, he wrote, riding in the "solemn, silent glare. . . . Here is what the early emigrants called the forty mile desert, well marked with bones and broken wagons. Strange how the very sunshine may become dreary." But Muir said he could find no real cause for the gold rushers' panic even in this apparently desolate spot, for there were "lovely tender abronias blooming in the fervid sand and sun, and a species of sunflower, and a curious leguminous bush crowded with purple blossoms, and a green saltwort, and four or five species of artemisia, really beautiful, and three or four handsome grasses." Nor was this all, for all about the desert rocks had their "grand geological story" to tell. Perhaps it all depended on the nature of your desires; for those whose prayers were all for the gold believed to be waiting on the other side of the mountains, the sink would have seemed bleak and forbidding enough.

By this time the Strentzels were no longer casual friends, and in fact Muir was in the first stages of a real courtship of the Strentzels' daughter, Louie Wanda. He was forty now, and if it is true, as some say, that we live our lives in decades, it must have seemed to him that real youth and its freedoms were pretty much behind him. What could he look forward to in what remained of life but an increasing sense of aloneness, emotional as well as social singularity? His letters to Sarah in this year and his remarks on Mormon marriage practices and his own lack of offspring strongly suggest that his fortieth birthday was a sort of watershed event in his mind.

As in so many instances, it had been Jeanne Carr who had been instrumental in introducing Muir to the Strentzels, and this was the last great service she would render him. From the first, her object had been a match between Muir and Louie. "I want you to know my John Muir," she had written Louie back in 1872. "I wish I could give him to some noble young woman 'for keeps' and so take him out of the wilderness into the society of his peers." Subsequently she had arranged a meeting between Muir and the Strentzels, but nothing much had come of it until Muir decided to drop in at the Strentzel ranch on his way back to San Francisco in the fall of 1877.

The letters he wrote the Strentzels from Utah and Nevada were all addressed to Dr. and Mrs. Strentzel and contain but a single fleeting reference to their daughter, but there is little doubt that he meant them more for her eyes than for theirs. In them he was at his engaging best—jocular, witty, now and again lapsing into broad Scots, telling thrilling tales of desert adventure, waxing lyrical about shrubs and stones and the virtues of anything wild.

Dr. John Strentzel was then a vigorous sixty-six-year-old who had been born in Poland and had taken part in the abortive Polish revolution of 1830–31 against the Russians. The battle of Ostrolenka had ended the hopes of the Polish patriots, and Strentzel was forced to flee his homeland when the Romanov troops moved into Warsaw in the fall of 1831. In Hungary, where Strentzel took refuge, he gained practical training in horticulture and viticulture and formal training in medicine at the University of Budapest. Then in 1840 Strentzel joined the swelling ranks of immigrants to America, ending up as a member of a pioneering colony near the site of present-day Dallas. The colony failed (as so many did in those years), and Strentzel moved on, this time to Lamar County, Texas, where he met and married a woman from Tennessee whose name was Louisiana Irwin. In a faded love poem that survives from the couple's courtship in the still-unsettled Texas country, the young doctor expressed his devotion to his beloved by his determination to exterminate all the Indians and so save his fair one from that fate worse than death. But when the alien conventions of poetry did not force him into such grim sentiments, he could write quite feelingly, and there exists a later account of the death of the couple's young son Johnny that is profoundly moving.

Louisiana herself wrote poetry, and from the fragmentary records seems to have been sensitive to the natural world. In a poem on mountains she writes:

By the cloud, the awe, the silence, sunshine, verdure, flowers and
    storm,
Let us bless God for the mountains! Let them float a solemn hymn,
Up to Heaven, from the vast temples, massy aisles and cloisters dim.

The Strentzels' daughter, Louie Wanda, was born in 1847, and two years later the family joined the great exodus to California when Dr. Strentzel accepted a post as medical adviser to one of the hundreds of expeditions heading west in '49. In 1853 they bought twenty acres of rich valley land south of the bayside hamlet of Martinez, and there Strentzel began to put to good use his training in horticulture and viticulture.

Wheat and oats had been the principal crops of Contra Costa County, but Strentzel shrewdly saw the commercial possibilities in fruit ranching. In the 1850s he set out pear orchards and subsequently added extensive vineyards, beginning with muscats and adding tokays and other varieties as the years went on. But Strentzel was not content with his own successes, urging valley residents to make the transition from what he called the "Rip Van Winkle slumber" of grain growing to fruit ranching. He organized the county's first grange and was as active in nurturing it as he was his own orchards and vineyards. By the time Muir came to be a regular visitor at the Strentzels', the doctor had greatly expanded his holdings and was a prosperous and highly respected man. Under his leadership the Alhambra Valley had become a center of California fruit culture with many thousands of acres in vineyards and extensive orchards of apple, pear, peach, apricot, orange, and mulberry.

When Muir began his circumlocutive courtship of Louie Wanda Strentzel in the spring of 1878, she was thirty-one, and in a state whose population was heavily male she was surely past the age when she might have been expected to marry. The only extant photograph from her youth (and one of the very few of her from any period) shows an attractive, if somewhat prim-appearing woman with high cheekbones, a full mouth, and somber eyes. She had been schooled at the Atkins Seminary for Young Ladies (now Mills College) at nearby Benecia and was a very accomplished pianist who some said could have had a concert career. Despite this talent and its promise, she was apparently content to live reclusively with her parents, where she took an active role in her father's fruit ranching operations.

Clearly, Jeanne Carr had recognized her qualities, had seen that she was far more than the retiring, dutiful daughter she appeared, but Carr's matchmaking had apparently proved a failure, and when the Carrs moved to Pasadena in 1877 the matter seemed at an end. Maybe Muir was really waiting for Jeanne Carr to quit the vicinity before beginning a suit; the timing of his first visits to the Strentzels is interestingly suggestive. At any rate, his initial callings were in the guise of a naturalist come to talk with a horticulturist and grape grower, but gradually the true object of his trips was revealed.

They made something of an odd couple as they strolled the valley lands and hills of the doctor's ranch, the bearded, casually dressed wanderer and the home-bound woman, careful in dress and deportment, as retiring in manner as he could be outgoing. Both of them were at ages where it seemed likely they would remain unmarried, both apparently confirmed in single habits that would last out their lifetimes. What passed between them in their walks that spring and in the months that followed remains unknown, nor do the letters Muir wrote Louie reveal much. In fact, in all of Muir's literary effects there is astonishingly little on his relationship with her. And for her part, though she would become the wife of a famous man, mother of two children, and mistress of a home that teemed with visitors, she would also retain her retiring habits. Very "old-fashioned" was the way one contemporary described her while attempting to account for the fact that so few actually knew much about Louie. That may not be as accurate a way of depicting her and the choices she made as to say that she was determined that to a real extent her life would be lived on terms that were hers and her family's, not those of the wider world.

Her view of the relationship with John Muir remains an unsolved, maybe insoluble mystery. She appears not to have kept a diary or to have written revealing letters to friends, but an early sequence of events may reveal something of the terms she accepted and abided by. Early in June 1879, Muir paid Louie a visit and declared his intentions. She accepted, and they became formally engaged, though this was kept a family secret. But at the same time that Muir declared himself, he told Louie that he was shortly to go on a sea voyage northward, that he did not know just how long he would be gone, that he might get as far north as Alaska, in which case he would be gone well into 1880.

At this moment in the relationship there must have been a discussion of the long-range implications of Muir's voyage; terms must have been stated and discussed. They seem to have been mostly his terms, and they were by no means easy or conventional. He would love and honor, but he must also be guaranteed a good measure of freedom for his explorations—which meant he must be allowed to reserve an essential part of himself from her forever. Here again, Louie seems less "old-fashioned" than determinedly individualistic, even "modern." For in accepting such terms she was also reserving a part of herself, that retiring, home-bound character she exhibited when Jeanne Carr and then Muir first knew her. At the same time, the role she accepted required generous amounts of resourcefulness and tolerant understanding, the first for those frequent times when Muir would be abroad with his work, the last to brave the disapproval of her parents and others who saw her husband's travels as irresponsibilities.

There is evidence in her early letters to Muir that these strictures were hard on her, that she suffered feelings of loneliness and abandonment and reactionary feelings of weakness and inadequacy. There is also abundant evidence that she proved at last fully equal to the terms, created her own secure place in life, and allowed her husband his.

As for Muir, with a glad heart he left his newly betrothed, writing to Jeanne Carr on July 9 (without so much as a mention of Louie or his engagement to her): "I'm going home—going to my summer in the snow and ice and forests of the north coast. Will sail tomorrow at noon on the Dakota for Victoria and Olympia. Will push inland and alongland. May visit Alaska."

Steaming out of Portland, he felt a sense of relief and release, perhaps partly occasioned by that feeling any passenger may experience once aboard ship: that you are now out where nothing of the land or landed concerns can reach you. In his journals, and later in the book he was making out of them in the last months of life, there is an unmistakable feeling of renewal and release, the continuation of that pattern commenced in childhood wherein a creative escape to nature was sought and found whenever the world pressed too closely. Now he reveled in the long breaking waves, in the ship racing through them half buried in spray, even in the fact that seasickness kept most of the other passengers below so that he had the decks to himself.

Then there were the whales. A half dozen of them, they showed their backs to him "like glaciated bosses of granite," and like Melville he was moved to think of that cavernous, antediluvian life, "of the hearts of these whales, beating warm against the sea, day and night, through dark and light, on and on for centuries; how the red blood must rush and gurgle in and out, bucketfuls, barrelfuls at a beat!" Whales, the sea, space, freedom, a landscape as freshly beautiful as if a "hundred Lake Tahoes were united end to end"—these were the delights of voyage northward along the coast, and Muir felt all "hard, money-gaining, material thoughts loosen and sink off and out of sight, and one is free from oneself and made captive to the fresh wildness and beauty, obeying it as necessarily as unconscious sun-bathed plants." But the real lure was Alaska, and Muir knew this, writing in a journal entry of July 15 that for a lover of pure wilderness no more magical place could be imagined.

Alaska had been a part of the United States barely a decade, but it was no longer virginal, as Muir was shortly to discover at Fort Wrangell and Sitka. That same insatiable haste and greed that Muir had so recently noted in the Nevada silences was now evident here as white civilization gnawed at the edges of a huge, primeval wilderness, creating its splintered outposts of progress, establishing trade relations with the tribes, eyeing economic potentials ever in advance of where it was. Muir had not been many days in this newest country before he saw all the future in a few frontier facts. The time is coming, he wrote in his journal," "when Alaska will seem nearer home, when her resources will be laid under contribution searching enough and intense enough for the most exacting of utilitarians. . . ."

Still, here was as magnificent an opportunity as it was a landscape, and he knew it. Coming to America so comparatively late, he had missed much of that primitive splendor that predecessors like Bartram, Catlin, Audubon, and his own countrymen, David Douglas and Sir William Drummond Stewart, had beheld—and that was in fact passing away even as they breathlessly beheld it. Now he had been given that kind of chance again by an odd turn in American history, "Seward's Folly." Here again, and for the last time, was the great, soaring wilderness and within it the tribes. He plunged into it as would one encountering the truth of a dream.

When the ship steamed into the messy little outpost of Fort Wrangell with its load of Christian divines come to save native souls, one of those awaiting it was the resident Presbyterian missionary, S. Hall Young. He noted a man standing apart from the missionizing party, a lean, sinewy, stoop-shouldered figure with a long reddish beard and wearing a Scots cap and tweed ulster. Subsequently, Young was introduced to "Professor" Muir, said to be a naturalist.

If Muir's position on the steamer's deck was physically set off from the missionaries with whom he had made the voyage, Young was quickly to learn that the "professor" was in almost every other way as well a man apart. At any hour of the day Muir might be found sauntering in the damp woods beyond the settlement or discovered down on hands and knees prying into the secret world of mosses, ferns, and liverworts that reminded him of the bogs of Canada. Nor were his investigations always confined to daylight, for one black and streaming night the village natives came to Young in great consternation: on a hill behind the village a strange, awful glow cut through the dark and the steady rain, and they were afraid of some evil. It was, as they subsequently learned, only the professor who had climbed the hill in the storm and built himself a huge bonfire so that he might observe how these Alaskan trees behaved in wind and rain and hear the songs they sang.

Young learned too that such behavior was no mere eccentricity but instead the inevitable, natural expression of a unique character. Soon enough the missionary found himself seeking out Muir at any available moment and accompanying him on his botanical hikes. They found certain tastes in common and quoted Burns, Keats, and

Shelley to one another. Young carried a volume of Emerson with him and read from it to Muir, who read to him from his volume of Thoreau.

To the youthful missionary whose work in this outpost was the serious business of conversion, there was something wonderfully compelling in watching Muir at his work. Though evidently a Christian, Muir's personal version of the faith seemed joyously free and untroubled with doctrinal questions. The woods and fields were alive within divinity, and Muir seemed in a state of suspended ecstasy when out in them. Young marveled to see the man in his long ulster, running from one flower cluster to another in a high mountain meadow, falling on his knees in worship before them, babbling in broad Scots a mixture of scientific language and baby talk. He greeted old flower friends he had known elsewhere— Tennessee or Shasta—and clasped unknown species to him like new loves.

At Glenora on the Stikine River above Wrangell, Young got an opportunity to experience the full force of Muir's expert and loving engagement with the natural world. A party including Muir had gone up the river to investigate the condition of the Tlingits near the old Hudson's Bay trading post, and in midafternoon of their last day out Muir announced he would hike to a group of mountains some seven miles distant, scale the tallest, and return before morning when the ship would return to Wrangell. Young begged to go with him, and Muir consented, though warning that it would be a strenuous outing and he could not be responsible for Young.

Young told Muir he was a good walker and that he had some climbing experience. On the way to the mountains he proved the first. Then the two botanized happily about the lower slopes until a lengthened shadow reminded Muir of the waning day and the sunset he wanted to catch from the summit. Then, as Young was to remember it,

> Muir began to *slide* up that mountain. I had been with mountain climbers before, but never one like him. A deer lope over the smoother slopes, a sure instinct for the easiest way into a rocky fortress, an instant and unerring attack, a serpent-like glide up the steep; eye, hand and foot all connected dynamically; with no

appearance of weight to his body—as though he had Stockton's negative gravity machine strapped on his back.

Once started, there was no hesitation in Muir, no pause for breath, and Young was hard-pressed just to keep him in view. And while Young's legs were sturdy and his wind sound, he now began to feel an old weakness he had concealed from Muir: ten years before when breaking colts in West Virginia, he had suffered dislocations of both shoulders, and since that time the shoulders had been out of joint more than once. Now as he scrambled after the flying Muir, he felt the head of his left humerus move from its socket. But he had no time—and perhaps no inclination, either—to call out to Muir.

As Muir worked carefully around a particularly dangerous shoulder, he called back a warning to Young and then continued on. But Young in his haste to keep up did not heed the warning. Stepping incautiously on an unsupported stone, he felt it drop away with sickening suddenness, and he plunged downward toward the brink of a slope beneath which was a thousand-foot drop onto a glacier. When he was able to arrest his slide, Young's feet hung over the brink and both shoulders were helplessly dislocated. His scream for help brought Muir back, and while last thoughts of wife and children flashed through the hanging man's brain, he heard Muir talking calmly to him, telling him he would soon have him out of this. Then Young heard him "going away, whistling 'The Blue Bells of Scotland,' singing snatches of Scotch songs, calling to me, his voice now receding as the rocks intervened, then sounding louder as he came out on the face of the cliff."

What Muir had done in perhaps ten minutes' time was to work below Young to a sliver of a shelf he found beneath that brink on which the missionary lay so perilously poised. Reaching up and over he grasped Young's pants at the waist, then commanded him to let himself slide downward. As Young did so, Muir crooked him onto the shelf with one iron arm and seized Young's shirt collar with his teeth. There they stood, looking down on the abyss, but Muir was not one to reflect on the tragedy that might have been —and still might be. He told Young that he was going to need both hands for climbing but that, helpless as Young's arms were, he could still help Muir by scrambling upward with his feet. Then, taking Young's collar in his teeth again, the man somehow climbed back the ten or twelve feet to that point from which Young had originally fallen. Pondering this incredible feat years later, Young could still not imagine how it had been accomplished, and the sheer wonder of it continued to grow on him.

Once on the ledge, Muir succeeded in setting one of Young's shoulders though the arm remained useless; the other arm he simply had to tie to Young's body using a suspender and a handkerchief. But the great difficulty still loomed ahead: how to get the pain-wracked and virtually helpless man back down the mountain in the gathering dusk. As Young said, the descent for an unencumbered climber would have been difficult enough, but at this hour and with this burden it seemed almost impossible. Yet Muir accomplished it. Carefully, painstakingly, he would cut heelholds for Young on the steepest places and place him in them, then work down farther, cut another succession of niches and carry the missionary down to these. So by long, weary ways Muir at last got his friend down upon the glacier around midnight. They took the long walk back to the ship in very short stages, and at each stop Muir would build a reviving fire and comfort Young as best he culd. Then on they would stagger in darkness, Muir half carrying Young, who was by now almost insensible.

They reached Glenora and a wrathful and anxious group of missionaries who awaited them at seven-thirty that morning. Muir was so exhausted that he cared nothing for the reproofs hurled from the deck but simply went to his bunk and immediately fell asleep, leaving Young to explain as best his condition permitted that this had been no irresponsible lark but a near-fatal accident.

That, obviously, was the highlight for Young of Muir's first Alaskan trip, and for years thereafter the missionary regaled friends and dinner-table audiences with his version of it. As for the hero himself, he never even mentioned it in his Alaskan notebooks and might never have gotten around to writing out his own account had not a "miserable, sensational" version (his words) appeared years afterward in a popular magazine.

For Muir, the highlight of his first Alaskan exploration was a canoe voyage of almost 800 miles to the mysterious, cloud-shrouded waters of Glacier Bay. As the days and season wore on at Wrangell and the time for the return to civilization drew closer, Muir found that the icy and largely unknown lands to the north burned in his brain as a great opportunity untaken. Some prospectors, learning of his fascination with storms, ice, and glaciers, told him that up there he would find these things in abundance, and though it was already mid-October Muir determined on the trip if arrangements could be made.

When he informed Young of his intentions, the missionary, eager for an opportunity to again accompany his extraordinary friend and to take survey of the spiritual state of distant tribes, immediately counted himself in and took over the making of arrangements. Their guides and assistants would be four Indians led by Toyatte, "a grand old Stickeen nobleman," as Muir described him, and owner of the canoe in which the party would travel. With him would be Kadachan, son of a Chilcat chief; John, like Toyatte a Stikine, who would serve as interpreter; and Sitka Charley. They left Wrangell on October 14.

If Muir's goal on this exploration was Glacier Bay, the ultimate if unsought result was a much deeper appreciation of Native Americans. His encounters with the tribes in the lower states had encouraged scant admiration or respect (though he had been somewhat sympathetic to the dispossessed natives of Wisconsin), and in fact up to this time he seemed generally uncharitable toward the Indians he had encountered in California. Maybe this was because when he had come into that country the heartless and incredibly rapid destruction of the tribal cultures had so reduced the survivors that Muir could find nothing wild or natural-seeming in their mendicant existence. If Indians had figured as part of that primal vision of America received through schoolboy reading in Dunbar, the Wisconsin and California realities so far failed to measure up that Muir seems to have closed that sympathetic, perceptive eye he turned on so much else of the American world. Now, however, circumstances forced an intense engagement with the aboriginal presence, and this was another unexpected gift of the Alaskan experience, another backward glance vouchsafed the latecoming explorer.

Thoreau—and Jefferson before him—had come to feel that somehow in the Indian all of the New World might be comprehended, and as a terminally ill man Thoreau made it as far west as Minnesota, where he had seen the Sioux on the eve of their bloody uprising there. Throughout his brief maturity he had been carefully gathering notes toward a book on Indians, and his last gasping words, "Moose . . . Indian . . . ," seemed to express his conviction that the Indian equaled the New World as it had once been and as Thoreau, in part at least, would have it yet. Muir would not become a student of Indian cultures as a result of this canoe trip, nor would his subsequent contacts with the Alaskan natives on his explorations of 1880, 1881, 1890, and 1899 result in much more than passing references to Indian life. Yet by the time he had returned to Wrangell from Glacier Bay in November of this year he had come to understand that the tribes of the New World had once enjoyed a relationship with their lands that so-called civilized men could not fathom.

Like Bartram, Catlin, and Audubon before him, Muir saw that profound and mysterious relationship being destroyed by the civilization of which he and Young were the advance personnel. "The agency fort-and-soldier system," he wrote in his journal, "begets only disease, crime, debauch, general demoralization, and death." And like Melville in the South Seas, he was not sanguine about the effects of Christianizing on the tribes, observing that in the process the natives "become very nearly nothing, lose their wild instincts, and gain a hymnbook, without the means of living." Then, he said, "they mope and doze and die on the outskirts of civilization like tamed eagles in barnyard corners. . . ."

On the Glacier Bay exploration Muir saw the process at work, the tribal groups already in various stages of bewilderment as an evidently "superior" civilization brought them news of the true and only God. How indeed could they hold to and honor their ancient traditions when the "Boston men" (as the natives styled all whites) came to them in great swift ships, with guns, gadgets, and everything in plenty, and then told the natives that all these wonders were the consequences of an intimate association with the Christian God? "You Boston men," said the chief of a Kupreanof Kake village whose words Muir recorded, "must be favorites of the Great Father. You know all about God, and ships and guns and the growing of things to eat. We will sit quiet and listen to the words of any teacher you send us."

But in Toyatte's canoe and in the sheltered, woody nooks where the party made their nightly camps, matters were otherwise, and Muir was allowed glimpses of that older, other world that had existed before the coming of the whites. He heard the native traditions; and more than just the interpreted words, he heard the melody of those traditions, the way they always meant more than they said. One night, while the Indians told the two whites prehistoric tales of the language and behavior of animals, their talk was interrupted by the howlings of a wolf, and Kadachan stumped the missionary by asking whether in his view wolves had souls. Apparently Young had never considered the question (though his religion had answered it in the negative centuries earlier). For the natives, the wolves, as well as other animals, plants, stones, and stars, did have soul life, and Kadachan went on to describe the special characteristics of the wolf clan and their methods of hunting the deer. "I inquired," wrote Muir, "how it was that with enemies so wise and powerful the deer were not all killed. Kadachan replied that wolves knew better than to kill them all and thus cut off their most important food-supply." Here was an ethic of conservation truly beyond the fathoming of most of the "Boston men."

The deeper Muir penetrated the aboriginal world, the more he found in it to admire. At a Hootsenoo village on Admiralty Island he said he had "never felt more at home" (a comment frequent among those whites capable of accepting Indian hospitality), and he dwelt with telling autobiographical emphasis on the unfailingly kind and wise behavior of Indian parents toward their children. He had precisely the same reactions in a Hoona village on Icy Strait, and everywhere he went he was impressed with the natives' generosity and sincerity. Plainly, the large, assumed contrasts between civilized and savage here were revealed as empty, baseless abstractions.

But the aspect of aboriginal Alaska that was to stay longest and best with Muir was the character of the old Stikine headman, Toyatte. Muir had the opportunity to witness the man in all manner of trying circumstances, both those of native life and those consequent to the coming of white civilization, and Toyatte's innate nobility was as unfailing as sunrise. "I saw Toyatte," Muir wrote, "landing at night in dark storms, making fires, building shelters, exposed to all kinds of discomfort, but never under any circumstances did I ever see him do anything, or make a single gesture, that was not dignified, or hear him say a word that might not be uttered anywhere."

Muir was present, too, at an episode more trying by far than any Toyatte would have experienced along the wonted pathways of native life—his examination for admission to the Presbyterian church. In this instance again the man's greatness of character was blazingly clear as he told of his spiritual life before the missionaries and of his subsequent conversion. "In all his gestures," Muir said, "and in the language in which he expressed himself, there was a noble simplicity and earnestness and majestic bearing which made the sermons and behavior of the three distinguished divinity doctors present seem commonplace in comparison." Muir named one of the Stikine glaciers he explored in honor of Toyatte—as high an accolade as the man the Indians called the "Ice Chief" could bestow.

When Muir, Young, and the Indians returned at last to Wrangell in late November, the missionary was eager for news. Muir was not; the only real news, he told Young, was in the wilderness. Still, whether the news of the day was a sham and the civilization that lived by it in some ways fraudulent, he knew he must now return to it and to its obligations and commitments.

Foremost, of course, was Louie, whose somewhat plaintive letters were awaiting him in Wrangell. She had received no word from him since before his long exploration of the north, nor would she until he reached Portland early in January 1880. And though she was trying her best to keep up her spirits and to match him in courage, it was a hard, lonely wait in Martinez.

When she did hear from him it was to tell her that, although he was on his way homeward, he would not be coming directly to her. First he would give a few lectures in Portland, and then he had further business to clear up in San Francisco. It was not until mid-February that he and Louie were together again, and then, as if the Alaskan expedition had served as an appropriate sort of engagement, a wedding date was set and plans for the couple's immediate future were drawn.

Muir and his bride would live in the ample home formerly

occupied by Louie's parents, and the older couple would take temporary quarters while they built a Victorian mansion in the middle of their valley lands. Muir was to rent land from Dr. Strentzel and embark on a new career as a fruit rancher, operating on his rented acreage as well as assisting his father-in-law in the management of holdings that had become too much for one man—2,600 acres in all.

April 14 was chosen as the wedding day, and when news of it filtered out to a select group of friends like the Swetts, the Keiths, and the Carrs, there was mingled disbelief and joy. Jeanne Carr wrote from Pasadena to say that the union had been foreordained —as perhaps from her point of view it had—and she told Mrs. Black, wife of the old Yosemite hotelkeeper, that in her opinion Louie Strentzel was the only woman in the world in every way worthy of Muir. Mary Louise Swett, John Swett's wife, wrote a friendly, congratulatory letter to Louie, telling her that she hoped Louie was good at "hair-splitting arguments. You will need to be to hold your own with him."

April 14 dawned gray and threatening, but Muir had always loved stormy weather, had often sought it out, so perhaps as he drove the buggy to the Martinez station to pick up the minister he was doubly happy: it was simply pouring. The Reverend Dwinell recalled years afterward that the bridegroom had driven him home "like the rush of a torrent down the cañon." And there at the home they would call theirs, Muir and Louie were married amid the rain and a profusion of booms from the doctor's orchards.

For the first time since leaving Hickory Hill, Muir had a home. Twenty years of wandering, solitary adventures had come to an end. Now was a new beginning, and he would once again have to learn to be easy in the harness of domestic life and the agricultural round he had left behind long ago in those rolling inland hills of Wisconsin.

PART
IV

A
Legacy

Against
the American
Grain

Robert Underwood Johnson had finished dressing for dinner on a late May evening in 1889 at San Francisco's Palace Hotel and still Muir had not appeared. The man's arrival at the hotel had been announced to Johnson a good while ago, surely long enough for the veteran mountaineer to have made his way to Johnson's room. Then Johnson heard his name being called down the hallway, "Johnson, Johnson! Where are you?" It was Muir, lost in what he called the artificial canyons and caverns of a city hotel and lacking those familiar, native signposts—trees, mosses, glacial striations—that in the wilderness had always told him where he was. What Johnson did not know but was to find out over subsequent years was that the old wilderness wanderer was comically helpless in any city, his best instincts blunted by buildings, blocks, and crowds.

The man Johnson rescued into the haven of the hotel room seemed on first glance a kind of farmer, casually, almost negligently dressed in a rough blue suit and black slouch hat, his shaggy beard graying, his face weathered by sun and wind. Johnson noted his bright blue eyes, one of them slightly off (the result, he was to learn,

of an old accident), and hollowed temples that seemed to speak of
age and anxieties. A torrential talker, Muir plunged directly into a
monologue almost without greetings, his speech charmingly
flavored with a Scots burr that for affect he would occasionally
broaden.

But, of course, Muir was much more than a rustic come to
town, and the New York editor knew it. Though this was their
first meeting, Muir was well known to Johnson through his writings and by a reputation that had acquired through the years
something of the legendary. Indeed, part of Johnson's editorial
mission to California was to recruit Muir's pen for the pages of
the *Century*. The two series that magazine had run on the Civil
War and on Lincoln had proven highly popular, and Johnson was
out here laying the groundwork for a new series on the gold rush.
But in addition, there was the intriguing prospect of John Muir.
He had been strangely silent for almost a decade, though editors
and other admirers had persistently asked him when he would
write again. Indeed Johnson himself had received no reply when
he had written Muir asking whether Muir had entirely forsaken
literature.

Initial contact made, Johnson went to his dinner party buoyed
by a hopeful sign, for Muir had invited him to visit at Martinez
when his gold-rush prospecting in the city should be completed.
And in a general way Muir had indicated the reasons for his silence
and had given Johnson some hope that he might now be ready to
resume his literary and public career. In recent years, Muir said, he
had been entirely taken up with another occupation, that of manag-
ing the Strentzel-Muir ranch and accumulating a store of money for
his family. Dr. Strentzel was now so aged that Muir had full responsibility for the running of all the acreage, both his and the doctor's.
He and Louie had the care of the old couple, too, along with that
of their own daughters. Wanda (born in 1881) was now eight, and
the frail Helen ("Midge" to her fond "Papa") only three. So, even
in this most general way, Johnson could begin to understand something of Muir's situation, and several days later at Martinez he saw
more fully into it.

Here was the sprawling ranch with its valley lands and undulant
hills intensively set to cherries, Bartlett pears, apricots, and zinfan-
del, muscat, and tokay grapes. Hired hands moved among the rows,

and Muir had the supervision of them as well as of all the livestock and equipment of a going enterprise. Dominating the ranch on a hillcrest was the tall, oddly blocky Victorian pile that Dr. Strentzel had built and in which he and Mrs. Strentzel still lived. Away to the east was the Muirs' home, a cheerful Dutch Colonial that Muir had made yet more cheerful by the addition of dormer windows that let in light and air and gave a fine view down the valley. There Johnson met Mrs. Muir, whom he found intelligent if somewhat retiring. She too, he found, deplored Muir's literary inactivity and had been urging him to either delegate some authority to a foreman or else lease out some acreage and so free himself from such daily duty.*

What neither Louie Muir nor John himself could have told their visitor was that Muir had felt positively driven to make a great deal of money now that he was a family man. The Strentzels had neither understood nor approved of his wilderness wanderings when he had married their daughter, and since his return from his third Alaskan voyage in the fall of '81 he had stayed close to home, bowing in part to the pressure of his in-laws but even more to an internal pressure that forbade solitary travel and compelled profitable work. He had taken hold here with a sort of vengeance, as if after all those years of having refused to take a normal part in what was called the "world's work" he would now prove something to those watching him. Though to many he had long appeared a shaggy, solitary, and impractical dreamer, they did not know of that strong vein of Scots practicality in him that had first been expressed

*In August 1885, while Muir was taking one of his too infrequent camping trips, Louie had written him, urging that he stay away from the ranch until he was well rested and relaxed. "My father and mother," she wrote, "at last realize your need of the mountains. Then as for the old ranch, why it is here, and a few grapes more or less will not make much difference." Then, the summer previous to Johnson's visit when Muir had gone into Oregon and Washington with William Keith, she had written him even more pointedly: "A ranch that needs and takes the sacrifice of a noble life ought to be flung away beyond all reach and power for harm. . . . The Alaska book and the Yosemite book, dear John, must be written, and you need to be your own self, well and strong, to make them worthy of you. There is nothing that has a right to be considered beside this except the welfare of our children" (Linnie Marsh Wolfe [ed.], *John of the Mountains: The Unpublished Journals of John Muir*).

in his backwoods inventions, that had last been expressed in the time-and-motion study done for his Indianapolis employers.

Now in the '80s it cropped out again. Dr. Strentzel's industry and acumen in building up fruit ranching on his own lands and throughout the Alhambra Valley were well known when Muir married Louie, but the doctor was still something of an Old World dreamer with a scientific, theoretical approach to fruit ranching. But once he gave his son-in-law full rein the ranch began to produce —and pay—as never before. Muir had neither a scientific nor a theoretical interest in fruit ranching—for him it was first and last a business. He loved the trees and vines; he retained that old fellow feeling, developed in Wisconsin, for the animals that had to do so much of the heavy work of any agricultural enterprise;* but still and all it was a business, and he went at it with a grimness that was the precise and telling opposite of the playfulness of his wilderness travels. He would not indulge in any of the doctor's agricultural experimenting but converted lands formerly in pasturage to vineyards and orchards and concentrated production on Bartlett pears, tokay grapes, and cherries, all good cash crops.

He made a great deal of money, just as he had intended, but it was not easy even with all his energy and Scots shrewdness. The period of the '80s was one of significant decline in agricultural prices, for even though the market continued to expand with the population, methods of production improved even faster, and the result was a glut. Compounding the farmers' problems were a deflated currency and a critical lack of information about the markets they aimed for. This was particularly true for California fruit growers, whose major markets were on the other side of the continent and who had little idea what a fair price for their products might be. The railroads routinely gouged them, and the commission merchants took full advantage of their ignorance and relatively weak bargaining position.

But neither the designs of shippers nor those of the middlemen could defeat Muir, in whom they found a sharp, tough adversary. He studied the markets enough to develop a good sense of what

---

*"Muir had the best horses in the valley," a ranch hand recalled. "If you ... mistreated them in any way, you were fired on the spot" (P. J. Ryan, *John Muir National Historic Site,* Point Reyes, California, 1977).

his corps were worth, and he drove hard bargains, occasionally calling the bluffs of the merchants and refusing to sell to them at all until they met his figure. Perhaps in the earliest days he could afford this strategy since he had Dr. Strentzel's considerable financial backing, but soon enough it was his own money and his own sense of the economics of the business that he used to his advantage.

In 1885 the citrus growers tried to break out of this strangling situation by combining into a cooperative, but the middlemen were still far too strong and easily crushed them. Their new terms exacted harsh retribution and were meant as a warning to others in the California fruit industry. Muir went his own way, and as the decade wore on his regular trips to the bank in Martinez, a laundry sack of cash behind his seat in the buggy, and his frost-damaged foot dangling over the side, excited both admiration and not a little envy in his Alhambra Valley neighbors. By the time Robert Underwood Johnson met him, Muir had made himself a rich man and had accumulated savings that would last the family his lifetime and more.

But the battle had been hard on him, and that produced the hollowness Johnson had noted about Muir's temples. Nor was the hardest part of it his dealings with shippers and middlemen, difficult as these were. Burning inside him like a subterranean lignite fire was the knowledge that the great spectacle of nature was going on while he had chained himself to a business with its thousand petty details. Sunrise and the spread of spangled glory across his lands seemed to mock him and his deadly earnest efforts. Sunset was a daily admonition, a reminder of the lengthening shadows of his own life: so much he would do and experience had he the time; so much he would tell the world of his adventures in the great, beating heart of nature. Yet his voluminous notes lay almost wholly unmined beneath the covers of his journals or stacked in hopelessly random fashion in the corners of his study. In the valley, moving in supervision among his rows, he still knew where the far mountains and glaciers were, and that knowledge was a daily agony.

He was devoted to his little girls (the "babies" he called them, long after they were past that), and he found genuine delight in taking them on nature walks through the hills, when he would name for them the flowers and trees and tell stories of those unsung lives, yet these were the poor flights of a clipped eagle. At the

dinner table the girls would make him tell other stories, long
fictional ones that might extend serially through weeks, but such
extemporaneous composition was an ineffectual substitute for his
literary work. Through it all, Louie was everything she could be for
him, solicitous, understanding, ever urging him to be less hard on
himself. But it all came nowhere near equaling contentment, and
he knew it never would. And *that* must have given him a private
sense of guilt that could make an unpleasant combination with the
large, agonizing contrast between his old life in nature and his
present one. So he had his irascible moods, flashes of temper when
his rich fund of profanity (learned, as Daniel Muir had feared, from
Dunbar's bad boys) would flow, even with the "babies" present.
He grew lean as a crow, was "nerve-shaken," as he would put it,
and developed a persistent, hacking cough. At such times, if possible, Louie would make arrangements for his relief and pack him off
—to Yosemite, perhaps, or to the northwestern states as in '88. But
the respites were far too few and inadequate in any case.

His companion of Alaskan days, S. Hall Young, visited Muir
on the ranch in 1883 and again five years later when Young had
ended his missionary days in the far north. On the first occasion,
Muir broke into what Young called a "passionate" voicing of his
discontent. "I am losing precious days," Young quoted him as
exclaiming. "I am degenerating into a machine for making money.
I am learning nothing in this trivial world of men. I must break
away and get out into the mountains to learn the news."

Young's visit of 1888 was unexpected, and when Muir spied
him, he dropped the basket of cherries he was holding and came
running to Young, crying out that he was certain his friend had
come to take him away from all this, up to the ice, snow, and
dreaming solitudes of the great north. He was aghast when Young
told him he was done with Alaska. It was a terrible mistake, Muir
said, for the Alaskan landscape with its white peaks and snow banners would haunt Young's dreams even as it did his own. Look at
me, he enjoined his visitor:

I'm a horrible example. I, who have breathed the mountain air
—who have really lived a life of freedom—condemned to penal
servitude with these miserable little bald-heads! [holding up a

bunch of cherries]. Boxing them up; putting them in prison! And for money! Man! I'm like to die of the shame of it.

He ran on about the details of the "sordid world" in which he lived, how just the other day a "Chinaman" had dumped a bucket of phosphorus over him and almost burned him up. How mean a death that would have been compared with a "nice white death in the crevasse of a glacier!" Then lapsing into broad Scots for emphasis, he confided, "Gin it were na for my bairnies I'd rin awa' frae a' this tribble an' hale ye back north wi' me." Through the remainder of that day and on into the night as they talked, the embattled explorer almost seemed to cling with a pathetic desperation to his old friend in an ironic reversal of their positions years ago when it had been Young who had clung to Muir on that mountainside above Glenora.

Perhaps it was Young's visit in early summer that jarred something loose in the Muir household. At any rate, by late June Louie had been successful in persuading Muir that at all costs he must get away. Irritable, his stomach a knot, he agreed and went camping and botanizing around Lake Tahoe with his friend Charles C. Parry. And from there he went northwestward with Keith into Oregon and Washington. It was to prove a momentous trip, for during it both John and Louie came to the realization that things simply could not continue as they had. Muir was miserably discontent too much of the time, and the sacrifices he felt compelled to make for the family no longer made sense. It was at this point that Louie wrote him saying that any enterprise that required the sacrifice of a "noble life" ought instantly to be abandoned. His real work, she told her husband, was his writing, and there was nothing that had a right to be considered before this "except the welfare of our children."

If she had called Muir's life a noble one, this was also a noble letter, and even he, driven as he was, could now see that she meant it and that it was the utter and absolute truth. It was precisely what he needed. His first journal entries of the trip with Parry had been brief and somewhat dispirited in tone as he noted the devastation loggers were creating along the Truckee River. The spirit of the entries picked up after a camp at Cascade Lake, and there Muir adapted a favorite line from Emerson—"the pomp of kings ridiculous!" By the time he and Keith were in the moist verdure of the Northwest and he had Louie's momentous letter in hand, he was observing and writing with his old-time vigor. He wrote a stirring account of a climb of Mount Rainier and included a fine description of his party's first full view of the mountain, "awful in bulk and majesty, filling all the view like a separate, new-born world, yet withal so fine and beautiful it might well fire the dullest observer to desperate enthusiasm."

But it was the forests of Oregon that truly released him. Wandering in them, he thought of that earlier Scots explorer, David Douglas, who had written the first description of these woods and of their noblest inhabitant, the sugar pine. When Douglas had first come upon the great tree and was busily examining its bark and seeds, he was surprised by a band of heavily armed Indians. The natives automatically assumed the white man was in their woods for plunder, for every white they had ever encountered had been so, most especially the trappers. But when they learned Douglas was after nothing but a knowledge of the woods, they left him in peace and christened him the "Man of Grass."

The anecdote seemed instructive to Muir, knowing what he did of the subsequent fate of this wilderness. In the long years since the first whites had entered these grand forests Douglas had been singular, no others having loved it as he evidently had, no others having been "men of grass." He thought of Lewis and Clark and of the mountain men who had followed those blazes to pursue the beaver with a "weariless ardor." Not even in the quest for gold, Muir thought, had a more "ruthless, desperate energy been developed." So the mountain men had gone their heedless way, slaughtering, trading, carousing "until at length a bullet or arrow would end all." Most of them, he wrote, lasted but a few short seasons, just like the beaver they trapped: after a relatively few years both the mountain men and their quarry had passed away leaving "scarcely the faintest sign of their existence."

The mountain men had rendered an important service to the country, Muir judged, by the deep and comprehensive knowledge of it they had acquired and passed on. Yet in the long view that history was disclosing, their influence had been pernicious, for they had been mighty contributors to the American tradition of wasting the wilderness. He sketched the beginnings of that tradition when the first whites came to the New World, "said their prayers with superb audacity," and plunged inland to the mindless work of destruction. From that time to this very moment the work had gone on without surcease, native cultures, game animals, landscape—all plundered, destroyed. What was the motive force behind this? What could be equal to it as an opposing force? Here in the Northwest the future was as unmistakable as the whine of the sawmills. Soon enough—and far sooner than either the loggers or the public imagined—there would be no more forests.

Witnessing the earlier destruction of the New England forests, Thoreau had thought it might be a good idea to preserve remnant woodlands in a kind of national park, if only so that all memory of what America once had been would not vanish into the maw of progress. In *The Maine Woods* he wrote with characteristic acerbity that even the ignorant monarchs of England had shown the sense to preserve certain tracts of forest, however selfish their motives. But not so the supposedly enlightened American democrats; they seemed bent on destroying every bit of woodland on the continent. "Why should not we," he wondered, "who have renounced the king's authority, have our national preserves . . . ?" The forests thus saved, he thought, would be grand sources of inspiration and "true recreation." Or were Americans fated to "grub up" all the woods, "poaching on our own national domains?"

In a similar mood, Muir now wondered whether out of all the immensity of Oregon's forest wealth a few specimens of the lordly sugar pine "might be spared to the world, not as dead lumber, but as living trees." A park of moderate extent, he mused,

> might be set apart and protected for public use forever, containing at least a few hundreds of these noble pines, spruces, and firs. Happy will be the men who, having the power and the love and the benevolent forecast to do this, will do it. They will not be forgotten. The trees and their lovers will sing their praises, and generations yet unborn will rise up and call them blessed.

With these recent experiences within Muir and with a new understanding between him and Louie, Johnson's prospects were brighter than he could have guessed. Muir still carried the same burdens of the past seven years, and in fact even after 1891 when he gave over a portion of the ranch supervision to his brother-in-law, John Reid, he continued to feel burdened and trapped.* But by this summer of '89, he had begun slowly to turn his attentions again to the wider world.

Nothing probably was better calculated to set ablaze old enthusiasms than a trip to Yosemite. He wanted to show it to the visiting easterner, perhaps as much as anything to prove that it really did "come up to the brag," as Emerson had said it did. They went by stage to Wawona and then into the valley itself, where Johnson was suitably awed. There Muir arranged a pack trip into the higher mountains, and with three mules and a cook/aide-de-camp named "Pike" they set off for Tuolumne Meadows. The entire way Muir was in a sustained flight of boyish glee, pointing out the natural features they encountered, telling stories of his earlier life here, filling in his personal background for Johnson. On their slow ascent to the meadows, Pike continued to urge his old friend to "wallop" the stubborn mule he rode, but Muir would not, content apparently to let the beast take its own good time to Soda Springs, where they made camp. From this base Muir planned arduous walking excursions and took some delight in Johnson's difficulties with the rocky terrain. But at night around their campfire Muir was solicitous and even gentle with Johnson, and under the brightest stars the latter had ever seen they talked intimately.

In the course of one of these conversations, Muir commenced

---

*Muir's ranch journals for the years 1895 and 1896, for example, reveal him still chafing under the routines and obligations of the ranch and family life. In the journal of the latter year he noted "another bright day" on April 17: "the old pomp over again—monotonous through small local cares & tasks, while like gophers we drive our trade of soil stirring almost in the dark how vast a multitude of interesting events are taking place over this busy loving, hating world." A week later he wrote: "How time flies, & how little of my real work I accomplish in the midst of all this ranch work & the petty details of a domestic kind. How grand would be a home in a hollow sequoia!" (Muir Papers, Holt-Atherton).

what Johnson called a "whimsical denunciation" of the supervisory work of the Yosemite Park commissioners. They had, in Muir's view, already greatly diminished the park's natural beauty by tolerating pigsties, hayfields, and corrals in the valley and by an injudicious cutting and pruning of the trees so that the eye was deprived of units of scale whereby to measure and set off the great precipices. Johnson then took up the theme, remarking that on their way up from the valley he had missed those marvelous mountain meadows whose luxuriant grasses and flowers Muir had described in his writings. He missed them, Muir rejoined, because they no longer existed. The "hoofed locusts," as Muir called the sheep, had destroyed them through years of summer pasturings. A portion of Yosemite, he explained, had been made a state park by President Lincoln in 1864, but the grant to the state protected neither the higher mountain meadows nor the headwaters of the streams that fell into the valley. And in any case, such was the attitude toward unimproved lands, whether public, private, or park that Muir doubted the sheepmen would respect any boundaries. Grazing, no matter how destructive it might prove, was regarded as a kind of natural right that had grown up with the country.

Obviously, said Johnson, the thing to do was to create a national park around the state park so as to protect the meadows and the headwaters of the streams. In a way, it was as ignorant a suggestion as it was bold: Johnson did not have a good understanding of western and especially Californian attitudes toward land. Muir patiently explained something of these and included the information that both he and Senator Newton Booth had tried to formulate legislation to widen the park's boundaries but that nothing had come of their efforts. Muir was highly skeptical that anything ever could: between the vested interests and public indifference the fate of Yosemite appeared sealed, and eventually only the inaccessible reaches of the Sierras would be safe from the hands of men.

Johnson listened, and in Muir's words it was not hard to hear a lament for the American wilderness, like the sighing of wind in the trees. But even if he was largely ignorant of these western and California realities of which his guide now spoke, Johnson thought he knew better than Muir the larger realities of contemporary American life.

Fifteen years Muir's junior, Johnson was, like William Dean

Howells, Mark Twain, and John Wesley Powell, a product of the democratic idealism of the prewar midwestern village, and he had never wavered in the beliefs that background had taught so well. Educated in the ferment of abolitionism, caught by the romance of the print shop and of the village bookshop with its unforgettable smell of leather bindings, he too had been thrilled and permanently inspired by Emerson, and he believed profoundly in the power of the written word to change things for the better. For almost two decades he had been in the public arena, fighting for causes he thought good. He had seen the appalling spectacle of venality and corruption in Washington under Grant and so had no illusions about what could happen to the republic if good people resigned themselves to the worst. But he had also seen and participated in the steady, heartening rise of reformist idealism since the early '80s, and he believed that something as significant as the preservation of Yosemite was not a lost cause and would find many adherents. He also saw in Muir a potentially magnificent recruit to the ranks of crusading writers like Howells, Henry George, and Henry Demarest Lloyd.

Johnson was persuasive in those evenings at Soda Springs as the two men lay wrapped in blankets over which the campfire spread its rich glow. He wanted Muir to write two articles for the *Century,* one to attract general attention to the threatened natural features of Yosemite, the other detailing the new boundaries of the national park as he and Johnson should draw them. If Muir would do this, Johnson would take the articles, lavishly illustrated, to Washington and there lobby for passage of a bill creating a Yosemite national park. Johnson had connections on the public lands committees of both the House and Senate, and he told Muir he had good hopes such a measure would be adopted without serious opposition. Surprised by hope, Muir agreed he would try.

A less optimistic man than Robert Underwood Johnson might have been moved to observe that as far as the protection of the American landscape was concerned there were as many ominous signs as hopeful ones as the nation entered the century's final decade. Chief among the former were two looming matters of history that had hardly been affected by the stirrings of reform in the 1880s: a deeply rooted American animus toward wild lands and a cavalier attitude toward the use of the public domain. Both matters would be significant in this campaign for a national park and both would be of continuing significance in the conservation and preservation battles that would consume the final years of Muir's life.

Of the first, it was clear to Muir at least that it had its genesis well before the birth of the American republic: his remarks in the journal of his thousand-mile walk indicate his early awareness that there was something in the culture of the Christian West that encouraged hostility to all of the natural world that was unimproved by man or that seemed to resist human use. Thoreau had seen this hostility as a "war with the wilderness," nor had he gone too far in so characterizing it. Muir had seen the consequences of this battle in his own life, and he could have been in little doubt that here lay the most serious obstacle to the creation of wilderness oases. Writing tongue in cheek to Johnson, Muir observed that among Californians love of unspoiled nature was "desperately modest" and "consuming enthusiasm almost wholly unknown." And what was true of Californians he had discovered in his travels was true of Americans generally so that it would have to be within this general cultural framework that any work of protection would be done.

Then there was the matter of the popular attitude toward the use of the public domain. The public domain itself was an odd and unlooked-for consequence of the American Revolution, and its history accurately reflected its accidental origins. Suddenly, the infant nation found itself nominal possessor of vast, largely uncharted lands lying west of the Appalachians. The seven larger states of the original thirteen all had claims of various sizes and degrees of fictionality in those western lands, and it was clear that if those claims were allowed to stand, the six smaller states would find themselves boxed in by the seaboard on one side and by the big seven on the other. Led by Maryland, the lesser six refused the Articles of Confederation until the bigger states had resigned their western claims and so acknowledged that those lands were common property.

The bigger states actually had no very precise understanding of what their western claims entailed; Virginia's claim, for instance, swept northwestward in a broad, hoggish swath up through the Great Lakes and into Canada. But soon enough they realized that there would be no such thing as a "United States" unless they relinquished their claims, and between 1780 and 1802 they did so. Thus by the latter date something had been created that became known as the public domain, a huge extent of unsettled landscape over which the federal government reluctantly assumed the position of trustee for the American people.

Given this background, it is not surprising that the government was from the first eager to convey the public domain into private hands as quickly as might be. Nobody had imagined the government as a great landlord (a specter from the Old World); nobody knew how it could effectively exercise its trusteeship responsibilities. Further, the strong states' rights feeling and the endemic lawlessness of the frontiersmen pushing into the western lands encouraged a sense of unease in the government over its position. And so began the great giveaway.

Through such legislation as the Ordinance of 1785, the Preemption Act of 1830 (and subsequent extensions of it), the Indian Removal Act (the same year), the Act of 1850 (commencing large-scale grants to railroads), the Homestead Act (1862), and the Timber Culture Act (1873), the federal government succeeded famously in alienating most of the public lands. By 1886 Henry George was able accurately to observe that the nation had arrived "on the verge of an event which is, in some respects, the most important that has occurred since Columbus sighted land—the 'fencing in' of the last available quarter section of the American domain." Three years later the census made it official: the frontier was gone and the public domain had been settled.

In the course of this incredibly rapid giveaway the government had unwittingly encouraged the habits of land speculation and land spoliation; by 1890 these had deepened into traits of the national character. As the population had continued its swift expansion through the nineteenth century, spreading westward into the public domain, individuals were encouraged to buy up more land than they themselves could ever want or use and hold it out for later sale at higher prices.* And since the government so obviously felt the

*Even Emerson had been persuaded by his lawyer and financial adviser to speculate in western lands and had turned a handsome profit in a Wisconsin land deal (Ralph L. Rusk, *The Life of Ralph Waldo Emerson,* New York, 1949).

public lands existed for the sole purpose of private exploitation, the habit of treating them ruthlessly became widespread. When the lands were worked out and their natural resources squandered, so what? Was this not what the lands were there for? And would there not be more public lands available at the cheapest prices?

By 1890, as Muir penned his Yosemite articles and Johnson prepared for his Washington lobbying, America remained saddled with a grotesquely outmoded philosophy of public-land use characterized by cynicism, greed, and carelessness. The creation of a Yosemite national park would by itself do little to change popular attitudes toward public-land use, but the debate the park proposal initiated would be an important step in raising the consciousness of the nation to a consideration of the best use of its remaining natural resources.

When Muir and Johnson went to work on a Yosemite bill there were some precedents. Yellowstone had been made a national park in 1872, and a forest tract in the Adirondacks had been set aside as "forever wild" in 1885. Yet in a way, their existence was about as much hindrance as help because they had drawn some unfavorable attention to the first faltering steps of what could hardly yet be called a conservation movement. Both Yellowstone and the Adirondacks reserve had been established primarily for commercial reasons and without much regard—none in the case of the Adirondacks reserve—for their scenic qualities or their potential as places of wilderness recreation. Even so there were some, both in public and private life, who decried their existence. After all, as one congressman said of Yellowstone, the federal government was supposed to be in the business of *selling* its lands, not *preserving* them. And if, as was the case in the Adirondacks, the reserve was necessary to ensure steady water flows in the Erie Canal and the Hudson River, still it was a question whether it was necessary to prohibit all exploitation of the timber within the reserve. The act providing for the permanent preservation of 715,000 acres of choice timberland went hard against an American grain more than a century in the forming.

The major impetus for the protection of Yellowstone had most likely been the fears of a powerful few that other individuals would acquire title to sites with geysers and hot springs and so be able to monopolize (and perhaps abort) a projected tourist trade. For this reason Jay Cooke's company, financier of the Northern Pacific, was interested in federal protection for Yellowstone. Seeing itself as owner of the only line serving the projected park, it offered its considerable lobbying strength to Ferdinand V. Hayden and other supporters of the park idea. Yellowstone became a national park partly because Cooke & Company had more power than the individual squatters and hucksters who wished to preempt the sites of the natural tourist attractions; and partly, too, because Congress became persuaded that the area was useless for anything except the tourist trade. Thereafter and for about a decade a vast indifference characterized political and public opinion about Yellowstone except for an occasional grumble to the effect that the park ought to be sold as other public lands had been and that it was an "expensive luxury."

Yet when a mining company and a railroad discovered in the mid-1880s that it would be expedient to have a line run through park lands, Yellowstone got its first sustained national attention, and a railroad spokesman told a congressional hearing that he found it incredible that there should be defenders of the park's inviolability against legitimate commercial interests. Were such interests, he asked, to be frustrated and actually defeated by a "few sportsmen bent on the protection of a few buffalo"?* In this instance, at least, defenders of Yellowstone were successful in defeating the designs of the "legitimate commercial interests," but a pattern emerged that would become much more obvious through subsequent years: a park or any sort of wilderness preserve would be inviolable until—and only until—commercial interests found a use for it. Then its existence would be put in jeopardy and its defenders stigmatized as selfish sentimentalists.†

---

*The last of the once gigantic herds of buffalo had been killed off by 1883; in 1884 only three hundred buffalo hides were reported shipped from the Great Plains. Several small herds of mountain buffalo remained in Colorado and one in Yellowstone, and their numbers probably did not exceed one hundred (David A. Dary, *The Buffalo Book: The Saga of an American Symbol,* New York, 1975, 1984).

†The pattern bears an interesting resemblance to that established in the creation and subsequent abolishment of Indian reservations, a pattern in evidence in the year Muir and Johnson met and discussed Yosemite prospects. Oklahoma,

The congressional defenders of Yellowstone had to make a case that natural scenery was good for you: that when people were exposed to the great and untouched features of the park, their souls received tonic and toning that would help make them better people, better citizens. Representative McAdoo of New Jersey spoke directly to this point when he claimed that Yellowstone National Park had been created so that Americans could come into contact with the West's "inspiring sights and mysteries of nature" and so be brought into "closer communion with omniscience. . . ."

If this was a hard thing to prove, the idea had an old and honored history in America and had existed as a minor tradition at least since the seventeenth century. For most of the American Romantics the idea had been central, and in their spiritual descendants it lived on. But by the 1890s the idea had achieved the honorific and empty status of a sentiment: an intellectual decoration that was pleasing if you could afford it but that must always yield to the higher truths of economics.

For Muir the healing powers of nature and the close if mysterious connection between nature and God were hardly intellectual decorations. Nor were they directly the bequests of the Romantics, of Wordsworth, Emerson, or Thoreau, however much he had learned from and been heartened by these men. They were home truths he had been learning and living with since his earliest childhood days in Dunbar. Now in writing his articles for the *Century,* these beliefs formed the heart of his argument, nor did he ever in subsequent pleas for the preservation of this or that natural feature feel the truths were by themselves insufficient. For him at least the old spiritual promise of America had been fulfilled. He was not incapable of speaking and writing on a recognizably "practical" plane in conservation and preservation matters and on occasion would do so. But the ultimate plane of reference remained elsewhere, and to those disposed to listen to him this lent a mysterious and even awesome power to his words. To others, he would always appear impractical, God-haunted, self-righteous.

In the autumn of 1890, Muir spoke in the diction his life in

formerly Indian territory forever, was opened to white settlement in February 1889, and eleven million acres of Sioux land were ceded to the United States in August.

nature had taught, especially in his first article, "Treasures of the Yosemite" (August 1890). For this, he went back into the talus of his notes and journals and exhumed his accounts of the spring of 1868 and the summer of '69, his primary contacts with Yosemite and the Sierras. The glow of those personally mythic moments was reflected across the decades into the pages of an essay that led ineluctably to this point:

> From the heights on the margins of these glorious forests we at length gain our first general view of the valley—a view that breaks suddenly upon us in all its glory far and wide and deep; a new revelation in landscape affairs that goes far to make the weakest and meanest spectator rich and significant evermore.

"Features of the Proposed Yosemite National Park" appeared in the next issue of the *Century* and was a somewhat more practical "how-to" approach to the park as it might be experienced by tourists. Like "Treasures," it was filled with illustrations, but whereas the first article included pictures of the devastation caused by the merchants and sheepman, "Features" contained illustrations of the surpassing beauties of the place as well as a map of the proposed new boundaries. At the end of the article, in a description of the nearby Hetch Hetchy Valley, Muir called forthrightly for federal intervention to save all he had so lovingly described. "Unless reserved or protected," he wrote, "the whole region will soon or late be devastated by lumbermen and sheepmen, and so of course made unfit for use as a pleasure ground." Already, he claimed, the ground in many areas had been "gnawed and trampled into a desert condition, and when the region shall be stripped of its forests the ruin will be complete."

Though he did not know it, in calling for federal intervention Muir was following the lead of Frederick Law Olmsted, who had been one of the original commissioners of the Yosemite and Mariposa grants when Lincoln had deeded them to the state in 1864. In the current campaign Johnson enlisted Olmsted's aid once again, and the latter responded with an open letter that several newspapers printed. Muir told Johnson he found the letter a "little soft," but there had been nothing soft about Olmsted's recommendations in 1865 for the care of Yosemite. In a very detailed report read to the Yosemite Commission in that year, Olmsted vigorously spelled out the duty of a democratic government to provide for the protection of places of special natural beauty. The physical and mental benefits citizens gained from experiencing such places, Olmsted argued, more than justified the expenses accrued in their acquisition and upkeep. Without government acquisition of such selected sites, they would inevitably become the private preserves of rich men, and thus America would recapitulate the history of Old World aristocracies. But, Olmsted stressed, unless the government was prepared actively to protect its parks and preserves, their existence would be nugatory. Already in 1865 he foresaw the lawless, cavalier treatment Yosemite would suffer at the hands of unregulated loggers and shake-makers, sheepmen, hostelers, and assorted merchants. Unfortunately for Yosemite, the comprehensive measures he advocated in his report cost money, a good deal of it by the standards of the time, and it was the state of California Olmsted was actually speaking to though his report looked, as it were, over the head of the state and toward the federal government for support. California had been given Yosemite to manage without federal money, and the state did not want to spend too much on its gift. Two of the Yosemite commissioners, William Ashburner and Josiah D. Whitney, succeeded in quashing Olmsted's report for fear that money spent on Yosemite might come out of appropriations for Whitney's Geological Survey—as indeed it might have.

The results were those Muir had pointed out to Johnson in the spring of 1889. Now the 200,000 subscribers to the *Century* could see for themselves the plowed valley lands dotted with ramshackle barns and messy haystacks, the stump forest of cut trees, the ruthlessly inartistic tree trimming that contributed to the beaten, frowsy look of the place. And they could see also, as Muir and Johnson meant them to, the sublime rocks towering over this scene as if making mocking gloss on the restless, improving hand of man.

Muir's articles and especially his specific recommendations for the enlarged boundaries of the park were of critical significance to the Yosemite campaign. No one involved in working for the new park had so comprehensive an understanding of the whole region and of the issues involved in its protection. The map he drew and sent to Johnson became the basis of the final bill (H.R. 12187) that was introduced in the fall of 1890. But it is likely that Robert

Underwood Johnson's work in New York and Washington was even more important to the bill's passage than was Muir's. His connections were wide and various, and he himself was a persuasive lobbyist and tireless worker. Under his leadership the campaign had generated great momentum well before Muir's second article appeared, and Johnson had succeeded in creating a large—and unlikely—coalition favoring the park, including the powerful Southern Pacific Railroad and the Hearst family.

The opposition was led by Colonel John P. Irish, secretary and treasurer of the Yosemite Commission, but it was slow to develop and so ineffective when it did that after the bill had passed the commissioners found it expedient to claim that they had actually favored the measure all along. Colonel Irish was successful, however, in slinging some mud that stuck to Muir for the rest of his life. In a heated reply to an article of Muir's in which the author said the valley, too, ought to be nationalized, Irish wrote in the Oakland *Tribune* that Muir himself had been a great despoiler of the valley. Muir, said Irish, was but a "pseudo-naturalist" who had "logged and sawed the trees of the Valley with as willing a hand as any lumberman in the Sierras." The charge as Irish made it was untrue, as he must have known. Muir had always said that the timber he milled for Hutchings in the early '70s was down timber, and maybe most of it was. But Galen Clark, the official valley guardian, had written Olmsted in July 1868 (well before Muir went to work for Hutchings) that Hutchings had defied the commission's order that he not establish a sawmill at that time and had felled four hundred trees in the valley. It is possible that Muir did mill this timber while ignorant of the circumstances. In any case, Muir felt compelled publicly to deny the charge; thereafter it became standard practice for Muir's allies to issue the denials for him, always carefully specifying that Muir had milled only down wood.

Irish's slander not availing, personal friends of Johnson's introduced the Yosemite bill in the House and Senate, and without much discussion it passed both houses on the last day of September 1890; the day following, President Harrison signed it into law. Johnson's coalition had hung together and accomplished its mission, but as the park's advocates were to learn, the victory was not by any means final, for soon after the bill had become law the opposition crystalized, hardened its objections, and began the process of trying to whittle away at the park's generous boundaries.

Nor was the victory final in another sense, for there as a symbol of the intransigent opposition to a Yosemite National Park was the valley itself, Yosemite's diadem. It remained thoroughly in state hands and largely subject to the desires of special interests. The campaign for its recession to the federal government and inclusion in the national park would not actively begin for another five years. When it did, it would engage the best energies of Muir, Johnson, and their allies, and it would drag on through eleven years before President Theodore Roosevelt would sign the measure including the valley in the national park in 1905.

The important thing, to be sure, was the passage of H.R. 12187, however much the bill might have seemed to Muir a tentative measure and qualified victory. As an important by-product of the campaign for its passage, Muir had discovered that he now had allies, unsuspected friends willing to stand up on behalf of the American landscape. Here indeed was evidence of what Johnson had tried to convince Muir of, that revival of reformist idealism now succeeding the moral interregnum of the late '60s and the decade of the '70s: a growing sense among Americans that national affairs had reached a critical stage where public participation was imperative. A century of unparalleled progress was rushing to its conclusion, and to many it seemed as if that progress had been random, uneven, and had brought along with it, like a flood, a ruck of problems, inequities, and painful discrepancies between professed ideals and actual practices. America, the reformers believed, needed direction badly.

A committed loner in his work, Muir now began to see and feel the advantages of association, both on a professional plane and on a personal one as well. Coming out again into the wider world under Johnson's prodding, he found that association was a watchword of the times: people banding together in corporations, trusts, unions, cooperatives, splinter parties, and special-interest groups to advance their interests or protect them.

And as he realized his own mortality he appeared to feel as never before the need of comrades. David Galloway, as close to Muir as blood and but ten years his senior, had died in 1884,

apparently inconsolable about the accidental death of his and
Sarah's teenaged son. It was the first death truly close to Muir, and
he felt it.

But of far greater significance to this change in Muir was the
death of his father the next year. He had not seen him since that
summer day in 1867 when they had angrily parted at Hickory Hill,
had hardly any communication with him in the intervening years.
Daniel Muir had attempted to intrude on his son's fledgling literary
career in 1874 by writing him that "the best and soonest way of
getting quit of the writing and publishing your book is to burn it
and then it will do no more harm either to you or to others," and
that had been about the extent of their contact.

But the beaten and tyrannized child lived on within the man,
and John carried Daniel Muir with him. He would tell almost
anyone he became familiar with of those events in his youth, and
so it is not surprising that he should have been seized with a powerful premonition of the father's impending death in the late summer
of 1885. He acted upon it, went east to gather up as many of the
family as he could, and then went to Kansas City, where Daniel
Muir was living with Joanna Muir Brown and her husband.

Muir had delayed his arrival about a month from the time of
the premonition, as if to give prophecy time to enact itself and so
prevent a calamitous meeting. When he did arrive, he found Daniel
Muir on his deathbed, and it was the eldest son who held the old
man's hand as he slipped away. He would go on telling of Daniel
Muir's cruelty until the end of his own life, would write feelingly
of it in his autobiography, but it was as if the death of his old
tormenter had deprived the son of something he could not do so
well without.

Most recently he suffered from the loss of Charles Parry, with
whom he had botanized less than a year before. Writing his friends
the Bidwells, Muir confessed Parry's death made him feel lonesome. Then there was this:

> The Scotch have a proverb, 'The evenin' brings a' hame.' And so,
> however separated, far or near, the evening of life brings all
> together at last. Lovely souls embalmed in a thousand flowers,
> embalmed in the hearts of their friends, never for a moment does

death seem to have had anything to do with them. They seem near, and are near, as if in bodily sight I wave my hand to them in loving recognition.

His own health continued to issue warnings that chimed with these losses, and he was sick enough in the summer of 1890 to leave family, ranch, and the pending Yosemite legislation and go once more to Alaska, where he imagined the microbe-killing cold would destroy whatever germs racked his lungs with a persistent cough and twisted his stomach.

He fled civilization and all cares with a "steady aim like a crusader bound for the Holy Land or a bird to its northern home following the flight of the seasons," as he wrote in his journal. Less than a month out, he was able to write Louie that his cough had disappeared and his appetite had returned with a savage voracity. As always, immersion in the natural world had healed what ailed him, and those thoughts of death which had come to him in civilization now shrank back into their proper proportions, dwarfed by the immense spectacle of the wilderness. He wrote in his journal that days

spent alone in the depths of the wilderness have shown me that immortal life beyond the grave is not essential to perfect happiness, for these diverse days were so complete there was no sense of time in them, they had no definite beginning or ending, and formed a kind of terrestrial immortality.

"After days like these," he concluded, "we are ready for any fate —pain, grief, death or oblivion—with grateful heart for the glorious gift as long as hearts shall endure."

So, as he pushed on into the Alaskan wilds, the old magic contentment enveloped him. He laughed at ravens, harbingers of death, who tracked him as he playfully slid down a glacier. "Not yet, you black imps," he wrote, "not yet." Neither morbid thoughts nor germs could withstand a wilderness fresh and sweet and green as life itself. These forests, he observed, are the clearest way into the feeling of oneness with the universe, while the mountains moved him to think of his own life's history. Mountains, he thought, have always been fountains of men as well as of rivers, great poets and prophets having been schooled in them for their work among men. Here was life, and like Thoreau, he exultantly wrote that in the wilderness "lies the hope of the world—the great fresh unblighted, unredeemed wilderness." Here the "galling harness of civilization drops off, and the wounds heal ere we are aware."

He would need all the cheerful fortitude he had gained in Alaska, for immediately upon his return in late summer his responsibilities increased. Dr. Strentzel died on the last of October, and by this time Muir was already hard at work on a new preservationist campaign aimed at enlarging the boundaries of Sequoia National Park, which had been created at the same time as Yosemite. In the remaining months of the year he and Louie made the move down the hill and into the "big house" where they could care for Mrs. Strentzel. Thus by January 1891 the old sense of crushing captivity had returned to Muir, and in a letter to his brother Dan he described himself as "stupidly busy" with the cares of ranch and family as well as with his literary tasks.

But there were consolations and, wherever found, Muir seized them. Chief among these was that new sense of community that had come out of the first Yosemite campaign. Now in the wake of that success some were talking of a kind of association that would formally bring together lovers of the western mountains. Muir was from the first amenable to approaches the early planners made to him.

Here again, American cultural history had created precedents. Beginning in the populous East, where the wilderness had disappeared with astonishing rapidity in the years after the revolution, associations had been formed in a sort of nostalgic reaction: the Williamstown Alpine Club (1863), the White Mountain Club (1873), and the Appalachian Mountain Club (1876). In the 1880s the American Ornithological Union and the Audubon Society had been organized, and these latter were more than outing or appreciation groups; they had distinctly preservationist objectives as well. Naturally, in the larger and more newly settled West such organizations came later: wildernesses and natural resources could not be

*||| (+ planet Earth too)

regarded as precious until they were understood to be finite and
endangered. In the West few understood this in the nineteenth
century; even fewer cared. In 1890 western popular attitudes toward the wilderness and the use of the public domain were about
what eastern attitudes had been a century earlier, and indeed this
very cultural lag was to prove a conspicuous feature of the land
battles of the next two decades.

Nevertheless, there were stirrings, especially in the Bay area,
where an informal network of hikers and university intellectuals
had begun talking of organization in the wake of the Yosemite
victory. But the prime movers were Robert Underwood Johnson,
a San Francisco attorney, Warren Olney, and Muir. It was apparently Johnson who first suggested something like a Yosemite defense league to protect the new park from what he was certain
would be the attempted depredations of special interests. Olney
gladly lent his services to the framing of the articles of incorporation as well as to the other legal matters attendant to organization;
the first meetings were held in his offices on Sansome Street in San
Francisco. And it was Muir who gave his prestige and enthusiastic
support to a club that surely would have seemed lame without him.

By the time the first organizational meeting was convened in
Olney's offices at the end of May 1892, the association had its name,
the Sierra Club, and on June 4 twenty-seven men signed its articles
of incorporation. Muir was the unanimous choice for president with
Olney as first vice president. Its articles stated that the club existed
to promote the exploration and enjoyment of the mountain regions
of the Pacific and also to "enlist the support and co-operation of the
people and the government in preserving the forests and other
features of the Sierra Nevada Mountains. . . ."

The list of charter members included old friends of Muir's such
as Keith, McChesney, Galen Clark, and Joseph Le Conte. Wanda
Muir was on the list, as were the San Francisco millionaire Adolph
Sutro, who would soon become the city's mayor, and Muir's old
employer and sometime antagonist, James M. Hutchings. Young
Sam Merrill of the Indianapolis Merrills happened to be staying
with the Muirs at the time, and years after he recalled vividly Muir's
delight when he returned to Martinez that evening. Never, said
Merrill, had he seen Muir so happy and animated as he was at the
dinner table that night. Surrounded now by kindred spirits, Muir

felt that something constructive might at last be done to protect the mountains and trees.

No doubt a more specific source of Muir's pleasure in the formation of the club was his view that Yosemite could be much more ably defended by an association than by one man speaking alone or by scattered lovers of the mountains raising their voices singly. Speedily the accuracy of this view was put to the test when a bill was prepared by Congressman Anthony Caminetti that would contract the park's boundaries. Responsive to the complaints of stockmen accustomed to running their sheep and cattle on public lands, Caminetti drew up a measure that would substantially affect the new park everywhere but on its southern boundary. Muir was instantly on the alert and with two other club members urged the Sierra Club to formally protest the bill.

Again, Johnson acted as Muir's man in Washington. He kept Muir and the club abreast of proceedings, and in February 1893 he judged the time was right for concerted protest since action on Caminetti's measure was imminent. The Sierra Club directed its protest to the House Committee on Agriculture, where presumably it had the desired effect. Caminetti's bill died in committee, and a month later Muir felt confident that the park was safe, "at least for this time."

This first concerted—and successful—club action may have been a significant factor in a decision Muir made in this spring. For years he and Keith had been talking of a European trip, and now suddenly in May Keith telegrammed to say that he could wait no longer and was starting east immediately. Surprisingly, Muir decided he too could wait no longer. He now had the daily help of his brother-in-law in the supervision of the ranch, and since the past summer his brother David had been on the property and was beginning to take good hold in the business after the disastrous failure of his dry-goods firm in Portage. The sense of available help with the ranch, the defeat of the Caminetti bill, and perhaps, too, the telling contrast between the season of the year and his own time of life all combined to send Muir east after his friend.

But, as always, he took a meandering, circuitous route. Never one to keep to fixed schedules or itineraries, the habit of purposeful sauntering now deeply ingrained, he paid his mother a visit in Portage and then went to the World's Columbian Exposition at Chicago before going on to New York. Writing Louie from Chicago, he told her he considered the Exposition a "cosmopolitan rat's nest" where men had gathered together "much rubbish and commonplace stuff as well as things novel and precious." For all this, he confessed his admiration for the paintings on exhibit, for the great, shimmering city the landscapers and architects had created in Jackson Park—Augustus Saint-Gaudens, Olmsted, Daniel H. Burnham, Louis Sullivan—for the miles of tiny electric lights that made "all a fairyland on a colossal scale. . . ." It was enough, he wrote in Twain-like fashion, to have made "the Queen of Sheba and poor Solomon in all their glory feel sick with helpless envy."*

Still, for all the marvels on exhibit he remained profoundly skeptical of much that went on under the huge banner of "Progress." At Machinery Hall, for example, huge crowds gathered to watch mill and woodworking machines turn out products for the nation's insatiable appetite for wood, and in a separate building four sawmills chewed their ways through lengths of raw timber. If Muir saw these exhibits—and considering his background and interests it is hard to imagine he did not—he had nothing to say about them. But in due time he would have a good deal to say about the uses of the forests and about the uncritical popular attitude evidenced in the crowds now gathered to witness these machines at work.

Then he went to New York but not to Keith, and not yet to Europe, either. Keith was caught up in a whirl of parties, and as soon as Robert Underwood Johnson got hold of Muir, the latter found himself similarly engaged. In a stunning succession of lunches at private clubs and champagne dinners, Muir met John Burroughs, Richard Watson Gilder (the *Century*'s chief editor), and a number of other literary celebrities, all of whom seemed to

---

*Had Muir visited the exposition in July, he could have attended a special meeting of the American Historical Association, for there another Portage native, Frederick Jackson Turner, was scheduled to give an address on "The Significance of the Frontier in American History." The address proved controversial in its claim that American democracy came not out of transplanted English institutions but out of a mobile people's constant, vitalizing contact with the great wilderness.

know Muir and count him among their number. "I had no idea I was so well known," he wrote Louie, "considering how little I have written."

Everywhere they went Johnson prompted Muir to the telling of his hairbreadth escape across an Alaskan glacial crevasse with the mongrel dog Stickeen in 1880. And that was but one, though it proved the most popular, of the hundreds of stories this visitor could spellbindingly spin. As his rich voice filled club rooms, bringing a white, wild world to the tables of the well-placed, the legend of John Muir bloomed in the eyes of his audiences. The bearded, spare figure with the weathered face and distant-seeming eyes was the authentic article, more wilderness man than author, and an oral tale-teller of such power that in his presence the written word seemed a cheapened, secondhand sort of thing. It was all very curious, Muir wrote Louie, adding that when he told his Stickeen story even the servants would listen from behind screens and half-closed doors.

But if his New York audiences were as entranced with Muir's presence as if a literate Boone had suddenly materialized among them, Muir easily kept his own head straight. He had always had ambition, yes, and had wrestled long and hard with the problem of vocation. He had wanted, too, to be found worthy by the world of his time, provided this could be achieved without sacrificing his essential self. Now, evidently, he had been found more than ordinarily worthy and wholly on his own terms. So the experience of New York had to have been gratifying, and in its aftermath it is possible to see Muir beginning to assume in public something of the masking persona of the legendary figure, as if he, too, now saw himself partly as a work of art. But within himself, in his own life and work, he remained mostly unmoved. For him the best encounters of this eastern exposure were the new friends he made in Henry Fairfield Osborn, the famous paleontologist, and Charles S. Sargent, the great student of the American forests, friendships that would nurture and sustain him for the rest of his days.

Neither did the other grand experience have anything to do with his rather spectacular reception in New York. Johnson took Muir north to Boston, Cambridge, and Concord, and here at last Muir encountered the presences of legends that truly meant something to him: Emerson, Thoreau, and (to a lesser extent) Hawthorne. He made a pilgrimage to Sleepy Hollow Cemetery in Concord, to the simple, unadorned graves of Hawthorne and Thoreau and to the more dramatic one of Emerson, whose headstone Muir discovered was a rugged shaft of quartz that looked as if dropped there by a glacier. The graves of these men made it appear to him as though a kindly Mother Earth had gently taken them back into her bosom, and Muir, musing beneath summer's young leaves, was strongly moved. "I could not help thinking," he wrote Louie, "how glad I would be to feel sure that I would also rest here."

From Sleepy Hollow he and Johnson walked to Walden Pond, "a mere saunter." Muir found it a beautiful lake "embosomed like a bright dark eye" in the wooded hills of moraine gravel and sand with a rich undergrowth of huckleberry, willow, and oak bushes. "No wonder," he said, "Thoreau lived here two years. I could have enjoyed living here two hundred years or two thousand."

Finally there was a meeting and a meal with Emerson's son and with the son's father-in-law, and Muir was able to see at last that home to which Emerson himself had long ago invited him. Here, too, he was to learn of his celebrity, for Emerson's son told him that in Emerson's last years "John Muir" had become a sort of household word.

Before they left the Boston area the indefatigable Johnson had introduced Muir to Josiah Royce, Sarah Orne Jewett, and Francis Parkman, now at the close of a career spent writing about the settlement of the wildernesses of the New World. Then it was back to New York, where Muir met Twain and Twain's collaborator on *The Gilded Age,* Charles Dudley Warner; also Rudyard Kipling, George Washington Cable, and the electronics genius, Nikola Tesla, with whom he and Johnson spent a hilarious (and perhaps bibulous) evening. One evening he had dinner with James Pinchot at the latter's Gramercy Park residence, and there Muir met Pinchot's young son, Gifford, who, Muir learned, was studying forestry. By the time Johnson consented to Muir's release from this social servitude Keith and his wife had long since sailed for Europe; Muir himself did not get away until the end of June.

Whatever his original plans for Europe may have been (and it is likely they were only sketchy at best), the heart of the trip must always have been Scotland and especially Dunbar. Between the end of June and mid-September he visited London, the Lake District,

Ireland, and Switzerland, where he paid homage to the great, glacial Agassiz. But first and last it was Scotland and Dunbar. When he arrived in Edinburgh he was feeling lonely and displaced, a man suddenly without a country, but with typical resolution he looked up the well-known author and publisher, David Douglas, who had known Hugh Miller and Scott, and after a long evening of talk ("the most wonderful night as far as humanity is concerned I ever had in the world," he wrote Louie) he was brought back into a "quick and living" contact with Scotland. Now, he said proudly, "I am a Scotchman and at home again." And so he was, especially on the day following, when he took the train for Dunbar.

There it was, just as in memory, the old red, weathered town on the sea and the castle, now a bit more crumbled, on which schoolboys still clambered. There, too, were his old homes on the high street, and he was especially interested in the second one, wishing to discover just what sort of an adventure it really had been when he and David had climbed out the dormer window and onto the high-pitched roof.

After a night at a hotel, he hunted up a cousin living in the Lammermuirs and was enthusiastically welcomed. Here, too, apparently he was known. In the town itself he found on his leisurely rambles a number of his old schoolmates, most of them, so he said, looking older and grayer than he. But there were many ghosts as well: those he had known as a child here—his maternal grandparents and the fiesty druggist, Peter Lawson, whose headstone, brown and stark, formed a melancholy greeting near the entrance to the kirkyard. These prompted him to copy some lines of poetry into his journal:

> When musing on companions gone
> We doubly feel ourselves alone

Beneath which he copied another line on the situation of a man in his time of life, poised between resignation and content.

He visited the old school at the foot of the Davel Brae where, as he wrote Helen, "the teacher used to whip me so much, though I tried to be good all the time and learn my lessons." He had dinner with the present master, a Mr. Dick, who had read Muir's *Century* articles, and Muir was amused when another of Mr. Dick's dinner guests asked the host if he didn't wish he had the "immortal glory of having whipped John Muir."

A hundred associations, personal and historical, leaped at him out of faces, buildings, and especially the landscape. He filled pages of his journal with notes on the battles, deaths, executions, and heroes of his country's past, tiny scraps of poems about Scotland, reflections on Scott's *The Black Dwarf,* observations on the geology of Scotland and its natural geographical divisions. The long twilights of summer here entranced him, and he wrote that no one could imagine anything half so beautiful as these, when the curtain of night was rung down so gradually that at last it met the misty rise of morning.

He ambled or even rode the old roads of the Lammermuirs where once he had run mile on mile. Now he stopped to chat with farmers whose predecessors perhaps had shouted after the truant, turnip-snatching boy, and they listened with wonder, he told Louie, "to the stories of California and Alaska." When the heather bloomed he felt he must camp out in it a week but settled for sending a sprig of it to his girls.

Near the end of his stay he took a stroll with his cousin, Maggie Lunam, along the shore where as a boy he had larked. The waves, he wrote Wanda, "made a grand show breaking in sheets and sheaves of foam, and [sang] grand songs, the same old songs they sang to me in my childhood, and I seemed a boy again and all the long years in America were forgotten while I was filled with that glorious ocean psalm."

The
American
Forests

Black weather and rain, Muir noted in his journal entry for January 18, 1896, and so time for indoor work while nature went on with its mission. He was "pegging away" on a book about his Alaskan adventures, he said, but it was "dolefully slow progress," and to make it worse he was ill again with bronchitis.* The next day there was more black weather, but Muir's attention was drawn from the wet fields and dripping boughs, for now he was writing descriptions of Alaskan scenery, and he found that his mind went there with a "marvelous vividness," enabling him to see the mountains and the glaciers flowing down their gorges to the sea.

Then came the California spring and with it the demanding work of the fields. On April 24, he noted the rapid growth of the vines, some varieties showing shoots a foot in length and the apri-

---

*Indeed it was slow progress. When Muir died in 1914 the Alaskan book still had not been completed, having in the interim years been set aside again and again for other literary and public projects. It was posthumously published as *Travels in Alaska* in 1915.

cots as big as hickory nuts; noted on this date, too, the desperately slow pace of his literary labors and pessimistically predicted that between the ranch and the family they woud be wrecked utterly.

By mid-June the pace of the ranch work had slackened enough for him to go into San Francisco on the fourteenth to have lunch with Keith and a chat with another old friend, Thomas Magee. Magee told Muir of a minister friend who refused to believe the age Muir gave to the sequoias because a seedling transplanted to Scotland had shot up so rapidly in its first years of growth. Back home, Muir confided to this journal that although the minister might know much of heaven he knew nothing about trees. According to his logic, Muir wrote with acerbity, a human being should weigh a ton at fifty years to judge by the rate of its baby growth.

Only a few days after this, Muir was sitting amid the clutter of his second-floor study when, as had been the case with his father's impending death, he had the unshakable feeling that his mother lay dying in Portage. If he would see her again in life, he must make all haste. He had been scheduled to go east, anyway, in a matter of days to receive an honorary degree from Harvard, but now he arose from his desk determined to start at once for Wisconsin.

When he arrived in Portage he found the truth of the mysterious message: Anne Muir was indeed gravely ill. But her son's arrival appeared to stir her, and by nightfall of that day she was greatly improved. During the next days she continued to rally, and meanwhile Muir had successfully prevailed on his physician brother Dan to come from Nebraska to watch her progress while he went on to New York and then Cambridge. But while in New York he received a telegram with the news that Anne Muir had died peacefully in her sleep. Muir wired back that he would go on to the Harvard commencement exercises and take the train out the day following.

The honor at "Ha-a-a-rvard," as he joshingly spelled it in a letter to Robert Underwood Johnson, must have been at least mildly gratifying, though as usual he harbored some reservations. Johnson had asked him in a letter of the previous spring whether there was anything to the story—another part of the Muir legend in the making—that Harvard had once offered him a professorship and that he had turned it down. All this personal stuff, Muir replied, is hateful, and apparently that included the business of receiving

awards and honors. But, he said, the answer was no, though Asa
Gray had invited him to Harvard back in the '70s just as Emerson
had invited him to Concord about the same time. You must surely
know, he wrote Johnson, "that I never for a moment thought of
leaving God's big show for a mere profship, call who may."

He left this reminiscence out of his remarks at a dinner following the commencement exercises, choosing to concentrate instead
on his warm memories of the Harvard men he had known and
loved—Emerson, Agassiz, and Gray. It is said, he began, that a
Scotchman cannot speak, he can only discourse, and admitted the
saying was surely true of him. He added that with two or three
hours at his disposal he might possibly get something said. Then he
told of his meeting with Emerson, the first great emissary from the
outer world to "find me and hail me as a brother," of those few
glorious days in the valley with him, and of Emerson's fond farewell
as he started back down the long trail that led to sunset. The next
day Muir himself was bound for the sunset on a fast train that got
him to Portage in time for the funeral.

On July 3, Muir wrote an affectionate letter to little Helen from a
sweltering Chicago, thanking her for the illustrated letters she had
been sending him. He gave her a brief annotated itinerary of his
travels since leaving home, telling her he had gone from Portage
to Madison and there visited with William Trout, "with whom I
used to live in a famous hollow in the Canadian woods thirty years
ago." Then he had gone to Indianapolis to renew ties with the
Moores family and the Merrills. Now, he said, bringing her up to
date, he was awaiting the arrival of the Forestry Commission and
would travel west with it on its inspection of the nation's forest
lands.

The commission was largely the creation of Charles S. Sargent
and the ubiquitous Johnson. Sargent, as the preemiment student of
the American forests, had impressed upon Johnson his belief that
unless remedial federal action were soon taken to check the fraud
and waste in timbering on public lands the nation's forest resources
would become permanently depleted. Already the damage was
great; a recent report by the inspector of the Public Land Service

calculated the value of only the most recent losses through illegal timbering, grazing and burning at $37 million. But there was a new law on the books, the Forest Reserve Act of 1891, and under its broad provisions something might possibly be done to protect remaining resources. Johnson had been a receptive listener, having already been initiated by Muir to the lore and plight of trees; now he went to work with customary inventiveness to create a fact-finding commission.

Jealous of its prerogatives and sensitive to pressures from lumbering, mining, and livestock interests, Congress was loath to approve the creation of such a commission, but Johnson and Sargent persuaded Grover Cleveland's secretary of the interior, Hoke Smith, to request the National Academy of Sciences to form a study group. Sargent was appointed commission chairman with the other academy members being Henry L. Abbot, Alexander Agassiz, William H. Brewer, Arnold Hague, and Wolcott Gibbs, the academy's president. Young Gifford Pinchot was appointed commission secretary, and Sargent asked Muir to come along in an ex officio capacity. Johnson was able to sweet-talk the powerful, autocratic Joe Cannon, chairman of the House Appropriations Committee, into a stipend of $25,000 for the commission's work, though its members were to serve without pay.

On July 5 Muir accompanied Sargent, Brewer, Hague, and Abbot westward by train across the broad green stretches of Iowa and Nebraska and on into the Black Hills, where they would begin their work. Here, Muir told his daughters in a letter, was the land that precipitated the last great clash between the Indians and whites, ending at the Little Big Horn. The Indians, he said, had wished to keep these hills because of their abundance of game, while the whites had wanted the gold found here. Now the game was gone, he told the girls, "for wherever the white man goes the game vanishes." And here as everywhere else the commission was to travel—Wyoming, Montana, Washington, Oregon, northern California—they found the littered and smoky evidence of timber theft and timber waste on a vast scale, the vital protective cover of the watersheds logged off and the ground scorched. In the foothills the fragile soil had been so overgrazed that it was questionable whether under the most careful management it could ever come back. Nor were the depredators any respecters of the boundaries between their own lands and those belonging to the public; if anything, their treatment of the latter lands was worse.

Pinchot joined the commission in Montana, and immediately the young forester was drawn to Muir and he to Pinchot. They spent considerable time together off from the main party, hiking, chatting, and sitting around campfires. At the Grand Canyon on September 29, for instance, Muir and Pinchot hiked the canyon rim, behaving like schoolboys in the joy of freedom with all that magnificence spread out beneath them. They stood on their heads to make the canyon colors even more vivid and at evening made their separate camp in a grove of pines and cedars.* They offered some cedar as incense to the gods, talked until midnight (Muir spinning stories such as Pinchot had never heard), and in the morning came back like truants to join the other commissioners.

But there were inherent, fundamental differences between these two in their appreciation of nature and its trees, and these surfaced that fall when the commission began the task of drawing up its report and recommendations. All the members could agree that some form of immediate federal regulation was needed to protect the nation's timberlands, but what kind of regulation and enforced by whom? Pinchot alone among the commission members had any real idea of practical forestry and the governmental administration of forest resources, having gained valuable experience in Europe, where forestry practices were now far in advance of America's. He was, moreover, a man of markedly practical bent, aware of the legitimate needs of the lumber industry, the stockmen and miners. While he was captivated by Muir's personal magnetism and deferential to Sargent with his vast fund of dendrological knowledge, he was not going to be persuaded by them simply to lock up broad swaths of highly valuable timberlands under the vigilant supervision of the U.S. Army. Instead Pinchot envisioned a civilian force of trained foresters administering forest reserves to which commercial interests had supervised access.

---

*In June 1890, while in Alaska, Muir wrote of the gains in perspective to be gotten from standing on your head. "Then," he claimed, "we behold a new heaven and earth and are born again, as if we had gone on a pilgrimage to some far-off holy land and become new creatures with bodies inverted. . . ." (Wolfe [ed.], *John of the Mountains*).

The final report was an obvious compromise that left all the commission members unhappy. In it, the commission recommended to the outgoing Cleveland that he set aside thirteen new forest reserves. The Muir-Sargent faction got its recommendation that these be policed by the military—but only until a trained civilian forestry corps could be placed in the field. They also were successful in including their proposal for a ban on sheep grazing in the reserves but had to accept wording that implied limited commercial accessibility.

Pinchot thought the report a miserable farrago and considered issuing a minority report. In a way, he was right, for the report left unaddressed the large question of use. Was it really responsible or realistic to lock up valuable public lands or to so narrow the routes of access to them that they became in effect as useless as if they had been deserts? He thought not and was confident a great many others would feel similarly. "The first principle of conservation is development," he was to write several years later, "the use of natural resources now existing on this continent for the benefit of the people who live here now." As for Sargent, Pinchot said he simply could not get practical matters through the older man's head, and he charged Sargent with having wrecked the commission's potential usefulness and having needlessly provoked western hostility.

Cleveland, however, accepted the commission's recommendations as given and with a sense of historical irony chose the birthday of the legendary tree-chopper, George Washington, to announce the creation of the new reserves, which together totaled more than 21 million acres. In doing so, the president formally opened the longest-running conservation battle in American history and perhaps the most significant one as well.

All of the new reserves were in the West, and the entire region from South Dakota to Washington to California exploded in rage. A mass meeting in Deadwood, South Dakota, drew 30,000 people to protest the closing of the Black Hills reserve, a move, it was claimed, that would ultimately ensure the depopulation of a region so dependent on mining and related industries. In Washington, the newest capital of the lumber industry, the Seattle *Post-Intelligencer* raised again the great question of the federal government's legal claim to lands in the public domain. "At best," the paper said, "the only title which the federal government ever had to the lands was based upon forced concessions which the new states were compelled to make as the price of their admission to the Union." It was time, the editorialist said, for the government to get out of the real-estate business and let the states take over. And the San Francisco *Chronicle* voiced a classic western sentiment when it styled the commissioners "wiseacres" and "amiable theorists" grotesquely out of touch with western realities. Naturally, all this speedily reached the nation's capital, where after fierce legislative wrangling the presidential order authorizing the new reserves was suspended until March 1, 1898, a grace period during which both legal and illegal activities in the affected areas could continue unchecked while the opponents of the reserves shaped their strategy.*

Behind the uproar was a great deal more than the specific local grievances of Deadwood or Seattle or even the outrage felt by particular commercial interests; at issue were attitudes toward the wilderness and land use developed over three centuries of American cultural history.

In the beginning of that history, the woods of the eastern seaboard had been the most visible and obvious manifestation of the wilderness the newcoming whites would have to open if they wanted to make homes here. William Bradford's famous, bleak description of the wall of winter woods that confronted the Pilgrims as they swung at anchor off Cape Cod has become a staple in anthologies of American literature, but it may also be seen as the announcement of an assault on the forests of North America, the first notice given of what would be a siege against the woods that resulted in the clearing of a continent.

All of the newcomers—English, Dutch, Spanish, French—were astonished at both the extent of the American forests and the size of the individual trees, for they had come from a continent mostly deforested, a process that began so far back that Plato had com-

*The measure new President William McKinley signed into law June 4, 1897, not only suspended the reserves until March 1, 1898, but also provided for mining, agriculture, and the allowance of free timber to settlers. In effect, the measure nullified the report of the Forestry Commission (Roy M. Robbins, *Our Landed Heritage: The Public Domain, 1776–1936,* Lincoln, 1942, 1962).

mented on it. Here they came into the looming presence of a gigantic climax forest centuries in the making and stretching from the eastern seaboard and the Gulf coast all the way to the big river —perhaps more than 400,000 square miles of woods.

But if they were astonished, they were not awed, for awe has in it the quality of reverence. The "primitive" sense of wonder, of reverence for the tree as a living, breathing, reproducing organism —that wonder evidenced in the tree rituals of the Eastern Woodland tribes (and indeed in the forgotten rites of "pagan" Europe) —was gone from those who now entered the New World armed with axes. In place of it was a mingled arrogance and a dread of all wild nature. The settlers had, of course, to make clearings for themselves and their settlements, and they had to utilize the woods for fuel and building materials, but the way they went about using up the forests of the eastern half of the continent had about it a kind of thoughtless rage, as if they really were at war with the wilderness, as Thoreau said.

A folk truth of that time had it that the eastern forests were originally so extensive that a squirrel could start in a tree on the seaboard and travel west all the way to the Mississippi without having to touch the earth. By 1800 the folk truth had been rendered a folk antiquity, for by that time the eastern forests had been broken to the western portions of Pennsylvania, and behind the heedlessly flashing axes were to be seen the sure signs of deforestation: spring floods followed by diminished stream flows, erosion, soil impoverishment, poorer crops, Much of the felled wood was simply wasted, the settlers leaving it to rot where it fell, believing they were doing good by letting light and air into the darkened land and ridding themselves and their civilization of what they appeared to regard as a species of pernicious weed, as Muir would soon observe. But of course not all the wood was wasted. In the early days almost everything was made at least in part of wood, and indeed to European travelers in early America the country was a wooden one: all forests, wooden towns, wooden tools, implements, dishware. American had already embarked on the road to the large-scale exploitation of its single greatest natural resource.

By the 1880s the great eastern forests had been logged out, and so had most of those in the Midwest. The commercial loggers were now shifting their attentions to the West Coast, to California and the Northwest. Here on the sites of the remaining large stands of virgin timber the historic pattern of overcutting, theft, and waste was repeated just as it had been in every region westward of the original settlements. And of all the abuses, timber theft was by far the most flagrant.

Since the creation of the public domain, stealing timber from Uncle Sam had been a recognized and popularly sanctioned practice. Individuals openly poached timber from public lands (as Daniel Muir was rumored to have done at Hickory Hill), and no one cared. Large companies did also, creating for themselves the notorious "round forties" of legally purchased land, from which bases they helped themselves to all of the publicly owned timber that lay convenient to them. Tanneries, turpentine distilleries, steamboat companies, mining companies, and especially the men who would eventually be recognized as "timber barons"—Alger, Weyerhaeuser, Vilas, Ryerson, Sage, Cornell—all stole on so grand a scale that few could believe it criminal. Instead, it was regarded as an American frontier tradition. In 1850, to give available estimates for a year, Wisconsin and Michigan together produced about 90 million board feet of lumber, and of this total half was estimated to have been stolen outright or else fraudulently obtained. (The estimate does not include several million illegally gotten railroad ties nor a million telegraph poles.) But when the fledgling Interior Department tried to prosecute the timber thieves in these states, Representative Eastman of Wisconsin voiced the sentiments of many when he said the federal government ought to be encouraging the hardy enterprisers instead of persecuting them. These are the men, he said, who have opened up and developed America, and the stolen timber should actually be allowed them as "a sort of bounty for their hardships. . . ."

The Interior Department was instructed not to pursue its cases, and from the early 1850s until the vigorous stewardship of Carl Schurz (1877–81) Interior did almost nothing about the despoilment of the nation's forests. The Timber Culture Act (1873) and the Timber and Stone Act (1878) were passed, but about all these really accomplished was to provide legal covers for the old practices. Schurz predicted future disaster if something was not done to protect the forests. His recommendations for the care and custody of the forests and his enunciation of the basic principle of sustained yield were eventually to form the essence of national forest policy, but that policy would not be implemented in the late 1870s nor in the early '80s, either.* Grant's administrations had gone, but it was not until 1891 that anything significant was done in the way of forest conservation.

The Forest Reserve Act of that year was symptomatic of the primitive state of governmental thinking on forest policy. The American Forestry Association had petitioned Congress in 1889 to withdraw all public forest lands from sale, and the same year the American Association for the Advancement of Science sent a memorandum to Congress suggesting the creation of national forest reserves for the purpose of ensuring favorable hydrological conditions in the nation's river systems. Late into an evening near the bedraggled end of the second session of the Fifty-first Congress, an amendment was added to the General Revision Act authorizing broad presidential discretion in setting aside forest reserves out of the public domain. The bill with its potentially explosive amendment went through the Senate without even being printed; in the House there was superficial debate, some attention being drawn there to the extraordinary powers granted the president in Section 24. On March 2, 1891, the General Revision Act was adopted without a recorded vote.

Nothing was said in the act nor afterward about what specifically the new reserves would be for, how they were to be protected, or how many in the future might be created. If the passage of the Forest Reserve Act symbolized a much-belated rise in conservation consciousness, it was hard to find evidence of it in the act itself; or indeed in the lack of public reaction when President Harrison created fifteen reserves in 1892–93, locking up 13 million acres of public forestland.

But this was not so in 1897, by which time the implications of

*For his forest recommendations Schurz was denounced by House Speaker James G. Blaine, a friend of the timbering interests. Blaine said Schurz's recommendations were Prussian, autocratic, and had no place in a democratic society— a charge eerily echoed in recent years when a secretary of the interior, James Watt, suggested environmentalists envisioned the same sort of state control the Nazis had achieved in Germany. Blaine did not denounce with impunity: Schurz was instrumental in denying him the Republican presidential nomination in 1884.

an emerging forest conservation policy had become clear to those interested. Before they became clear to Johnson, Sargent, and Muir, it became obvious to the special interests that you could not take valuable forestlands out of the public domain and put a legislative padlock around them. If this was reform in resource management, it did not say a great deal for the reformist frame of mind. Plainly, a more substantive statement of intent was required of those who would conserve national forest resources, and by general consent among active conservationists the man to make the statement was Muir.

Earlier advocates of American forest conservation like George Perkins Marsh (whose book on the consequences of deforestation Johnson had used in his persuasions of Secretary Smith and Joe Cannon) and Franklin B. Hough had made their arguments from a practical base. They explained how a tree works to hold soil in place and thus helps to regulate water flow. They understood, too, the multiple, long-term results of deforestation; their projections of the estimated current annual cuts indicated to them that the time was not far ahead when America would suffer from a timber shortage as well as from other consequences of deforestation.

Muir, of course, knew these arguments well. He had made his own studies of tree life and tree history, and he knew from firsthand experience in Wisconsin, parts of the South, California, and the Northwest the results of predatory timbering practices. Yet in the articles he now prepared, he deliberately relegated more obviously practical considerations to secondary status.* Nor was this Scots perversity: instead, it was the manifestation of his determination to greatly expand the definition of "use" in the public dialogue on the American landscape. For him the kind of religiously followed utilitarianism he had first seen in Wisconsin was a disaster, a critical misuse of resources. The dominant impression he had carried away from his own unwilling participation in that process was that none of the Wisconsin settlers had truly known how to use the great gift nature had made them in the lands they lived on. It had been in Wisconsin that he had begun to discover for himself a way of living

*The articles were "Forest Reservations and National Parks," *Harper's Weekly,* June 5, 1897; "The American Forests," *Atlantic,* August, 1897; and "The Wild Parks and Forest Reservations of the West," *Atlantic,* January, 1898.

not on the land but *with* it, so that he might receive its gifts of the spirit. In his view that was what America had been for all along, its mysteriously vouchsafed discovery having a higher use than the mere grubbing out of wealth. This was the bold tack he took now in his forest-reserve articles. Charged with a sense of mission and crisis and inspired by a unique sense of advocacy of trees as living beings, Muir created here some of the most remarkable pieces he ever wrote, deeply personal literary bequests to his adopted culture.

This was particularly true of "The American Forests." Here Muir powerfully evoked the myth of America as the Garden of the World that had lain waiting through centuries for the spiritually jaded whites to find it and be healed. Like Columbus, whose first American journal was filled with delighted descriptions of the trees he encountered on the island, Muir began with a description of America as it must have been before the forests were scarred by progress. "The American forests," he wrote in his opening lines, "however slighted by man, must surely have been a great delight to God; for they were the best he ever planted. The whole continent was a garden, and from the beginning it seemed favored above all the other wild parks and gardens of the globe." He narrated the slow and careful preparation of the continent's landscape, from its emergence from the sea, through its glacial scouring, folding, and crimping, to the blooming of its jewel, the forests, waving high in the wind, monarch trees "proclaiming the gospel of beauty like apostles." He called their names, from east to west, with an Old Testament amplitude: in the East, oak and elm, walnut and maple, chestnut, beech, ilex, locust, tupelo, ash, "a leafy translucent canopy along the coast of the Atlantic over the wrinkled folds and ridges of the Alleghenies,—a green billowy sea in summer, golden and purple in autumn, pearly gray like a steadfast frozen mist of interlacing branches and sprays in leafless, restful winter."

In the South, cypress, magnolia, palm, "glossy-leaved and blooming and shining continually." In the far North, the pines, "spiry, rosiny evergreens," seeking the sky with their points and brightening all the landscape. And westward following the sun, the juniper and spruce, aspen and willow, until at last the forests of the Pacific were reached, and there were found the giant cedars and spruces, silver firs, and the sequoias, "kings of their race, growing close together like grass in a meadow . . . towering serene through the long centuries, preaching God's forestry fresh from heaven." These were the American forests, "the glory of the world!" Surveyed thus, he went on,

> they are rich beyond thought, immortal, immeasurable, enough and to spare for every feeding, sheltering beast and bird, insect and son of Adam; and nobody need have cared had there been no pines in Norway, no cedars and deodars on Lebanon and the Himalayas, no vine-clad selvas in the basin of the Amazon. With such variety, harmony, and triumphant exurberance, even nature, it would seem, might have rested content with the forests of North America, and planted no more.

This then was the New World into which human beings entered, and Muir observed that the Indians scarred it about as much as did a beaver or a browsing moose. But then came the invaders from the Old World, and when the "steel axe of the white man rang out on the startled air" the "doom" of the American forests was sealed. Every tree, he wrote, "heard the bodeful sound, and pillars of smoke gave the sign to the sky."

Having invoked the myth of America and the fall from its unscarred paradise of trees into white history, Muir briefly and bitterly sketched the westward way of what he called the "invading horde of destroyers," who left the lands behind them cleared and "scorched into melancholy ruins" until at last they ran out of land and reached the Pacific. Soon enough they would run out of forests, too, unless the government stepped in to protect what was left of the public timberlands. Drawing in part on information Pinchot had provided on the more enlightened forestry practices of Europe, and perhaps also on the information in Marsh's *Man and Nature,* Muir concluded that it was the righteous duty of any good government to protect its public forests so as to "keep in view the common good of the people for all time." But so far our government, he claimed, has done "nothing effective with its forests . . . , but is like a rich and foolish spendthrift who has inherited a magnificent estate in perfect order, and then has left his fields and meadows, forests and parks, to be sold and plundered and wasted at will, depending on their inexhaustible abundance."

He described the grosser forms of timber theft and fraud and remarked on the vast amount of cut timber that was wasted (about five-eighths of each tree, a contemporary estimate judged). Muir claimed somewhere between five to ten times as much timber was destroyed annually as was used, chiefly through running forest fires, and cited Thoreau to the effect that logging practices would some-day render America so bald that men would be obliged to cultivate whiskers to hide behind.

If this was a melancholy picture of what had happened to the American Garden, it was also an indictment of "use" as popularly sanctioned over the years. But all was not as black as the skies above a forest fire, and in his closing paragraphs Muir adverted to the dawning of a better, brighter day. The signs of this were the creation of Central Park in New York, of national parks in the West, and, most significantly, of the forest reserves. The country was apparently passing, he guessed, out of the long period of public indifference into the period of protest and strife wherein "the plunderers, who are as unconscionable and enterprising as Satan," would vociferously voice their complaints at the highest reaches. But, Muir predicted, "light is surely coming, and the friends of destruction will preach and bewail in vain." Right use, regulated use, of the forests was so obvious a necessity that it must ultimately prevail.

"Any fool," he wrote in his concluding lines, "can destroy trees. They cannot run away; and if they could, they would still be destroyed,—chased and hunted down as long as fun or a dollar could be got out of their bark hides, branching horns, or magnificent bole backbones." Through the centuries before the coming of the whites God had cared for these trees and saved them from all manner of natural disasters. But "he cannot save them from fools, —only Uncle Sam can do that."

Except for a very few vaguely worded lines near the end of this passionate essay, Muir said nothing about what right use of the forests was, and he said nothing at all about what ought to be done with the newly created reserves. But the implication was unmistakable that the reserves existed and should be protected so that Americans could avail themselves therein of the spiritual blessings wild forests had to give, the same argument, in other words, that had been made in the campaigns for the first national parks.

What Muir had to say here about the timber barons, sheepmen, and shake-makers and the impassioned, bibical language he used to say it makes it clear that he expected this argument to be dismissed out of hand by such people. Moreover, he had already had sufficient contact with Gifford Pinchot to surmise that forestry to Pinchot and his allies was actually resource engineering, that Pinchot's definition of use was far narrower than Muir could live with; so narrow in fact, that it seemed to preclude the kind of use Muir argued for here while at the same time it encouraged other kinds of use that to Muir were plainly disastrous.

By the time Muir's second forest article, "The American Forests," appeared in August 1897, he had split with Pinchot on the issue of use, though the schism had in fact always been there, however unrecognized. In a confrontation that month in a Seattle hotel lobby, Muir had asked Pinchot if the latter had been accurately quoted by a reporter to the effect that sheep grazing did no real harm to forests. Pinchot replied that the quote was accurate, and Muir turned abruptly away from him in repudiation. But the confrontation was essentially unimportant in the issue of use, for both men had long before developed their positions, and Muir surely knew this even as he was writing "The American Forests." To such as Pinchot, prayer and recreation in forest temples looked rather like a species of waste, and Muir and his friends the fools from whom Uncle Sam had to protect the reserves.*

In "The Wild Parks and Forest Reservations of the West" Muir advanced yet more boldly his vision of the cultural mission of the reserves. The demands and discontents of modern American civilization, he claimed, were so great and the rewards so fraudulent that wilderness preserves were a spiritual and psychological necessity. Referring to the trend of recent years that had seen more Americans seeking outdoor recreation, he wrote that these "tired, nerve-shaken, over-civilized people are beginning to find out that going

---

*Pinchot's position on grazing in the forests was actually more complex than Muir was willing to grant. He was in favor of allowing grazing on national forest lands, believing that it was far wiser to regulate the practice than to altogether forbid it. But he was vigorously opposed to overgrazing and as early as 1900 remarked publicly on this practice. Still later, he said Muir was right in calling sheep "hoofed locusts" (Gifford Pinchot, *Breaking New Ground,* Seattle, London, 1947, 1972).

to the mountains is going home; that wildness is a necessity; and that mountain parks and reservations are useful not only as fountains of timber and irrigating rivers, but as fountains of life." Yet the wild parts of America were quickly passing out of existence, and at the very time when they were more than ever needed.

In illustration of this alarming trend, he drew on his own experiences in California, beginning with his first view of the great Central Valley, then a bed of gold and purple flowers, now "ploughed and pastured out of existence, gone forever. . . ." So too with the Sierran forests, where the ground, "once divinely beautiful, is desolate and repulsive, like a face ravaged by disease." What had happened in California, he noted, was what had happened in those portions of the country settled first, and it is what will happen to even the most inaccessible parts of it in due time "unless awakening public opinion comes forward to stop it."

This said, Muir took readers on a leisurely literary tour of the forest reserves, pointing out to them in the manner of a friendly guide the grand natural features particular to each, everywhere extolling the spiritual benefits travelers could infallibly expect in these places. Writing of the Bitter Root reserve, "the wildest, shaggiest block of forest wilderness in the Rocky Mountains," Muir enjoined the "nerve-shaken" and "over-civilized" to "wander here a whole summer if you can. Thousands of God's wild blessings will search you and soak you as if you were a sponge, and the big days will go by uncounted." So it had been for him, so it must be for others, the deep authority of his own experiences showing him that there was no personal crisis, no anguish of night, that nature could not heal. *That* was the best, highest use to which the yet unscarred portions of the American landscape might be put. All other uses, legitimate as they might be in their ways, ought to give precedence to this one.

To Muir there was no one among his friends and colleagues who felt about trees the way he did except Sargent. In the late summer of 1897 he had taken an extended trip with Sargent and William Canby, a Delaware botanist, studying trees and forest conditions, and it had been a delight. Now in the spring of 1898, Sargent sent him the eleventh volume of his *The Silva of North America,* which

Muir found was dedicated to him. And along with the handsome gift, Sargent proposed that the three take another such trip, this one devoted to the forests of the East and South.

Muir was ecstatic, writing that the idea had "stirred up wild lover's longings" to renew acquaintances with his old forest friends. "I don't want to die," he wrote Sargent back, "without once more saluting the grand, godly, round-headed trees of the east side of America that I learned to love and beneath which I used to weep with joy when nobody knew me." He said he wanted to travel light as in the old days, avoiding cities, society, and society dinners. "If tree-lovers could only grow bark and bread on their bodies," he exclaimed, "how fine it would be, making even handbags useless!"

But he could not avoid the "bread-line" as he had in his Sierra days. Sargent and Canby had the "house habit," as Muir once put it, and all three of them were along in years. Muir himself, to his somewhat rueful surprise, discovered that he too liked comforts and was progressively more disinclined to rough it. Besides, when he arrived in Boston late that summer he was in such poor health he could not get meals down: grippe, a nervous stomach, and his old cough again plagued him. It was only will that kept him pushing eastward, that and his belief that a tour of the woods, even if by rail and carriage, would cure him.

As it happened, it was Sargent whose illness influenced the trip; he took sick in Tennessee, and this forced the three friends to go back to Brookline until he recovered. But by the time they had gotten to Chattanooga Muir was cured and waxing so enthusiastic over mountain views and forest groves that his more staid companions were beginning to look more at his antics than at the scenery. He did not care: a view from Grandfather Mountain in North Carolina rendered human decorum ridiculous by contrast.

At Chattanooga before their enforced departure north, Muir rode an electric car to the summit of Lookout Mountain and visited the battlefield at Chickamauga, where he found that once-bloody terrain now studded with monuments to an action he had missed. Then, on the way back to Brookline, he read William Bartram's *Travels,* which Sargent had given him, thus creating a kind of triple-layered effect for the trip, Bartram's travels forming the bottom-most layer with his own now and in '67 superimposed.

Waiting for Sargent to recover, Muir stayed busy, his revived

∂Plattsburgh!

health and spirits spurring him to Albany, Lake George, Montreal, Burlington, and Stowe. In the countryside near Stockbridge in western Massachusetts he made some journal entries on the flight from the farm to the cities, regarding it as folly and conveniently overlooking his own flight from the farm. He also visited a rake factory and noted with satisfaction that he could make rakes at half the cost of those produced there. He visited with his friends the Henry Fairfield Osborns at their palatial Hudson River residence, "Wing-on-Wing," and from there he wrote his "Darling Helen" on November 4, jocularly describing his luxurious circumstances, how he loved to lie abed in the morning and have a cup of coffee served him by a household servant. This morning, he told her,

> when I was sipping coffee in bed, a red squirrel looked in the window at me from the branch of a big tulip-tree, and seemed to be saying as he watched me, "Oh, John Muir! camping, tramping, tree-climbing scrambler! Churr, churr! why have you left us? Chip churr, who would have thought it?"

Six days later they were heading south again. Muir wrote Louie from Savannah, reminiscing on his lonesome and momentous arrival there on his long walk. There had been many changes in old Bonaventure Cemetery, he told her, "and how many in my life!" On a Miami morning he botanized peacefully in the hot sun of a vacant lot, then went in to a hotel breakfast. On November 20, now evidently consumed with a nostalgic curiosity about the young unknown of '67, he went to Cedar Key and put up at the Dutch Hotel. There he learned that two of his old benefactors, Mr. Hodgson and his son, were dead; but Mrs. Hodgson was still alive and living at Archer, and Muir visited her there. On the twenty-first, he described the meeting to Louie:

> I asked her if she knew me. She answered no, and asked my name. I said Muir. *"John* Muir?" she almost screamed. *"My* California John Muir? My California John?" I said, "Why, yes. I promised to come back and visit you in about twenty-five years, and though a little late I've come."

There the travelers parted company, Sargent and Canby heading home while Muir, filled with wanderlust and perhaps a sense of old mortality again, went on to Live Oak, Florida, then New Orleans, and so westward toward home. He had wanted to just go on traveling with his friends, had hoped they would go down to Mexico, but the other two had had enough, and when they left him as he told Sargent later, he had felt "childishly lonesome and woe-begone." They must do much more of this, he urged once back in Martinez; they should see the trees of Japan and eastern Asia. "It will soon be dark," he said. "Soon enough our good botanical pegs will be straightened in a box and planted, and it behooves us as reasonable naturalists to keep them trampling and twinkling in the woods as long as possible. . . ."

Other
Yosemites

On a warm September afternoon in 1901, President William McKinley stood in a reception line in the Temple of Music at Buffalo's Pan-American Exposition. There a young man approached him and, as the president extended his hand in greeting, fired two pistol shots into McKinley's body.

The assailant, instantly apprehended, was subsequently alleged to have said he was an anarchist, inspired to this act by the writings of Emma Goldman. As the president lingered between life and death the nation murmured angrily. Since the Haymarket riot of 1886, public fears about the rise of anarchism had steadily mounted, and here at Buffalo was apparent proof that the very foundations of the republic were indeed threatened by misrule. Leon Czolgosz, the assailant, was one of that barbaric horde of which Henry George and others had been warning.

On September 6 when McKinley was shot, the vice president was on an outing of the Vermont Fish and Game League at Lake Champlain. Then came the telegram with its news, and Theodore Roosevelt boarded a special train for Buffalo. But by the time he arrived there the president was rallying, and so on the tenth Roose-

velt left the city for the Adirondacks, where he would do some
mountain climbing.

On the thirteenth, Roosevelt was high on the slopes when a
breathless messenger caught up with him: the rally was over, and
the president was dying. It was now late in the afternoon, and there
ensued a wild fifty-mile buckboard dash through sunset and evening to the nearest train station. While Roosevelt was en route to
Buffalo, McKinley died of gangrene, and Roosevelt was president.
He was sworn in on the afternoon of September 14.

On so inauspicious a note began the brightest period of the
American conservation movement. The new president was widely
known and admired as an avid outdoorsman, and he lost no time
setting in motion fact-finding groups on the state of the nation's
natural resources. As part of this process, Muir received a letter that
October from C. Hart Merriam with the good news that the president shared their views on forest preservation and on the danger
of sheep grazing on forest-reserve lands. More, the president
wanted specifically to hear from men like John Muir the unvarnished facts about the forests and how best to conserve other natural resources.

Muir was happy to contribute. He did not apparently share the
fin de siècle pessimism of many who feared anarchism or entropy.
He had noted in an undated journal entry of perhaps the year
previous that, despite the fears of many that things were sliding
from bad to worse, there were some definite bright spots in the
national picture. Chief among them was what he called "this righteous uprising in defense of God's trees." The wrongs done to trees,
he wrote, "are done in the darkness of ignorance and unbelief, for
when light comes, the heart of the people is always right." Now the
elevation of Roosevelt, tragic and accidental though it was, and his
swift call for information on conservation measures, seemed another part of an emerging, optimistic pattern. Never before had an
American chief executive shown such frank and direct interest in
hearing the voices of conservationists, and in Roosevelt's first message to Congress in early December conservation was a strong
theme.

So here he was, an adviser to the president, another of those
unlooked-for developments that had made his life a sort of story-
book. In the years since the late '80s when he had reemerged into

public view, honors and recognition had come upon him with astonishing swiftness and with equally astonishing regularity, so that at last he had with some bemusement begun to regard himself as a kind of legend-in-the-flesh. This was the tone of a long, rambling, surprisingly personal letter he now wrote to Harry Randall, his old friend of the earliest Yosemite days. "I have no lack of friends & have acquaintances in every rank almost everywhere nowadays," he told Randall, "but I never forget old friends & those of early pioneer days in the grand Sierra are my especial delight." He gave Randall a sketch of his life since those long-ago days, down to his recent experiences with the Harriman Alaska Expedition (1899); brought him up to date on the personages of the valley— Hutchings and his first wife, Galen Clark, James Lamon—and said with typical candor that Randall might have gone "a little farther ahead" had he stayed with Muir and followed the less-beaten path. But, he added, "Heaven guides us more than we know & our fate, none of us can forsee [*sic*]."

On Christmas Day Muir presided over a family gathering that now included, in addition to Louie and the girls, half of Muir's Wisconsin family, for Sarah had come to Martinez in this year to join David and Maggie. Slowly through the years Muir, like a magnet, had drawn them to him out of that Wisconsin farmscape that he could love in memory but never go back to. And clearly the eldest son, so long disparaged in his mission by the father, now took considerable pleasure in being able to underwrite handsomely the late comforts of the others.

Just after Christmas it was learned that Clarence King had died on December 24 in Arizona. Doubtless the news provoked comment from Muir, but there is no written record of it. He and King had felt a rivalry in their Sierra years, and Muir had not forgotten the derisive scorn the better-known man had then heaped on him for his glacial theories. Subsequently, Muir had taken available occasions to belittle King's mountaineering skills. Now King was dead at fifty-nine, and what had that meteoric life meant, anyway? Henry Adams had found King the perfect representation of the young nation, a man who with any luck would have died at eighty, "the richest and most many-sided genius of his day." He and Robert Underwood Johnson were but two among a great many in high places who had permanently fallen under the spell of King. But

King himself had fallen under the spell of the America that took shape out of the war, had abandoned the brilliant promise of a scientific career to devote himself to a frantic scramble for wealth. Leading at least a double life, wasted and deranged, he had lived only long enough to see his America as a Roman nightmare relived. There was a moral here, and Muir, sensitive as ever to morals and moral lessons, might possibly have seen King's career as paradigmatic of the worst tendencies in the culture. Maybe in an unintended way Adams had been right after all—King was the perfect representation of modern America.

However this might be, Muir saw his own duty clearly in the dawn of the new century and the new administration. He would remain proof against the seductions of power and influence, just as earlier he had remained proof against the lure of fabulous wealth. On the Harriman Alaska Expedition he had dared to tell Harriman that he, Muir, was richer than the magnate, for he knew how much he really needed and Harriman did not. And remaining proof against wealth and power, he would continue to make his voice heard in the land, countering what he styled the "gobble-gobble" school of economics and land use with his singular vision of a landscape cared for and in places preserved for prayer and true recreation.

Although some of the signs were propitious for the cause of conservation, others were at least mixed. The new president seemed favorably disposed to the efforts of the conservationists—had publicly committed himself to the cause—but there was something too drily utilitarian in the view of conservation he had expressed to Congress, and Muir had reason to fear Roosevelt's attention would be wholly captured by resource engineers like Gifford Pinchot. In that case, conservation would surely be defined and practiced so as to exclude the less obviously practical sorts of land use in which Muir so passionately believed, that he and the Sierra Club had sworn to promote.

Indeed, Pinchot had gotten the presidential ear. On the day he arrived in Washington to assume command after McKinley's death, Roosevelt had summoned Pinchot and Frederick H. Newell, both known to him from earlier days, to a private meeting and had asked

them to assist him in that part of his congressional message dealing
with natural resources. In that message there was a decidedly utilitarian slant to the conservation section and no mention whatever of
other, less demonstrably productive land uses.

Having boldly claimed that the forest and water problems were
perhaps the most vital ones facing the nation, Roosevelt stated with
equal boldness that the "fundamental idea of forestry is in the
perpetuation of the forests by use." Forest protection is not an end
in itself, he said, but a "means to increase and sustain the resources
of the country and the industries which depend on them." In describing the "practical usefulness" of the forest reserves, the president said that such usefulness "should be increased by a thoroughly
businesslike management." To Muir that sounded a good deal like
Pinchot, and writing to Merriam early in 1902 he voiced his fear
that between politics and bureaucracy the forests would continue
to be mismanaged despite all the talk of efficiency and conservation
and the creation of Pinchot's spanking new Bureau of Forestry.

The issue was more complex than Muir was willing to admit.
Excepting him, hardly any of the ardent preservationists (a term
then coming into use to distinguish those like Muir from those like
Pinchot) could argue much with the sweeping conservation measures devised and pushed to enactment by the Roosevelt administrations. Roosevelt had overseen passage of the nation's first
broad-gauged reclamation act providing for the construction of
twenty-eight western dams. Then, over a span of six years, Roosevelt, working with Pinchot, was successful in setting aside 132
million acres of national forestland. Working with Muir's close
friend, C. Hart Merriam, Roosevelt gave wildlife conservation federal status and high priority, and the President smiled on John
Lacey of Iowa in his successful efforts to create a law protecting
places of special scenic and historic importance.

Nor was any of this easy. Roosevelt enjoyed immense personal
popularity, but that popularity was not sufficient to blanket with
grace all of his programs. Conservation, even in this heyday, was
no more popular with the large majority of Americans than it had
been in the 1870s, and it was held especially suspect in those
western regions where it was most comprehensively applied.
Roosevelt, Pinchot, Frederick Newell, Francis Newlands, and the
others bucked the long trend of American cultural history quite as

much and with equal courage as did Muir and the Sierra Club. And it might be argued that both the difficulties they faced and their achievements were substantially larger. It might also be argued that they were forced to emphasize the utilitarian aspects of their programs as much as they did, for anything less hard-headed would surely have faced almost insuperable opposition.

Nonetheless, there was something disturbing in the way they conceived of the American landscape. It was as if a consortium of shopkeepers and technocrats had taken a new, hard look at the land and determined that it could be used more efficiently to yield greater and more sustained economic benefits. In the rise of conservation the new leaders were mostly drawn from the ranks of science —hydrology, forestry, geology—and for many of them the ultimate sociopolitical model was the perfectly functioning machine that would run to maximum productivity with a mimimum of waste. There was scant room in their thinking for any turn-of-the-century despair, few Adams-like broodings among them on the cultural implications of the second law of thermodynamics; nor did they see themselves as spiritual and intellectual descendants of the New England Transcendentalists. Science and technology had opened exciting new vistas wherein they could see the rational management of all natural resources and ultimately the rational management of society as a whole. They were optimistic, energetic, and devoted to the ideal of efficiency in all human endeavors. There was scarcely a jot of mysticism in any of them. Nature was not a "Thou"; it was a thing to be inventoried and managed. At a conservation meeting in 1908 the president of the American Society of Civil Engineers forcefully illustrated the new attitude when he said that the aesthetics and historical significance of Niagrara Falls and the ancient monuments of the Nile were alike of negligible significance compared with the power and irrigation potentials of these sites. Preservation of such sites, he claimed, is an archaism having no place in modern-day thinking. What remains of significance in assessing such sites is "that which confers the greatest good on the greatest number."

Pinchot typified the new conservationist. Honest, ambitious, energetic as he was, yet there was a spareness to him more than physical. The woods were not home to him, and he seems never to have been touched by their mystery. Muir had suggested that he get out into them alone, do some solitary hiking and camping, and Pinchot wrote a respectful letter to the older man saying he had been trying to put into practice Muir's suggestions; but they went against the grain of his temperament, and he must have wondered what he was doing out there in the woods all by himself. Plainly, he could not become another Muir, but he could become Gifford Pinchot and blaze his own trail as America's first professional forester.

Almost from the beginning he saw the woods in terms of production and waste, and he never wavered from a forthright promotion of that view. So at the outset of his government career he vigorously opposed the efforts of those who would have prohibited commercial use of the forest reserves. His equally vigorous campaign for managed use of the reserves and his early support for grazing on reserve lands won him the endorsement of westerners and timber men who otherwise would have fought his conservation measures bitterly. At a March 1903 meeting of the Society of American Foresters, Pinchot summed up his position on use: "The object of our forest policy," he said, "is not to preserve the forests because they are beautiful or wild or the habitat of wild animals; it is to ensure a steady supply of timber for human prosperity. Every other consideration comes as secondary." In order to make his position perfectly clear, Pinchot sent a copy of this address to Robert Underwood Johnson. And in an article for the *Century* in 1904, Pinchot went even further by stating that "no lands will be permanently reserves which can serve the people better in any other way."

This suggested that no lands currently reserved from sale or entry were to be considered permanently exempt from future commercial uses as the pressures for these uses might become clear in time. This was bound to make the preservationists uneasy since it apparently called into question all their hard-won victories in the cause of forest and scenic preservation. It also raised by implication the question of whether this doctrine might be extended to include the national parks. If use was the measure by which all reserved lands were to be judged, who was to say that in some future time the perceived needs of "the people" might not dictate commercial

appropriation of sections of national park land? And how in the case
of either the forest reserves or the parks could Pinchot and the
other resource engineers presume to speak for the long-term needs
of the people with any more authority than the defenders of the
wilderness? These were weighty questions, and as the tenor of the
new conservation movement became clear in the early Roosevelt
years, they troubled Muir, Johnson, and other preservationists.

From Muir's point of view Roosevelt was a more promising audience for preservationist sermons than were those who worked
under him. Roosevelt, like many of his subalterns, was devoted to
the ideal of efficiency in government, resource management—in
almost everything. Sometimes this led him into ludicrous positions,
as when he championed the cause of simplified spelling as an example of orthographical efficiency.* But he was serious about waste,
which was to him a species of sin, and he was a great believer in
inventories, fact-finding commissions, and conferences to assess
current states of affairs.

Roosevelt was also an outdoorsman and an amateur naturalist
of some accomplishment. He had a genuine if rough love for unspoiled nature, and he was an avid and expert hunter, hiker, and
mountain climber. These qualities made him attractive to a nation
still uncritically sentimental about the old wildlife imagined for
preindustrial America, and they also made Roosevelt attractive to
Muir and like-minded wilderness advocates. Moreover, Roosevelt
had himself experienced those very healing powers of the natural
world that Muir wished to preserve for this specific use. As a college
youth in 1876, Roosevelt had gone into the Maine woods to physically build himself up and had discovered unsuspected personal
resources in the process. He had returned to civilization with a new
confidence and sense of well-being. Then in 1884, his mother and

---

*This was a ludicrous campaign as it was run, and Roosevelt finally came to
see it. So in September, 1907, while reviewing a naval display off his retreat at
Oyster Bay, the President was delighted by a launch that churned past him labeled
"Pres Bot" (Henry F. Pringle, *Theodore Roosevelt: A Biography,* New York, 1931,
1956).

his young wife had died within hours of one another, and the broken man had retreated to the Dakota Badlands. In those wide, jagged spaces peace had finally come to him, and he had been enabled to go on with public life. These intensely personal experiences remained a private part of the public man, and occasionally they would manifest their continuing existence in oblique ways, as now they did in the spring of 1903 when the president said he wanted to meet John Muir on a western presidential trip in May.

When it was communicated to Muir, the request presented a problem, for it conflicted with a European and Asian tour he had long been planning with Charles Sargent and his son. And just as he had as a young unknown rejected the invitations of great men —Emerson and Agassiz—to follow his own course, so now he was strongly minded to tell the president he had other things planned for May. But he did not. Instead, it was Sargent he wrote, apologizing for a necessary change in plans. "An influential man from Washington wants to make a trip into the Sierra with me," he wrote his friend, "and I might be able to *do some forest good* in freely talking around the campfire." Sargent sent back a hot reply, including the observation that Roosevelt took but a "sloppy unintelligent" interest in forests and that he was "altogether too much under the influence of that creature Pinchot." But he agreed to wait for Muir.

It is doubtful Muir would have agreed to delay his tour to meet with Roosevelt had the conditions not been so promising for the kind of talk he had in mind. Chester Rowell, California state senator, had told Muir that the president wanted to camp out alone with Muir in the Sierras. If the president should do this, Rowell wrote, "he wishes it to be entirely unknown, carried out with great secrecy so that the crowds will not follow or annoy him, and he suggested that he could foot it and rough it with you or anybody else."

Muir liked that, and maybe especially so the implied challenge from the president. Muir never acknowledged any man's equality with him as hiker or mountaineer (Galen Clark, he said, came closest), and he was not one to duck even Theodore Roosevelt on this ground. If he had any lingering disposition to go with the Sargents as scheduled, it was dispelled by a subsequent personal message from Roosevelt in which the president said with characteristic boyish frankness, "I do not want anyone with me but you, and

I want to drop politics absolutely for four days, and just be out in the open with you." That settled it.*

The fate of the forests was not the only item on the agenda Muir now prepared for the meeting with Roosevelt. There was also the lingering, vexed issue of Yosemite Valley. Since the creation of the national park surrounding it thirteen years before, the valley had remained under state jurisdiction, both anomaly and increasingly an eyesore. Since 1897, a movement had been afoot to have the state recede the valley to the federal government as it had the surrounding lands, and there were some in the legislature who now saw that the divided jurisdiction of the Yosemite region was un-workable and illogical. The efforts at recession had thus far failed, but in 1903 the issue was very much alive. So when Muir learned that the state's new governor, George Pardee, was to be included in the presidential party, he saw this as a unique, in situ opportunity to impress both state and national chief executives with the necessity of recession.

On the evening of May 14, Muir, wearing a new suit bought for the occasion, came into San Francisco to meet the presidential train. It was late, and so the old man, saying loudly that he would not lose his sleep for anyone, went back to Oakland to spend the night. The next morning he and Roosevelt met and, forgetting its explosive language, Muir handed Roosevelt Sargent's letter, apparently as a way of verifying the difficulties he had faced in arranging this meeting. As Roosevelt read some of Sargent's words aloud, Muir tried to retrieve the letter, which only increased Roosevelt's mirth.

A large crowd had gathered to see the president at the train station at Raymond, and he was obliged to greet them briefly. He apologized for his rough camping outfit, saying he had "only come prepared to go into the Yosemite with John Muir. . . ." The crowd, delighted as Roosevelt's audiences always were with the living image of their Rough Rider president, cheered the party as it boarded stages for Wawona.

*Later, Muir told a journalist that he had no more interest in meeting Roose-velt just because he was president of the United States than he had in meeting the next man. But, he added, he finally decided he shouldn't refuse Roosevelt's request "just because he happen[ed] to be President" (Bailey Millard, "A Skyland Philosopher," *Bookman's,* February, 1908).

The Yosemite Park Commission, charged with the care and keeping of the valley, had laid elaborate plans for Roosevelt's stay. They were fully aware of the recession rumors, aware too that Muir would be with Roosevelt, and they wished to demonstrate to the president just how carefully the valley was kept, how conscientiously they exercised their stewardship. But they swiftly learned to their dismay that Roosevelt had been utterly serious in his desire to travel alone with Muir. And that is practically what the two men did: when they went into camp in the Mariposa Grove (near where Emerson had only paused, not camped, with Muir three decades before), there were only two rangers and a cook accompanying them, and these men made themselves as inconspicuous as possible. The huge, columnar trunks of the sequoias towered above the two campers as they talked: Roosevelt of birds, Muir of flowers, forests, rocks. The old mountaineer, who had spent so many silent, solitary nights in this region with only the snapping of a campfire for company, now found himself in the presence of a man as talkative as himself. He was pleasantly surprised by the other's comprehensive knowledge of natural history, and that, combined with bluff, hearty ways and joyful boyishness, endeared the man to Muir. Roosevelt so evidently enjoyed the escape into the woods and away from public responsibilities that Muir could hardly help feeling that here was a kindred soul. So on this night and the two thereafter two major figures in American history enacted in microcosm one of the culture's persistent dreams: creative truancy in the wild heart of the New World.

If anything, the experience was more impressive to the younger man than it was to Muir. The latter had made himself native to this place, had truly lived out the truant dream. Roosevelt had experienced the dream's edge, but always the lure of the political arena had compelled his behavior. With the craggy, bearded mountaineer he was allowed fleetingly to imagine all of it, and he remembered the experience for years thereafter with a striking vividness. As his guide showed him the grand and smaller wonders of this place, and as he spun his stories of years lived in close communion with rocks, meadows, and water ouzels, Roosevelt saw further into the possibilities he had brushed in the Maine woods and the Badlands.

When it was over and the president had to turn again to the affairs of state, he had become convinced of the necessity of extend-

ing federal protection to the forest lands north of the valley, and
he subsequently directed his secretary of the interior, Ethan Allen
Hitchcock, to take steps to extend the Sierra reserve all the way to
Mount Shasta. At Sacramento, ablaze with Muir's passion for forest
protection, Roosevelt gave a very Muir-like speech in which he said
that trees had not only great and strategic commercial values but
aesthetic and moral ones as well. The sequoias deserve protection,
he said, "simply because it would be a shame to our civilization to
let them disappear. They are monuments in themselves." He went
on to sketch an historical vista for his audience, telling them that
as Californians and as Americans they were obligated to take the
long view. "We are not," he said, "building this country of ours
for a day. It is to last through the ages." It was, of course, this long
view of national needs that Muir and the preservationist forces were
trying so hard to promote. And as for Yosemite Valley, while they
had camped together Roosevelt had promised Muir that if a bill for
the valley's recession should ever reach his desk, he would sign it.
The trick would be to get such a measure out of California.

So at the end of May, Muir was free to go with the Sargents. E. H.
Harriman, a warm friend to Muir since the Harriman Alaska Expedition of 1899, generously assisted in the planning, arranging special accommodations and free passes on his steamship lines, quite
as a king might do for favored subjects of his far-flung domain.
Despite Harriman's arrangements and Muir's longtime affection
for Charles Sargent, the trip was pretty much a failure, and it was
tribute to Muir's amazing constitution and recuperative powers that
he survived it. He was older than he would really acknowledge, and
though he could make jokes about his advancing age, the strain of
more than a year's continual travel was simply too much for him.
      He was tired before they had completed the European portion
of the tour. Europe seemed weary to him with its museums filled
with "old armor and murder implements," and he was glad to leave
it behind. His spirits picked up a bit in Russia and even more in
Finland, the rural landscape of which charmed him with visions
of peace and rest. But back in Russia he became ill, and when the
little party took a train for the Black Sea and the Caucasus he
had to be put aboard on a stretcher.

Compounding his condition were nagging fears about his family. Helen's health was precarious again, and since his departure no word had arrived from home. On his return to Moscow, he cabled Martinez and received a reassuring answer; thereafter both health and spirits improved. Still, he remained incapable of truly enjoying much that he was seeing, and the experience of traveling in company was daily proving more unsatisfactory. All was wearisome and boring, and he was glad to leave behind all the cities for Siberia and Manchuria at the beginning of August. As the train rattled and swayed through the immense landscape, the exhausted traveler gazed from its grimy windows on vast forests of birch and larch and on wheatfields with peasants bent in attitudes of immemorial toil, a sight that perhaps fleetingly brought back those dog days in the fields of Wisconsin.

In Manchuria he fell ill again, this time with ptomaine poisoning. Numbed with morphine and stupefied with brandy, he spent the blank days hoping for health as his weight steadily dropped below a hundred pounds. He scrawled occasional lines in a travel notebook as if to prove he was still alive.

At Shanghai he made a decision: ill and weak as he was, he would separate from the Sargents and head toward India, toward the clean whiteness of the Himalayas and toward those almost mythical deodar trees he had long wished to behold. He cabled Harriman for transportation advice and assistance and got it. En route to India, he cabled Louie, telling her that with mountains in prospect he felt revived and that never again would he travel with others.

He saw the Himalayas at Darjeeling, saw them each morning at sunrise when he would climb the hill behind his hotel. He would not climb the mountains, however, would never climb them at this hour of life; but at least he had been given a glimpse of them, and he was both old enough and wise enough to make himself content with that. He saw the deodar trees, too, and at Simla he had both the deodars and the Himalayas at once.

Here again came the fears for Helen, and so he wrote another cable and received another reassurance. Now, feeling considerably heartened, he took a hitch in his belt and set his face toward even farther places. "There are a few more places I should see before I die," he wrote Louie. He saw Egypt and surveyed its pyramids with a mountaineer's eye, felt better still in Australia and New Zealand, the flora and fauna of these places delighting him and making him a beginner again in botany. Then he began the long homeward swing, courtesy of Harriman, aboard whose vessels he was treated like royalty. When his girls saw him coming down the plank at San Francisco on May 27, 1904, they were amazed and delighted to find Papa tanned and weighing more than he ever had before.

He had survived a year of rigorous travel, a mortal weariness, and great sickness, and his boyish behavior about the place in Martinez announced to his family that for now his eagerness for life remained intact.

For Muir the rest of that year was largely taken up with elaborate planning for the 1905 session of the California legislature, in which a bill would be introduced calling for the recession of Yosemite Valley to the federal government. Like President Roosevelt, Governor Pardee had assured Muir that he favored recession and would sign such a bill if it passed the legislature; in the summer of 1904, Pardee instructed staff members to assist recession advocates in the planning of strategy.

Earlier, there had been some uncertainty within the Sierra Club about just what role the organization should properly play in this campaign, and this undercurrent of indecision and even dissent (a harbinger of things to come) had hurt and angered its president. He found it an intrusion of "politics" into the club and said so. Like an aging father whose favorite child had disappointed him, Muir lashed out at the club's alleged politicians and displayed some uncharacteristically autocratic behavior. But now, with the chips down and the legislative session looming, the club swung unanimously behind Muir and William Colby in their efforts, and despite the expected vocal opposition of those who would wrap themselves in the state flag and argue for continued state control of the valley, things looked especially bright in January 1905.

In addition to the Sierra Club's carefully orchestrated plan and the effective personal lobbying efforts of Muir and Colby, the bill was supported by two influential California groups, the Native Sons of the Golden West and the State Board of Trade. But perhaps of even greater consequence was the strong but covert support of

Harriman's Southern Pacific Railroad. The Southern Pacific, under the rapacious and unscrupulous Collis P. Huntington, had long been an ogre in the California popular imagination, and the railroad was widely believed to dictate policy to the legislature and to dispose of California state matters generally as best suited its own interests. There was some truth in the belief, but in 1905 the Southern Pacific was not quite what it once had been. Huntingon was dead, Harriman had taken over, and the railroad had suffered some reverses and diminishment of its power. The railroad still had its men in the legislature, though it could no longer use them as openly as once it had, and it also still had a shrewd and well-organized executive in William H. Mills, the company's chief land agent. Assessing all of this, Colby prevailed on Muir to make use of his friendship with Harriman, and Muir did so.

Apparently at Harriman's insistence, Mills helped Colby in the drafting of the recession bill, and he and William Herrin, the Southern Pacific's chief counsel in California, lined up the crucial votes. The bill passed the legislature on February 23, and on March 3 Roosevelt signed Senate Joint Resolution 115, which called for federal acceptance of the valley and specified an annual $20,000 for its administration. In June of the year following, Yosemite Valley formally became a part of the surrounding national park, preserved thus for future generations to admire. And so the singular dream of a man who had come into the valley an unknown wanderer and found it home had now almost forty years later been translated into a national reality: the valley would now be a sort of home to the American people forever.

Throughout the last stages of the process, Muir had been badly worried about Helen. She had suffered another attack of pneumonia, and her recovery from this one was so slow and problematic that on the advice of a specialist Muir took her to Sierra Bonita Ranch near Wilcox in the Arizona desert where it was said Helen would have to live for a year to strengthen her lungs. Muir and Wanda accompanied her south and helped arrange her living conditions.

Her anxious Papa at least was instantly convinced the move was the right one. The air felt wonderful, and he wrote confidently in his journal that he had "never breathed air more distinctly, palpably good." It was clean, fresh, and "pure as the icy Arctic air," he continued. "It fairly thrills and quivers, as if one actually felt the beatings of the infinitely small vital electric waves of life and light drenching every cell of flesh and bone, bringing on a complete resurrection after the death of sound sleep."

Believing as ever in the resurrection nature could effect, Muir was startled out of his desert confidence by trouble from another quarter. A telegram from home on June 24 told him he must return there immediately: Louie was gravely ill. Only three days before Louie had telegrammed that she had been ill but was recovering. Leaving Helen behind, Muir and Wanda hurried to Martinez. Once there, it was clear that for Louie nature could not effect a resurrection from this illness. She had lung cancer, and the case was pronounced hopeless. She lasted little more than a month, dying on August 6, and was buried on the ranch next to her parents in a shaded little plot beyond an orchard. Stunned and suddenly immensely tired, Muir could do nothing other than return with Wanda to the Arizona desert and Helen.

Man and wife had spent much more time apart than was conventional—whole years in sum—and it may be that his youthful attachment to Jeanne Carr was the most powerful emotion he had ever felt for another human being. But he had loved Louie deeply in his singular way, had honored her for her family skills, and had long known that she had understood and supported him as no one else ever could have, patiently, consistently, through all the difficulties his personality and calling had presented. With a superb intuition she had known how to balance her husband's needs with those of the family, and at the critical moment she had turned him again toward the wider world, away from the ranch and family life. Now she was gone and with her that solid, stable home base that had allowed Muir his creative freedom. Roosevelt wrote him now, urging him to get out into the mountains and forests, for they would do "more for you than either man or woman could." But for much of that autumn Muir was too broken and dazed to take old comforts from the sun and bracing air.

They were living now at Adamana, Arizona, at the Forest Hotel, a large rambling place by the railroad tracks run by a couple who gave guided tours of the Petrified Forest six miles south.

Helen had a tent pitched beside the hotel and, hoping to strengthen her lungs, slept out in it even when the temperature sank toward zero. From the hotel Muir could look across the desert with its spiky plant life to the gray and tumbled mesa to the southeast. Behind it lay the Blue Forest (now Blue Mesa), and gradually as his spirits and energy revived he began making regular trips there, alone or accompanied by the girls. The huge stumps, petrified through centuries of seeping silica-rich water, looked as cleanly sawed at their bases as though cut by a race of prehistoric loggers who had left them where they fell and gone on to other, unimaginable tasks.

Muir had once written his mother that he must have been born with bog juices in his veins, so drawn throughout life had he been to alpine meadows, glaciers, and all watery, green places. Yet now in his bereaved age he found a strange sort of balm in this silent and outwardly inhospitable place. At sunrise, the desert was blood red, and all day long the unchecked winds scoured its treeless stretches with blowing sand. At high noon and on cloudy days the vivid colors of the iron oxide folds became bleak and sombre-seeming, then at sunset they were blood red again. There had once been human dwellers here but so long ago that the place was uninhabited when the Spaniards first stumbled across it in the six-teenth century. Muir found abundant evidence of the ancient Indian life, their dwellings, pottery, and pictographs. He spent long days patiently excavating and piecing together shards or studying the pictographs of animals, humans, and sidereal formations.

But there was current life here, too, amazingly abundant and varied in the polychromatic wasteland. As ever and even in grief, Muir found it. If it was not that alpine lushness nor the templed forest splendor, nor still less the utter white cleanliness of the Alaskan glaciers, it was yet something unique and wonderful. The Painted Desert told him once again and in a time of great need of the inexhaustible capacity of natural things to flourish where they were, nothing amiss, nothing out of place or fragmented. The desert, if you looked carefully, was no wasteland; it was simply, wonderfully an abode of specialized life, the hardy, tough, clinging variety that Muir so admired, like the whitebark pine of the Sierras. Here were the tough annuals—Indian paintbrush, prince's plume, desert primrose, evening primrose, painted cup, globe mallow— and the even tougher perennials, juniper, rubber rabbitbush, ephedra. There were the remarkable animals, too, like the gopher snake and the lizard that could withstand and even prosper in so unforgiving a climate. Most amazing of all was the kangaroo rat, which manufactured its own water while living on a totally dry diet.

In January 1906, a family from Maine stopped at Adamana in the midst of a lengthy sight-seeing tour, and the young daughter, Alice Cotton, immediately fell under the spell of the thin, shaggy-bearded man who sat down to dinner with them that first night in the hotel's capacious dining room. His talk flowed in amazing quantity on subjects both native to this place and exotically remote. When he smiled, as he did in extolling the singular virtues of Mrs. Stevenson's baked potatoes, a captivating twinkle lit his eyes. Through dinner she tried hard to place him and then did: he was the famous naturalist, John Muir.

During the precious days that followed, Muir and his daughters appointed themselves the Cotton family's guides, showing them in loving detail the multiple wonders of the place. Muir seemingly knew every fold, hollow, and Indian site in the whole area, and Wanda and her sister were hardly less interesting than their famous father. Wanda could drive a six-horse rig like a man and whip it through pockets of quicksand with expert determination. Helen, said an awed Alice Cotton, rode a horse like a cowboy, sixty miles a day—and wore divided skirts.

To this remote spot the despoilers had come also, as they had to the more accessible and obvious garden spots of the West, and Alice Cotton learned that Muir had gone into battle with them as soon as he had arrived here and discovered their operations. Vandals dynamited the petrified logs to get at their crystal innards, and at Adamana a mill had been set up to crush the logs into abrasives. Muir, according to Alice Cotton, said he made a special trip to Washington to bring this abuse to official attention, and he was confident something would soon be done to remedy it.*

At the end of the Cottons' stay, Muir gave Alice Cotton an

---

*Something soon was. Under the vigorous sponsorship of the environmentally conscious John F. Lacey of Iowa, Congress passed the Antiquities Act, June 8, 1906. The act empowered the president to set aside areas of historic and scientific value. Under its provisions, Roosevelt created the Petrified Forest National Monument on December 8, 1906, and there can be little doubt that Muir was influential in the creation of the nation's second national monument (Sidney

Indian pot that she so treasured she refused to allow it out of her sight on the long train trip home. All her life she would continue to prize the artifact and, even more than the thing itself, the man who had given it to her and had made the family the gift of himself.

Shortly after the Cottons departed, Muir made a long entry in his journal in commemoration of the anniversary of the birth of Robert Burns. It is glorious to know, he said (using a favored word that Robert Underwood Johnson and other editors had urged him to put out to pasture), that one of the greatest men of the nineteenth century was a Scotsman, for Burns's lessons of love and sympathy for mice and men "have gone ringing and singing around the globe, stirring the heart of every nation and race." Perhaps on this occasion he was moved to think back on his own life, so much of which had been lived in Burns's century, and to that walk he long ago took outside Dunbar with Grandfather Gilrye when he had sat in a haymow and heard the squeaky distress of a mother mouse. That moment had touched him so that he remembered it forever, and among his special favorites of Burns's was "To a Mouse."

Then, thinking of himself and of his hero, he went on to observe that the "man of science too often loses sight of the essential oneness of all living beings. . . ." But the eye of the "Poet, the Seer, never closes on the kinship of all God's creatures, and his heart ever beats in sympathy with great and small alike as 'earth-born companions and fellow mortals' equally dependent on Heaven's eternal love."

Weeks later, he was back in Martinez with Wanda. The big house seemed ghostly now with only the two of them and the silent Chinese servant, Ah Fong, in it. To fight off his sense of isolation he threw himself into the study of petrified forests and got out of the house to Berkeley, where he spent long hours in the university library reading on the subject. "I sit silent and alone," he wrote Helen, "from morn til eve in the deeper silence of the enchanted old old forests of the coal age. The hours go on neither long or short, glorious for imagination . . . but tough for the old paleontological body nearing 70."

In June, Wanda married Thomas Rae Hanna, a civil engineer

R. Ash and David D. May, *Petrified Forest: The Story Behind the Scenery,* Holbrook, Arizona, 1969, 1981).

she had met at school, and the young couple came to live in the old
Martinez adobe below the big house. Then in August, Helen came
home from the desert, and the two of them, the indomitable old
man and the young woman, set about creating a new order of
living. Muir's second-floor study, which before Louie's death had
seemed in its sacrosanct clutter a normal, functioning part of the
household, now looked utterly chaotic and forlorn like the raveled
residue of life itself. But Helen would help him shape some order
here, would sort through the dozens of versions of a single episode,
selecting toward coherent manuscripts, and type them. Scattered
throughout the room were the materials for perhaps a dozen books,
but so far he had published but two, *The Mountains of California*
(1894) and *Our National Parks* (1901), despite more than thirty
years of literary effort. Now, with Louie gone, Wanda married, and
the business of Yosemite satisfactorily concluded, he could with
Helen's assistance spend his remaining time trying, as he would
later write a friend, to arrange his notes "in something like lateral,
medial, and terminal moraines on my den floor." "I never imagined," he said in surprise, "I had accumulated so vast a number.
The long trains and embankments and heaped-up piles are truly
appalling."

In October 1907, Muir went with Keith into the Sierras. He was
again badly worried about Helen, whose hacking cough had returned, and on this trip he could not get the sound of it out of his
ears. Still, there were moments of relative pleasure, especially during the week the two old friends camped out in Hetch Hetchy
Valley. Hetch Hetchy had long been a spot Muir was especially
fond of, and after this experience in it his friend Keith reportedly
pronounced it superior even to Yosemite Valley in its high-walled
beauty.

It is possible that Muir chose Hetch Hetchy as their campsite
because he wanted to reacquaint himself with its features so as to
be better prepared to defend it against the designs of the city of San
Francisco. As Muir well knew, the city had been casting about for
a cheap and reliable source of municipal water for more than a
quarter century and since 1900 had been looking more and more
closely at Hetch Hetchy. The main channel of the Tuolumne River

ran east through the valley's three-mile length, and the valley floor
was very level. Moreover, at the end of the valley where the river
exited, the walls were high and steep and the exit was narrow. Not
only would Hetch Hetchy be easy to dam as a reservoir for city
water, but it could also serve as a source of hydroelectric power.

For years San Francisco had suffered under the monopolistic
control of the Spring Valley Water Company and had even tried to
buy the company as a means of gaining control of its water supply.
But no solutions to the problem had appeared until the energetic
administration of Mayor James D. Phelan (1896–1902), one of the
earlier and most successful of San Francisco's reform politicians.
Phelan and his associates had quietly conducted feasibility studies
on the Tuolumne River system and had become convinced the city
must acquire rights to Hetch Hetchy. The problem of course was
that the valley lay within a national park. But before any of the
park's defenders were aware, moves were made to get around this
problem: Representative Marion De Vries of Stockton introduced
a measure in Congress that would authorize the secretary of the
interior to grant rights of way through national parks for canals,
pipelines, tunnels, or other water conduits, provided such facilities
were not incompatible with the public interest. The measure went
through Congress with little opposition and was signed into law on
February 15, 1901.* Here was perhaps the earliest important application of the operating doctrine of the new conservationists, "the
greatest good for the greatest number." It was also an indication
of the unsanctified status of reserved lands to which Pinchot would
refer in his *Century* article of 1904.

Between the largely unremarked passage of the Right of Way
Act and Muir's camping trip with Keith in the autumn of 1907
there occurred the cataclysm of the San Francisco earthquake. Previous to it, Roosevelt's secretary of the interior, Ethan Allen Hitchcock, had frowned on San Francisco's efforts to secure rights to
Hetch Hetchy and to Lake Eleanor, a part of the Tuolumne system

---

*Holway Jones, whose careful chronology of the Hetch Hetchy controversy
I follow here, shrewdly observes that in a way the battle for the valley was over
before its defenders knew it had begun. The Right of Way Act, as he suggests,
created a significant precedent that proponents of the reservoir plan consistently
referred to in the debate that was waged from 1906 to 1913 (Jones, *John Muir and
the Sierra Club,* San Francisco, 1965).

lying northwest of the valley. As for Pinchot, he had forthrightly supported the Phelan group's petition and had told Colby he did so in 1905, but he was not in a position to make policy. By 1906 he had, however, gone a good way toward convincing the president that the city ought to have rights to the valley and the lake. Then came the earthquake, the damage from which was predominantly caused by fire. In its aftermath the entire Bay area was water conscious as never before. No system could have survived the earthquake to deliver the water necessary to quench the hundreds of fires that raked the city on those April days, but ex-Mayor Phelan charged that Secretary Hitchcock's denial of the city's petition for the Tuolumne River sites had contributed to the disaster, and in the climate of that time it is understandable that he was widely believed.

Among other fallout from the quake was the publication of an opinion of the year previous by Roosevelt's assistant attorney general to the effect that the secretary of the interior had the authority to grant the city the river sites in question, no congressional approval being necessary. In any case, Hitchcock had left the administration and James R. Garfield had replaced him. Now all the conditions were changed, and Pinchot advised the city to renew its quest, indicating that the new secretary would be favorably disposed. Thus in 1907 the San Francisco Board of Supervisors resubmitted the city's petition and was not disappointed: in May 1908, Garfield granted the city rights to the Hetch Hetchy and Lake Eleanor sites.

In making the grant, Garfield remarked that the public interest dictated the use of the sites for a municipal water supply and that this must take precedence over the arguments of the park's defenders. He was obligated, Garfield wrote William Colby, to "consider what use will give the greatest benefit to the greatest number." Besides, he said, Hetch Hetchy was not unique even in its immediate locality, for there was the lordly Yosemite Valley relatively close to it. Garfield did urge, however, that the Lake Eleanor site be fully developed first and only then the Hetch Hetchy Valley site. This presumably would be a good many years into the future.

Here was a wedge of sorts, though it was to prove as useful to proponents of the dams as to the preservationists. The former pointed out that there was no present reason to mourn the loss of the beautiful Hetch Hetchy since it would remain undeveloped beyond the lifetimes of those now defending it. The latter asked why it was necessary now to grant San Francisco rights to a site all agreed would not be necessary for perhaps a generation to come.

For Muir the issue was starkly clear: the national parks had been reserved from the rush of real estate speculation and development as monuments to the aboriginal natural splendor of the New World as well as to the nation's memory of that splendor. They existed, supposedly, in a kind of temporal/spatial vacuum, unspoiled and forever inviolable, there for the perpetual recreation of the American people. Now a precedent had apparently been established changing all that: the national parks, it seemed, might be carved up piecemeal to satisfy the currently perceived needs of this outfit or that. They were to be treated like every other portion of the national landscape, subject to the same pressures, the same utilitarian standards. For Muir the contemplated development of Hetch Hetchy was a fraud and a betrayal of the national trust.

And, of course, there was something deeply and intensely personal involved as well. This was, after all, his home ground, the very fount of his inspiration and the place of his best, most intensely creative days. Coming down from it, he had subsequently worked long and imaginatively—denying certain strong, antisocial, apolitical tendencies in himself—to preserve Yosemite from the ceaseless raids of the developers. "This playing at politics," he once remarked to C. Hart Merriam, "saps the very foundations of righteousness." Yet he had forced himself to play, and he had played well in what he regarded as an unarguably just cause. In a real sense, it might pardonably have seemed to him as though Yosemite National Park was his gift and bequest to the American people, a thing incomparably greater and more enduring than any book he would ever write. The other pioneers and discoverers—voyageurs, conquistadores, mountain men—had died intestate.

Nor had those ardent lovers of the American world, Emerson and Thoreau, succeeded so well as Muir in translating that love into an accessible bequest. Emerson had confronted the central philosophic issue of the republic, the inherent antagonism between individualism and community, and had at last drawn back into the sanctity of his study, believing that the exemplary preservation of his own individualism was all he could finally give his society. Yet he was too honest a man and thinker not to realize that he had joined but not resolved the issue. Having outlived Thoreau, he had pronounced judgment on both of them when he said it was a waste of a great life that the younger man had so resolutely refused a wider role, preferring to remain "the captain of a huckleberry-party."

Muir, urged by Emerson, Jeanne Carr, and by some inner sense of social duty (perhaps ultimately Calvinistic in origin), had fought past those anti-societal impulses, had reluctantly acted publicly on his love for the American land. His most significant American discovery had been a way to love the land and to extend that love to the society at large. In his own life he had reconciled the conflict between democratic individualism and participatory democracy. Roosevelt, apostle of strenuous participation in the public arena, recognized this singular achievement, writing in a posthumous tribute to Muir that he was unique in that he was a lover of nature who was also a good citizen, "a man able to influence contemporary thought and action on the subjects to which he ha[d] devoted his life."

Now not only was Yosemite's integrity called into question but also the principle of the national parks and forests, and Muir found himself publicly stigmatized as a selfish obstructionist, his motives for defending Yosemite suspected. Phelan, writing Garfield in November 1907, put this accusation most bluntly when he charged that Muir considered Yosemite his private preserve and that was why the old man was so fanatic in his opposition to San Francisco's plans. Later, at House hearings on Hetch Hetchy in 1909, Phelan brought up the accusation again and extended it by saying he felt certain Muir would "sacrifice his own family for the preservation of beauty." Nor was Phelan the only one making such statements. In a generally sympathetic magazine article published in 1908, Bailey Millard felt compelled to defend Muir against the popular belief that Muir cared more for a tree than he did for a man.

Muir was sensitive to the charges: there *was* something proprietary in his attitude toward Yosemite. Who after all knew it better, had loved it as well, fought for it as long? And only he himself knew just how hard he had had to battle that strain of the anchorite in his character and to actively love mankind in the mass. He had come a long way from the morally vain young man who lectured the innocent sports at the Mondell House in Prairie du Chien. He had traveled a long way, too, from the guide of Yosemite days in the early '70s who privately scorned the blundering, upholstered efforts of tourists to appreciate God's granite grandeur. But he had not traveled *all* the way to some Christlike love of all mankind, and he knew this. It is likely also that he still felt he had gotten things from a sequoia or a sugar pine he never got from man or woman. Still, he had come far—too far, he felt, to be criticized so.

As the pressures of the Hetch Hetchy fight mounted and intensified through more than six years of his late age, something of the old moralistic and antisocial strains recurred. Some years before he had scrawled on a scrap of paper these words: "Heaven knows that John Bap was not more eager to get all his fellow sinners into the Jordan than I to baptize all of mine in the beauty of God's mountains." A noble sentiment perhaps, but not too much of a slip would be necessary to transform it into the arrogant utterance of a wilderness prophet pronouncing judgment on a wayward people. During the prolonged anguish of Hetch Hetchy, Muir lost some of the hard-won philosophical balance of his mature years and spoke like a desert father. Always a tough man in any contest and a formidable verbal antagonist, more and more in these years he adopted the charged and vivid language of the Old Testament. There recurred too an Augustinian sense of humans' departure from the divine plan, as if at the end of his life the revenant form of old Daniel Muir had arisen to hound his freed son, warping his perceptions into the paternal pattern. Right was blazingly clear; wrong was absolute. The motives of the proponents of the dam scheme were stained and even Satanic. "But what can you expect?" he asked rhetorically of the despoilers. "The Lord Himself couldn't keep the devil out of the first reservation that was ever made." And as for those many citizens who did not care much whether the park was violated or not, they did not deserve such beauty anyway. In an interview printed in 1906, Muir said that those who would not make the simple effort to "walk out of the smoke of the cities" had "no right" to God's freely bestowed natural beauties. He had forgotten how hard it was for city dwellers to actually get out into unspoiled nature, and maybe he had never truly understood how mentally and economically circumscribed were the lives of so many of the working class for whom, presumably, Yosemite was preserved.

The "enemy" was everywhere, even within his beloved Sierra Club, where some members who lived in San Francisco considered themselves citizens of that city first and club members second. Believing that the Hetch Hetchy and Lake Eleanor sites offered the best, least expensive solution to the city's water problems (a belief subsequently supported in an independent survey by the Advisory Board of Army Engineers), these members had from the first opposed the vigorous campaign Muir and William Colby mapped for the club. Warren Olney, who next to Muir had been most instrumental in the formation of the club, was the most conspicuous of these, and his defeat in the club elections of 1909 was charged by many to the efforts of Muir. Olney had enjoyed wide popularity among club members and his defeat brought a bitter taste to some mouths.

For Muir the dissension was a stab in the back from an unexpected source, and he was so hurt and angered that he thought seriously of resigning the presidency and even of resigning from the club. Instead, Colby convinced him that the better course would be to form a kind of rump organization out of the Sierra Club membership and use it to wage the Hetch Hetchy fight. In the spring of 1909, they formed the Society for the Preservation of National Parks with Muir as president and Colby, Joseph N. Le Conte, Robert Underwood Johnson, Harriet Monroe, and former Secretary of the Interior John W. Noble as prominent members.

In the fight's terminal stages, Muir came to suspect that even Colby was not entirely sound on Hetch Hetchy, that in the end no one cared as much about the integrity of the park as he. He was probably right about that, anyway. Even the indefatigable Johnson at last saw that the cause had become hopeless and that, having made their point, it would be best for the defenders to let the issue pass and get on with the rest of life. So in the end, Muir felt alone. The Senate passed the Raker Bill granting San Francisco the use of Hetch Hetchy on December 6, 1913, and on December 19 President Woodrow Wilson signed it into law. On December 27, Muir wrote a friend that the loss of the valley was "hard to bear." The destruction of its groves and gardens, "the finest in all California," went right to his heart, but, he dared to hope, "in spite of Satan &

Co. some sort of compensation must surely come out of this dark damn- dam-damnation."

For him the compensation was immediate if unspectacular. Near the end of the long battle he had written Helen, saying that however the business should turn out he would be glad when it was over, for it was killing him. He was right in more than the literal way he intended. There is little doubt that the fight badly depleted his remaining resources; but it was also damaging Muir's devotion to his country and its long-term needs, and, at the same time, his national reputation. At the battle's end, however, he performed an act of remarkable psychological resiliency: he recollected himself, expunged the bitterness from his soul, and resumed his amicable relations with the world.

This was as well for his country as it was for him personally. He had become a national treasure in his old age. Reporters sought him out and recorded his rambling observations on everything from evolution to the proper way to take a hike. William Howard Taft felt he, too, must have Muir guide him about Yosemite just as he had his predecessor, though Taft was no outdoorsman. He received honorary degrees from Yale and his alma mater, Wisconsin. A magnificent grove of redwoods across the bay from San Francisco had been made a park by gift of California Representative William Kent and named Muir Woods.* When he toured South America and Africa in 1911–12 in belated fulfillment of a lifetime dream, reporters covered his itinerary much as they would that of some international celebrity. At Buenos Aires they quoted him to the effect that he was really a tramp, not some famous author, and, he said, "I'm seventy-four, and still good at it." The image of the kindly faced, white-bearded sage who knew wilderness tales had become as much a part of the national consciousness as the image of Buffalo Bill Cody. Here was America's emissary from the wilderness, one who could teach a thoroughly modern nation how to love what of the old wild world it had left. If the image was something

*In the last stages of the Hetch Hetchy controversy, Representative Kent, who favored the cause of the city, had characterized Muir as a fanatic.

of a caricature, still it was a constructive one. For the Muir of the image was potentially at least a teacher, a guide, a wilderness guardian, and he might continue to function as such through future generations.

But the image had begun to show tarnish in the late years of Muir's intransigent opposition to the damming of the valley. Newspaper cartoons depicted him as a sour old curmudgeon, and some of his most ardent admirers turned away from him as from one who had betrayed that admiration. Even Willie Keith came to suspect his old friend had lost his balance over Hetch Hetchy. At the governors' conference of 1908, a national meeting in Washington on the state of conservation, Muir, the grand old man of the entire movement, was pointedly excluded—as were his friends—because of the Hetch Hetchy controversy. But as bitter a blow as this was to him, it was still worse for the conservation movement, deprived temporarily at least of a powerful voice and vision. As it turned out, the governors' conference was a somewhat dessicated and mechanical inventory of national resources.

But in the aftermath of Hetch Hetchy there was time, scant though it would prove, for everyone to recollect the more benign and beneficent John Muir, to cherish anew the gift of his character and influence. The brightening of the image began with Muir himself who simply, resolutely turned away from defeat and faced toward life again.

It is probable that in the last year or so of Hetch Hetchy he had admitted to himself that the fight was hopeless. That is one way to understand his extended tour of Africa and South America, as if he knew he had better relent and relax. And there were other signs in his activities upon returning from the tour in March 1912 that he had made up his mind to save himself at least even if he could not save the valley. Some of his comments on Hetch Hetchy began to show glimmers of that humor that in the past so often had saved him from dourness and moralism. Then in May 1913 he and his old friend and neighbor, John Swett, were honored with degrees by the University of California at Berkeley. Both men went down to Berkeley for the ceremonies, each believing he was humoring the other by doing so. But humoring or no, Muir appeared pleased with the recognition from the state's major school. Here was a home reward for all his efforts and a sign that on the very ground of the controversy there were still a great many who admired him for his stand.

On the last day of May he wrote a lovely, relaxed letter to Mina Merrill that contained not a single reference to Hetch Hetchy. He was, he told her, turning to his remaining literary tasks, principally his book on Alaska and an autobiographical volume that would show how he got to California. "It is now seven years," he continued on the autobiographical plane,

> since my beloved wife vanished into the land of leal. Both of my girls are happily married and have homes of their own. Wanda has three lively boys, Helen has two and is living at Daggett, California. Wanda is living on the ranch in the old adobe, while I am alone in the big house on the hill. . . .
>
> As the shadows lengthen in life's afternoon, we cling all the more fondly to the friends of our youth. And it is with the warmest gratitude that I recall the kindness of your family when I was lying in darkness.

Mina Merrill had written to ask certain questions about the first volume of his autobiography. *The Story of My Boyhood and Youth* had appeared serially (1912–13) and then in this year in book form. Like many other readers, Miss Merrill had been shocked by Muir's depiction of the harsh disciplines of school and home, and in his letter he assured her he had told the unvarnished truth.

Like the other deferred tasks, some of which would never be completed, Muir had long had this one in the back of his mind, and it probably would have stayed there had it not been for E. H. Harriman. For years Muir had been urged by admirers to tell the story of his life, but he had always put it off, believing there were more important jobs to be done and feeling leery of what he called "this personal rubbish." In the late summer of 1908, however, Muir was almost cudgeled by Harriman into a start on the project. He had told Harriman that he could not accept an invitation for a long visit at the Harriman lodge on Klamath Lake, Oregon—he was too busy writing, he said. "Well," Muir records Harriman as saying, "you come up to the Lodge and I will show you how to write books. The trouble with you is you are too slow in your

beginnings. You plan and brood too much. Begin, begin, begin!"
Not bad advice for any writer, and Muir, perhaps amused with this
wisdom from so unliterary a source, accepted.

Once he had gotten Muir to Pelican Bay Lodge, Harriman had
sicced his personal secretary on Muir with instructions to follow
him everywhere and take down whatever he said. Muir could not
shake Thomas Price. Wherever he walked, along the shores of the
lake with Mount Pitt rising with startling abruptness in the distance,
beneath the arrowy pines, along the winding road that led from the
lodge buildings through the woods, Price was there at his elbow,
taking dictation. The result was a large, amazingly coherent mass
of reminiscences interspersed with asides, remarks to local squirrels
and birds, and exclamations. Reporters who interviewed Muir in
these late years often remarked on his incredible memory for incident and detail, his ability to compose complex sentences on the
wing, and in the record Thomas Price took at Pelican Bay Lodge
the evidence of this is abundant and striking.

But in typical fashion, Muir did nothing with the material Price
typed and sent to him. Hetch Hetchy pressed him, of course, but
other literary matters still seemed more significant, though these
too were of an autobiographical nature. He went back into the
battered blue notebooks of that glorious first summer in the high
Sierras and without significant revision published them as *My First
Summer in the Sierras* in 1911. Then, he gathered together a manageable bundle of Yosemite notes and published these as *The Yosemite*
two years later. Only then did he turn fully to the shaping of the
Pelican Bay material.

The narrative took the young man up to that point at which with
"streaming eyes" he bade farewell to the University of Wisconsin,
and while it was a hymn to the natural beauties of his native Scotland and the Wisconsin farmlands, it was also unsparing in its portrait of the cruelties visited upon children by their teachers and
parents. When Daniel Muir had died, the elder son had composed
a conventionally tender eulogy. Now, he told the bleak truth as he
had been compelled to experience it. His sister, Joanna, now living
in Richmond, Virginia, wrote to say that she too remembered it this
way. "The portion relating to yourself and the family," she told
him, "was read in tears, and I wished with all my heart it had not
been so true. In other words, that the hard things had never oc-

curred so they would not be there to record."

In mid-August Muir left his dusty, almost barren house for a sentimental journey to the Harriman ranch at Island Park, Idaho. However this time he had not been invited by E.H.Harriman. The railroad czar who knew so well how to goad others to high levels of productivity had not known how to manage so well his own efforts and had worked himself into an early grave. Now it was his widow who invited Muir to visit, and he went, for auld lang syne, to honor the memory of a friend, to reminisce with Mrs. Harriman about the high times on the H.A.E. of 1899.

On the way he had a stop in Salt Lake City where so many years before he had wandered in lonely bachelorhood through the prolific "Latter Days." This time he heard the Mormon Tabernacle Choir sing "Nearer My God to Thee" and was profoundly moved, so devout, so sweet, so whispering low it seemed to him. Recently so many of his friends had, like Harriman, gone to the gathering host of the dead, nearer presumably to God than those like himself who yet stayed on: Jeanne Carr, his sister Maggie, Keith, A. H. Sellers, and John Hooker of happy Pasadena memories, and, just two months before, John Swett, who had stood white-haired and honored with Muir at the Berkeley exercises in May. It was all very mysterious and saddening. When Keith had died he had wondered aloud whether the brittle leaves that clung to boughs felt lonely when they saw their fellows fall. All flesh was grass indeed.

But it was not frightening. He was inclined to doubt that individuals survived intact the translation from this life into another existence, but he had seen too closely how life sprang eternally from death to doubt there was some kind of survival beyond the grave. "This grand show is eternal," he had written on one of his unnumbered and undated scraps:

> It is always sunrise somewhere; the dew is never dried all at once; a shower is forever falling; vapor is ever rising. Eternal sunrise, eternal sunset, eternal dawn and gloaming, on sea and continents and islands, each in its turn, as the round earth rolls.

In Louie's passing he had felt for the first time the tremendous pain of irremediable loss, had wondered then whether something, somehow might be done to alleviate this pain as so many other pains had been by science. Though he never quite got over that first great pain—nor did the clustering deaths of so many loved ones permit him to do so—something like his old mystical sense of the insepara- bility of life and death returned to him, as if the sense itself in its inevitable return were part of that cosmic wheeling visible in sun- rises and seasons. Death, like many another phenomenon, was mysterious only because humans knew just the first, outermost portion of it; the rest, like a chain stretching to God, was hidden from human sight. Everything taught that death was a going home, a rediscovery and an atonement. The Norse, he observed in an- other random jotting, "spoke of death as *Heimgang*—home-going.

> So the snow-flowers go home when they melt and flow to the sea, and the rock ferns, after unrolling their fronds to the light and beautifying the rocks, roll them up close again in the autumn and blend with the soil.

There was a certain something of this home-going feeling to the Island Park trip. Walking the meadows fringed with pine, the Snake River sparkling and dancing through, and the Tetons upthrust to the south, he felt an almost ancient serenity. The jottings in his notebook evened and smoothed themselves, and for the first time in years he sketched. When he met a Mr. Sherwood here, it was almost as if he were being vouchsafed a last backward glance over the trail of a long life. Sherwood was a storekeeper, farmer, inven- tor, millwright, and naturalist who possessed a "telling" collection of birds and mammals. Muir was instantly drawn to him and pro- nounced him a "remarkable man."

The California winter of 1914 was stormy and foggy. Muir caught the grippe again but did not know how seriously it had infected his right lung. He kept doggedly on with his writing, trying to shape his Alaskan notes into a book. Mrs. Marion Randall Parsons, re- cently widowed by Muir's Sierra Club ally, E. T. Parsons, had become a secretary to him and visited each day at the ranch. Ill and tired as she saw he was, yet she recorded that often he would insist on staggering twelve-hour work days, storing each finished chapter in an orange crate. His mind was bright, Mrs. Parsons recalled, his perceptions fresh, and his feeling for that faraway time and place marvelously vivid.

A reporter, Melville Anderson, was also making periodic visits to the ranch at this time, and his impressions tallied with those of Mrs. Parsons: the old man still had incredible mental and spiritual vigor, still had, too, his congenital dislike of writing, a task, so he said, that made your head hot, your feet cold, and your stomach restless. Anderson, like McChesney and Swett, found Muir ever ready to drop his writing for talk.

In June, Helen, now living with her husband and children on a ranch at the edge of the Mojave Desert at Daggett, had another son. That same month Silas Christofferson achieved a record altitude on his flight over Mount Whitney, sailing in his airplane high above the height so laboriously and lovingly achieved by the old mountaineer more than forty years before. In August the guns erupted in Europe.

All that late summer and on into the fall Muir was acting on an impulse to modernize the empty house. He bought curtains, rugs, and furniture to replace what he had given away, installed electricity, and had the place thoroughly cleaned—all but his study. Writing Helen on December 3, he told her he wished her back there with him, but at least the place had been "put in comparative order." That same day he wrote a note to his Dunbar cousin, Maggie Lunam: "Here is fifty dollars for yourself & the poor with all good wishes for the new year. Let me know when you need more."

As the month drew to a close, Muir told Wanda he wanted to go south to Daggett to see Helen and his new grandson. Wanda got him ready for the trip, and he packed along the typescript of the Alaska book, intending to work on it there. When he arrived in evening a sharp and bitter wind blew on the desert, and by the time he got to the ranch he was plainly unwell.

Another sunrise, "the old pomp," revived him. He and Helen walked out in the desert, he glad of its clean cold and stopping as ever to chat with the plants and to breathe deeply. But evening brought him low again: arising from fireside work on his manuscript, he staggered and was helped to his bed. The local physician came and pronounced it pneumonia. Dr. George L. Cole, who had seen Muir previously in Los Angeles, was now summoned to Dag-

gett and made an even graver diagnosis—double pneumonia—but
he thought it worth the risk to move the patient by train the eighty
miles southwest to the California Hospital in Los Angeles where
Cole could supervise treatment. Muir made the trip and was admitted to the hospital on December 23 at 11:45 p.m.

By the next morning he was rallying. He had passed death by
many times before, avoiding those premature "home-goings"
through the guidance of an inner sun that brought him through
crisis, and in the early hours of Christmas Eve morning as he steadily
improved he talked amiably with Dr. Cole and the nurse. The Alaska
manuscript lay ready to hand. There were always revisions . . . .

There was a sudden sinking, morning's gains lost; when he was
alone for a moment, he went. At the end there was no great wrestling against the fading of the light, but rather a simple saunter on
into the next season. In that it was like his life, for which he
provided the best summation. His retirement from the world for
the wilderness, he said,

was no solemn abjuration of the world. I only went out for a walk,
and finally concluded to stay out till sundown, for going out, I
found, was really going in.

Lake tenaya

El
capitan

Yosemite
Falls

TISSIAK
Half Dome

merced R,   Yosemite memories

Notes on Sources

At the outset of my work on John Muir, a friend of mine, author of distinguished biographies of Lincoln and Martin Luther King, Jr., succinctly defined his literary method for me. "A biographer," he said, "knows only what he's told."

Never having written biography before, I was grateful for the advice and for his subsequent encouragements at those times when the formidability of my task was borne in upon me—a not infrequent occurrence during the first years of work on this book.

There are many other lines to my friend's method, but what he was trying to do by so simplifying it for me was, I think, to warn me against the seductions of narrative. He is himself a wonderfully gifted raconteur. He is also a would-be novelist who has come to terms with his limitations in that literary form and has gone on to write stories where he invents nothing except design.

Many nonfiction writers yearn to write fiction, whether poetry or prose, if only because the fictive mode seems to promise liberation from libraries, archives, and notes—all those laborious and necessary steps that must be made before a single word is committed to the page. So in writing biography where there is a story to be told, the temptation is great to use the occasion for invention. We've all read—and been disappointed by— biographies in which the failed novelist can be observed peeping out from beneath the sober robes of the historian and inventing conversations, even incidents, which to him at least seem plausible.

Forewarned about the seductions of storytelling, I went to my work, but it was not long before it became clear to me that I could not write the kind of biography that my friend does so handsomely. More and more, it came to seem to me that even as a rough, cautionary maxim, "A biographer knows only what he's told" begged as many questions as it answered. *How,* I increasingly wondered, is a biographer told things? Are his sources to be confined to the documents? What of inference, surmise, even intuition? Are there significant, real differences between these kinds of "sources" on the one hand and the inventions mentioned above; or are all equally sins against the historian's trade?

Early on in the research for this book, I tacked to the shelving above my desk lines of Henry James to the effect that it is a useless endeavor to

try to live over the lives of others unless we're prepared to try to live over
their perceptions. That, to be sure, is advice from a novelist and so perhaps
dangerously misleading for a biographer. But for me, even taking into
account the inherent risks, this was better, more useful advice. "We too
must write Bibles," said Emerson, by which he meant, among other
things, that each of us must write our own books and write them out of
our own convictions rather than to the prescription of another, however
that prescription may be sanctified by age or acclaim.

So I have written a different sort of biography than I believe my friend
would be comfortable with, and I have no doubt others will share his
misgivings. I have invented nothing here, either of conversation or incident, but I have ascribed to Muir some perceptions for which there is no
precise proof and I have characterized certain large events in ways for
which there was no specific warrant in previous writings on John Muir.

Of the latter practice, fairly common and to certain minds the less
reprehensible of the two, I want only to say that I believe it to be a
significant job of a writer on history to tell us not only what happened but
how that "what" looks to him. To some extent, of course, any interpretation is personal and thus fallible, but it is saved from being *merely* personal
and idiosyncratic by the writer's understanding of the broad context
within which the interpretation is ventured and by his carefully acquired
understanding of his specific subject. I have characterized Muir's youthful
intellectual struggles, his relationship with Jeanne Carr, his ambivalent
feelings about family life, and the battle over Hetch Hetchy in ways for
which no definite, documented proof exists. In explanation, I can say no
more—or less—than that after more than twenty years of studying American cultural history and after four years of living with John Muir, so these
matters looked to me.

About the former practice—ascribing to Muir certain perceptions for
which there is no documented proof—something more needs to be said.

In the chapter I call "The Lessons of a Long-Distance Runner" I claim
that the deepest locus of Muir's Dunbar experience was not the sea but
the Lammermuir hills that rise behind the town. In "Discovering the New
World" I go into some detail about farm work, how the fields looked, felt,
smelled, how it felt to dive into Fountain Lake. In "The Thousand-Mile
Walk" I describe what Muir saw as he followed the Hiwassee River from
Tennessee into North Carolina. In "First Summer" I describe the alpine
meadow where Muir and Billy the shepherd made their final camp with
the sheep and the way other places in Yosemite looked to him in that first,
magical summer up there. For none of these is there any definite extant
proof in the Muir papers I have studied. There are, however, suggestions
here and there, muted directions, as it were, for a script yet to be written,

and in the instances cited here these became blazingly clear to me when I went to these sites and meditated on Muir's experiences in them.

In both the published and unpublished versions of his autobiography, Muir pays tribute to what the sea at Dunbar gave him. In the long after-years, however far inland he might have been living, he could always be brought instantly back to the North Sea at Dunbar by a whiff of vagrant salt air, so deeply was that element a part of him. Yet, as I say, there seem to be suggestions here and there that the land lying westward was ultimately more significant for him. Partly, I think this was because the Lammermuirs offered greater possibilities than did the sea and shore for what I have called "creative truancy": he could get lost in them beyond easy recall; he was much more accessible to adult surveillance along Dunbar's harbor and shoreline. And partly it may have been simply because he could go farther into the country along the lanes and across fields, encountering surprises and splendors, than as a boatless boy he could on the seashore.

But the precise reasons why Muir might have been drawn more to the hills than to the sea are not too significant, even supposing they exist and could be discovered. What is significant for me as a writer trying for an understanding of his subject is that I obscurely felt that preference in Muir's reminiscences of his Scots childhood and that it seemed to explain a number of important things. Then, standing in the main room of the Muir family home on Dunbar's high street, I *saw* that preference suddenly, and a great light shone across a stretch of his years. The buildings across the street blocked a view of the sea, but from this room as from that above it where John and David Muir slept the Lammermuirs were fully, beguilingly in view. They beckon like some remembered freedom, calling one beyond town, walls, fences, even family. This was the truth I sensed in Muir's words about the excursions of his childhood and that I had come so far to find—without understanding what it was I was seeking there.

So too with my descriptions of the farm, its tasks and look, except that in this instance the directions were not found on any pages but in myself. I spent my boyhood summers in Wisconsin and, reaching through Muir's words for some fuller sense of his time at Fountain Lake and Hickory Hill, I came at last to my own indelible recollections and drew on them.

I know the look of Wisconsin clouds, the heat of corn-belt summers, the sudden violence of thunderstorms, the way the earth steams in their aftermath. I know too the damp cut of Wisconsin winters. Walking the cornfields of Hickory Hill with the owner, Harry Kearns, I smelled the heat and the milk of the corn, imagined the Muir children laboring in those deeps and yearning for noon dinner, the end of a dog day. Diving into Fountain Lake, I felt the rushes trail the length of my body. Watching the play of light on the lake, I was taken back to my own boyhood days when with my brother and sister I spent happy, placid days doing nothing more than watching water bugs zig over a Wisconsin lake or the ways the afternoon sun shafted down through the iron-filtered waters.

Hiking in Yosemite, following Muir's precise directions (in *The Yosemite*) to the sheepcamp in the meadow above Dog Lake and spending a day there gazing at pines and peaks; hiking the Hiwassee in Tennessee; walking about Cedar Key in search of the site of the Hobson house—these are not effective substitutes for a close experience with the documents of Muir's life and career, nor am I offering them as such. But for me, they proved of immeasurable adjunctive value in understanding that life, in trying to live it over. They gave me discoveries I could never have made in libraries.

As for the other kinds of discoveries deriving from a reading of documents, I have very few to offer readers here. I did find Daniel Muir's deed of sale for the house in Dunbar. With the help of a friend, I found a charming and revealing reminiscence of Muir in Arizona in 1906, and I found an important early photo of Muir (possibly the very first) mislaid among the Muir papers at the Holt-Atherton Library at the University of the Pacific. I have made, I think, fuller and better use of Jeanne Carr's papers at the Huntington Library than anyone before me, but the existence of these papers has of course long been known to Muir scholars.

But really, these are pitifully niggling things to trot out as the fruits of hundreds of hours at the Holt-Atherton, the Huntington, the Yosemite National Park Research Library, the State Historical Society of Wisconsin, the Bancroft Library, the archives of the John Muir National Historic Site at Martinez, and a dozen other places holding Muir and Muir-related materials. If they were all I had to show for these hours and for the four years of thought and writing spent on this book, I would be ashamed to offer so large a volume to further clog the already choked stream of human communication. What I have to offer instead of startling "new" discoveries is a new perspective on John Muir, one that places him in the context of his time and that seeks to establish his relationship to our own.

All the essential facts of Muir's life have been known since William Frederic Badè (*The Life and Letters of John Muir*, 1923) and Linnie Marsh Wolfe (*Son of the Wilderness*, 1945) established them. In the years since Wolfe published her Pulitzer Prize-winning book nothing of transforming significance has come to light. Rumors of unpublished Muir letters may still be heard, especially in the vicinity of Yosemite, but these letters are almost always said to concern but one episode of a long and rich life, and even if they should exist, I doubt they would substantially change what is now known of the man.

Both Badè's book and Wolfe's were authorized by the Muir family. Badè had been a colleague of Muir's at the Sierra Club and after Muir's death was appointed his literary executor. Wolfe was a family friend, and after Badè's death was appointed his successor. The family was highly pleased with her skillful editing of the unpublished portions of the journals (*John of the Mountains,* 1938) and subsequently encouraged her to write a biography.

The advantages Badè and Wolfe enjoyed in their pioneering efforts were about equal to the disadvantages at which they worked. They had the advantage of the cooperation of the family, access to the primary materials in their raw, original state, access also to those who had known Muir. Of these great advantages, only the last-mentioned is not also a disadvantage. There is a gingerly quality to their work, the mark almost always of family cooperation and participation; a tentativeness that is the mark of that largely unmapped way through which they had to write. And there is a lack of dimension to their portraits of Muir that is the inevitable consequence of the absence of historical perspective, that steadily enlarging view that only time discloses.

After Wolfe had had her say a sort of literary interregnum ensued, as if she had wrapped it all up and there was nothing important left to say. Edwin Way Teale did a handsome edition of Muir's essays culled from various sources (*The Wilderness World of John Muir,* 1954), but for a surprisingly long period of time this was about all. The Age of Assessment began with what might be described as the better sort of coffee-table book, *John Muir's America* (1976), text by T. H. Watkins, photos by Dewitt Jones. The book, however, was far other than that, for Watkins—prying, searching for another Muir behind the established portraits—invented conversations with Muir's ghost and in this way revealed the quirky, competitive, sharp-tongued Scot who awaited such a discovery. This was a brilliant stroke and unrepeatable, but it had the effect of opening the way into the second stage of literature on Muir.

Watkins was certainly my way into a search for another, fuller John Muir, but his path-breaking invention did not suggest Muir to me as a subject. That, oddly, happened in dream.

In the dream, I was walking the stacks of a large library, seemingly in search of something, when my eye was drawn to a book pulled out of its line on a shelf. Its spine read, simply, "John Muir" in that gold stamping used in rebinding. The morning following, I acted on the dream, canvassing the area libraries, where I found that despite his fame relatively little had been written on Muir—far less, for instance, than on the comparable figure, Thoreau.

The dream of course is hardly mysterious, even less so if I add that at the time I was a writer between books and searching for a subject. Then, too, my previous book had been an examination of Western civilization's historic attitudes toward the wilderness, in the course of which I had encountered John Muir.

Reading Badè and Wolfe was not, however, very encouraging, and it wasn't until I came across Watkins' text that I began to see the possibilities for another kind of biography. The flatness of the established portraits of Muir and their critical lack of historical and cultural perspective defined for me the shape of my intention. I wanted to create a picture of a man slowly and painfully coming to creative terms with his extraordinariness and then bringing the full force of that extraordinariness to bear on his adopted culture. And I wanted such a picture to be merged securely in the context of Muir's own time.

If I have been successful, my picture of Muir will point not only to that past in which he lived; it will point also at our present in which we are making the future, for here is where John Muir must have his meaning for us. Once I dreamed Muir's name; now I dream that the reading of this book about him will be a sort of action, one involving readers in that life lived over but also in its implications for us in our lands and times. Writing in "History," Emerson spoke of this need to read history actively. We ought, he told us, truly to sympathize in the "great moments of history, in the great discoveries, the great resistances, the great prosperities of man; because there the law was enacted, the sea was searched, the land was found . . . *for us.* . . ."

But first it is the responsibility of the writer to so place the reader that the sympathy will be felt. It is the writer who must show the reader that here in truth was a life lived for us. In the biography of John Muir that I hope I have composed, this would be, finally, to show that one man's rediscovery of America may also be our own.

As I hope I have sufficiently indicated, my debts to William Frederic Badè and Linnie Marsh Wolfe are great indeed. Muir traveled widely and often on itineraries known only to him. He wrote steadily, compulsively from about 1863 until his death half a century later. Yet it was not until the latter 1880s that he began to think of himself seriously as having a career of sorts, and he never began a systematic recording of his life or his writings. His love of the wilderness and the personal freedom available in it occasioned a profound ambivalence in him about both career and authorship, and the evidence of that ambivalence is in the chaos of the papers he left behind and in his reluctance to write a formal autobiography.

Badè and Wolfe were the inheritors of this. They had the task of sifting through what Muir late in life called the "lateral, medial, and terminal moraines" of his papers. The task was further complicated by Muir's lifetime habit of writing on any available scrap of paper, under any conditions, with soft, smudgy pencils or adamantine ones that left hardly a trace. In his later years he composed sometimes as many as half a dozen versions of a single incident.

Badè made a brave beginning at establishing a chronology, especially for the letters. There are largish gaps in his two-volume *Life and Letters*, though, and it was left to Wolfe to fill these in. Anyone who has spent time with her papers at the Holt-Atherton Library knows how painstakingly she labored to put the pieces together, and still for some episodes the chronology can be only approximate.

In the individual bibliographic essays that follow, I have not cited either Badè or Wolfe since to do so for every chapter would have been tedious. This general citation serves notice that I have relied on their chronology throughout except in those instances (rare) when I have found them to be in error. This does not mean, however, that I have accepted their evaluation and characterization of the events of Muir's life and career, as indeed very often I have not. The citations of documents from various institutions holding Muir materials indicate the numerous instances in which I have found the documents lead to other and fuller interpretations.

Prologue:
Peru Again

As far as I know, Badè was the first to suggest in print the symbolic contrast between the motives of the gold rushers and those that took John Muir to California two decades thereafter. Badè made the suggestion only in passing, but it is as fruitful as it is arresting, and others studying Muir's career have been struck by it. So was Muir himself. In his extensive travels through California from 1869 on, he encountered the multifarious evidence of what the gold rush had meant to the state, beginning with his relationships with his earliest employers and with the look of the Sierra foothills, where he first lived and worked. Ultimately, the gold rush became for him a metaphor for that get-rich-quick mentality that resulted in so much environmental abuse. In *Steep Trails: California, Utah, Nevada,*

Washington, Oregon, the Grand Cañon (Boston, 1918), Muir made numerous references to that mentality as he had encountered its effects in California and elsewhere in the West.

Muir's primitive image of America and his childhood fascination with Wilson's descriptions of American wildlife come from Muir's very late autobiographical book, *The Story of My Boyhood and Youth,* (Boston, 1913). *Story* began as the rambling, though internally coherent reminiscences Muir dictated to E. H. Harriman's personal secretary in the summer of 1908 when Muir was seventy. At first blush, it would not seem wise to trust the strict accuracy of such reminiscences, yet there are both general and specific reasons for doing so. First, there is the well-known fact that in elderly persons who have not suffered significant mental impairment as the result of stroke or other disease, long-term memory often is remarkably accurate. Even if short-term memory may have been affected by the aging process, long-term memory may actually improve in reach and clarity. And when the specific content of those first memories happens (as here with Muir) to bear a vital relationship with the rest of a person's life, we are called to respect their essential truth. Then there is the matter of Muir's memory, which all who knew the man attest was truly phenomenal and which remained in force into his last days. (See here the reminiscences of Marion Randall Parsons, his secretary during the last year, "John Muir and the Alaska Book," Sierra Club *Bulletin,* January, 1916.) Whatever of nature there was in this faculty of Muir's, it is certain there was much of nurture, too: Daniel Muir practically beat a memory into his eldest son, forcing him to commit to mind great swatches of the Bible, and the Scots school system helped in the same way. In adolescence, isolated on his family's Wisconsin farm, Muir discovered an ironic benefit of all that learning-by-sore-flesh: he could memorize almost anything—literature, mathematical problems, mechanical ones—and muse on these as he went about his daily chores.

I dwell at this length on the point not merely to attempt to justify my acceptance of Muir's first memories of a fabulous, undiscovered America but also to indicate why I have accepted so much of his account of his first twenty years. I do not believe, as others apparently do, that Muir's autobiography, both the published portion and that which remains in manuscript, represents a late, flawed patching of the record by an old man grown great. (See in this regard Michael Cohen, *The Pathless Way: John Muir and the American Wilderness,* Madison, 1984.) To be sure, I do not uncritically accept everything, and I find Muir's record of the years after he left the University of Wisconsin spotty and occasionally evasive. In some instances, too, his record of crucial experiences of the mature years represents autobiographical artistry, and here Michael Cohen's comparison of Muir and Thoreau is instructive. But for the early years, I have trusted my guide. So too did his sister Joanna. When Muir sent her a copy of what he then projected as the first of a multivolume autobiography, Joanna Muir Brown replied that what he had written was all too true (see letter, Joanna Muir Brown to John Muir, October 7, 1913, Muir Papers, Holt-Atherton Library, University of the Pacific).

As for the record of Daniel Muir's early years, we have almost nothing to go on. We know what his famous son has told us, and we have the family reminiscences collected by Linnie Marsh Wolfe. As for the rest of the early picture, historical context must supply what it can.

In that connection, my reconstruction of Scots history and culture was derived from R. L. Mackie, *A Short History of Scotland,* ed. Gordon Donaldson (New York, 1962); Mackie's discussion of Scots agricultural practices and land use was especially helpful. Also, Agnes Mure Mackenzie, *Scotland in Modern Times: 1720–1939* (London, Edinburgh, 1942), was good on religious life and the Scots' schismatic tendencies. Gordon Donaldson, *Scotland: Church and Nation Through Sixteen Centuries* (Edinburgh, London, 1960), provided a useful overview of a subject that is of critical importance in understanding Muir's religious inheritance and development. No book I know of more brilliantly illustrates the cankered, crabbed byways into which one might be led by the Scots brand of Calvinism than James Hogg's classic *The Private Memoirs and Confessions of a Justified Sinner* (1824; New York, 1959). Henry Thomas Buckle, *On Scotland and the Scotch Intellect,* ed. H. J. Hanham (Chicago, London, 1970), is a classic, too, though the author's virulent anticlericism makes one read with some caution. But for my understanding of the Scots national character, I ultimately owe most to Francis Quinn, a Glaswegian, with whom I have spent many glorious hours over twenty years and who gave me a guided tour of his native country that provided what no book could have.

ADDITIONAL SOURCES:

John Walton Caughey. *The California Gold Rush* (Berkeley, London, 1948, 1975).

J. Hector St. John Crevecoeur. *Letters from an American Farmer* (1782; New York, 1963, 1981).

Bernard De Voto. *The Year of Decision: 1846* (Boston, 1942).

Janet Glover. *The Story of Scotland* (London, 1960, 1977).

Marcus Lee Hansen. *The Atlantic Migration, 1607–1860: A History of the Continuing Settlement of the United States* (New York, 1940, 1961).

Donald Dale Jackson. *Gold Dust* (New York, 1980).

W. G. Johnston. *Experiences of a Forty-Niner* (New York, 1892, 1973).

Eugene I. McCormac. *James K. Polk: A Political Biography* (Berkeley, 1919).

John Muir. Letter to Mary Muir, Indianapolis, April 22, (1866?). Yosemite National Park Research Library.

Milo Milton Quaife (ed.). *Pictures of Gold Rush California* (Chicago, 1949).

n.a. Article III (on the prospects for emigration), *Edinburgh Review* (July, October, 1848).

The Lessons of a
Long-Distance Runner

The primary sources here are Muir's *Story of My Boyhood and Youth;* the unpublished autobiographical manuscript with the Muir Papers at the Holt-Atherton Library, University of the Pacific; photographs and other Dunbar memorabilia collected by Muir and now with his papers at the Holt-Atherton; and a trip my wife and I made to Dunbar in the early summer of 1980. On that occasion we spent a week poking about Dunbar, walking the Lammermuirs, experiencing the strength of a summer blow on the North Sea, watching the changes of light on old stones and streets. I also found some useful facts in James Miller, *The History of Dunbar* (Dunbar, 1859).

As a former folklorist, I may perhaps be pardoned for relying so much here on folklore as a window through which we may get a unique view of history and culture. But having read in various histories of Scotland, I found their generalities confirmed and sharpened by returning to the Scots ballads, border legends, and nature lore I studied more than twenty years ago. It is no wonder the ancient airs stuck with John Muir in all his long travels away from the place of their provenance: in them his native culture is perfectly realized and preserved for memory. The mother lode here, of course, is Sir Walter Scott, *Minstrelsy of the Scottish Border,* ed. T. F. Henderson, 3 vols. (1802–3; New York, 1902). Albert B. Friedman (ed.), *The Viking Book of Folk Ballads of the English-Speaking World* (New York, 1956); George Douglass (ed.), *Scottish Fairy and Folk Tales* (New York, 1901, 1977); and Eve Blantyre Simpson, *Folklore in Lowland Scotland* (West Yorkshire, 1908, 1976), are useful compilations of Scots lore. Raphael Holinshed's famous *Chronicles of England, Scotland, and Ireland* (London, 1577, 1807) is a virtually inexhaustible mine of folklore and history—as Shakespeare was perhaps first to discover. Holinshed narrates the career of Sir William Wallace and its savage conclusion.

Discovering
the New World

On my trip to Dunbar, I discovered with the help of Eric Simmons of that town the deed of sale of the Muirs' property to Dr. John Lorn. This document as well as the Muirs' deed of purchase are now with the Muir Papers at the Holt-Atherton. The Muirs' second home on the high street eventually became the Lorne Temperance Hotel, and the spelling of the name of this establishment brings up a small point. The documents spell John Lorn's name without the *e* it somehow subsequently acquired. On the other hand, though both Badè and Wolfe give "Ann" as the spelling of John Muir's mother's name, the documents give "Anne." So too does the gravestone at Portage, Wisconsin, and so that is the spelling I have followed throughout.

For the background on the Disciples of Christ, I found David E. Harrell, Jr., "A Social History of the Disciples of Christ" (unpublished Ph.D. dissertation, Vanderbilt University, 1962), and the Wisconsin Historical Records Survey (W.P.A.), *Inventory of the Church Archives of Wisconsin: Disciples of Christ* (Madison, 1942), helpful. Mark Twain's reminiscence of the sect's great Alexander Campbell is embedded in a hilarious anecdote in *The Autobiography of Mark Twain,* ed. Charles Neider (New York, Hagerstown, San Francisco, London, 1917, 1975).

For the background of the Muirs' emigration to America, I used Marcus Hansen, *The Atlantic Migration;* William J. Brownell, *History of Immigration to the United States . . .* (New York, 1856); and Oscar Handlin, *A Pictorial History of Immigration* (New York, 1972). For more specific remarks on the situation of Scots emigrants, I used Douglas Hill, *Great Emigrations: I: The Scots to Canada* (London, 1972); William C. Lehmann, *Scottish and Scotch-Irish Contributions to Early American Life and Culture* (Port Washington, London, 1978); and Andrew Hook, *Scotland and America: A Study of Cultural Relations, 1750–1835* (Glasgow, London, 1975).

The basic source of my portrait of the Muirs in Wisconsin is John Muir's autobiographical writings, both published and unpublished. I also drew on some undated jottings of his on the town of Portage; these latter are in the Muir Papers at the Holt-Atherton. But Muir's recollections have been supplemented in various ways. Robert C. Nesbit, *Wisconsin: A History* (Madison, 1973), is a model of clarity and comprehensiveness in the writing of state history. William Rudolph Smith, *Observations on the Wisconsin Territory* . . . (New York, 1838, 1975), and Fredrika Bremer, *The Homes of the New World; Impressions of America,* tr. Mary Howitt, 2 vols. (New York, 1854), provided roughly contemporary views of the rapidly evolving place in which the Muir family settled. Bremer's book, of course, is a classic well known to students of American culture. Increase I. Lapham, one of America's early environmentalists, gave a significant contemporary overview of the Wisconsin landscape at the time of the Muirs' settlement in his *Wisconsin: Its Geography and Topography* (New York, 1846, 1975). The maps of Robert W. Finley, *Orginal Vegetation Cover of Wisconsin; Compiled from U.S. General Land Office Notes* (St. Paul, 1976), and E. F. Bean, *Geologic Map of Wisconsin* (Madison, 1949; rev. 1965), gave me a basis on which to reconstruct the Muirs' journey from Milwaukee to Fountain Lake. They also provided valuable data for a portrait of the landscape of John Muir's youth and young manhood.

But the roots of my sense of that landscape lie in the soil of personal experience, as I have already indicated. Then, too, I had local help of an invaluable sort. Millie Stanley of Pardeeville, Wisconsin, devoted three days to guiding me to sites associated with Muir's Wisconsin years. Mrs. Stanley probably knows more about Muir's life there than anyone else, having spent many years in researching and interviewing on the subject. She not only took me to important places I would otherwise have missed but in subsequent letters and telephone calls patiently answered my questions and saved me from as many mistakes as she could.

It was Mrs. Stanley who introduced me to the Kearns family, which has owned for many years the Muirs' Hickory Hill farm. Harry Kearns, a vigorous ninety when I met him, took me on foot about the farm, showing me the near-fatal well, taking me down into the cellar within whose gloomy confines Muir began to improvise escape from his serfdom, walking with me the rolling cornfields in which Muir and the other children labored under the harsh exactitude of their father.

It was Harry Kearns who told me of the persistent neighborhood rumor that Daniel Muir ordered John to poach government timber. For three excellent overview of American attitudes toward such practices and toward landscape in general, see Roy M. Robbins, *Our Landed Heritage: The Public Domain, 1776–1936* (Lincoln, 1942; 1962); Peter Matthiessen, *Wild Life in America* (New York, 1950); and Wendell Berry, *The Unsettling of America: Culture and Agriculture* (New York, 1978). See the notes to "The American Forests" chapter of this book for further sources on land and forest usage.

William Dean Howells is the author—in *Years of My Youth* (New York, London, 1916)—of the poignant observation that one generation cannot communicate to another its most deeply felt convictions and frustrations. Howells was temperamentally too genial a man to write much of the deprivations of a nineteenth-century midwestern childhood. Besides, his own had been relatively benign, though beset with fears and phobias enough. But he knew enough of the region's life to honor the intentions and achievements of younger writers who late in the century attacked the sentimentalized image of America's heartland. Hamlin Garland was perhaps chief among these younger writers, and I have relied for details on *A Son of the Middle Border* (New York, 1917, 1927), *Main-Travelled Roads* (New York, 1891, 1962), *Boy Life on the Prairie* (Lincoln, 1899, 1961), and *A Daughter of the Middle Border* (New York, 1921, 1957). The critical literature on the "revolt" of the literary generation of the 1890s is extensive. Larzar Ziff, *The American 1890s: Life and Times of a Lost Generation* (New York, 1966, 1968), supplies perhaps the broadest cultural context for the phenomenon. Werner Berthoff, *The Ferment of Realism: American Literature, 1884–1919* (Cambridge, London, New York, New Rochelle, Melbourne, Sidney, 1965, 1981), is excellent on specific works.

ADDITIONAL SOURCES:

Black Hawk. *Black Hawk: An Autobiography,* ed. Donald Jackson (Urbana, 1833, 1955).

Josie Greening Croft. "A Mazomanie Pioneer of 1847." *Wisconsin Magazine of History* (December, 1942).

Walter Havinghurst (ed.). *The Great Lakes Reader* (New York, London, 1966, 1978).

George D. Lyman. *John Marsh, Pioneer: The Life Story of a Trail-blazer on Six Frontiers* (New York, 1930).

Lawrence Martin. *The Physical Geography of Wisconsin* (Madison, 1916, 1977).

J. M. Peck. *A Guide for Emigrants, Containing Sketches of Illinois, Missouri, and the Adjacent Parts* (New York, 1831, 1975).

Carl O. Sauer. "Conditions of Pioneer Life in the Upper Illinois Valley," in *Land and Life: A Selection from the Writings of Carl Ortwin Sauer,* ed. John Leighly (Berkeley, Los Angeles, 1963).

John R. Swanton. *The Indian Tribes of North America* (Washington, D.C., 1953).

n.a. *The American Almanac and Repository of Useful Knowledge for the Year 1849* (Boston, 1848).

n.a. *The American Almanac . . . for the Year 1851* (Boston, 1850).

n.a. London *Times* (February 19, 20, 1849).

Terms of Challenge

My reconstruction of Muir's teenage years and arrival at manhood is again largely based on the autobiographical materials he left behind. But the writer is here obliged to admit that the crucial inner record is not very full. Except for what the mature Muir cared to recall there is little more than those few surviving documents I cite in this chapter: the poem on the old schoolhouse; the letter to Bradley (both of these with the Muir Papers at the Holt-Atherton); a few drawings he kept of his inventions (these with the Muir Papers at the Holt-Atherton and at the State Historical Society of Wisconsin); and scattered recollections of neighbors and descendants of neighbors in the Portage area (most of these collected by Wolfe). The Archives Division of the State Historical Society of Wisconsin also has a recorded interview with Jessie Duncan, daughter of that William Duncan who so befriended the young Muir during a crucial period in his development.

Harry Kearns, owner of the Muirs' Hickory Hill property, made a point of emphasizing to me that young Muir was regarded by his peers as a "kind of nut, always going around looking for plants or bugs while they were working." It was not, Kearns alleged, until Linnie Marsh Wolfe began interviewing residents of the Portage/Pardeeville area that anyone thereabouts began to regard John Muir as having a legitimate claim to distinction. Local recognition is often slow. In late years Muir remarked with some sarcasm that it was not until he had been granted an honorary degree by Harvard that his own University of Wisconsin thought it proper to follow suit.

Kearns's views of the young Muir raise several points of significance in attempting to reconstruct Muir's life from 1850 to 1860. I have already alluded to the paucity of documentary evidence. Second is the reasonable inference that Muir probably was regarded as something of a "nut" or at least as an oddity in that sober, predominantly Scots agricultural community. Here as elsewhere with Muir's life the parallels with that of Thoreau are inescapable: a hero to many, Thoreau was regarded as anything from a pest to a crank by most of his townsmen. With Muir, the possibility also exists that, knowing some of his peers found him odd, he was occasionally at pains to behave eccentrically in their presence. Several local tales suggest this. Third, Kearns's remark that Muir sparked a kind of resentment by collecting flora and fauna while others labored in the fields can only be understood as referring to the period 1861–64, after Muir had left the home farm and was shuttling back and forth between Madison, Hickory Hill, and the Galloways' home at Fountain Lake. Certainly he had no leisure time before this to pursue such activities, and his serious interest in botany did not begin until his college years. I make the point at this length because it serves to emphasize that most of the information we have on Muir in Wisconsin dates from the period *after* he had left the farm for the wider world of Madison.

Some light is shed on the pre-Madison years by David Gray, *Letters, Poems and Selected Prose Writings of David Gray* (Buffalo, 1888), vol. 1. Gray was Muir's contemporary and friend in the years before Muir left the farm. Gray preceded Muir in that move, going east to Buffalo in 1865 where he established a literary career and became a friend of Mark Twain's. In his memoirs, he has little to say about Muir, but he does remark that Muir years later reminded him of the day of road work when Muir first heard the "twa Davies" talking of Dickens and literature. Gray himself had forgotten the episode. But scant as are Gray's recollections of Muir, the parallels between the lives of these farm boys are striking and serve as confirmation of the authenticity of Muir's autobiographical portrait of his hard apprenticeship. Like Muir, Gray was born in Scotland (in 1836 and in Edinburgh, scarcely fifty miles from Dunbar) in middle-class circumstances. Like Muir's father, Gray's was converted to the Disciples of Christ. Like the Muir family, the Grays emigrated to America in 1849 and settled near Portage because they knew there was a group of coreligionists there. Like Muir, David Gray was impressed into the round of farm labor, but, unlike Muir, Gray appears never to have found any comforts or delights in his backwoods surroundings. Recalling his first glimpse of the prairie and woods in an early morning's light, Gray said he felt he was on the outskirts not only of civilization but of life itself. So, when he could escape the farm and the countryside, he did so. By that time, the hard life he had been forced to lead had cast a sort of shadow over him, and his brother remarked that David's once sunny disposition had darkened under the strain of continual manual labor. Writing a friend from Buffalo, Gray confessed that to him it was "rather a comfortable thing to keep your hands clean and your back dry in all weathers, and never to feel the oppression of labor, dragging at your boots and making you an inch shorter at night than at morn."

But if David Gray suffered the same generic hardships as his neighbor and peer, he also enjoyed some inestimable advantages, as did the other of the "twa Davies," David Taylor. Compared to John Muir, David Gray and David Taylor had Harvard and Yale in their homes. Their parents not only allowed the boys their enthusiasm for literature but actively encouraged it. Gray's home, like Taylor's, was filled with books and newspapers and periodicals imported from New York. And when Gray got his opportunity to leave for Buffalo, the family sent him off with its blessing, believing that their David might be meant for something else and that he had his right to a chance in the wider world.

David Taylor, by Gray's account the more talented of the two, never left the Portage area. A photo of him in the Muir Papers at the Holt-Atherton shows a white-bearded man with something of the wistful child about the face whose eyes seem haunted with disappointment. When Muir returned to Portage in 1896, he spent some hours with Taylor, and among some undated jottings in his papers at the Holt-Atherton is the remark that "David T." drank to deaden his loneliness. "I have no exchange of thought . . . with any living soul," Muir quotes him as saying. Here, it seems, was a man of talents who missed his opportunity for growth and so turned inward upon himself. The phenomenon was a familiar one of that time and place, and some of those who left the midwestern hinterlands to become writers took note of it. Hamlin Garland did so in writing of the obscure destiny of his boyhood idol, Burton Babcock.

One other aspect of the early Wisconsin years deserves mention, and that is Muir's reading. Occasionally in his maturity Muir made comments that disparaged books as repositories of potential experience, and, compared to the great out-of-doors that he had come so intimately to know, perhaps it really did seem to him that he had derived relatively little from them. Yet there can be no doubt that in the 1860s literature was a powerful and wholly beneficial influence on him and that without books his way toward intellectual growth and emancipation would have been much more tortuous, not to write impossible. Reading Park, Humboldt, Campbell, Akenside, and Plutarch enabled me to go over Muir's formative intellectual tracks, as it were, though of course there is no way of knowing precisely which passages in the works of these authors particularly struck his attention. I list below under "Additional Sources" the editions I used.

ADDITIONAL SOURCES:

W. H. Auden and Norman Holmes Pearson (eds.). *The Portable Romantic Poets: Blake to Poe* (Harmondsworth, New York, 1950, 1978).

Douglas Botting. *Humboldt and the Cosmos* (New York, Evanston, San Francisco, London, 1973).

Frederika Bremer. *The Homes of the New World.*

Thomas Campbell. *The Complete Poetical Works of Thomas Campbell,* ed. J. Robertson Logie (London, New York, 1907).

David Douglas. *Douglas of the Forests: The North American Journals of David Douglas* ed. John Davies (Edinburgh, 1979).

Alexander von Humboldt and Aimé Bonpland. *Personal Narrative of Travel in the Equinoctial Regions of America, During the Years 1799–1804,* tr., ed. Thomasina Ross, 3 vols. (London, 1900).

William C. Lehmann. *Scottish and Scotch-Irish Contributions to Early American Life and Culture.*

Hugh Miller. *The Footprints of the Creator; or, The Asterolepis of Stromness* (Boston, New York, Cincinnati, 1847, 1866).

Stephen Nissenbaum. *Sex, Diet, and Debility in Jacksonian America: Sylvester Graham and Health Reform* (Westport, 1980).

Mungo Park. *The Life and Travels of Mungo Park* (Edinburgh, 1870).

Roy Harvey Pearce. *Savagism and Civilization: A Study of the Indian and the American Mind* (Baltimore, 1953, 1965).

Plutarch. *The Lives of the Noble Grecians and Romans,* tr. John Dryden; rev. Arthur Hugh Clough (New York, n.d.).

Millie Stanley. "John Muir, as remembered by one who knew him." Portage *Daily Register* (July 15, 1972).

David Wright (ed.). *The Penguin Book of English Romantic Verse* (Hardmondsworth, New York, 1968, 1978).

Books of Life, Drums of Death

In this chapter I have tried to narrate the more intensive and formal beginning of Muir's intellectual odyssey, though, as I hope is already clear, I believe that journey really stretches back to his Dunbar days. To some, I have no doubt, it will seem as if I have made overmuch of Muir's fragmentary studies at the University of Wisconsin. As I have already suggested in the notes to the previous chapter, there has been a tendency to view Muir as an untutored, natural genius who owed little to books, less to formal study—as if this would make him even more securely in the American grain. To some extent, Muir encouraged the tendency. And to be sure, there was always something freestyle about Muir's learning, never more so than in his university years. Jeanne Carr's comment on Muir in Madison makes it clear that others saw this at the time. In some way impossible for us to define, Muir always seemed to understand what it was he needed to learn, and he took many an untrodden path to his appointed intellectual destinations. Some of his contemporaries as well as some of his subsequent assessors have considered him essentially a gifted amateur in botany and geology.

All this said, and rightly so, it remains to be added that Muir made himself into a deeply learned man with an abiding respect for what could be gained from books and from formal study. He remained indebted to Professor Carr and to James Davie Butler for their instruction and for introducing him to what he called the great book of life, nor should his phrase be taken wholly as a metaphor pointing to the world beyond books themselves. By the end of his life, Muir had accumulated a very large library (now at the Holt-Atherton), and an inspection of its volumes shows plainly that he read most of it with scrupulous attention. Thus my emphasis on a process that began in earnest in his university years.

By this point in Muir's life the biographer begins to be considerably aided by the existence of letters Muir wrote. Jefferson believed that a person's letters "form the only full and genuine journal of his life." That may be more true of Jefferson than of Muir, but there is no doubt that the latter's letters, which commence in these Madison years, are of great benefit in enlarging our picture of the young man. From 1860 to the end of his life, Muir was a wonderfully prolific correspondent—so much so that he made several unsuccessful resolves to cut back on this activity. Though in some sense reluctant to speak of his feelings about others as well as to reveal his own inner feelings, Muir's letters are often more revealing than he intended. Late in life he recognized this to be the case with letters he had written Jeanne Carr in the late 1860s and early '70s. I list below manuscripts of the early letters I have used in this chapter. Badè, as I have said, has made the fullest printed collection of them.

For my picture of the University of Wisconsin during the late 1850s and early '60s, I used the Board of Regents of the University of Wisconsin, *Annual Reports* (Madison, 1860, 1861, 1862, 1863); C. W. Butterfield, *History of the University of Wisconsin from its First Organization to 1879 . . .* (Madison, 1879); Reuben Gold Thwaites et al., *Wisconsin in Three Centuries, 1634–1905* (New York, n.d.); vol. 3; and Robert C. Nesbit, *Wisconsin: A History.*

As for Muir at the university, the record is sketchy. According to Frank Cook, director of university archives, fires have destroyed all academic records for the period of Muir's attendance. There thus remain a number of minor mysteries. Muir said he took chemistry, mathematics, physics, "a little Greek and Latin," botany and geology. As for the length of his stay, he recalled in *Story of My Boyhood and Youth* that he was at the university four years. This is either a lapse of memory, the reflection of an occasionally casual attitude about dates and durations, or else a curious, possibly defensive, fudge. In the unpublished portion of the autobiography, Muir said it wasn't until the fall of 1861 that he was admitted to regular student status. The regents' *Annual Report* for the year ending September 30, 1861, does list John Muir as a first-year student in the scientific course of study. He is so listed again in the report for 1862, indicating that he was not following a course of study that would lead to graduation. In the report for 1863, the identifications of the students' courses of study are not supplied, but Muir is listed as in attendance both terms. We know that he left the university for good in June 1863. Thus, including his weeks in the preparatory school and the three months he spent teaching in the winter of 1861–62, this would make a total of two and a half years.

The sources for the portrait of Muir in Madison are Jeanne C. Carr's undated notes on Muir, which are with the Jeanne C. Carr Papers at the Huntington Library; Charles E. Vroman, "John Muir at the University," *Wisconsin Alumni Magazine* (June, 1915); Charles H. Vilas, "Reminiscences of John Muir as a Student," *Public Exercises in Honor of John Muir* [pamphlet] (Madison, 1916); Milton S. Griswold, "Remarks," at the Muir Knoll Dedicatory Exercises, *Wisconsin Alumni Magazine* (August, 1918); and Charles E. Brown, *John Muir: Little Stories of His Boyhood and University Years* [pamphlet] (Madison, 1938). Each of these is pretty slight. Vroman's recollections have been drawn upon by everyone who has tried to piece together a narrative of the university years. The recollections are not, however, without their problems, the most conspicuous of which is that by the time Vroman got around to writing them down more than half a century had passed and his old roommate had become a national legend. Then, too, Vroman had clearly read Muir's *Story of My Boyhood and Youth;* some of its language shows up as Vroman's own. Still, I prefer to accept the essential authenticity of Vroman's recollections and assume he drew on *Story* to refresh his memory as well as to fill in gaps. That he borrowed from Muir's writing would be, I think, a natural deference to a famous writer.

For material on the Carrs, I drew on Jeanne Carr's papers at the Huntington; these include some biographical information on Ezra S. Carr as well as texts of some of his lectures.

For material on James Davie Butler, I used his "Commonplace Books: A Lecture" in the Muir Papers at the Holt-Atherton. The date of the lecture is 1884, well after Muir was his student, but many of its illustrations date from the Civil War era, and it seems likely to me that Butler had been urging the use of commonplace books for many years in lectures like this one.

George P. Merrill, *Contributions to the History of American Geology* [No. 135] from the *Report of the United States Museum for 1904* (Washington,

D.C., 1906), was valuable in tracing the evolution of the earth sciences to the turn of the present century. Carroll Lane Fenton and Mildred Adams Fenton, *Giants of Geology* (Garden City, 1945, 1952), Ruth Moore, *The Earth We Live On: The Story of Geological Discovery* (New York, 1956), and Loren Eisley, *Darwin's Century* (Garden City, 1958, 1961), provided good overviews of the history of geological study and summaries of the contributions of the major figures.

ADDITIONAL SOURCES:

Gay Wilson Allen. *Waldo Emerson: A Biography* (New York, 1981).

Ralph K. Andrist. *The Long Death: The Last Days of the Plains Indians* (New York, 1964, 1969).

John Burroughs. "Remarks," in *Public Exercises in Honor of John Muir* [pamphlet] (Madison, 1916).

Bruce Catton. *The Army of the Potomac: A Stillness at Appomattox* (New York, 1953).

————. *The Coming Fury* (New York, 1961, 1967).

Henry Steele Commager (ed.). *The Blue and the Gray: The Story of the Civil War as Told by the Participants* (New York, Scarborough, 1950, 1973), vol. 1.

Adrian Cook. " 'Ashes and Blood': The New York City Draft Riots," *American History Illustrated* (August, 1977).

David Donald et al. *Divided We Fought: A Pictorial History of the Civil War, 1861–1865* (New York, 1952).

Ralph Waldo Emerson. *The Complete Essays and Other Writings of Ralph Waldo Emerson,* ed. Brooks Atkinson (New York, 1940, 1950).

David Galloway. Letter to John Muir, Fountain Lake, December 21, 1860. Muir Papers, Holt-Atherton Library.

Peter Levine. "Draft Evasion in the North during the Civil War, 1863–1865." *Journal of American History* (March, 1981).

John Muir. Letter to family, Madison, September 1860. Muir Papers, Holt-Atherton Library.

————. Letter to Sarah Galloway, Madison, October 1860. Muir Papers, Holt-Atherton Library.

————. Letter to Daniel Muir (Jr.), Prairie du Chien, November 19, 1860. Huntington Library.

————. Letter to Sarah Galloway, Prairie du Chien, December 1860. Muir Papers, Holt-Atherton Library.

————. Letter to Mary, Anna, and Joanna Muir, Madison, May 1861. Yosemite National Park Research Library.

————. Letter to Daniel Muir (Jr.), Fountain Lake, December 20, 1863. Huntington Library.

————. Autobiographical fragments, c. 1870s. Muir Papers, Holt-Atherton Library.

Muir Family. Letter to John Muir, Hickory Hill, October 14, 1860. Muir Papers, Holt-Atherton Library.

Vernon L. Parrington. *Main Currents in American Thought: The Romantic Revolution in America, 1800–1860* (New York, 1927, 1954).

Stephen E. Whicher. *Freedom and Fate: An Inner Life of Ralph Waldo Emerson* (New York, 1953, 1961).

n.a. Wisconsin *State Journal,* September 25, 1860. State Historical Society of Wisconsin.

The Eye Within

Attempting to trace Muir's Canadian wanderings, Badè wondered whether Muir might possibly have left any personal effects with his Indianapolis friends. It was a good surmise and handsomely rewarded when portions of Muir's herbarium with its identifying place slips were found in the attic of Charles W. Moores, son of Julia Merrill Moores. A typescript of a portion of the herbarium, beginning with an entry for April 20, 1864, is with the Muir Papers at the Holt-Atherton Library.

Also at the Holt-Atherton are reminiscences of William H. Trout, who employed Muir at the Meaford factory. Trout's recollections constitute the only independent source of information on Muir's Canadian interlude, and I have depended on them heavily in drawing my picture of Muir, 1864–66. In general, Trout paid high tribute to Muir, both as a mechanic and as a man, though it is also evident he and the others at Meaford found their guest a bit prickly and opinionated at times. It is also evident that Muir's loosening scriptural literalism and his growing conviction that divinity was best approached through nature caused friction. But whatever their disagreements on these matters, Trout did not let them affect his regard for Muir as a man. He remarked that in all Muir's inventing and botanizing Muir never assented for a moment to

what Trout regarded as the atheistical spirit of the new sciences just then
coming to public attention. He saw, said Trout, God's hand in all things.
When it came time for the final financial reckoning, Trout said Muir
would only accept a figure of $200 as eventually due him. It was not
until Muir was engaged to marry (nearly a decade later) that he reminded Trout of the debt owed.

For the Indianapolis period, I have used Muir's autobiographical man-
uscript at the Holt-Atherton as well as the letters he wrote various family
members from that place. I cite the specific documents below. Muir's
remarkable time-and-motion study with its graphs and text is in the State
Historical Society of Wisconsin. On the eye injury he suffered at the
Osgood & Smith factory, there are various accounts; mine is based on
Muir's notes found among his autobiographical fragments at the Holt-
Atherton.

The notes Muir made on his botanizing trip north from Indianapolis
to Portage in the spring of 1867 are with his papers at the Holt-Atherton.
There is also a fragment of an essay he began on the experience; it is titled
simply "A Walk" and is of considerable interest to those interested in the
development of Muir's literary style and aesthetics.

ADDITIONAL SOURCES:

Bruce Catton. *The Army of the Potomac.*

Stephen Crane. *The Red Badge of Courage* (New York, 1895, 1962, 1976).

Bernard De Voto. *The Year of Decision.*

William R. Holloway. *Indianapolis: A Historical and Statistical Sketch of the
Railroad City . . .* (Indianapolis, 1870).

John Muir. Pelican Bay manuscript of the unpublished autobiography.
Muir Papers, Holt-Atherton Library.

———. Letter to Daniel Muir (Jr.). Trout Hollow (Canada), February 18,
1866. Muir Papers, Holt-Atherton Library.

———. Letter to Daniel Muir (Jr.), Indianapolis, May 7, 1866. Huntington Library.

———. Letter to Daniel Muir (Jr.), Indianapolis, August 12, 1866. Huntington Library.

———. Letter to Daniel Muir (Jr.), Indianapolis, undated but probably
fall 1866. Huntington Library.

———. Letter to Anne G. Muir, Indianapolis, March 9, 1867. Yosemite
National Park Research Library.

————. Letter to Jeanne C. Carr, Indianapolis, April 6, 1867. Muir Papers, Holt-Atherton Library.

————. Letter to Daniel Muir (Jr.), Indianapolis, September 1, 1867. Huntington Library.

The Thousand-Mile Walk

This chapter is based almost exclusively on Muir's *A Thousand-Mile Walk to the Gulf,* (Boston, 1916). Michael Cohen, in *The Pathless Way,* says there are significant differences between the journal version of the experience and the book published from the journal. I have examined both the original journal and the typescript prepared from it (both with the Muir Papers at the Holt-Atherton), and I do not share this view.

The journal itself is a small, brown, leather-bound volume that would easily fit into a suitcoat pocket. It is profusely illustrated with the author's vigorous and often amusing sketches. Its contents bear the marks of heavy editing, the original entries having apparently been made in ink and the additions, deletions, and emendations in pencil. In every instance in which I compared crucial passages in the journal with those as eventually published I found no substantive changes, though to be sure textual scholars will find a great many inconsistencies of a minor nature. There is one exception, but this strengthens my reading of a particular passage rather than calling that reading into question. In Muir's meditation on death in Bonaventure Cemetery, he originally wrote that Christians were taught to regard death as an "Evemade" accident, a characterization that sharpens the point of his attack on both Milton's epic and the traditional Christian interpretation of Genesis 1–3 on which the great apologist drew.

There remains, however, the question of *when* Muir did the editing of the journal. If he went back to it some years after the original experience, then my analysis of his intellectual and spiritual development and the critical significance of the walk in that development is largely invalidated. The question can never be definitively answered, but both internal and external evidence convince me that Muir went back through the journal at no great remove from the time of his writing it. I suggest he was revising both in Cedar Key and in Cuba. Many of the penciled corrections are in the way of amplifications of quite specific details about plants, flowers, and trees. Even taking into account the man's astonishing powers of recall, the addition of such small details suggests that he went back through the entries while the experiences were still spanking fresh. Certainly in the weeks following his partial recovery in January 1868, he would have had ample opportunity to do this work, and, considering the momentousness

of the adventure as well as the adventure's near-fatal conclusion, it would
have been odd and uncharacteristic of Muir if he had not been driven by
curiosity to inspect what he had written before his illness.

As to the external evidence, the journal is really the first extended
appearance of Muir on paper that we have. As such its observations on
God, man, and nature appear perhaps more radical and startling than they
may actually have been to the writer himself. I do think, as I have said,
that they evince a genuine, significant breakthrough for him. But against
the argument that they look too radical and must therefore have been
added in more mature years, there is evidence that Muir was moving to
these observations before he took the walk and that immediately after it
he was saying many of the very same things. On the far or prior side of
the walk is the evidence of his letters and his actions while in Canada and
Indianapolis. Most striking here is his letter to Jeanne Carr of January 21,
1866, from Trout Hollow. The important passage here is by no means
unambiguous, perhaps because its author was still working his way toward
the emancipation he detailed in his Savannah and Cedar Key entries. It
reads as follows:

> Nature is so replete with divine truth, it is silent concerning the
> fall of man and the wonders of Redeeming Love. Might she not
> have been made to speak as clearly and eloquently of these things
> as she now does of the character and attributes of God? It may
> be a bad symptom, but I will confess that I take more intense
> delight from reading the power and *goodness* of God from "the
> things which are made" than from the Bible. The two books,
> however, harmonize beautifully, and contain enough of divine
> truth for the study of all eternity (John Muir, *Letters to a Friend*
> [Boston, 1915]).

I read the sense of this as a precursor to the Bonaventure Cemetery
meditation with Muir saying that nature tells us nothing of sin, the fall,
or even of Christ's redeeming us from death to life everlasting through
the power of His love. Nature, however, *could* speak of these things had
its creator so desired. But instead nature tells only of God's love and
power. In that sense, then, nature is potentially at least a more direct
avenue to the appreciation of divinity and of God's plan for man than
either the Bible or Christianity. And an emphasis on sin, death, and
damnation is simply not supported by the visible facts of the God-made
world. This reading is supported, I think, by Muir's behavior in Canada
and Indianapolis. He studiously refrained from going to church in either
place, argued with the Trouts about the Disciples of Christ kind of literal-

ism, and took his Sunday school children out into the great tabernacle of the Indiana fields for worship and instruction. My feeling is that now that he had broken with his father, he could break also with the father's insistent emphasis on sin and damnation, with, in fact, almost all of the Puritan cosmology.

On this side of the long walk the evidence for the contemporaneity of the journal's penciled editings is even stronger. In a little marble-bound notebook Muir used on his passage to California through Panama in the spring of 1868, he went on in a vein identical with that of his meditations in Georgia and Florida, remarking on the narrowness of human sympathies, on human arrogance, and on that meanly utilitarian view of the natural world that valued everything merely in terms of its presumed usefulness to man. The sea on which he was riding (and which, apparently, made writing so difficult that some of his words are illegible) seemed to him a magnificent metaphor for the limitations of our knowledge of and sympathy with the natural world. The journal is with the Muir Papers at the Holt-Atherton.

Once Muir had arrived in California, his letters and journal entries of 1868–69 plainly reveal the views so forcefully expressed in the journal of the thousand-mile walk. But here I begin to anticipate, and for a full narration of those first California days I refer the reader to "First Summer."

In a large, general way, the route Muir took to Savannah is known by the place names he mentions, but the specific route can never be wholly traced. Tom Melham and Farrell Grehan (*John Muir's Wild America,* Washington, D.C., 1976) include photographs taken along Muir's conjectured route, and these were helpful to me in trying to visualize what Muir would have encountered. I have also walked that portion of Muir's way that took him from Madisonville, Tennessee, to Murphy, North Carolina, and I did this—as Muir did—in late September. I incorporate my observations of the scenery into the account I give of Muir's passage along this way. In addition, I have had considerable experience with the mountainous borderlands of Tennessee and North Carolina through the generous guidance of Robert Card, Sr., and Hoyle Rymer, both of Cleveland, Tennessee, and the late Bob Barker of Andrews, North Carolina. These men introduced me to the legends of the region, particularly those relating to the Civil War era.

For the Florida portion of the walk I have drawn on Charles Fishburne, Jr., *The Cedar Keys in the Civil War and Reconstruction, 1861–1876* (Cedar Key, 1982); *Cedar Key Booming: 1877–1886* (Cedar Key, 1982); *The Cedar Keys in Decline* (Cedar Key, 1982); and his "Hodgson Hill in Cedar Key," an unpublished monograph. I have also visited Cedar Keys and had the benefit of a tour, courtesy of Bill Roberts. The railroad Muir followed from Fernandina to Cedar Key was the project of the fabulously colorful David Levy Yulee; for details on his career and road, see Gloria Jahoda, *The Other Florida* (New York, 1967, 1978). The Hodgsons who so solicitously cared for Muir during his illness and slow convalescence were Richard W. B. Hodgson and Sarah A. Hodgson. At the time of Muir's visit, Hodgson was part owner of a sawmill at the port town of Cedar Key, having come there from Georgia at the end of the 1850s when the Cedar Keys were a profitable timbering area.

ADDITIONAL SOURCES:

Melville Anderson. "The Conversation of John Muir," *American Museum Journal* (March 1915).

John Bakeless. *Daniel Boone* (New York, 1940).

———. *The Eyes of Discovery: America as Seen by the First Explorers* (New York, 1950, 1961).

William Bartram. *Travels* (1796; Salt Lake City, 1980).

Charles Darwin. *The Voyage of the Beagle* (New York, 1839, 1958).

Loren Eisley. *Darwin's Century.*

J. S. Hurlburt. *The History of the Rebellion in Bradley County, East Tennessee* (Indianapolis, 1866).

Horace Kephart. *Our Southern Highlanders: A Narrative of Adventure in the Southern Appalachians and a Study of Life Among the Mountaineers* (Knoxville, 1913, 1976).

John Milton. *Paradise Lost: A Poem in Twelve Books* (1667; Indianapolis, 1962).

John Muir. Letter to Jeanne C. Carr, near Burkesville, Kentucky, September 9, 1867. Muir Papers, Holt-Atherton Library.

Eliot Porter. *Appalachian Wilderness: The Great Smoky Mountains,* text by Edward Abbey (New York, 1970).

William Trout. Reminiscences. Muir Papers, Holt-Atherton Library.

First Summer

For my account of Muir's passage to California through Panama, I used his brief journal of the spring of 1868, now with the Muir Papers at the Holt-Atherton.

For the walk with Chilwell into the Sierras, I drew on a long letter to

Jeanne Carr and on his autobiographical notes as printed by Badè (vol. 1, pp. 178–189). I also drew somewhat on a motor trip I made out of San Francisco, following Muir's approximate route to Gilroy and then east over the Pacheco Pass and up through Coulterville, where there is a sign telling of Francisco Bruschi and the general store he ran there at the time of Muir's arrival. Since Muir mentions that the storekeeper from whom he and Chilwell bought provisions was Italian, I have assumed it was Bruschi.

The journals of Muir's first mountain summer are badly cut up and crossed over. In 1910 Muir went back into those battered blue notebooks to make a book out of them; *My First Summer in the Sierra* was published the following year (Boston: 1911). Wherever it is possible to compare the journal entries with the published version it is clear that Muir made few substantive changes. He corrected his overreliance on such words as "glorious" and "noble," changed the dates of a few entries, and in one instance lifted an experience out of its original context and transported it to an adjacent entry. For the most part, however, it would appear that *My First Summer* is a faithful depiction of his experiences, and I have quoted from it in this chapter. The journals themselves are with the Muir Papers at the Holt-Atherton Library.

The religious phrasing of much of what eventually became *My First Summer* is obvious to any reader and indicates that for Muir this truly was a conversion experience, as he said in his entry of June 6. It was prepared for, of course, by a considerable novitiate, as most conversion experiences seem to be. But his entrance into the mountains and the sudden "turning in the seat of the soul," as the Zen Buddhists term it, is remarkably paradigmatic of this great spiritual event as it has been studied and described by religious historians and psychologists. Compare Muir's June 6 entry—indeed much of *My First Summer*—with the definition of conversion in Arthur Darby Nock's classic *Conversion* (London, Oxford, 1933, 1961): "the reorientation of the soul of an individual, his deliberate turning from an earlier form of piety to another, a turning which implies a consciousness that a great change is involved, that the old was wrong and the new right." Nock goes on, following William James in *The Varieties of Religious Experience* (see particularly lectures IX and X), to remark that the conversion experience is often characterized by a "passion of willingness and acquiescence, which removes the feeling of anxiety, a sense of perceiving truths not known before, a sense of clean and beautiful newness within and without and an ecstasy of happiness. . . ." Such feelings indeed characterize Muir in the summer of 1869 and carry over into much of his first two years in Yosemite.

On earlier naturalists and explorers in America, see John Bakeless,

The Eyes of Discovery, and Robert Elman, *First in the Field: America's Pioneering Naturalists* (New York, Cincinnati, Toronto, London, Melbourne, 1977). For Powell's explorations, which so nearly coincide with Muir's entry into California, see Wallace Stegner, *Beyond the Hundredth Meridian: John Wesley Powell and the Second Opening of the West* (Boston, 1953). Stegner devotes several pages to the significant parallels between Powell and Muir.

The standard work on the mountain men is Bernard De Voto, *Across the Wide Missouri* (Boston, 1947, 1975). For the southerly version of the breed, see Robert Glass Cleland, *This Reckless Breed of Men: The Trappers and Fur Traders of the Southwest* (New York, 1950). More specialized works include Stanley Vestal, *Jim Bridger, Mountain Man* (Lincoln, 1946, 1970); Mae Reed Porter and Odessa Davenport, *Scotsman in Buckskin: Sir William Drummond Stewart and the Rocky Mountain Fur Trade* (New York, 1963); James P. Beckwourth, *The Life and Adventures of James P. Beckwourth,* ed. T. D. Bonner (New York, 1931); William Goetzmann, *Exploration and Empire: The Explorer and the Scientist in the Winning of the American West* (New York, 1966, 1978); and Lewis O. Saum, *The Fur Trader and the Indian* (Seattle, London, 1965). A. B. Guthrie, Jr., *The Big Sky* (New York, 1947), is a vivid and accurate depiction of mountain-man life, and though it is fiction it may be about as close as we can get to how that life seemed to those who led it. How much Muir thought about the mountain men during his first summer of apprenticeship to becoming a mountaineer is, as I say in the text, uncertain. But he did think of the meaning of these lives later in the 1870s and again in the 1880s. Obviously, the subject was of some interest to him.

ADDITIONAL SOURCES:

Lafayette Bunnell. *Discovery of the Yosemite in 1851* (Golden, 1880, 1980).

Francis P. Farquhar. *History of the Sierra Nevada* (Berkeley, Los Angeles, London, 1965).

John Muir. *John Muir: To the Yosemite and Beyond: Writings from the Years 1863 to 1875,* eds. Robert Engberg and Donald Wesling (Madison, 1980).

———. *A Thousand-Mile Walk to the Gulf.* Muir Papers, Holt-Atherton Library.

———. Journal of "A Thousand-Mile Walk to the Gulf." Muir Papers, Holt-Atherton Library.

———. Letter to Annie Muir, Hopeton, California, August 15, 1868. Yosemite National Park Research Library.

————. Letter to Daniel Muir (Jr.), Hopeton, California, April 17, 1869. Huntington Library.

Carl P. Russell. *100 Years in Yosemite: The Story of a Great National Park* (Berkeley, Los Angeles, London, 1947, 1968).

The Secret Pass

The details of Muir's mountaineering techniques are from an autobiographical fragment in the Muir Papers at the Holt-Atherton. Some confusion exists on a minor point here: the identity of the trusty "Brownie" who accompanied Muir on so many of his lonely travels. At one point he is described as a mustang, as I have indicated in the text. Yet on several other occasions "Brownie" is plainly a mule. Perhaps there were two beasts of the same name?

At a 1980 Muir conference convened by Ronald Limbaugh, archivist of the Muir Papers at the Holt-Atherton Library, several of the participants, myself included, realized that independently they had been struck with the numerous similarities between Muir's Sierran experiences of the '70s and descriptions of the Zen experience. The subject is not easy to discuss, and surely there is nothing to be gained by a foolish "point by point" listing of the alleged similarities. Yet these seem to exist and are a way to a partial understanding of what Muir was experiencing in these years of his solitary splendor.

Over the years a great deal of misleading effort has been expended on the subject of oriental influences in American intellectual history. Emerson and Thoreau have been described as Hindu converts or crypto-Buddhists, and it has been soberly argued that through them orientalism entered the stream of American Romanticism. That would make Muir potentially at least an inheritor of the influence. It is true that both older men read widely in translations of oriental religious and philosophical texts, but really they owe little in the way of formative influence to Eastern thought, and the subject, for my money, is correctly and curtly dismissed by James Baird in his brilliant *Ishmael: A Study of the Symbolic Mode in Primitivism* (New York, 1956, 1960). As for Muir, I am unaware of any direct experiences he had with oriental texts, so that for me there is no question of influence, only of suggestive similarities between that calm, acceptant balance Muir achieved in the Sierras in the early '70s and the Zen experience.

It took Muir a while to learn that truly it made no real difference how he lived his life, that finally one can do *no other* than live according to the "way things are." To attempt to go against this stream or force is to

guarantee a life of fruitless struggle. That, I think, is the great inner sense
of calm that one senses in the Muir of the early '70s. And I think Muir
was led to this position by the ability he developed to contemplate natural
facts simply and directly. When this ability is achieved (or reachieved),
then the natural facts become modi of liberation. D. T. Suzuki, the foremost explicator of the Zen experience for Westerners, quotes the Zen
master Gensha as responding thus to a monk who asked him how to enter
upon the path of truth: "Do you hear the murmuring stream? There is a
way to enter" (*Zen Buddhism,* ed. William Barrett [Garden City, 1956]).
And R. H. Blythe notes that the enlightenment of Tōzan began with his
understanding of the teachings of inanimate things, at which point Tōzan
wrote:

> Marvellous! Marvellous!
> How mysterious the Inanimate-Teaching!
> It is difficult to hear with the ears;
> When we hear with the eyes, then we know it!
> *Zen and Zen Classics,* comp. Frederick Franck
> [New York, 1960, 1978].

For the background of Muir's glacial investigations, I drew again on
George P. Merrill, *Contributions to the History of American Geology;* Ruth
Moore, *The Earth We Live On;* Loren Eisley, *Darwin's Century;* Francis
Farquhar, *History of the Sierra Nevada,* which contains the best general
account of the achievements of the California state geological survey;
and Francois E. Mathes, *The Incomparable Valley: A Geological Interpretation
of the Yosemite,* ed. Fritiof Fryxell (Berkeley, Los Angeles, London,
1950).

Of Muir's relationships with Elvira Hutchings and Jeanne Carr, Jack
Geyer, curator of the Yosemite National Park Archives, told me of the
persistent rumors around Yosemite of Muir's romantic involvement with
Mrs. Hutchings. Without lending his own support to these, he said, "For
years, people around the valley have been saying that Muir 'ran off with
Hutchings's wife.' " Just how this feat could have been accomplished is
another matter, but then rumor is no respecter of particulars. The case for
anything more than an emotionally loaded attachment to Mrs. Hutchings
remains in my view unproved and unlikely.

With Jeanne Carr the matter is more complex, but I incline to the view
that nothing physical ever transpired between them. Mrs. J. B. McChesney, who with her husband opened her Oakland home to Muir in 1873–
74, was adamant in reminiscences collected by Badè that the entire
relationship had been misunderstood and distorted. Her remarks are in-

cluded with the Muir Papers at the Holt-Atherton. Muir certainly went
to lengths to retrieve his letters to Jeanne Carr, whatever they once contained. Stephen Fox, *John Muir and His Legacy: The American Conservation
Movement* (Boston, Toronto, 1981), speculates that Muir's efforts were
exerted because these letters contained material relating to his relationship
with Elvira Hutchings. I think it entirely likely that this was part of the
reason Muir was so anxious to get those letters back but not the entire
reason. These letters also contained material on his relationship with
Jeanne Carr. Some of the letters are now missing and others have been
crudely mutilated. There are letters missing that predate his relationship
with Elvira Hutchings; others, particularly the "moonlight rapture" letter
he wrote Jeanne Carr in 1871, are so devoted to matters between the two
correspondents that it is difficult to imagine they once contained passages
about Elvira Hutchings as well. Still other now missing or mutilated letters
postdate Muir's involvement with either Mrs. or Mr. Hutchings. In any
case, to say that Muir wanted certain passages stricken from the record is
hardly to prove that they once contained evidence of a genuine love affair
with anyone. By 1903–04 when the threat of George Wharton James's
publication of the letters became clear, Muir was a national figure, a friend
of presidents and heavily involved in controversial conservation issues. It
is therefore entirely understandable that he would not have wanted letters
in public circulation that might so easily have been misconstrued.

   Jeanne Carr's papers, which I drew on for my portrait of her, are in
the Huntington Library. A minor figure in all this, Thérèse Yelverton is
portrayed in words and pictures in *Frank Leslie's Illustrated Newspaper*
(April 6, 1861).

   For Emerson's impact on Muir, I used James Bradley Thayer, *A Western Journey with Mr. Emerson* (Boston, 1884), the contemporary account
of their meeting in Yosemite; Muir's notes on the meeting, made in
preparation for his Harvard commencement remarks in 1896 (Muir Papers, Holt-Atherton); Emerson's letter to Muir, Concord, February 5,
1872 (Yosemite National Park Research Library); and Muir's annotated
copy of Emerson's *Prose Works* (Boston, 1870), vol. 1 (Beinecke Rare
Book and Manuscript Library).

ADDITIONAL SOURCES:

Gay Wilson Allen. *Waldo Emerson: A Biography.*

Lafayette Bunnell. *Discovery of the Yosemite in 1851.*

Alice and Phoebe Cary. *The Poems of Alice and Phoebe Cary,* ed. Katherine
Lee Bates (New York, 1903).

Robert Glass Cleland. *This Reckless Breed of Men.*

Ralph Waldo Emerson. *The Complete Essays and Other Writings of Ralph Waldo Emerson.*

——. *Journals of Ralph Waldo Emerson,* ed. Edward Waldo Emerson and Waldo Emerson Forbes (Boston, New York, 1909–14), vol. 10.

Theodore Gaster. *The Oldest Stories in the World* (Boston, 1952, 1958).

Clarence King. *Mountaineering in the Sierra Nevada* (Lincoln, London, 1872, 1970).

Bailey Millard. "A Skyland Philosopher." *Bookman's* (February, 1908).

John Muir. Field Journal, 1872. Muir Papers, Holt-Atherton Library.

——. Letter to Jeanne C. Carr, Yosemite, c. April 3, 1871. Yosemite National Park Research Library.

——. *My First Summer in the Sierra.*

——. *The Mountains of California* (Berkeley, 1894, 1977).

——. Pelican Bay manuscript of autobiography. Muir Papers, Holt-Atherton Library.

——. *The Yosemite* (Garden City, 1912, 1962).

Margaret Sanborn. *The Yosemite: Its Discovery, Its Wonders, Its People* (New York, 1981).

Henry David Thoreau. *The Maine Woods* (New York, 1864, 1961).

Thurman Wilkins. *Clarence King: A Biography* (New York, 1958).

Civilization and Its Discontents

Reading Ruskin's *Modern Painters,* it is easy enough to see why Muir would have assented to the author's intellectual and literary greatness while vehemently rejecting many of his specific contentions about the natural world. *Modern Painters* is a work of stupendous erudition, but the tone of arrogant assurance would surely have failed to cow and convince Muir where Ruskin wrote of subjects he knew but partially. Muir would have been offended, for example, by Ruskin's observation that plants were probably incapable of pleasure and that, since this was the case, humans could not feel a genuine love for them. But it was Ruskin's remarks on mountains that particularly irked his mountaineer reader. In volume 4, Ruskin spoke often of mountain "gloom," of mountains as "objects of terror" that made the villages that cowered beneath them dark, somber, gloomy places. Mountain slopes were said to look "lifeless, like the walls of a sepulchre," while glaciers were described as masses of "blackened ice . . . as if out of some long and foul excavation. . . ." Muir can hardly be imagined as setting out on a literary and (later) political career to refute Ruskinian notions of mountains and the whole natural world. Still, Ruskin and the anthropocentric view of nature he so fully represented were the opposition as Muir came to see it, and he became progressively more determined to convert his audience to what he believed were more authentic views of the natural world and its relationship to men and civilization. For the intellectual and historical background of Ruskin's views, see Marjorie Hope Nicolson, *Mountain Gloom and Mountain Glory: The Development of the Aesthetics of the Infinite* (New York, 1959, 1963). For the specifically American portion of the politics of alpine perception and landscape perception in general, see Barbara Novak, *Nature and Culture: American Landscape Painting, 1825–1875* (New York, 1980).

Reminiscences used here on Muir in the McChesney household during the winter of 1873–74 are those of Mrs. J. B. McChesney and are with the Muir Papers, Holt-Atherton Library.

"Studies in the Sierra" were never collected in book form; perhaps this was one of the many long-deferred projects Muir left for his last years. The essays in the series that appeared in the *Overland Monthly* are as follows: "Mountain Sculpture," May 1874; "Origin of Yosemite Valleys," June 1874; "Ancient Glaciers and Their Pathways," July 1874; "Glacial Denudation," August 1874; "Post-Glacial Denudation," November 1874; "Formation of Soils," December 1874; "Mountain Building," January 1875.

The most comprehensive survey of ancient beliefs about forests and trees is, of course, Sir James G. Frazer's classic *The Golden Bough*. Fortunately, for those who have need of this monument of nineteenth-century armchair scholarship, Theodore Gaster has done a skillful abridgment based on modern anthropology's refinements of Frazer's often highly speculative formulations: *The New Golden Bough* (New York, 1959, 1964).

Reminiscences of Muir in the Swett household and of John Swett's influence on Muir at that time and afterward were given me by Margaret Plummer, Swett's granddaughter, at Martinez, California, March 1980.

Muir's remarks in "God's First Temples: How Shall We Preserve Our Forests?" (Sacramento *Record-Union*, February 9, 1876), may owe something to the work of Ezra S. Carr, who with the editorial assistance of his wife had written forcefully on forestry practices in America compared with those of Europe: "Forestry: Its Relation to Civilization" is with the Jeanne

C. Carr papers at the Huntington Library. The ultimate source here may be George Perkins Marsh's path-breaking *Man and Nature* (Cambridge, 1864, 1965), which first attempted a global survey and analysis of forestry practices.

The place to begin to discover the elegaic note in nineteenth-century American culture is Henry Nash Smith's *Virgin Land* (Cambridge, London, 1950, 1970). Lee Clark Mitchell, *Witnesses to a Vanishing America: The Nineteenth-Century Response* (Princeton, 1981), surveys those observers like Audubon, Catlin, George Bird Grinnell, and Muir's late adversary in the Muir-Carr letters controversy, George Wharton James, who expressed the national ambivalence about the fate of the wilderness. Catlin's *Letters and Notes on the Manners, Customs, and Conditions of the North American Indians,* 2 vols. (New York, 1844, 1973), is a brilliant and poignant description of Plains life on the eve of its destruction. Grinnell's best works are *Blackfoot Lodge Tales: The Story of a Prairie People* (Lincoln, 1892, 1962), and *The Cheyenne Indians: Their History and Ways of Life,* 2 vols. (Lincoln, 1923, 1972). Perhaps the ultimate in this elegaic mode is James Willard Schultz, *My Life as an Indian: The Story of a Red Woman and a White Man in the Lodges of the Blackfeet* (New York, 1907), a classic of Americana too little recognized.

In my discussion of the broad changes in American culture, 1830–76, and especially those of the years 1861–76, I follow the standard historical interpretation laid out by Charles and Mary Beard, *The Rise of American Civilization* (New York, 1930); Lewis Mumford, *The Brown Decades: A Study of the Arts in America, 1865–1895* (New York, 1931, 1955); Matthew Josephson, *The Robber Barons: The Great American Capitalists, 1861–1901* (New York, London, 1934, 1962); and Louis M. Hacker, *The Triumph of American Capitalism* (New York, 1940). In recent years a certain amount of historiographical tinkering has gone on with the interpretation of this period as a great cultural watershed, tending to suggest that the Civil War was not so decisive as the Beards et al. had claimed. In fact, in some of the essays in Ralph Andreano (ed.), *The Economic Impact of the Civil War* (Cambridge, 1967), it is claimed that statistical evidence shows the war actually retarded the industrialization of America, and so, presumably, delayed consequent cultural developments. I am about as persuaded by this evidence as I am by the statistically based conclusions of Fogel and Engerman in *Time on the Cross* (Boston, 1974) wherein it is claimed that in some ways we have an exaggerated view of the harshness of southern chattel slavery and that the institution was actually a bit more benign and efficient than popularly believed, which is to say not persuaded at all. Louis M. Hacker, *The World of Andrew Carnegie: 1865–1901* (Philadelphia, New York, 1968), offers what is to me an entirely convincing rebuttal of those revisionists he styles "econometricians."

Other works on the cultural trends of the decades on either side of the war years include Leo Marx, *The Machine in the Garden* (London, Oxford, New York, 1964, 1977); John F. Kasson, *Civilizing the Machine: Technology and Republican Values in America, 1776–1900* (Harmondsworth, 1976, 1977); Daniel Boorstin, *The Lost World of Thomas Jefferson* (New York, 1948); Daniel Aaron, *Men of Good Hope: A Story of American Progressives* (New York, 1951); and Ray Ginger, *Age of Excess: The United States from 1877 to 1914* (New York, London, 1975).

ADDITIONAL SOURCES:

Henry Adams. *The Education of Henry Adams* (New York, 1913, 1955).

Brother Cornelius. *Keith: Old Master of California* (New York, 1942).

William Dean Howells. *Years of My Youth.*

Roland Morgan. *San Francisco Then and Now* (San Francisco, Toronto, Vancouver, 1978).

John Muir. Letter to J.B. McChesney, Yosemite, January 9, 1873. Yosemite National Park Research Library.

———. *The Mountains of California.*

———. *Steep Trails.*

———. Undated fragment on trodden gardens and the plight of city dwellers. Muir Papers, Holt-Atherton Library.

Lawrence N. Powell. *New Masters: Northern Planters During the Civil War and Reconstruction* (New Haven, 1980).

Henry David Thoreau. "Walking," in *The Portable Thoreau,* ed. Carl Bode (New York, Harmondsworth, 1947, 1981).

T. H. Watkins. *California: An Illustrated History* (Palo Alto, 1973).

Walt Whitman. "Specimen Days" and "Democratic Vistas," in *Leaves of Grass and Selected Prose,* ed. John Kouwenhoven (New York, 1950).

Home

In reconstructing Muir's fieldwork of 1877, I have relied on the letters he sent the Strentzels as printed by Badè, and on *Steep Trails,* a posthumously assembled collection of newspaper pieces he wrote at the end of the '70s, most of them for the San Francisco *Bulletin.*

For anyone seeking an understanding of Muir's relationship with

Louie Strentzel Muir, the present situation with the Strentzel family papers at the Holt-Atherton is disappointing. Apparently, much valuable material exists that has yet to be made available while other material to which Badè and Wolfe once had access has been removed. Wolfe seems to have had a look at a diary Louisiana Strentzel was keeping in the 1870s, but since then the diary has disappeared. The paucity of information, including photographs, on Louie Strentzel Muir is almost astonishing. She was by nature retiring, and Mrs. J. B. McChesney described her as very old-fashioned and fiercely protective of her daughters. Since she permitted herself to be known by very few, this would mean that there might not be much in the way of contemporaneous recollections. But an almost absolute lack of them? Did she write and receive no letters? This part of the Muir story remains for me a mystery.

In reconstructing Muir's Alaskan adventures of 1879, '80, and '81, I have used the journals; Muir's *Travels in Alaska* (Boston, 1915, 1979), at which he was at work when he died and which his secretary, Marion Randall Parsons, completed from his manuscript; and S. Hall Young, *Alaska Days with John Muir* (New York, 1915, 1972). Of this last work, it must be said that Young had a kind of hero worship of Muir, understandable in view of the incident at Glenora. On the other hand, Muir inspired hero worship in a good many others who knew him in far less wild and perilous circumstances. Young's portrait of the mature Muir in action (and later on his Martinez ranch) is in my view trustworthy and valuable. For a deft synopsis of Muir's evolving attitudes toward Indians, Alaskan and otherwise, see Richard Fleck, "John Muir's Evolving Attitudes Toward Native American Cultures," *American Indian Quarterly* (February, 1978).

ADDITIONAL SOURCES:

Daniel Aaron. *Men of Good Hope: A Story of American Progressives.*

Henry Adams. *The Education of Henry Adams.*

Walton Bean. *California: An Interpretive History.* (New York, San Francisco, St. Louis, Toronto, Sydney, 1968).

Anna George de Mille. *Henry George: Citizen of the World* (Chapel Hill, 1950).

Henry George. *Progress and Poverty: An Inquiry into the Cause of Industrial Depressions and of Increase of Want with Increase of Wealth: The Remedy* (New York, 1879, 1938).

Ray Ginger. *Age of Excess.*

Lee Clark Mitchell. *Witnesses to a Vanishing Landscape.*

Nicholas C. Polos. "The Educational Philosophy of John Swett and John Muir." *Pacific Historian* (Spring, 1982).

Mae (Fisher) Purcell. *History of Contra Costa Country* (Berkeley, 1940).

Kevin Starr. *Americans and the California Dream, 1850–1915* (New York, 1973).

T. H. Watkins. *California: An Illustrated History.*

R. Hal Williams. *The Democratic Party and California Politics, 1880–1896* (Stanford, 1973).

Against the American Grain

On the meeting between Robert Underwood Johnson and Muir at the Palace Hotel in 1889 et seq., I used Johnson, *Remembered Yesterdays* (Boston, 1923); Johnson, "Personal Reminiscences of John Muir," *Outlook* (June 3, 1905); Johnson, "John Muir as I Knew Him," Sierra Club *Bulletin* (January, 1916); and Stephen Fox, *John Muir and His Legacy.*

For Muir's life during the decade of the 1880s, see his *Travels in Alaska; The Cruise of the Corwin* (Boston, New York, 1917); *Stickeen* (Berkeley, 1909, 1981), his stirring account of his adventure on an Alaskan glacier with a mongrel dog; the relevant portions of his journals; P. J. Ryan, *The John Muir National Historic Site* (Point Reyes, 1977); and *The Muir-Strentzel Ranch* [pamphlet] (John Muir Memorial Association in cooperation with the U.S. Department of the Interior and the National Park service, n.d.).

Muir's sketches of the landscapes of the Northwest on his trip of 1888 were eventually collected in *Steep Trails.*

On the history of the public domain, by far the best single work remains Roy M. Robbins, *Our Landed Heritage: The Public Domain, 1776–1936.* It is dated only in the sense that almost a half century of subsequent history has occurred since its publication; the fundamental issues remain precisely as Robbins defined them, and his explication of often tangled legal and political matters is a model of clarity. For more recent, specialized treatments of the public domain, see Vernon Carstensen (ed.), *The Public Lands: Studies in the History of the Public Domain* (Madison, Milwaukee, London, 1968); the essays here on the railroads and the role of the speculator seek to stimulate reappraisals of two historical "legends." For yet more specialized works that consider attitudes toward the public domain, see Henry Nash Smith, *Virgin Land;* Roderick Nash, *Wilderness and the American Mind* (New Haven, London, 1967, 1970); and Hans Huth, *Nature and the American: Three Centuries of Changing Attitudes* (Lincoln, 1957, 1962).

On the creation of Yosemite National Park, Nash's *Wilderness and the American Mind* is excellent on the background as is Huth's *Nature and the American.* Huth's monograph, *Yosemite: The Story of an Idea,* originally published in the Sierra Club *Bulletin* (1948), has been conveniently reprinted by the Yosemite Natural History Association (1975). See also Carl P. Russell, *100 Years in Yosemite.* Laura Wood Roper's biography of Frederick Law Olmsted, *FLO* (Baltimore, London, 1973, 1983), contains valuable information on the earliest years of the state park and on Olmsted's efforts to establish an official rationale for its operation and maintenance. Holway Jones, *John Muir and the Sierra Club: The Battle for Yosemite* (San Francisco, 1965), is the most detailed account of the specifics of the first recession battle.

Muir's Yosemite articles for the *Century* have been reprinted with their accompanying illustrations as *The Proposed Yosemite National Park— Treasures & Features* (Olympic Valley, 1976).

On the rise of reformers and the Progressive movement, see Daniel Aaron, *Men of Good Hope;* Ray Ginger, *Age of Excess;* Samuel P. Hays, *The Response to Industrialism, 1885–1914* (Chicago, London, 1957); and Hays's study of the conservation movement within this general context, *Conservation and the Gospel of Efficiency: The Progressive Conservation Movement, 1890– 1920* (Cambridge, 1959). Jackson Lears, *No Place of Grace: Anti-Modernism and the Transformation of American Culture, 1880–1920* (New York, 1981), is not about reform per se, yet it is in many ways an absorbing survey and analysis of various off-beat reformlike movements such as the artisan ideal, the martial arts ideal, the vogue of interest in the mind of the Middle Ages, and orientalism. Richard Hofstadter, *The Age of Reform: From Bryan to F.D.R.* (New York, 1955), is in many ways a brilliant, cold-eyed analysis of the reform movement and what happened to it, but it strikes me that its author was strangely out of sympathy with his subject. Hofstadter is at his best describing the perceived alienation of the individual from society and of various groups from the mainstream of the culture. Larzar Ziff, *The American 1890s,* is an excellent analysis of the literary response to rapid cultural change.

On the Sierra Club and the background of its formation, the prime source is Holway Jones, *John Muir and the Sierra Club.* To date, Jones has made the most extensive and effective use of the club's archives.

On Muir's return to Scotland and his evident delight in the natural and human history of his native country, see his notebook on the trip with the Muir Papers, Holt-Atherton.

ADDITIONAL SOURCES:

Walton Bean. *California: An Interpretive History.*

Ray Allen Billington. *Frederick Jackson Turner: Historian, Scholar, Teacher* (New York, 1973).

David Douglas. *Douglas of the Forests.*

Howard Mumford Jones. *The Age of Energy: Varieties of the American Experience, 1865–1915* (New York, 1971).

Richard G. Lillard. *The Great Forest* (New York, 1947).

William Morwood. *Traveler in a Vanished Landscape: The Life and Times of David Douglas* (New York, 1973).

John Muir. Letter to Daniel Muir (Jr.), Martinez, January 13, 1891. Huntington Library.

———. Journal, 1895. Muir Papers, Holt-Atherton Library.

———. Journal, 1896. Muir Papers, Holt-Atherton Library.

Henry David Thoreau. *The Main Woods.*

T. H. Watkins. *California: An Illustrated History.*

The American Forests

Roderick Nash, *Wilderness and the American Mind,* is good on both the background and the personalities of the tour of the Forestry Commission; so, too, is Robert Underwood Johnson, *Remembered Yesterdays.* Gifford Pinchot described his experiences with the commission and with Sargent and Muir in *Breaking New Ground* (New York, 1947). Muir himself wrote out fragmentary notes, some of which Wolfe published in *John of the Mountains;* the rest are with the Muir Papers, Holt-Atherton.

Richard Ketchum, *The Secret Life of the Forest* (New York, 1970), is a fine, clear introduction to the way trees live and work. John Fowles, *The Tree* (Boston, Toronto, 1979), and Sir James G. Frazer, *The Golden Bough,* suggest something of the mysterious hold trees have had on the human imagination.

For a history of wood usage and the background of American national forests, I may perhaps be pardoned for regarding my own "The Language of the Forest," *Wilderness* (Summer, 1983), as a serviceable overview. Behind that essay stand a number of good works, chief among which are George Perkins Marsh, *Man and Nature;* Richard G. Lillard, *The Great*

Forest; Michael Frome, *Whose Woods These Are: The Story of the National Forests* (Garden City, 1962); Jack Shepard, *The Forest Killers: The Destruction of the American Wilderness* (New York, 1975); Peter Matthiessen, *Wildlife in America;* and John Bakeless, *The Eyes of Discovery.*

On a closely related subject, Huth, *Nature and the American,* Hays, *Conservation and the Gospel of Efficiency,* and Robbins, *Our Landed Heritage,* provide solid information on the legislative battles over use of public forest lands.

Muir's forest articles, with the exception of "Forest Reservations and National Parks," were collected in *Our National Parks* (Boston, New York, 1901). The journal of his trip with Sargent and Canby, July 2– November 28, 1898, is with the Muir Papers, Holt-Atherton.

ADDITIONAL SOURCES:

Ezra S. Carr. "Forestry: Its Relation to Civilization."

John Muir. Journal, 1896. Muir Papers, Holt-Atherton Library.

————. Notes for after-dinner speech at Harvard University, June 24, 1896. Muir Papers, Holt-Atherton Library.

Gifford Pinchot. *The Fight for Conservation* (Seattle, London, 1910, 1967).

Other Yosemites

Of the Harriman Alaska Expedition, May 30–July 30, 1899, Muir wrote a fair amount. He contributed a chapter on Pacific Coast glaciers to a collection, and there are numerous references to the expedition in a memorial pamphlet he wrote on E. H. Harriman, *Edward H. Harriman* (n.p., 1911, 1978). There are also the journal entries. The voluminous scientific reports of this seagoing "think tank," as one writer styled it, were edited by C. Hart Merriam, *Harriman Alaska Expedition,* 13 vols. (New York, Washington, D.C., 1901–14). Those interested in this aspect are free to take a dive into this ocean of material. More entertaining and revealing is William Goetzmann and Kay Sloan, *Looking Far North: The Harriman Expedition to Alaska* (New York, 1982). The authors have gone extensively into the literature of the H.A.E. and its photographic records and have created a lively, comprehensive narrative.

To judge from the reminiscences collected by Goetzmann and Sloan, Muir was not an unmixed delight on the H.A.E. To begin with, it wasn't his sort of outing, this big, ornate expedition, mounted by a man known to him only as a railroad magnate. And considering the deservedly bad odor in which the Southern Pacific line remained in California, it would not be too much to suppose that Muir held a low opinion of railroad executives in general and Harriman in specific. But Merriam talked him into coming, and probably the opportunity to see Alaska once more was compelling. Perhaps, too, at this time in his life, there was an unacknowledged appeal in the prospect of doing his exploring in comfort.

So, with mixed feelings, he went. But all the heavily upholstered arrangements, the structure Harriman imposed, the committees, lectures, hymn-singing sessions, etc., probably got on his nerves, exaggerating certain character traits that were not unfailingly winning to colleagues and friends. He was always a nonstop talker, and in the close quarters of a ship this habit became the more obvious. He was by national character as well as by personal background disputatious; here in the company of officially certified scholars, he was even more so. He believed he had learned about glaciers all by himself—and learned the hardest of ways—and would allow no one else an opinion on the subject. He balked at Harriman's benign brand of dictatorship and contentiously told a group of listeners that he was richer than Harriman because he knew how much money he needed and Harriman didn't. Finally, he thought all the committee work and plans for a full scientific report of the expedition "much ado about nothing."

That Muir should ever have become a warm friend of Harriman's may be, as Stephen Fox says in *John Muir and His Legacy,* one more illustration of opposites attracting. But possibly Harriman was not quite the ogre that some have thought him (including Theodore Roosevelt, who came to view him as one of the foes of righteousness). Surely he was not wholly responsible, as some thought then, for all the evils associated with the Southern Pacific's heavy hand in California life and politics around the turn of the century. In any case, a revisionist view of the Southern Pacific is beginning to emerge in historical circles. Richard J. Orsi, professor of history, California State University (Hayward), is developing evidence suggesting that the help Harriman lent Muir and the cause of conservation was not purely a matter of personal affection. According to Orsi, the Southern Pacific had been fairly consistent since the 1890s in supporting water and timber conservation, seeing these measures as in its own interest. In any case, says Orsi, the "Robber Baron" image of Harriman is too simplistic to be of much use. By the turn of the century corporate structures had become far too complex to admit of a baronial approach, and often decisions were made that had little to do with the titular head of a corporation. In the case of the Southern Pacific, for example, the essential figure was not Harriman but William H. Mills, the company's chief land agent and a man who made an enviable record in various state reform movements. See Orsi, "The Octopus Reconsidered: The Southern Pacific and Agricultural Modernization in California, 1865–1915," *California Historical Quarterly* (February, 1975).

For my discussion of Muir in Arizona in 1905–06, I have followed notes made at that time by Alice Cotton Fletcher as well as her unpublished sketch, "Along the Way I Met John Muir." These were kindly donated to me by Mrs. Fletcher's son, John E. Fletcher, and are now with the Muir Papers at the Holt-Atherton. I also derived valuable background information from Sidney R. Ash and David R. May, *Petrified Forest: The Story Behind the Scenery* (Holbrook, 1969, 1981); and John Wagner, *This Is Painted Desert* (Holbrook, 1971). I made a trip to the Petrified Forest National Monument and to the abandoned dwellings at Adamana in March 1983.

The history of the Hetch Hetchy controversy is, of course, a great deal more complex than I could afford to acknowledge in my narrative. As I have said, the best, most detailed and dispassionate discussion of Hetch Hetchy is Holway Jones's *John Muir and the Sierra Club*. Other useful discussions are found in Roderick Nash, *Wilderness and the American Mind* and Stephen Fox, *John Muir and His Legacy*. Robert Underwood Johnson, *Remembered Yesterdays*, necessarily lacks the historical breadth that comes to later commentators, but Johnson's account is vivid and immediate and suggests how heated and personal the battle became. Generally a fair-minded man, Johnson evinced a personal dislike of Gifford Pinchot and came close to saying that had it not been for Pinchot the Hetchy Hetchy takeover would not have occurred.

I think the facts are otherwise. Pinchot was from the first entirely open in his support of the city's petition, a position consistent with his philosophy of conservation. Though Pinchot did apparently influence Roosevelt in San Francisco's direction, he had little influence on Taft, who fired him for insubordination in 1910; and he had no influence at all on the administration of Woodrow Wilson. Pinchot seems to have been a factor in 1906–08 in encouraging the city to petition for Hetch Hetchy and Lake Eleanor, but after that many other forces took over.

Three other matters may be briefly suggested. First, there was an interesting precedent set for what San Francisco had in mind for its water supply. Since the 1880s communities in southern California had been tapping mountain water systems to meet the needs of expanding populations. Los Angeles found itself in a critical water shortage in 1904, and with the support of Roosevelt and the U.S. Reclamation Service it developed plans for the Owens River aqueduct that eventually delivered water to the city from Long Valley, 200 miles away in the Sierras. What is especially significant here is that, in the early stages of the project, Roosevelt extended the boundaries of the Inyo National Forest to include the site of the proposed reservoir, thus protecting it from potential encumbrances that might hamper the developers' plans. Here then was an early example of federally protected land being used for private development. Indeed, as San Francisco was to learn, from a developer's point of view the fact that the site in question was federally protected constituted a unique virtue, for such an area would not be dotted with private holdings, which would be more difficult to retire than would a large federal one.

Second is the question raised early and often by opponents of the Hetch Hetchy plan: might not the city have obtained its water from other sites without violating the sanctity of the park? The answer is, yes it could have. Here, as in almost every other instance of the issue, the interpretation of the answer turns on one's position. Opponents of the city's plan claimed that ex-mayor Phelan and his associates had invested too much money, time, and prestige into the plan to honestly consider alternatives. Proponents cited the report of the Advisory Board of Army Engineers (1913), which favored Hetch Hetchy and estimated other sites would cost the city an additional $20 million. Since city voters had in 1908 gone heavily in favor of incurring a bonded debt of $600,000 for the purpose of acquiring rights to the Hetch Hetchy and Lake Eleanor sites, it was probably out of the question in the wake of the board's report to go back to them and ask that they consider alternative sites.

Third, was Muir blind to the predicament and needs of San Francisco? Writing to Roosevelt in 1908, Muir said he was "heartily in favor of a Sierra or even Tuolumne water supply for San Francisco." But, he argued, "all the water required can be obtained from sources outside the park, leaving the twin valleys, Hetch-Hetchy and Yosemite, to the use they were intended for when the Park was established." By 1909, Muir had gone further, indicating his willingness that Lake Eleanor be used for the city's needs. But he would go no further, and, as I have suggested in the text, there appears to have been a hardening of his attitude toward the whole business the longer it dragged on. So on July 15, 1913, he wrote his old friend Henry Fairfield Osborne: "This is the twenty-third year of almost continual battle for the preservation of Yosemite Park, sadly interrupting my natural work. Our enemies now seem to be having most everything their own wicked way, . . . spending millions of the people's money for selfish ends. Think of three or four ambitious, shifty traders and politicians calling themselves 'The City of San Francisco,' bargaining with the United States for half of Yosemite Park like Yankee horse-traders, as if the grandest of all our mountain playgrounds, full of God's best gifts, the joy and admiration of the world, were of no more account than any of the long list of tinker tariff articles."

On Muir's final illness, the record is sketchy. Muir's records at the California Hospital have either been destroyed or misplaced. His chart, #36550, is listed in the entry book, but the chart itself is missing (Medical Records Office, California Hospital Medical Center, Los Angeles).

ADDITIONAL SOURCES:

Henry Adams. *The Education of Henry Adams.*

Melville Anderson. "The Conversation of John Muir."

Clara Barrus. "With John O' Birds and John O' Mountains in the Southwest." *Century* (August, 1910).

Walton Bean. *California: An Interpretive History.*

Joanna Muir Brown. Letter to John Muir October 7, 1913. Holt-Atherton Library.

Michael Cohen. *The Pathless Way: John Muir and the American Wilderness.*

Benard De Voto. *Across the Wide Missouri.*

Michael Frome. *Whose Woods These Are: The Story of the National Parks.*

Samuel P. Hays. *Conservation and the Gospel of Efficiency: The Progressive Conservation Movement, 1890–1920.*

C. Hart Merriam. "To the Memory of John Muir." Sierra Club *Bulletin* (January, 1917).

John Muir. Field Journal, 1872. Holt-Atherton Library.

———. Journal, 1913. Holt-Atherton Library.

———. Letter to Harry Randall, Martinez, December 20, 1901. Yosemite National Park Research Library.

———. Letter to Mary Muir Hand, Martinez, April 30, 1911. Yosemite National Park Research Library.

———. Letter to Mary Muir Hand, Martinez, January 3, 1914. Yosemite National Park Research Library.

———. Letter to Maggie Lunam, Martinez, December 3, 1914, Yosemite National Park research Library.

———. *The Yosemite.*

———. *Travels in Alaska.*

Maribeth Patrick. "A Visit with John Muir." Sierra Club *Bulletin* (September/October, 1982).

Gifford Pinchot. *Breaking New Ground.*

———. *The Fight for Conservation.*

Henry F. Pringle. *Theodore Roosevelt: A Biography* (New York, 1931, 1956).

French Strother. "Three Days with John Muir. *World's Work* (November, 1906).

G. W. Townsend. *Memorial Life of William McKinley . . .* (Washington, D.C., 1901).

Stephen F. Whicher. *Freedom and Fate: An Inner Life of Ralph Waldo Emerson.*

Thiurman Wilkins. *Clarence King: A Biography.*

n.a. "Earth He Loved Reclaims Him" (Muir's obituary). Los Angeles *Times* (December 25, 1914).

Index